Sixth Edition

I Never Knew I Had a Choice

OTHER BOOKS BY GERALD COREY:

Theory and Practice of Group Counseling, 4TH EDITION
    (and *Manual*) (1995)

Case Approach to Counseling and Psychotherapy, 4TH EDITION
    (1996)

Theory and Practice of Counseling and Psychotherapy, 5TH EDITION
    (and *Manual*) (1996)

BY GERALD COREY AND
MARIANNE SCHNEIDER COREY:

Groups: Process and Practice, 5TH EDITION (1997)

Group Techniques, 2ND EDITION (1992, with Patrick Callanan
    and J. Michael Russell)

Becoming a Helper, 2ND EDITION (1993)

Issues and Ethics in the Helping Professions, 4TH EDITION
    (1993, with Patrick Callanan)

Sixth Edition

I Never Knew
I Had a Choice

GERALD COREY
California State University, Fullerton
Diplomate in Counseling Psychology,
American Board of Professional Psychology

MARIANNE SCHNEIDER COREY
Private Practice

Brooks/Cole Publishing Company
I T P® An International Thomson Publishing Company

Pacific Grove · Albany · Bonn · Boston · Cincinnati · Detroit · London · Madrid · Melbourne
Mexico City · New York · Paris · San Francisco · Singapore · Tokyo · Toronto · Washington

 A CLAIREMONT BOOK

Sponsoring Editor: *Eileen Murphy*
Marketing Team: *Gay Meixel and Margaret Parks*
Editorial Associate: *Patricia Vienneau*
Production Coordinator: *Fiorella Ljunggren*
Production: *Cecile Joyner, The Cooper Company*
Manuscript Editor: *Kay Mikel*
Permissions Editor: *Lillian Campobasso*
Cartoonist: *Andy Myer*
Interior Design: *Terri Wright*

Cover Design: *Vernon T. Boes*
Cover Photo: *Macduff Everton, West Stock*
Photo Research: *Terri Wright*
Indexer: *Glennda Gilmour*
Typesetting: *ColorType, Inc.*
Cover Printing: *Phoenix Color Corporation, Inc.*
Printing and Binding: *Courier Westford, Inc.*
Photo credits appear on page 441.

For more information, contact:
BROOKS/COLE PUBLISHING COMPANY
511 Forest Lodge Road
Pacific Grove, CA 93950
USA

International Thomson Publishing Europe
Berkshire House 168-173
High Holborn
London WC1V 7AA
England

Thomas Nelson Australia
102 Dodds Street
South Melbourne, 3205
Victoria, Australia

Nelson Canada
1120 Birchmount Road
Scarborough, Ontario
Canada M1K 5G4

International Thomson Editores
Campos Eliseos 385, Piso 7
Col. Polanco
11560 México D. F. México

International Thomson Publishing GmbH
Königswinterer Strasse 418
53227 Bonn
Germany

International Thomson Publishing Asia
221 Henderson Road
#05-10 Henderson Building
Singapore 0315

International Thomson Publishing Japan
Hirakawacho Kyowa Building, 3F
2-2-1 Hirakawacho
Chiyoda-ku, Tokyo 102
Japan

Printed in the United States of America

10 9 8 7 6 5 4 3 2 1

Library of Congress Cataloging-in-Publication Data

Corey, Gerald
    I never knew I had a choice / Gerald Corey, Marianne Schneider
Corey — 6th ed.
        p. cm.
    Includes bibliographical references and index.
    ISBN 0-534-34339-2
    1. Self-perception. 2. Choice (Psychology) I. Corey, Marianne
Schneider, [date]. II. Title
BF697.5.S43C67   1997
158 — dc20   96-5075
                                                  CIP

In memory of our friend Jim Morelock,
a searcher who lived and died
  with dignity and self-respect,
who struggled and questioned,
who made the choice to live his days fully
  until time ran out on him at age 25.

Preface

I Never Knew I Had a Choice is intended for college students of any age and for all others who wish to expand their self-awareness and explore the choices available to them in significant areas of their lives. It is also used by counselors in private practice settings and in public and private mental health organizations for workshops and groups. The topics discussed include choosing a personal style of learning; reviewing childhood and adolescence and the effects of these experiences on current behavior and choices; meeting the challenges of adulthood and autonomy; becoming the woman or man one wants to be; balancing work and leisure; maintaining a healthy body and pathways to wellness; managing stress; appreciating the significance of love, sexuality, and intimate relationships; dealing creatively with loneliness and solitude; understanding and accepting death and loss; and choosing one's values and philosophy of life.

This is a personal book, because we encourage readers to examine the choices they have made and how these choices affect their present level of satisfaction. (It is also a personal book in another sense, inasmuch as we describe our own concerns, struggles, decisions, and values with regard to many of the issues we raise.) The book is designed to be a personal workbook as well as a classroom text. Each chapter begins with a self-inventory that gives readers the chance to focus on their present beliefs and attitudes. Within the chapters, sections called "Time Out for Personal Reflection" offer an opportunity to pause and reflect on the issues raised. Additional activities and exercises are suggested at the end of each chapter for use in the classroom or outside of class. We wish to stress that this is an *unfinished* book; readers are encouraged to become coauthors by writing about their personal reactions in the book and in their journals.

What are some of the changes from the fifth to this sixth edition? Although the themes underlying the book are basically the same, whenever possible we have updated material to reflect current thinking. The introductory chapter continues to emphasize the importance of self-exploration and invites students to consider the values and excitement, as well as the commitment and work, involved in learning about oneself, others, and personal growth. However, social concerns must balance self-interests, and although we still emphasize self-actualization, we also maintain that self-fulfillment can occur only if individuals have a sense of social consciousness. Chapter 1 includes a brief discussion of the lives of four key figures — Maslow, Rogers, Jung, and Adler — and examines how their lives are revealed through their theories and ideas. Cultural identity is discussed throughout the chapters, focusing on the cultural factors that influence choice and behavior. New to this edition is a discussion of the concept of multiple intelligences and learning styles. "Personal Stories" are a new feature found in many of the chapters. These first-person accounts of an individual's struggles and the choices made in response to challenging life events convey a powerful message, one that needs little amplification or commentary.

Chapters 2 and 3 provide theoretical material on personality development from a life-span perspective, as well as practical tools to help readers modify the design of their present and future existence in their struggle toward autonomy. Chapter 4 continues with a developmental theme but focuses on how life experiences influence beliefs about gender identity. This chapter takes into account some current trends in the psychology of women and men. Chapter 5, "Work and Leisure," discusses college education as work, specific factors in vocational decision making, the relation between personality types and occupational choices, and active career planning. It also offers practical guidelines for career decision making and addresses the role of leisure in providing a balance to work. Chapter 6, "Your Body and Wellness," deals with wellness as a lifestyle, ways to stay healthy, body image, and touch and sensuality. Dreams and counseling are explored as pathways to both wellness and self-understanding. Chapter 7, "Managing Stress," is a continuation of Chapter 6 in that it examines the impact of stress on the body, causes of stress, destructive and constructive reactions to stress, and stress and the healthy personality. In Chapters 6 and 7 we challenge readers to look at the value they place on health and well-being rather than merely avoiding illness. In the previous edition the topics of body image, wellness, and stress were all covered in one chapter, but because we added a good deal of new material, these topics have been divided into two chapters for this edition.

Chapter 8, "Love," has been updated in certain sections. Chapter 9, which deals with sexuality, contains an updated section on the AIDS crisis and its effects on sexual behavior. An expanded section on sexual abuse and harassment looks at timely subjects such as incest, date and acquaintance rape, and sexual harassment on the campus and in the workplace.

Chapter 10, "Relationships," contains guidelines for meaningful interpersonal relationships. This chapter covers a broad range of relationships: friendships, couple relationships (including gay and lesbian relationships), and family relationships. Recognizing and dealing with anger and conflict in relationships still retains a central place in the chapter. Chapter 11, "Loneliness and Solitude," discusses the creative dimensions of solitude. The remaining two chapters, "Death and Loss" and "Meaning and Values" (Chapters 12 and 13), deal with fears of death, the interdependence of life and death, the importance of grieving, suicide, and finding meaning in life. In addition, Chapter 13 contains a new section on embracing diversity, one way we can all expand our personal values to the broader community of humankind. The Epilogue, which is new to this edition, reminds readers that their journey toward personal growth is only beginning and offers a variety of avenues for growth that readers may wish to pursue now and in the future.

Fundamentally, our approach in *I Never Knew I Had a Choice* is humanistic and personal; that is, we stress the healthy and effective personality and the common struggles most of us experience in becoming autonomous. We especially emphasize accepting personal responsibility for the choices we make and consciously deciding whether and how we want to change our lives.

Although our own approach can be broadly characterized as humanistic and existential, our aim has been to challenge readers to recognize and assess their own choices, beliefs, and values rather than to convert them to a particular point of view. Our basic premise is that a commitment to self-exploration can create new potentials for choice. Many of the college students and counseling clients with whom we work are relatively well-functioning people who desire more from life and who want to recognize and remove blocks to their personal creativity and freedom. It is for people like these that we've written this book.

In talking about the contents of this book with both students and instructors, we have found that students select a personal growth course because of their interest in discovering more about themselves and their relationships with others. Most of them are looking for a *practical* course, one that deals with real issues in everyday living and that will provide an impetus for their own personal growth. Accordingly, we have focused on helping readers recognize blocks to their creative and productive energies, find ways of removing these obstructions, and make conscious choices to modify their attitudes and behaviors.

The experiences of those who have read and used the earlier editions of *I Never Knew I Had a Choice* reveal that the themes explored have application to a diversity of ages and backgrounds. Readers who have taken the time to write us about their reactions say that the book encouraged them to take an honest look at their lives and challenge themselves to make certain changes. Many readers who have used this book for a college course have told us that they have shared it with friends and relatives.

Choice was developed for use in college courses dealing with the psychology of adjustment, personality development, applied psychology, personal growth, and self-awareness. But *Choice* has also been adopted in courses ranging from the psychology of personal growth on the undergraduate level to graduate courses for training teachers and counselors. It is also used in group counseling courses as a catalyst for small-group interaction and for workshops in training group leaders. Courses that make use of an interactive approach will find *Choice* a useful tool for discussion.

We've written this book to facilitate interaction — between student and instructor, among the students within a class, between students and significant people in their lives, between the reader and us as authors — but most important of all, our aim is to provide the reader with an avenue for reflection. This is not a book that can be read passively; it is designed to provoke thoughtful reflection. Readers are encouraged to look at the direction of their lives to see if they like where they are heading. Our experience has been that active, open, and personal participation in these courses can lead to expanded self-awareness and greater autonomy in living.

An updated and expanded *Instructor's Resource Manual* accompanies this textbook. It includes about 25 test items, both multiple-choice and essay, for every chapter; a student study guide covering all chapters; suggested reading; questions for thought and discussion; numerous activities and exercises for classroom participation; guidelines for using the book and teaching the course; examples of various formats of personal-growth classes; guidelines for maximizing personal learning and for reviewing and integrating the course; and a student evaluation instrument to assess the impact of the course on readers.

Acknowledgments

We would like to express our deep appreciation for the insightful suggestions given to us by friends, associates, reviewers, students, and readers. The following people, many of whom had used *Choice* in earlier editions, provided helpful reviews for this revision: John Brennecke of Mt. San Antonio College, Kathy Carpenter of the University of Nebraska at Kearney, L. William Cheney of the Community College of Rhode Island, James Dailey of Vincennes University, Herb Goldberg of California State University at Los Angeles, Robert Levine of Hillsborough Community College, Robert D. Lock of Jackson Community College, Sebastian Mudry of Manchester Community Technical College, Glenda Nichols of Tarrant County Junior College, Jana Preble of Saint Cloud State University, Valerie Scott of College of Satint Elizabeth, Troy D. Smith of North Shore Community College, Veronika Tracy of California State University at Fullerton, Bonnie Tyler of the University of Maryland, and Joseph Zielenewski of the University of Cincinnati.

We appreciate our student reviewers who provided insightful comments and constructive suggestions: Suzanne Cios, Gary Kerr, Michelle Muratori, Judy VanderWende, and Christiana Woodward. Thanks also to Mimi Fairbanks of Franklin University and James Morrow of Western Carolina University, who reviewed the work and leisure chapter, to Sam Cochran of the University of Iowa, who reviewed the chapter on gender roles, and to Mark Biddell of the University of California at Santa Barbara, who reviewed the chapter on sexuality. Special thanks are extended to our students who contributed personal stories for this edition.

We are indebted to our friends and colleagues — Patrick Callanan, in private practice in Santa Ana, California; Soraya and Ron Coley; Helga Kennedy; Mary Moline of Seattle Pacific University; and J. Michael Russell of California State University at Fullerton — for many provocative discussions concerning the ideas raised in this book. We also thank Glennda Gilmour for preparing the index.

Finally, as is true of all our books, *I Never Knew I Had a Choice* continues to develop as a result of a team effort, which includes the combined talents of several people in the Brooks/Cole family. It is a delight to work with a dedicated staff of professionals who go out of their way to give their best. These people include Claire Verduin, who recently retired from a 25-year career with Brooks/Cole; Eileen Murphy, who is the new editor of counseling and psychology; Fiorella Ljunggren, production services manager, who carefully oversees the production of our books; Cecile Joyner, of The Cooper Company, who coordinated the production of this book; and Kay Mikel, the manuscript editor of this edition, whose talented editorial assistance we greatly appreciate. We also want to recognize the work of the late Bill Waller, who edited most of the previous editions of *Choice*—and whose influence has carried over into this edition. We appreciate Patricia Vienneau, editorial associate, who facilitated the reviewing process and who always managed to keep a sense of humor; Terri Wright, the interior designer and photo researcher for the book; and Andy Myer, who created the original cartoons for this edition. We are grateful to all of these people, who continue to devote extra time and effort to ensure the quality of our books.

Gerald Corey
Marianne Schneider Corey

Brief Contents

Contents

3   *Adulthood and Autonomy*   *70*

4   *Becoming the Woman or Man You Want to Be*   *108*

8   *Love*   *235*

9   *Sexuality*   *258*

13   *Meaning and Values*   *391*

Epilogue: Where to Go from Here — Pathways to Continued Growth   *416*

1

Invitation to Personal Learning and Growth

The unexamined life is not worth living.
—*SOCRATES*

Choice and Change

■ We Do Have Choices!

If you are interested in examining your life and living by choice, this book is for you. Is your life fully satisfying? If not, you may want to learn more about yourself. You may decide to make some changes. You may feel powerless right now and think that external circumstances prevent you from making any real change. You may say: "If my parents weren't so critical of me, I'd feel much better." "When my partner becomes more affectionate toward me, I'll feel worthwhile." "I'd like to say what I feel, but I'm afraid I'll lose my friends if I do." "I know I'm shy, but it's too late for me to change. I've been this way since I was a kid." "I would be fine if the people around me were different." While it is true that you can't change others, you are a powerful person — you can examine your own life and choose another path.

Our hope is that this book and this course will inspire you to reflect on the quality of your life and decide for yourself how you want to change. We encourage you to challenge your fears rather than being stopped by them. Socrates, in his wisdom, said, "The unexamined life is not worth living." Examine your values and your behavior. If you have struggled with various crises in your life, for example, you can come to realize that a crisis represents a significant turning point. The Chinese symbol for crisis represents both *danger* and *opportunity.* As you engage yourself in this book, consider ways to use critical life situations as opportunities for personal growth.

It is exciting for us when our students and clients discover that they can be in charge of their own lives to a greater degree than they ever dreamed possible. As one counseling client put it: "One thing I can see now that I didn't see before is that I can change my life if I want to. *I never knew I had a choice!*" This remark captures the central message of this book: We are not passive victims of life; we *do* make choices, and we *do* have the power to change major aspects of our lives as we struggle toward a more authentic existence. This book will lead you through the process of becoming a *proactive* person rather than a *reactive* person.

■ Are You Ready to Change?

One way to begin focusing on the quality of your life is by reflecting on such questions as: To what extent do you like the way you are living now? Are there some things in your life that you'd like to change? Do you feel that change is even necessary?

It is not uncommon to hear comments like these: "I don't know if I want to rock the boat." "Things aren't all that bad in my life." "I'm fairly secure, and I don't want to take the chance of losing this security." "I'm afraid that if I start probing around, I may uncover things that will be tough for me to handle." It is not a sign of cowardice to have doubts and fears about making changes. In fact, it is a mark of courage to acknowledge your resistance to change and your anxiety over taking increased control of your life. It is a challenge and a struggle to take an honest look at your life and begin to live differently. Those who are close to you may not ap-

Peanuts cartoon reprinted by permission of United Features Syndicate, Inc.

prove of or like your changes, and they may put up barriers to your designing a new life. Your cultural background may make it more difficult for you to assume a new role and modify certain values. These factors are likely to increase your anxiety as you contemplate making your own choices rather than allowing others to choose for you.

Self-exploration, being honest with yourself and others, thinking for yourself, and making a commitment to live by your choices entail diligent effort. Taking charge of your life exacts a price. A degree of discomfort and even fear are associated with discovering more about yourself. You may prefer to remain unaware—allowing others to choose for you and being content with the status quo. Or you may question but decide that change is not necessary. After all, you don't have to change. Ask yourself if you are willing to pay the price for taking the personal risks involved in choosing for yourself. Change is a proactive process, and only you can decide what you are willing to risk and how much change is right for you.

Throughout this book both of us make disclosures about our own lives and our values. We use a personal style and openly share with you how we arrived at some of the beliefs and values we write about. We hope that knowing our assumptions, biases, and struggles will help you evaluate your own position more clearly. We are not suggesting that you adopt our philosophy of life. Rather, ask yourself how the issues we raise concern *you*. It is not our intention to provide simple answers to complex life issues. Although self-help books provide insights and useful information for many people, we have concerns about the kind of books that give an abundance of advice or attempt to offer easy answers. The same can be said of television talk shows or therapists who offer counsel on the radio to callers with personal problems. Information and even suggestions can be useful at the right time, but rarely can an individual's problems be resolved by uncritically accepting others' advice or directives.

In the chapters that follow, we will offer a great deal of information that we hope you'll reflect on and use as a basis for making better choices. Our aim is to raise questions that lead to thoughtful reflection on your part and to meaningful dialogue with others. We encourage you to develop a tolerance for examining questions that engage you. Instead of searching for advice or for simple solutions to your problems, we hope you will increasingly make time for personal reflection and consider the direction of your life. We encourage you to listen to others and consider what they say, but even more important is learning to look inside yourself for direction. Listen to your inner voice.

This book can become a personal companion. You can use it to reflect on questions that are personally significant to you such as: What are your answers? How can you trust yourself to discover what is best for you and for others? What are the choices you've made for yourself? What choices do you want to make now? How can you best live with your choices?

■ What about Other People?

Making choices for yourself and being in control of your life is important, but we are certainly not encouraging you to ignore the reality that you are a social being and that many of your decisions will be influenced by your relationships with significant people in your life. The focus of this book is on becoming your own person, but at the same time you need to consider others in your quest for self-development. In *Habits of the Heart* the authors assert that the goal for most Americans is to "become one's own person, almost to give birth to oneself" (Bellah, Madsen, Sullivan, Swidler, & Tipton, 1985). But in their many interviews they also found as a common theme the notion that the good life cannot be lived alone, that we do not find ourselves in isolation, and that connectedness to others in love, work, and community is absolutely essential to our self-esteem and happiness: "We find ourselves not independently of other people and institutions but through them. We never get to the bottom of ourselves on our own. We discover who we are face to face and side by side with others in work, love, and learning" (p. 84).

However, if you wait for others to become different, or if you blame them for the fact that you're not as happy as you'd like to be, you diminish your power to take full control of your life. If you want a closer relationship with your father and insist that he talk to you more and approve of you, for example, you are likely to be disappointed. He may not behave the way you want him to, and if you make changing him your central goal, you are keeping yourself helpless in many respects. But if you make some significant changes in the way you talk to your father and in the way you treat him, you may be greatly surprised at how he might change. You will increase your chances of success if *you* do what you want *him* to do.

As this example shows, the idea of personal choice does not imply doing whatever you want without regard for others. Making a commitment to examine your life does not mean becoming wrapped up in yourself to the exclusion of everyone else. Unless you know and care about yourself, however, you won't be able to develop caring relationships with others.

A Model for Personal Growth

One of the obvious benefits of choosing to change your life is that you will grow by exposing yourself to new experiences. But just what does personal growth entail? In this section we contrast the idea of *growth* with that of *adjustment* and offer a humanistic model of what ideal growth can be. We also deal with divergent perspectives on what constitutes the ideal standard of personal growth.

■ Adjustment or Growth?

Although this book deals with topics in what is often called "the psychology of adjustment," we have an uneasy feeling about this common phrase. The term *adjustment* is frequently taken to mean that some ideal norm exists by which people should be measured. This notion raises many problems. You may ask, for example: What is the desired norm of adjustment? Who determines the standards of "good" adjustment? Is it possible that the same person could be considered well adjusted in our culture and poorly adjusted in some other culture? Do we expect people who live in chaotic and destructive worlds to adjust to their life situations?

One reason we resist "adjustment" as a goal of human behavior is that those who claim to be well adjusted have often settled for a complacent existence, with neither challenge nor excitement. Within the limits imposed by genetic and environmental factors, we have many possibilities for creating our own definitions of ourselves as persons. No single standard of measurement exists for identifying universal qualities of the well-adjusted or psychologically healthy person. The concept of adjustment cannot be understood apart from the person-in-the-environment, for cultural values and norms play a crucial role. For example, if you are in your twenties and still live with your parents, some would view this as dependent behavior on your part and think that you should be living apart from your family of origin. Yet, from another cultural perspective, others would see this as the expected lifestyle and consider it inappropriate for you to be living on your own.

Instead of talking about adjustment, we tend to talk about *growth*. A psychology of growth rests on the assumption that growth is a lifelong adventure, not some fixed point at which we arrive. Personal growth is best viewed as a process rather than as a goal or an end. We will face numerous crises at various stages of our lives. These crises can be seen as challenges to change, giving our lives new meaning. Growth also encompasses our relationship with significant others, our community, and our world. We do not grow in a vacuum but through our engagement with other people. To continue to grow, we have to be willing to let go of some of our old ways of thinking and acting so new dimensions can develop. During your reading and studying, think about the ways you've stopped growing and the degree to which you're willing to invest in personal growth. Some questions to ask yourself are:

- What do you want for yourself, for others, and from others?
- What aspects of your life are working for you?
- What is not working in your life?
- How would you like to be different?
- What are possible consequences if you do or do not change?
- How will your changes affect others in your life?
- What range of choices is open to you at this time in your life?
- How has your culture laid a foundation for the choices you have made, and how might your cultural values either enhance or inhibit your ability to choose something different?

■ A Humanistic Approach to Personal Growth

I Never Knew I Had a Choice is based on a humanistic view of people. A central concept of this approach to personal growth is *self-actualization*. Striving for self-actualization means working toward fulfilling our potential, toward becoming all that we are capable of becoming. Humanistic psychology is based on the premise that this striving for growth exists but is not an automatic process. Because growth often involves some pain and considerable turmoil, many of us experience a constant struggle between our desire for security, or dependence, and our desire to experience the delights of growth.

Although other people have made significant contributions to humanistic psychology, we have chosen to focus on four key people who devoted much of their professional careers to the promotion of psychological growth and the self-actualization process: Alfred Adler, Carl Jung, Carl Rogers, and especially Abraham Maslow, who did extensive research on the process of self-actualizing individuals. It is particularly interesting to note the close parallels between the struggles of these men in early childhood and the focus of their theories. Based upon a set of life experiences, each of these men made a choice that influenced the development of his theory.

Alfred Adler (1958, 1964, 1969) made major contributions during Sigmund Freud's era and was a forerunner of the humanistic movement in psychology. In opposition to Freud's deterministic views of the person, Adler's theory stresses self-determination. Adler's early childhood experiences were characterized by a struggle to overcome weaknesses and feelings of inferiority, and the basic concepts of his theory grew out of his willingness to deal with his personal problems. Adler is a good example of a person who shaped his own life as opposed to having it determined by fate.

Adlerian psychologists contend that we are not the victims of fate but are creative, active, choice-making beings whose every action has purpose and meaning. Adler's approach is basically a growth model that rejects the idea that some individuals are psychologically sick. Instead of sickness, Adlerians talk of people being discouraged. Adlerian therapists view their work as providing encouragement, so people can grow to become what they were meant to be. They teach people better ways to meet the challenges of life tasks, provide direction, help people change unrealistic assumptions and beliefs, and offer encouragement to those who are discouraged.

One of Adler's basic concepts is *social interest,* an individual's attitudes in dealing with other people in the world, which includes striving for a better future. Adler equates social interest with identification and empathy with others. For him, our happiness and success are largely related to a sense of belonging and a social connectedness. As social beings we need to be of use to others and to establish meaningful relationships in a community. Adler asserted that only when we feel united with others can we act with courage in facing and dealing with life's problems. Since we are embedded in a society, we cannot be understood in isolation from our social context. Self-actualization is thus not an individual matter; it is only within the group that we can actualize our potential. Adler maintained that the degree to which we successfully share with others and are concerned with their welfare is a measure of our maturity. Social interest becomes the standard by which to judge psychological health. M. Scott Peck (1987) captures this idea of social interest: "It is true that we are created to be individually unique. Yet the reality is that we are inevitably social creatures who desperately need each other not merely for sustenance, not merely for company, but for any meaning to our lives whatsoever" (p. 55).

The Western concept of social interest is grounded in individualism, which affirms the uniqueness, autonomy, freedom, and intrinsic worth of the individual and emphasizes personal responsibility for our behavior and well-being. The ultimate aim of this orientation is the self-actualization of the individual, or becoming everything that one is potentially able to become. By contrast, the Eastern concept of social interest rests on collectivism, which affirms the value of preserving and enhancing the well-being of the group as the main principle guiding social action. This collective orientation emphasizes unity, unification, integration, and fusion. It does not view self-actualization as the ultimate good. Instead, it emphasizes cooperation, harmony, interdependence, achievement of socially oriented and group goals, and collective responsibility.

Carl Jung (1961), who was a contemporary of Adler, made a monumental contribution to the depth of understanding of the human personality. His pioneering work sheds light on human development, particularly during middle age. Jung's personal life paved the way for the expansion of his theoretical notions. His

loneliness as a child is reflected in his personality theory, which focuses on the inner world of the individual. Jung's emotional distance from his parents contributed to his feeling of being cut off from the external world of conscious reality. Largely as a way of escaping the difficulties of his childhood, Jung turned inward and became preoccupied with pursuing his unconscious experiences as reflected in his dreams, visions, and fantasies. At age 81 he wrote about his recollections in his autobiography *Memories, Dreams, Reflections* (1961). He made a choice to focus on the unconscious realm in his personal life, which also influenced the development of his theory of personality.

According to Jung, humans are not merely shaped by past events but strive for growth as well. Part of the nature of humans is to be constantly developing, growing, and moving toward a balanced and complete level of development. For Jung, our present personality is determined both by who and what we have been and also by the person we hope to become. The process of self-actualization is oriented toward the future. Jung's theory is based on the assumption that humans tend to move toward the fulfillment or realization of all their capabilities. Achieving individuation — or a fully harmonious and integrated personality — is a primary goal. To reach this goal we must become aware of and accept the full range of our being.

The public self we present is only a small part of who and what we are. For Jung, both constructive and destructive forces co-exist in the human psyche, and to become integrated we must accept the dark side of our nature with our primitive impulses such as selfishness and greed. Acceptance of our dark side (or shadow) does not imply being dominated by this dimension of our being but simply recognizing that this is a part of our nature.

Carl Rogers (1980), a major figure in the development of humanistic psychology, focused on the importance of nonjudgmental listening and acceptance as a condition for people to feel free enough to change. Rogers's emphasis on the value of autonomy seems to have grown, in part, out of his own struggles to become independent from his parents. Rogers grew up fearing his mother's critical judgment. In an interview, Rogers mentioned that he could not imagine talking to his mother about anything of significance, because he was sure that she would have some negative judgment. He also grew up in a home where strict religious standards governed behavior. In his early years, while at a seminary studying to be a minister, Rogers made a critical choice that influenced his personal life and the focus of his theory. Realizing that he could no longer go along with the religious thinking of his parents, Rogers questioned the religious dogma he was being taught, which led to his emancipation and his psychological independence. As a college student he took the risk of writing a letter to his parents telling them that his views were changing from fundamentalist to liberal and that he was developing his own philosophy of life. Even though he knew that his departure from the values of his parents would be difficult for them, he felt that such a move was necessary for his own intellectual and psychological freedom.

Rogers built his entire theory and practice of psychotherapy on the concept of the "fully functioning person." Fully functioning people tend to reflect and ask basic questions such as: Who am I? How can I discover my real self? How can I become what I deeply wish to become? How can I get out from behind my facade and become myself? Rogers maintained that when people give up their facade and accept themselves, they move in the direction of being open to experience (that is, they begin to see reality without distorting it), they trust themselves and look to themselves for the answers to their problems, and they no longer attempt to become fixed entities or products, realizing instead that growth is a continual process. Such fully functioning people, Rogers wrote, are in a fluid process of challenging and revisiting their perceptions and beliefs as they open themselves to new experiences.

In contrast to those who assume that we are by nature irrational and destructive unless we are socialized, Rogers exhibited a deep faith in human beings. In his view, people are naturally social and forward-moving, strive to function fully, and have at their deepest core a positive goodness. In short, people are to be trusted, and since they are basically cooperative and constructive, there is no need to control their aggressive impulses.

Abraham Maslow was one of the most influential psychologists contributing to our understanding of self-actualizing individuals. He built on Adler's and Jung's works in some significant ways, yet he distinguished himself in discovering a psychology of health. Maslow was concerned with taking care of basic survival needs, and his theory stresses a hierarchy of needs, with satisfaction of physiological and safety needs prerequisite to being concerned about actualizing one's potentials. Self-actualization became the central theme of the work of Abraham Maslow (1968, 1970, 1971). Maslow uses the phrase "the psychopathology of the average" to highlight his contention that merely "normal" people may never extend themselves to become what they are capable of becoming. Further, he criticized Freudian psychology for what he saw as its preoccupation with the sick and crippled side of human nature. If our findings are based on observations of a sick population, Maslow reasoned, a sick psychology will emerge. Maslow believed that too much research was being conducted into anxiety, hostility, and neuroses and too little into joy, creativity, and self-fulfillment.

In his quest to create a humanistic psychology that would focus on our potential, Maslow studied what he called self-actualizing people and found that they differed in important ways from so-called normals. Some of the characteristics Maslow found in these people included a capacity to tolerate and even welcome uncertainty in their lives, acceptance of themselves and others, spontaneity and creativity, a need for privacy and solitude, autonomy, a capacity for deep and intense interpersonal relationships, a genuine caring for others, a sense of humor, an inner-directedness (as opposed to the tendency to live by others' expectations), and the absence of artificial dichotomies within themselves (such as work/play, love/hate, and weak/strong). Maslow's theory of self-actualization, along with the implications for the humanistic approach to psychology, is presented next.

■ Overview of Maslow's Self-Actualization Theory

Maslow postulated a hierarchy of needs as a source of motivation. The most basic are the physiological needs. If we are hungry and thirsty, our attention is riveted on meeting these basic needs. Next are the safety needs, which include a sense of security and stability. Once our physical and safety needs are fulfilled, we become concerned with meeting our needs for belonging and love, followed by working on our need for esteem, both from self and others. We are able to strive toward self-actualization only after these four basic needs are met: physiological, safety, love, and esteem. Maslow emphasized that people are not motivated by all five needs at the same time. The key factor determining which need is dominant at a given time is the degree to which those below it are satisfied. Some people come to the erroneous conclusion that if they were "bright" enough or "good" enough, they would be further down the road of self-actualization. The truth may be that in their particular cultural, environmental, and societal circumstances these people are motivated to work toward physical and psychological survival, which keeps them functioning at the lower end of the hierarchy.

We can summarize some of the basic ideas of the humanistic approach by means of Maslow's model of the self-actualizing person. He describes self-actualization in his book *Motivation and Personality* (1970), and he also treats the concept in his other books (1968, 1971). Keep in mind that an individual is not much concerned with actualization, nor is a society focused on the development of culture, if the basic needs are not met.

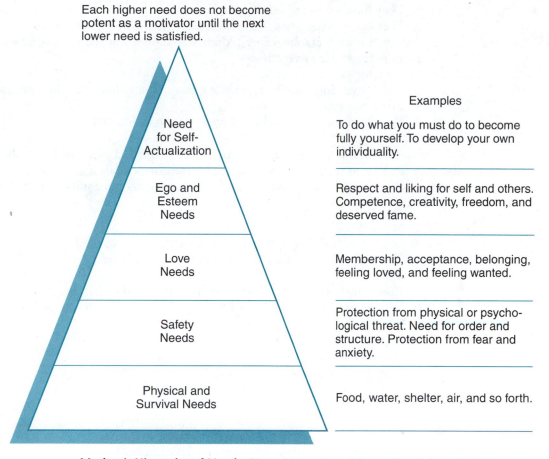

Each higher need does not become potent as a motivator until the next lower need is satisfied.

	Examples
Need for Self-Actualization	To do what you must do to become fully yourself. To develop your own individuality.
Ego and Esteem Needs	Respect and liking for self and others. Competence, creativity, freedom, and deserved fame.
Love Needs	Membership, acceptance, belonging, feeling loved, and feeling wanted.
Safety Needs	Protection from physical or psychological threat. Need for order and structure. Protection from fear and anxiety.
Physical and Survival Needs	Food, water, shelter, air, and so forth.

Maslow's Hierarchy of Needs. (From *Motivation and Personality*, 3/e by A. H. Maslow. Revised by Robert Frager, James Fadiman, Cynthia McReynolds, and Ruth Cox. Copyright 1954, © 1987 by Harper & Row, Publishers, Inc. Copyright © 1970 by Abraham H. Maslow. Reprinted by permission of HarperCollins Publishers, Inc.)

Self-Awareness.   Self-actualizing people are more aware of themselves, of others, and of reality than are nonactualizing people. Specifically, they demonstrate the following behavior and traits:

1. *Efficient perception of reality*
    a. Self-actualizing people see reality as it is.
    b. They have an ability to detect phoniness.
    c. They avoid seeing things in preconceived categories.
2. *Ethical awareness*
    a. Self-actualizing people display a knowledge of what is right and wrong for them.

    b. They have a sense of inner direction.

    c. They avoid being pressured by others and living by others' standards.

3. *Freshness of appreciation.* Like children, self-actualizing people have an ability to perceive life in a fresh way.

4. *Peak moments*

    a. Self-actualizing people experience times of being one with the universe; they experience moments of joy.

    b. They have the ability to be changed by such moments.

Freedom.   Self-actualizing people are willing to make choices for themselves, and they are free to reach their potential. This freedom entails a sense of detachment and a need for privacy, creativity and spontaneity, and an ability to accept responsibility for choices.

1. *Detachment*

    a. For self-actualizing people, the need for privacy is crucial.

    b. They have a need for solitude to put things in perspective.

2. *Creativity*

    a. Creativity is a universal characteristic of self-actualizing people.

    b. Creativity may be expressed in any area of life; it shows itself as inventiveness.

3. *Spontaneity*

    a. Self-actualizing people don't need to show off.

    b. They display a naturalness and lack of pretentiousness.

    c. They act with ease and grace.

Basic Honesty and Caring.   Self-actualizing people show a deep caring for and honesty with themselves and others. These qualities are reflected in their interest in humankind and in their interpersonal relationships.

1. *Sense of social interest*

    a. Self-actualizing people have a concern for the welfare of others.

    b. They have a sense of communality with all other people.

    c. They have an interest in bettering the world.

2. *Interpersonal relationships*

    a. Self-actualizing people have a capacity for real love and fusion with another.

    b. They are able to love and respect themselves.

    c. They are able to go outside themselves in a mature love.

    d. They are motivated by the urge to grow in their relationships.

3. *Sense of humor*

    a. Self-actualizing people can laugh at themselves.

    b. They can laugh at the human condition.

    c. Their humor is not hostile.

Trust and Autonomy.   Self-actualizing people exhibit faith in themselves and others; they are independent; they accept themselves as valuable persons; and their lives have meaning.

1. *Search for purpose and meaning*
   a. Self-actualizing people have a sense of mission, of a calling in which their potential can be fulfilled.
   b. They are engaged in a search for identity, often through work that is a deeply significant part of their lives.
2. *Autonomy and independence*
   a. Self-actualizing people have the ability to be independent.
   b. They resist blind conformity.
   c. They are not tradition-bound in making decisions.
3. *Acceptance of self and others*
   a. Self-actualizing people avoid fighting reality.
   b. They accept nature as it is.
   c. They are comfortable with the world.*

This profile is best thought of as an ideal rather than a final state that we reach once and for all. Thus, it is more appropriate to speak about the self-actualizing process rather than becoming a self-actualized person.

How do we work toward self-actualization? There is no set of techniques for reaching this goal, but in a sense the rest of this book, including the activities and "Time Out" sections, is about ways of beginning this lifelong quest. As you read about the struggles we face in trying to become all we are capable of becoming, we hope you will begin to see some options for living a fuller life.

➤ *Time Out for Personal Reflection*

The "Time Out" sections in this book are an opportunity for you to pause and reflect on your own experiences as they relate to the topic being discussed. Unlike most quizzes and tests you have taken, these inventories have no right and wrong answers. Taking them will probably be a different experience for you, and you may have to make a conscious effort to look within yourself for the response or answer that makes sense to you rather than searching for the expected response that is external to you.

1. To what degree do you have a healthy and positive view of yourself? Are you able to appreciate yourself, or do you discount your own worth? Take this self-inventory by rating yourself with the following code: 4 = this statement is true of me *most* of the time; 3 = this statement is true of me *much* of the time; 2 = this statement is true of me *some* of the time; 1 = this statement is true of me *almost none* of the time.

_____ I generally think and choose for myself.
_____ I usually like myself.
_____ I know what I want.
_____ I am able to ask for what I want.

_____   I feel a sense of personal power.
_____   I am open to change.
_____   I feel equal to others.
_____   I am sensitive to the needs of others.
_____   I care about others.
_____   I can act in accordance with my own judgment without feeling guilty if others disapprove of me.
_____   I do not expect others to make me feel alive.
_____   I can accept responsibility for my own actions.
_____   I am able to accept compliments.
_____   I can give affection.
_____   I can receive affection.
_____   I do not live by a long list of "shoulds," "oughts," and "musts."
_____   I am not so security-bound that I will not explore new things.
_____   I am generally accepted by others.
_____   I can give myself credit for what I do well.
_____   I am able to enjoy my own company.
_____   I am capable of forming intimate and meaningful relationships.
_____   I live in the here and now and do not get stuck dwelling on the past or the future.
_____   I feel a sense of significance.
_____   I am not diminished when I am with those I respect.
_____   I believe in my ability to succeed in projects that are meaningful to me.

Now go back over this inventory and identify not more than five areas that keep you from being as self-accepting as you might be. What can you do to increase your awareness of situations in which you do not fully accept yourself? For example, if you have trouble giving yourself credit for things you do well, how can you become aware of times when you discount yourself? When you do become conscious of situations in which you put yourself down, think of alternatives.

2. Take a few minutes to review Maslow's theory of self-actualization and then consider the following questions as they apply to you:

- Which of these qualities do you find most appealing? Why?
- Which would you like to cultivate in yourself?
- Which of Maslow's ideal qualities do you most associate with living a full and meaningful life?
- Who in your life comes closest to meeting Maslow's criteria for self-actualizing people?

Are You an Active Learner?

The self-actualization process of growth implies that you will be an *active learner:* that is, you will assume responsibility for your education, you will question what is presented to you, and you will apply what you learn in a personally meaningful way. Your schooling experiences may not have encouraged you to learn actively. Instead of questioning and learning to think for yourself, you can easily assume a passive stance by doing what is expected, memorizing facts, and giving back information on tests. This section asks you to review your school experiences and assess whether you are an active learner.

During my own (Jerry's) childhood and adolescence, school was a largely meaningless and sometimes painful experience. In addition, my educational experiences from grammar school through graduate school often taught me to be a passive learner; I learned that:

- pleasing the teacher was more important than pleasing myself
- accepting the opinions of an authority was more valuable than becoming a questioner
- learning facts and information was more valuable than learning about myself
- learning was motivated by external factors
- there was a right answer to every problem
- school life and everyday life were separate
- sharing personal feelings and concerns had no place in the classroom
- the purpose of school was mainly to cultivate the intellect and acquire basic skills rather than to encourage me to understand myself more fully and make choices based on this self-awareness

I do think it is essential to learn basic skills, but I also think academic learning of content is most fruitful when combined with the personal concerns of the learners.

How did I make this shift in my thinking toward personal learning? I am fairly clear that a key motivation for becoming a teacher was my conviction that there had to be a better way of teaching and learning than I had experienced as a student. I wanted to make a difference. I wanted to be a teacher who could help his students relate classroom learning to their personal lives.

In my 35-year teaching career I have found a great deal of satisfaction in being instrumental in helping students believe in themselves. My experiences as a high school teacher, a psychology instructor at a community college, and a professor of counseling at a university continue to show me that an effective educator must be a perpetual learner—both about one's subject and about one's own life. Challenging my students to stretch their personal boundaries has always been more important than merely presenting knowledge. After many years of passive learning on my part, I have done whatever I can to encourage students to become active learners—to raise questions and to find ways to apply whatever they are learning to their lives and their future careers.

A number of writers espouse the values of personal learning. One of the leaders of humanistic approaches to learning who has influenced us both personally and professionally is Carl Rogers. In his thought-provoking and classic book, *Freedom to Learn for the '80s,* Rogers (1983) deals with the challenges of the teaching/learning process. He advocates "whole-person learning," wherein what is learned becomes a basic part of the person and the attitudes and values are at least

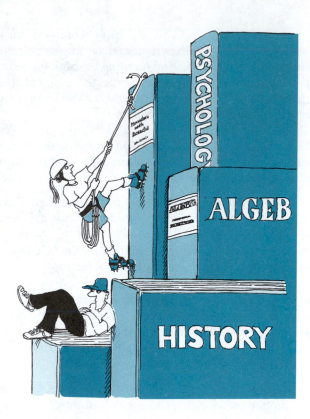

as important as the factual knowledge. Several key elements are involved in the personal learning that Rogers proposes:

- It is self-initiated, in that there is a sense of discovery, reaching out, and comprehending that comes from within the learner.
- It is pervasive, meaning that it makes a difference in the behavior, attitudes, and personality of the learner.
- The locus of evaluation is within the learner; that is, the learner determines whether what is being learned is meeting his or her needs.
- It is significant and matters to the learner; that is, it is holistic in that it combines the logical and cognitive with the intuitive and feeling dimensions.

If you think of learning from this perspective, it becomes a very different matter from simply taking in information that is external to the self, devoid of meaning, and quickly forgotten.

We challenge you to find ways to bring meaning to your learning by being active in the process. You can get the most out of your courses if you develop a style of learning in which you raise questions and search for answers within yourself. Since this kind of active learning may be different from most of your previous experiences in school, here is a "Time Out" that will help you review your own experiences as a learner and think about the effects your education has had on you.

➤ *Time Out for Personal Reflection*

How do you rate your education? In taking this inventory, respond quickly by giving your initial reaction. Indicate your response by circling the corresponding letter. You may choose more than one response for each item, or if none of the responses fit you, you may write your own response on the blank line.

1. How would you evaluate your experience in elementary school?
   a. It was a pleasant time for me.
   b. I dreaded going to school.
   c. It taught me a lot about life.
   d. Athough I learned facts and information, I learned little about myself.

   e. _____

2. How would you evaluate your high school experience?
   a. I have mostly favorable memories of this time.
   b. I got more from the social aspects of high school than I did from the educational ones.
   c. I remember it as a lonely time.
   d. I was very involved in my classes.

   e. _____

3. How do you evaluate your present college experience?
   a. I like what I'm getting from my college education.
   b. I see college as an extension of my earlier schooling experiences.
   c. I'm learning more about myself as a result of attending college.
   d. I'm here mainly to get a degree; learning is secondary.

   e. _____

4. To what degree do you see yourself as a "teacher pleaser"?
   a. In the past I worked very hard to gain the approval of my teachers.
   b. I'm now more concerned with pleasing myself than I am with pleasing my teachers.
   c. It's very important to me to please those who are in authority.
   d. Good grades are more important than what I learn.

   e. _____

5. To what degree have you been a questioner?
   a. I generally haven't questioned authority.
   b. I've been an active learner, and I've raised many questions.
   c. Basically, I see myself as a passive learner.
   d. I didn't raise questions earlier in my schooling, but now I'm willing to question the meaning of what I do in school.

   e. _____

6. Have you been motivated externally or internally?
   a. I've been motivated primarily by competition and other forms of external motivation.
   b. I've learned things mainly because of the satisfaction I get from learning.
   c. I see myself as having a lot of curiosity and a need to explore.
   d. I've generally learned what I think will be on a test or what will help me get a job.

   e. _____

7. To what degree are you a confident learner?
   a. I'm afraid of making mistakes and looking foolish.
   b. I often look for the "correct way" or the "one right answer."
   c. I trust my own judgment, and I live by my values.
   d. I think there can be many right answers to a problem.

   e. _____

8. To what degree has your learning been real and meaningful?
   a. School has been a place where I learn things that are personally meaningful.
   b. School has been a place where I mostly perform meaningless tasks and pursue meaningless goals.
   c. I've learned how to apply what I learn in school to my life outside of school.
   d. I've tended to see school learning and real life as separate.

   e. _____

9. To what degree have feelings been a part of your schooling?
   a. School has dealt with issues that relate to my personal concerns.
   b. I've believed that what I feel has no place in school
   c. The emphasis has been on the intellect, not on feelings.
   d. I've learned to distrust my feelings.

   e. _____

10. How much freedom have you experienced in your schooling?
   a. Schooling has taught me how to handle freedom in my own learning.
   b. I've found it difficult to accept freedom in school.
   c. I've experienced schools as places that restrict my freedom and do not encourage me to make my own choices.
   d. I've experienced schools as sources of encouragement to make and accept my own choices.

   e. _____

Now that you've taken this inventory, we have some suggestions for applying the results to yourself. Look over your responses and then decide which of the following questions might be meaningful follow-up activities for you.

1. How would you describe yourself as a learner during elementary school? during your high school years? as a college student?
2. What effects do you think your schooling has had on you as a person?

3. If you don't like the kind of learner you've been up until now, what can you do about it? What changes would you like to make?

4. What important things (both positive and negative) did you learn about yourself as a result of your schooling?

When you've completed your review of your school experience, you might consider (1) bringing your responses to class and sharing them or (2) using a journal to write down memories of school experiences that have had an impact on you and to keep an ongoing account of significant events in your present learning. Many students find that keeping a journal helps them personalize the topics addressed in this book, and they value looking back over what they wrote earlier. Further suggestions for journal writing are given in the section of this chapter on "How to Use This Book."

Multiple Intelligences and Multiple Learning Styles

Part of the process of getting the most out of your education consists of knowing where your talents lie and how you learn. People differ in how they learn best and in what kinds of knowledge they tend to learn most easily. For example, auditory learners tend to understand and retain ideas better from hearing them spoken, while visual learners tend to learn more effectively when they can literally see what they are learning. Some students learn best by listening to lectures and reading, others by hands-on experience. By learning as much as you can about your own learning style, you can maximize your success in college regardless of your field of study.

Behind differences in learning styles may lie basic differences in intelligence. Intelligence itself is not one single, easily measured ability but a group of abilities (Gardner, 1983). Howard Gardner, a professor of education at Harvard University, has discovered that we are capable of at least seven different types of intelligence and learning. His theory of *multiple intelligences* identifies the following forms of intelligence:

- verbal-linguistic
- musical-rhythmic
- logical-mathematical
- visual-spatial
- bodily-kinesthetic
- intrapersonal
- interpersonal

For the most part, traditional approaches to schooling—teaching methods, class assignments, and tests—have been geared to and measure the growth of verbal-linguistic and logical-mathematical abilities, what we generally refer to as IQ. Yet several, if not all, of the other forms of intelligence and learning are equally vital to success in life.

The implications of this are enormous, for both teaching and learning. For example, if you have trouble learning in the logical-mathematical sense, you should not assume you aren't "intelligent." You may well have strengths in one or several other areas. Moreover, if you have difficulty learning in one form of intelligence, you can probably compensate by using the forms of intelligence in which you are stronger to learn similar material.

Let's examine the specific characteristics of each of the seven kinds of intellectual abilities and then consider the implications for college learning.

■ If you are a *verbal-linguistic* learner, you have highly developed auditory skills, enjoy reading and writing, like to play word games, and have a good memory for names, dates, and places; you like to tell stories; and you are good at getting your point across. You learn best by saying and hearing words. People whose dominant intelligence is in the verbal-linguistic area include poets, authors, speakers, attorneys, politicians, lecturers, and teachers.

■ If you are a *musical-rhythmic* learner, you are sensitive to the sounds in your environment, enjoy music, and prefer listening to music when you study or read. You appreciate pitch and rhythm. You probably like singing to yourself. You learn best through melody and music. Musical intelligence is obviously demonstrated by singers, conductors, composers, but also by those who enjoy, understand, and use various elements of music.

■ If you are more *logical-mathematical,* you probably like to explore patterns and relationships, and you enjoy doing activities in sequential order. You are likely to enjoy mathematics, and you like to experiment with things you don't understand. You like to work with numbers, ask questions, and explore patterns and relationships. You may find it challenging to solve problems and use logical reasoning. You learn best by classifying information, engaging in abstract thinking, and looking for common basic principles. People with well-developed logical-mathematical abilities include mathematicians, biologists, medical technologists, geologists, engineers, physicists, researchers, and other scientists.

■ If your intellectual orientation is primarily *visual-spatial,* you probably feel at home with the visual arts, maps, charts, and diagrams. You tend to think in images and pictures. You are able to visualize clear images when you think about things, and you can complete jigsaw puzzles easily. You are likely to engage in imagining things and daydreaming. You probably like to design and create things. You learn best by looking at pictures and slides, watching videos or movies, and visualizing. People with well-developed visual-spatial abilities are found in professions such as sculpting, painting, surgery, and engineering.

■ If you are a *bodily-kinesthetic* learner, you process knowledge through bodily sensations and use your body in skilled ways. You have good balance and coordination; you are good with your hands. You need opportunities to move and act things out. You tend to respond best in classrooms that provide physical activities and hands-on learning experiences, and you are able to manipulate objects with finesse. You learn best by touching, moving around, and processing knowledge through bodily sensations. People who have highly developed bodily-kinesthetic abilities include carpenters, television and stereo repairpersons, mechanics, dancers, gymnasts, swimmers, and jugglers.

■ If you are an *intrapersonal* learner, you prefer your own inner world, you like to be alone, and you are aware of your own strengths, weaknesses, and feelings. You tend to be a creative and independent thinker; you like to reflect on ideas. You probably possess independence, self-confidence, determination, and are highly motivated. You may respond with strong opinions when controversial topics are discussed. You learn best by engaging in independent study projects rather than working on group projects. Pacing your own instruction is important to you. People with intrapersonal abilities include entrepreneurs, philosophers, and psychologists.

■ If you are an *interpersonal* learner, you enjoy being around people, like talking to people, have many friends, and engage in social activities. You learn best by relating, sharing, and participating in cooperative group environments. People with strong interpersonal abilities are found in sales, consulting, community organizing, counseling, teaching, or one of the helping professions.

These categories of intelligence and learning styles should not be thought of in a rigid or deterministic way. Intelligence is not a singular entity; it is complex and multidimensional. You may find that you have strengths in several different areas. The model of multiple intelligences is best used as a tool to help you identify areas you may want to pursue. As you'll see in Chapter 5, other factors besides ability (or intelligence) need to be weighed in deciding on a field of study or a career. The more you can view college as a place to use all your talents and improve your learning abilities in all respects, the more meaningful and successful your college journey will be.

■ Choices in Learning

You can use the knowledge of your own learning strengths to improve your college learning. In addition to the seven kinds of intelligences and the learning styles that flow from them, consider three different kinds of learners: auditory, visual, and kinesthetic. As you read the following descriptions, consider how you can best learn — and reflect on the choices you have open to you as a learner.

■ If you are an *auditory learner,* it is important that you hear the message. Your learning is facilitated by opportunities to listen and to speak. You prefer to learn by listening to lectures or audiotapes, and by discussing what you've heard. You'll probably profit more from reading *after* you've heard about the material you are to read. You may learn best by taping lectures and listening to them again or by listening to your textbook on audiotape. Reciting information and teaching others what you know are useful ways for you to learn.

■ If you are a *visual learner,* you prefer to learn by reading, watching videotapes, and observing demonstrations. You will learn better by seeing pictures and graphically mapping out material to learn rather than relying mainly on listening to lectures. It is important that you envision the big picture. You are likely to get more from a lecture *after* you've read the material. Besides the printed word, you may learn well by seeing pictures and forming images of what is to be learned. You learn by looking at pictures, watching movies, and seeing slides. You may rely on word processors, books, and other visual devices for learning and recall.

■ If you are a *kinesthetic learner,* you prefer to learn by doing, by getting physically involved through movement and action. It is a good idea to figure out ways to participate in movement exercises while learning or to use body language in learning. You tend to learn best by experimenting and figuring out ways of solving a problem. As a kinesthetic learner, if you had a problem with your computer, car, or videocassette recorder, you might lack the patience to plow through a manual. Instead, you'd probably manipulate gadgets until you figured out for yourself what was wrong with the equipment. You acquire and remember information best through movement, hands-on experience, role playing, working with materials, dramatic improvisation, games, and participatory workshops.

Although you may have a preference for one of these ways of learning, remain open to incorporating elements from the other styles as well. You are likely to find that you learn best by blending many pathways.

■ Different Ways of Thinking and Approaching Learning

To be challenged to think for yourself and to search within for direction may be a new experience for many of you. It may be unsettling when you do not get definite answers to your questions. Some of you may have a high need for structure and little tolerance for ambiguity. You may have been conditioned to find the "one correct answer" to a problem and to support whatever statements you make with some authoritative source. Our experience with university students repeatedly shows us how hesitant many of you are when it comes to formulating and expressing your position on an issue. You are often apologetic for using the word "I" in a paper, even when you support your position with sound reasoning and material from other sources. Yet many of you are disenchanted with mechanical and impersonal learning and truly want to learn how to think through issues and find meaning in the courses you take. One of the ways to do this involves employing what is known as divergent thinking.

Using Divergent Thinking.   In approaching a problem you can use either convergent thinking or divergent thinking. In *convergent thinking* the task is to sort out alternatives and arrive at the best solution to the problem. A multiple-choice test taps convergent thinking; you must select the one best answer from a list of alternatives given. *Divergent thinking,* in contrast, involves coming up with many acceptable answers to the problem. Essay tests have the potential to tap divergent thinking. Divergent thinking is an important skill to master if you choose to be an active learner. Part of being an active learner is having the capacity to raise questions, to brainstorm, and to generate multiple answers to your questions. This process implies a personal involvement with the material to be learned. This book is based on divergent thinking; the themes it addresses do not have simple solutions. It is designed to engage you in exploring how these themes apply to you and to help you find your own answers.

■ Taking Responsibility for Learning

At the beginning of a new semester some college students are overwhelmed by how much they are expected to do in all their courses while maintaining a life outside of

school. One reaction to this feeling of being swamped is to put things off, which results in getting behind with your assignments, which typically leads to discouragement.

If you take responsibility for your own learning, you are much more likely to succeed. Students who fail to see their own role in the learning process often blame others for their failures. But if you are dissatisfied with your education, first take a look at yourself and see how much you're willing to invest in making it more vital.

It is also essential that you develop effective study habits and learn basic time management skills. Although acquiring these skills alone does not guarantee successful learning, knowing how to organize your time and how to study can contribute significantly to assuming an active and effective style of learning. One aid to learning, found in the "Activities and Exercises" section at the end of this chapter, is the five-step SQ3R technique for studying, reading, and reviewing. We have also included the Rogers Indicator of Multiple Intelligence self-evaluation, which can help you understand how you learn best.

Think about how your present values and beliefs are related to your experiences in school. You might pause and reflect on a particularly positive school experience and how it might be affecting you today. Consider your educational experiences up to this point and think about your attitudes and behaviors as a student. What kinds of experiences have you had as a student so far, and how might these experiences influence the kind of learner you are today? If you like the kind of learner you are now, or if you have had mostly good experiences with school, you can build on that positive framework as you approach this course. You can continue to find ways to involve yourself with the material you will read, study, and discuss. If you feel cheated by a negative educational experience, you can begin to change it now. Are you waiting for others to do something to motivate you? How much are you willing to do to change the things you don't like?

Regardless of the format or structure of the course in which you are using this book, you can find ways to become personally involved in the course. For example, this book deals with personal topics such as reviewing your childhood and adolescence, loneliness, love, sexuality, intimate relationships, work and leisure, your body, and death and loss. You can make the choice to be actively engaged or only marginally involved in applying the themes in this book in your life. You can make this class different by applying some of the ideas discussed in this chapter. Once you become aware of those aspects of your education that you don't like, you can decide to change your style of learning.

One way to begin to become an active learner is to think about your reasons for taking this course and your expectations concerning what you will learn. The following "Time Out" will help you focus on these issues.

➤ *Time Out for Personal Reflection*

1. What are your main reasons for taking this course?

   _____

   _____

   _____

   _____

2. What do you expect this course to be like? Check all the comments that fit you.

   _____   I expect to talk openly about issues that matter to me.
   _____   I expect to get answers to certain problems in my life.
   _____   I hope that I will become a more fulfilled person.
   _____   I hope that I will have less fear of expressing my feelings and ideas.
   _____   I expect to be challenged on why I am the way I am.
   _____   I expect to learn more about how other people function.
   _____   I expect that I will understand myself more fully by the end of the course than I do now.

3. What do you most want to accomplish in this course?

   _____

   _____

   _____

   _____

4. What are you willing to do to become actively involved in your learning? Check the appropriate comments.

_____   I'm willing to participate in class discussions.
_____   I'm willing to read the material and think about how it applies to me.
_____   I'm willing to question my assumptions and look at my values.
_____   I'm willing to spend some time most days reflecting on the issues raised in this course.
_____   I'm willing to keep a journal and to record my reactions to what I read and experience.

Getting the Most from This Course: Suggestions for Personal Learning

Few of your courses deal primarily with _you_ as the subject matter. Most of us spend years acquiring information about the world around us, and we may even equate learning with absorbing facts that are external to us. Although such learning is essential, it is equally important to learn about yourself. To a large degree, what you get from this course will depend on what you're willing to invest of yourself; so it's important that you clarify your goals and the steps you can take to reach them. The following guidelines will help you become active and involved in personal learning as you read the book and participate in your class.

1. _Preparing._ Reading and writing are excellent devices for getting the most from this class. Many students have been conditioned to view reading as an unpleasant assignment, and they tolerate textbooks as something to plow through for an examination. As an active learner, however, you can selectively read this book, reflecting on those sections that have special meaning to you. Read this book for your personal benefit, and make use of the "Time Out" sections and exercises to help you apply the material to your own life. Writing can also give you a focus. Write brief reactions in the margins as you read and come to class prepared to share your thoughts on the topics. You can increase your chances of having a profitable experience in class by taking the time and effort to think about the problems and personal concerns you're willing to explore.

2. _Dealing with fears._ Personal learning entails experiencing some common fears: the fear of taking an honest look at yourself and discovering terrible things; the fear of the unknown; the fear of looking foolish in front of others (especially your instructor); the fear of being criticized or ridiculed; and the fear of speaking out and expressing your values. It's natural to experience some fear about participating personally and actively in the class, especially since this kind of participation may involve taking risks you don't usually take in your courses. How you deal with your fears is more important than trying to eliminate your anxieties about getting involved in a personal way. You have the choice of remaining a passive observer or acknowledging your fears and dealing with them openly, even though you will likely experience some degree of discomfort. Facing your fears takes

courage and a genuine desire to increase your self-awareness, but by doing so you take a first big step toward expanding the range of your choices.

3. *Taking risks.* If you make the choice to get personally involved in the course, you should be prepared for the possibility of some disruption in your life. You may find yourself changing certain attitudes, beliefs, and behaviors. It can be a shock to discover that those who are close to you do not appreciate your changes. They may prefer that you remain as you are. Thus, instead of receiving their support for your changes, you may encounter their resistance.

4. *Establishing trust.* You can choose to take the initiative in establishing the trust necessary for you to participate in this course in a meaningful way, or you can wait for others to create a climate of trust. Students often have feelings of mistrust or other negative feelings toward an instructor, yet avoid doing anything. One way to establish trust is to talk with your instructor outside of class.

5. *Practicing self-disclosure.* Disclosing yourself to others is one way to come to know yourself more fully. Sometimes participants in self-awareness courses or experiential groups fear that they must give up their privacy to be active participants. However, you can be open and at the same time retain your privacy by deciding how much you will disclose and when it is appropriate to do so. Although it may be new and uncomfortable for you to talk in personal ways to people whom you don't know that well, you can say more than you typically would in most social situations. You will need patience in learning this new communication skill, and you will need to challenge yourself to reveal yourself in meaningful ways.

6. *Being direct.* You can adopt a direct style in your communication. You'll be more direct if you make "I" statements than if you say "you" when you really mean "I." For example, instead of saying "You can't trust people with what you feel, because they will let you down if you make yourself vulnerable," try instead, "I can't trust people with what I feel because they will let me down if I make myself vulnerable." Make eye contact and speak directly *to* a person rather than *at* or *about* the person. Of course, directness may not be part of your cultural repertoire. You may have been taught that being direct is rude and that indirect communication is highly valued. You'll need to adapt these guidelines to fit your cultural context.

7. *Listening.* You can work on developing the skill of really listening to what others are saying without thinking of what you will say in reply. The first step in understanding what others say about you is to listen carefully, neither accepting what they say wholesale nor rejecting it outright. *Active listening* (really hearing the full message another is sending) requires remaining open and carefully considering what others say instead of rushing to give reasons and explanations.

8. *Thinking for yourself.* Only you can make the choice whether to do your own thinking or to let others do your thinking and deciding for you. Many people seek counseling because they have lost the ability to find their own way and have become dependent on others to direct their lives and take responsibility for their decisions. If you value thinking and deciding for yourself, it is important for you to realize that neither your fellow students nor your instructor can give you answers.

9. *Avoiding self-fulfilling prophecies.* You can increase your ability to change by letting go of ways you've categorized yourself or been categorized by others. If you start off with the assumption that you're stupid, helpless, or boring, you'll proba-

bly convince others as well. Your negative self-talk will certainly get in the way of being the person you'd like to be. For example, by telling yourself that you have little to offer and that you are basically boring, you'll act this way. If you see yourself as boring, you'll probably present yourself in such a way that others will respond to you as a boring person. If you like the idea of changing some of the ways in which you see yourself and present yourself to others, you can experiment with going beyond some of your self-limiting labels. Allowing yourself to believe that a particular change is possible is a large part of experiencing that change. And once you experience yourself differently, others might experience you differently too.

10. *Practicing outside of class.* One important way to get the maximum benefit from a class dealing with personal learning is to think about ways of applying what you learn in class to your everyday life. You can make specific contracts with yourself (or with others) detailing what you're willing to do to experiment with new behavior and work toward desired changes.

At this point, pause and assess your readiness for taking an honest look at yourself. You may feel some hesitation in exploring these personal topics. If so, leave the door open and give yourself and the course a chance. If you open yourself to change and try the techniques we've suggested, you may well experience a sense of excitement and promise.

How to Use This Book

This book was not written to tell you how you should be; rather, its purpose is to challenge you to think of how you want to be. Once you become aware of the way you function, you will be in a position to decide what you want to do about yourself.

Many of the exercises, questions, and suggested activities will appeal differently to different readers. Considerations such as your age, life experiences, and cultural background will have a bearing on the meaning and importance of certain topics to you. We have written this book from our own cultural framework. Some of the points we make may seem strange within your cultural context. Most of these topics, however, do seem to be personally significant to most readers, regardless of their background. In our workshops with people from various cultures, we continue to find that many of the issues we explore are common human themes that transcend culture and unite us in our life struggles. Before you reject these ideas too quickly, reflect on ways you might be able to adapt them to your own cultural background. We hope you'll treat this book in a personal way and attempt to apply it to yourself. With this in mind, here are some suggestions:

1. At the beginning of each subsequent chapter is a self-inventory designed to involve you personally with each subject. For the most part, they consist of personal statements to stimulate your thinking about the topics of discussion. We encourage you to assess your attitudes and beliefs before reading each of the chapters. If you're reading this book alone, you may want to have a close friend or your partner answer some of the questions and react to the statements in the inventories. Doing this is a good way to stimulate meaningful dialogue with a person close to you.

2. In one sense this is an *unfinished* book. You are challenged to become a coauthor by completing the writing of this book in ways that are meaningful to you. In many of the chapters, examples are drawn from everyday life. You can extend the impact of these examples by thinking and writing about how they apply to you. Rather than reading simply to learn facts, take your own position on the issues raised. As much as possible, put yourself into what you read.

3. The "Time Out" sections are designed to help you focus on specific topics. It will be most valuable if you do these exercises as you read. Actually writing down your responses in the text will help you begin to think about how each topic applies to you. Then you can look for common themes, go back to review your comments, or share them with a few friends or others in class. This process of reflecting and writing can help you increase your motivation. Here again you have many opportunities to become a co-author in finishing this book.

4. At the end of each chapter are additional activities and exercises suggested for practice, both in class and out of class. Ultimately you will be the one to decide which activities you are willing to do. You may find some of the suggested exercises too threatening to do in a class, yet exploring the same activities in a small group in your class could be easier. If small discussion groups are not part of the structure

of your class, consider doing the exercises alone or sharing them with a friend. Don't feel compelled to complete all the activities; select those that have the most meaning for you at this time in your life.

5. One activity we suggest throughout the book is keeping a journal. You might purchase a separate notebook in which to write your reactions. Later you can look for patterns in your journal; doing so can help you identify some of your critical choices and areas of conflict. We frequently give concrete suggestions of things you might include in your journal, but the important thing is for you to decide what to put in and how to use it. Consider writing about some of the following topics:

- what I learned about others and myself through today's class session
- the topics that were of most interest to me (and why)
- the topics that held the least interest for me (and why)
- the topics I wanted to talk about
- the topics I avoided talking about
- particular sections (or issues) in the chapter that had the greatest impact on me (and why)
- some of the things I am learning about myself in reading the book
- some specific things I am doing in everyday life as a result of this class
- some concrete changes in my attitudes, values, and behavior that I find myself most wanting to make
- what I am willing to do to make these changes
- some barriers I encounter in making the changes I want to make

It is best to write what first comes to mind. Spontaneous reactions tend to tell you more about yourself than well-thought-out comments.

At this time we also suggest that you do the exercise on writing your philosophy of life, which is at the end of Chapter 12. It would be good to at least write a rough draft of your life's philosophy early in the course and then to rewrite this exercise toward the end of the course.

Chapter Summary

We do not have to passively live out the plans that others have designed for us. With awareness we can begin to make significant choices. Taking a stand in life by making choices can result in both gains and losses. Changing long-standing patterns is not easy, and there are many obstacles to overcome. Yet a free life has many rewards.

One of these benefits is personal growth. Growth is a lifelong process of expanding self-awareness and accepting new challenges. It does *not* mean disregard for others but rather implies fulfilling more of our potentials, including our ability to care for others. Four scholars who have made significant contributions to the concept of personal growth in a framework of humanistic psychology are Alfred Adler, Carl Jung, Carl Rogers, and Abraham Maslow. Perhaps the best way to conceptualize personal growth is by considering Maslow's ideal of *self-actualization*. Keep in mind that until our basic needs have been met we are not really much concerned about becoming a fully functioning person. If you are hungry or are living on the streets, you are not likely to reflect on the meaning of becoming an actualized individual. Remember also that self-actualization is not something that we do in isolation; rather, it is through meaningful relationships with others and through social interest that we discover and become the person we are capable of becoming. Paradoxically, we find ourselves when we are secure enough to go beyond a preoccupation with our self-interests and become involved in the world with selected people. Striving for self-actualization does not cease at a particular age but is an ongoing process. Rather than speaking of *self-actualization* as a product we attain, it is best to consider the process of becoming a *self-actualizing person*. Four basic characteristics of self-actualizing people are self-awareness, freedom, basic honesty and caring, and trust and autonomy. This course can be a first step on the journey toward achieving your personal goals and living a self-actualizing existence while at the same time you contribute to making the world a better place.

Growing obviously entails learning. We've encouraged you to review your school experiences and make an inventory of the ways your present attitudes toward learning have been influenced. Becoming aware of the effects schooling has had on you gives you the power to choose a new learning style that will make a significant difference in your life and will involve both your thoughts and your feelings.

People differ in how they learn best and the kind of knowledge they tend to learn most easily. Understanding the various learning styles will enable you to approach learning in a personal and meaningful way. Intelligence is not a singular entity; rather, it is complex and multidimensional. Discovering your dominant forms of intelligence can help you identify areas for study or career options.

A major purpose of this chapter is to encourage you to examine your responsibility for making your learning meaningful. It's easy to criticize impersonal institutions if you feel apathetic about your learning. It's more difficult but more honest to look at *yourself* and ask these questions: "When I find myself in an exciting class, do I get fully involved and take advantage of the opportunity for learning?" "Do I expect instructors to entertain and teach me while I sit back passively?" "If I'm bored, what am I doing about it?"

Even if your earlier educational experiences have taught you to be a passive learner and to avoid risks in your classes, awareness of this influence gives you the power to change your learning style. We invite you to decide how personal you want your learning to be in the course you're about to experience.

Activities and Exercises

1. The following are exercises you can do at home. They are intended to help you focus on specific ways in which you behave. We've drawn the examples from typical fears and concerns often expressed by college students. Study the situations by putting yourself in each one and deciding how you might typically respond. Then keep an account in your journal of actual instances you encounter in your classes.

   Situation A: You'd like to ask a question in class, but you're afraid that your question will sound dumb and that others will laugh.

   - *Issues:* Will you simply refrain from asking questions? If so, is this a pattern you care to continue? Are you willing to practice asking questions, even though you might experience some anxiety? What do you imagine will happen if you ask questions? What would you like to have happen?

   Situation B: You feel that you have a problem concerning authority figures. You feel intimidated, afraid to venture your opinions, and even more afraid to register a point of view opposed to your instructor's.

   - *Issues:* Does this description fit you? If it does, do you want to change? Do you ever examine where you picked up your attitudes toward yourself in relation to authority? Do you think they're still appropriate for you?

   Situation C: Your instructor seems genuinely interested in the students and the course, and she has extended herself by inviting you to come to her office if you have any problems with the course. You're having real difficulty grasping the material, and you're falling behind and doing poorly on the tests and assignments. Nevertheless, you keep putting off going to see the instructor to talk about your problems in the class.

- *Issues:* Have you been in this situation before? If so, what kept you from talking with your instructor? If you find yourself in this kind of situation, are you willing to seek help before it's too late?

2. Review Maslow's characteristics of self-actualizing people. Then consider the following questions:
   a. To what degree are these characteristics a part of your personality?
   b. Do you think Maslow's ideal of self-actualization fits for individuals of all cultural and ethnic groups? Are any characteristics inappropriate for certain cultures?

3. In keeping with the spirit of developing active learning habits, we suggest that you tackle your reading assignments systematically. A useful approach is Robinson's (1970) SQ3R technique (*survey, question, read, recite, review*). It is intended to get you actively involved with what you are reading. The technique does not have to be applied rigidly; in fact, you can develop your own way of carrying it out. This five-step method involves breaking a reading assignment down into manageable units and checking your understanding of what you are reading. The steps are as follows:

   Step 1: Survey. Rather than simply reading a chapter, begin by skimming it to get a general overview of the material. Look for the ways topics are interrelated, strive to understand the organization of the chapter, and give some preliminary thought to the information you are about to read.

   Step 2: Question. Once you get the general plan of the chapter, look at the main chapter headings. What questions do they raise that your reading of the chapter should answer? Formulate in your own words the questions that you would like to explore as you read.

   Step 3: Read. After skimming the chapter and raising key questions, proceed to read one section at a time with the goal of answering your questions. After you've finished a section, pause for a few moments and reflect on what you've read to determine if you can clearly address the questions you've raised.

   Step 4: Recite. In your own words, recite (preferably out loud) the answers to your questions. Avoid rote memorization. Attempt to give meaning to factual material. Make sure you understand the basic ideas in a section before you go on to the next section. Writing down a few key notes is a good way to have a record for your review later. Then go on to the next section of the chapter, repeating steps 3 and 4.

   Step 5: Review. After you finish reading the chapter, spend some time reviewing the main points. Test your understanding of the material by putting the major ideas into your own words. Repeat the questions, and attempt to answer them without looking at the book. If there is a chapter summary or listing of key terms, be sure to study this carefully. A good summary will help you put the chapter into context. Attempt to add to the summary by listing some of the points that seem particularly important or interesting to you.

4. At the end of each chapter, we identify a few sources for further reading on the topics addressed by each chapter. For a full bibliographic reference for each

book, consult the "References and Suggested Readings" at the end of this book. For this chapter we highly recommend: *The Different Drum: Community Making and Peace* (Peck, 1987); *Freedom to Learn for the 80's* (Rogers, 1983).

5. The *Rogers Indicator of Multiple Intelligences* (RIMI) is a self-inventory created by Dr. Keith Rogers, a professor at Brigham Young University. By taking this inventory you can pinpoint your dominate intelligences. It should take you approximately 15 minutes to complete the inventory. Use the grid at the end of the RIMI to interpret each of your scores on the seven kinds of intelligences, indicating low intensity, moderate intensity, and high intensity areas. After you've scored the RIMI, ask yourself: Do the scores I received on the RIMI correspond to what I know about myself? Based on this inventory, what are the implications of my style of learning? How might I want to change the way I approach learning? How can I best learn?

The Rogers Indicator of Multiple Intelligences

DIRECTIONS: For each statement, mark a box for your most accurate response according to descriptors above the boxes. Think carefully about your knowledge, beliefs, preferences, behavior, and experience. Decide quickly and move on. There is no right or wrong, no good or bad, no expected or desirable response. Use your heart as well as your head. Focus on the way you really are, not on the way you "ought to be" for someone else.

	Rarely 1	Occasionally 2	Sometimes 3	Usually 4	Almost always 5
1. I am careful about the direct and implied meanings of the words I choose.	❑	❑	❑	❑	❑
2. I appreciate a wide variety of music.	❑	❑	❑	❑	❑
3. People come to me when they need help with math problems or any calculations.	❑	❑	❑	❑	❑
4. In my mind, I can visualize clear, precise, sharp images.	❑	❑	❑	❑	❑
5. I am physically well-coordinated.	❑	❑	❑	❑	❑
6. I understand why I believe and behave the way I do.	❑	❑	❑	❑	❑
7. I understand the moods, temperaments, values, and intentions of others.	❑	❑	❑	❑	❑
8. I confidently express myself well in words, written or spoken.	❑	❑	❑	❑	❑

(continued)

The Rogers Indicator of Multiple Intelligences (continued)

	Rarely 1	Occasionally 2	Sometimes 3	Usually 4	Almost always 5
9. I understand the basic precepts of music such as harmony, chords, and keys.	❏	❏	❏	❏	❏
10. When I have a problem, I use a logical, analytical, step-by-step process to arrive at a solution.	❏	❏	❏	❏	❏
11. I have a good sense of direction.	❏	❏	❏	❏	❏
12. I have skill in handling objects such as scissors, balls, hammers, scalpels, paintbrushes, knitting needles, pliers, etc.	❏	❏	❏	❏	❏
13. My self-understanding helps me to make wise decisions for my life.	❏	❏	❏	❏	❏
14. I am able to influence other individuals to believe and/or behave in response to my own beliefs, preferences and desires.	❏	❏	❏	❏	❏
15. I am grammatically accurate.	❏	❏	❏	❏	❏
16. I like to compose or create music.	❏	❏	❏	❏	❏
17. I am rigorous and skeptical in accepting facts, reasons, and principles.	❏	❏	❏	❏	❏
18. I am good at putting together jigsaw puzzles, and reading instructions, patterns, or blueprints.	❏	❏	❏	❏	❏
19. I excel in physical activities such as dance, sports, or games.	❏	❏	❏	❏	❏
20. My ability to understand my own emotions helps me to decide whether or how to be involved in certain situations.	❏	❏	❏	❏	❏
21. I would like to be involved in "helping" professions such as teaching, therapy, or counseling, or to do work such as political or religious leadership.	❏	❏	❏	❏	❏
22. I am able to use spoken or written words to influence or persuade others.	❏	❏	❏	❏	❏
23. I enjoy performing music, such as singing or playing a musical instrument for an audience.	❏	❏	❏	❏	❏

The Rogers Indicator of Multiple Intelligences (continued)

	Rarely 1	Occasionally 2	Sometimes 3	Usually 4	Almost always 5
24. I require scientific explanations of physical realities.	❏	❏	❏	❏	❏
25. I can read maps easily and accurately.	❏	❏	❏	❏	❏
26. I work well with my hands as would an electrician, seamstress, plumber, tailor, mechanic, carpenter, assembler, etc.					
27. I am aware of the complexity of my own feelings, emotions, and beliefs in various circumstances.	❏	❏	❏	❏	❏
28. I am able to work as an effective intermediary in helping other individuals and groups to solve their problems.	❏	❏	❏	❏	❏
29. I am sensitive to the sounds, rhythms, inflections, and meters of words, especially as found in poetry.	❏	❏	❏	❏	❏
30. I have a good sense of musical rhythm.	❏	❏	❏	❏	❏
31. I would like to do the work of people such as chemists, engineers, physicists, astronomers, or mathematicians.	❏	❏	❏	❏	❏
32. I am able to produce graphic depictions of the spatial world as in drawing, painting, sculpting, drafting, or map-making.	❏	❏	❏	❏	❏
33. I relieve stress or find fulfillment in physical activities.	❏	❏	❏	❏	❏
34. My inner self is my ultimate source of strength and renewal.	❏	❏	❏	❏	❏
35. I understand what motivates others even when they are trying to hide their motivations.	❏	❏	❏	❏	❏
36. I enjoy reading frequently and widely.	❏	❏	❏	❏	❏
37. I have a good sense of musical pitch.	❏	❏	❏	❏	❏
38. I find satisfaction in dealing with numbers.	❏	❏	❏	❏	❏

(continued)

The Rogers Indicator of Multiple Intelligences (continued)

	Rarely 1	Occasionally 2	Sometimes 3	Usually 4	Almost always 5
39. I like the hands-on approach to learning when I can experience personally the objects that I'm learning about.	❑	❑	❑	❑	❑
40. I have quick and accurate physical reflexes and responses.	❑	❑	❑	❑	❑
41. I am confident in my own opinions and am not easily swayed by others.	❑	❑	❑	❑	❑
42. I am comfortable and confident with groups of people.	❑	❑	❑	❑	❑
43. I use writing as a vital method of communication.	❑	❑	❑	❑	❑
44. I am affected both emotionally and intellectually by music.	❑	❑	❑	❑	❑
45. I prefer questions that have definite "right" and "wrong" answers.	❑	❑	❑	❑	❑
46. I can accurately estimate distances and other measurements.	❑	❑	❑	❑	❑
47. I have accurate aim when throwing balls or in archery, shooting, golf, etc.	❑	❑	❑	❑	❑
48. My feelings, beliefs, attitudes, and emotions are my own responsibility.	❑	❑	❑	❑	❑
49. I have a large circle of close associates.	❑	❑	❑	❑	❑

(continued)

Multiple Intelligence Scores

DIRECTIONS: In the chart below, the box numbers are the same as the statement numbers in the survey. You made a rating judgment for each statement. Now, place the numbers that correspond to your ratings in the numbered boxes below. Then add down the columns and write the totals at the bottom to determine your score in each of the seven intelligence categories. Then, for the meanings of the scores, consult the interpretations below the chart.

Verbal/ Linguistic	Musical/ Rhythmic	Logical/ Mathematical	Visual/ Spatial	Bodily/ Kinesthetic	Intrapersonal	Interpersonal
1	2	3	4	5	6	7
8	9	10	11	12	13	14
15	16	17	18	19	20	21
22	23	24	25	26	27	28
29	30	31	32	33	34	35
36	37	38	39	40	41	42
43	44	45	46	47	48	49
Totals						
Interpretations of knowledge, belief, behavior						

(continued)

Interpretation of Scores

To some degree we possess all of these intelligences, and all can be enhanced. We are each a unique blend of all seven; however, we all differ in the degree to which we prefer and have the competence to use each of the intelligences. Below are presented interpretations for the scores in the three ranges of low, moderate, and high.

Score	Intensity of Preference and/or Competence

7–15

(3)

Low Intensity: You tend to "avoid" it, and are probably uncomfortable when required to use it. Tertiary preference (3). This intelligence probably is not one of your favorites. In most circumstances, you lack confidence and will go out of your way to avoid situations involving intensive exercise of this intelligence. Your competence is probably relatively low. Unless you are unusually motivated, gaining expertise might be frustrating and likely would require great effort. All intelligences, including this one, can be enhanced throughout your lifetime.

16–26

(2)

Moderate Intensity: You tend to "accept" it, or use it with some comfort and ease. Secondary preference (2). You could take or leave the application or use of this intelligence. Though you accept it, you do not necessarily prefer to employ it. But, on the other hand, you would not necessarily avoid using it. This may be because you have not developed your ability, or because you have a moderate preference for this intelligence. Your competence is probably moderate also. Gaining expertise would be satisfying, but probably would require considerable effort.

27–35

(1)

High Intensity: You tend to "prefer" it, and use it often with comfort and facility. Primary preference (1). You enjoy using this intelligence. Applying it is fun. You are excited and challenged by it, perhaps even fascinated. You prefer this intelligence. Given the opportunity, you will usually select it. Everyone knows you love it. Your competence is probably relatively high if you have had opportunities to develop it. Becoming an expert should be rewarding and fulfilling, and will probably require little effort compared to a moderate or low preference.

2

Reviewing Your Childhood and Adolescence

What we resist persists.

✔ *Prechapter Self-Inventory*

Use the following scale to respond: 4 = this statement is true of me *most* of the time; 3 = this statement is true of me *much* of the time; 2 = this statement is true of me *some* of the time; 1 = this statement is true of me *almost none* of the time.

_____ 1. I'm capable of looking at my past decisions and then making new decisions that will significantly change the course of my life.

_____ 2. "Shoulds" and "oughts" often get in the way of my living my life the way I want.

_____ 3. To a large degree I've been shaped by the events of my childhood and adolescent years.

_____ 4. When I think of my early childhood years, I remember feeling secure, accepted, and loved.

_____ 5. As a child I was taught not to express negative feelings such as rage, anger, hatred, jealousy, and aggression.

_____ 6. I had desirable models to pattern my behavior after when I was a child and an adolescent.

_____ 7. In looking back at my early school-age years, I think that I had a positive self-concept and that I experienced more successes than failures.

_____ 8. I went through a stage of rebellion during my adolescent years.

_____ 9. My adolescent years were lonely ones.

_____ 10. I remember being significantly influenced by peer-group pressure during my adolescence.

Here are a few suggestions for using this self-inventory:

- Retake the inventory after reading the chapter and again at the end of the course, and compare your answers.
- Have someone who knows you well take the inventory for you, giving the responses he or she thinks actually describe you. Then you can discuss any discrepancies between your sets of responses.
- In your class, compare your responses with those of the other members and discuss the similarities and differences between your attitudes and theirs.

Introduction

This chapter and the next one lay the groundwork for much of the rest of the book by focusing on our lifelong struggle to achieve psychological emancipation, or autonomy. The term *autonomy* refers to mature independence *and* interdependence. As you'll recall from the previous chapter, becoming a fully functioning person occurs in the context of relationships with others and with concern for the welfare of others. If you are an autonomous person, you are able to function without constant approval and reassurance, are sensitive to the needs of others, can effectively meet the demands of daily living, are willing to ask for help when it is needed, and can provide support to others. In essence, you have the ability both to stand alone and to stand by another person. You are at home with both your inner world and your outer world. Although you are concerned with meeting your needs, you do not do so at the expense of those around you. You are aware of the impact your behavior may have on others, and you consider the welfare of others as well as your own self-development. Achieving personal autonomy is a continuing process of growth and learning, not something you arrive at once and for all.

Your attitudes toward gender-role identity, work, your body, love, sexuality, intimacy, loneliness, death, and meaning—the themes we'll be discussing in later chapters—were originally shaped by your experiences and decisions during your early years. But each stage of life has its own challenges and meanings, and you continue to develop and change, ideally in the direction of autonomy. In this chapter we will describe the stages from infancy through adolescence; in Chapter 3 we will take up early, middle, and late adulthood.

Stages of Personality Development: A Preview

In much of this chapter we describe a model that draws on Erik Erikson's (1963, 1982) theory of human development, but we also highlight some major ideas about development from a Freudian psychoanalytic perspective.

Sigmund Freud, the father of psychoanalysis, developed one of the most comprehensive theories of personality. He emphasized unconscious psychological processes and stressed the importance of early childhood experiences. According to his viewpoint, our sexual and social development is largely based on the first six years of life. During this time, Freud maintained, we go through three stages: oral, anal, and phallic. Our later personality development hinges on how well we resolve the demands and conflicts of each stage. Most of the problems people wrestle with in adulthood seem to have some connection with unresolved conflicts dating from early childhood.

Freud developed a model for understanding early development, especially its psychosexual aspects. Erikson built on and extended Freud's ideas, stressing the psychosocial aspects of development and carrying his own developmental theory beyond childhood. Although intellectually indebted to Freud, Erikson suggested that we should view human development in a more positive light, focusing on health and growth. Erikson also emphasized the rational side of human nature, whereas Freud emphasizes the irrational aspects of development. The id is the part of the personality that seeks immediate gratification; the ego is the component of the self that is in contact with the outside world through cognitive processes such as thinking, perceiving, remembering, reasoning, and attending. Freud's work emphasized aspects of the id, whereas Erikson's psychosocial theory maintains that the ego, not the id, is the life force of human development (Erikson, 1963). Erikson's theory focuses on the emergence of the self and the ways in which the self develops through our interactions with our social and cultural environment. Later in this chapter we will return to a more detailed discussion about development and protection of the self.

Erikson's theory of development holds that psychosexual and psychosocial growth occur together and that we face the task of establishing an equilibrium between ourselves and our social world at each stage of life. Psychosocial theory stresses integration of the biological, psychological, and social aspects of development. A combination of the Freudian psychosexual view and this psychosocial view of development provides a conceptual framework for understanding trends in development; major developmental tasks at each stage of life; critical needs and their satisfaction or frustration; potentials for choice at each stage of life; critical turning points or developmental crises; and the origins of faulty personality development, which leads to later personality conflicts.

Erikson described human development over the entire life span in terms of eight stages, each marked by a particular crisis to be resolved. You may think of a crisis as a gigantic problem or a catastrophic happening. But for Erikson, crisis meant a *turning point* in life, a moment of transition characterized by the potential to go either forward or backward in development. At these turning points we can achieve successful resolution of our conflicts and move ahead, or we can fail to resolve the conflicts and regress. To a large extent, our lives are the result of the choices we make at each stage.

By getting a picture of the challenges at each period of life, we will be able to understand how earlier stages of personality development influence the choices we make later in life. These stages are not precise categories that people fall into neatly. In reality there is great variability among individuals within a given developmental phase. Although there are general developmental tasks and problems associated with adolescence, for example, each adolescent reacts to the challenges of this period uniquely. The important point is that there is continuity in our lives. Our childhood experiences have a direct influence on how we approach the adolescent years. How well we master the tasks of adolescence has a bearing on our ability to cope with the critical turning points of adulthood. If we do not develop a clear sense of identity during adolescence, finding meaning in adult life becomes extremely difficult. As we progress from one stage of life to the next, we at times meet with roadblocks and detours. These barriers are often the result of having failed to master basic psychological competencies at an earlier period. When we encounter such obstacles, we can accept them as signposts and continue down the same path or use them as opportunities for growth.

Although the life-span perspective presented in these two chapters relies heavily on concepts borrowed from Freud's and Erikson's theories, we also draw on ideas from other writers who describe crises as individuals pass through life's stages: Berne (1975), Elkind (1984), Gould (1978), Mary and Robert Goulding (1978, 1979), Hamachek (1988, 1990), Havighurst (1972), Sheehy (1976, 1981, 1995), and Steiner (1975). Table 2–1 provides an overview of the major turning points in the life-span perspective of human development.

TABLE 2-1   OVERVIEW OF DEVELOPMENTAL STAGES

Life stage	Freud's psychosexual view	Erikson's psychosocial view	Potential problems
Infancy (First year of life)	*Oral stage.* Most critical stage in terms of later development. Failure to have one's need for basic nurturing met may lead to greediness later on. Material things may become a substitute for love. Infant's nursing satisfies the need for both food and pleasure.	*Infancy.* Basic task is to develop a sense of trust in self, others, and the environment. Infants need a sense of being cared for and loved. Absence of a sense of security may lead to suspiciousness and a general sense of mistrust toward human relationships. Core struggle: *trust* versus *mistrust.* Theme: hope.	Later personality problems that stem from infancy can include greediness and acquisitiveness, the development of a view of the world based on mistrust, fear of reaching out to others, rejection of affection, fear of loving and trusting, low self-esteem, isolation and withdrawal, and inability to form or maintain intimate relationships.
Early childhood (ages 1–3)	*Anal stage.* Child experiences parental demands and faces frustration. Toilet training is first experience with discipline. Attitudes toward body and bodily functions are direct results of this period. Problems in adulthood such as compulsive orderliness or messiness may stem from parental disciplinary practice.	*Early childhood.* A time for developing autonomy. Failure to master self-control tasks may lead to shame and doubt about oneself and one's adequacy. Core struggle: *self-reliance* versus *self-doubt.* Theme: will.	Children experience many negative feelings such as hostility, rage, destructiveness, anger, and hatred. If these feelings are not accepted, individuals may not be able to accept their feelings later on.
Preschool age (ages 3–6)	*Phallic stage.* Gender-role identity is a key issue. Child's interest in sexual matters increases; sexual attitudes are formed. Sexual dysfunctions in adulthood often have their roots in early conditioning and experiences.	*Preschool age.* Characterized by play and by anticipation of roles; a time to establish a sense of competence and initiative. Children who are not allowed to make decisions tend to develop a sense of guilt. Core struggle: *initiative* versus *guilt.* Theme: purpose.	Parental attitudes can be communicated verbally and nonverbally. Negative learning experiences tend to lead to feelings of guilt about natural impulses. Strict parental indoctrination can lead to rigidity, severe conflicts, remorse, and self-condemnation.

(continued)

TABLE 2-1   OVERVIEW OF DEVELOPMENTAL STAGES   *(continued)*

Life stage	Freud's psychosexual view	Erikson's psychosocial view	Potential problems
Middle childhood (ages 6–12)	*Latency stage.* Socialization takes place as children turn outward toward relationships with others. New interests emerge: school, playmates, sports, books. The sexual impulses are relatively quiescent, and social interests become prominent.	*School age.* Central task is to achieve a sense of industry; failure to do so results in a sense of inadequacy. Child needs to expand understanding of the world and continue to develop appropriate gender-role identity. Learning basic skills is essential for school success. Core struggle: *industry* versus *inferiority.* Theme: competence.	Problems that can originate during middle childhood include negative self-concept, feelings of inferiority in establishing social relationships, conflicts over values, confused gender-role identity, dependency, fear of new challenges, and lack of initiative.
Adolescence (ages 12–18)	*Genital stage.* Old themes of phallic stage are revived. Interest develops in opposite sex, with some sexual experimentation. Genital stage is the longest, beginning at puberty and lasting until later adulthood. In face of social restrictions and taboos, adolescents can redirect sexual energy by engaging in socially acceptable activities.	*Adolescence.* A critical time for forming a personal identity. Major conflicts center on clarification of self-identity, life goals, and life's meaning. Struggle is over integrating physical and social changes. Pressures include succeeding in school, choosing a job, forming relationships, and preparing for future. Core struggle: *identity* versus *role confusion.* Theme: fidelity.	A time when individual may anticipate an *identity crisis.* Caught in midst of pressures, demands, and turmoil, adolescent often loses sense of self. If *role confusion* results, individual may lack sense of purpose in later years. Absence of a stable set of values can prevent mature development of a philosophy to guide one's life.

TABLE 2-1   OVERVIEW OF DEVELOPMENTAL STAGES   *(continued)*

Life stage	Freud's psychosexual view	Erikson's psychosocial view	Potential problems
Early adulthood (ages 18–35)	*Genital stage* (continues). Core characteristic of mature adult is the freedom "to love and to work." The move toward adulthood involves developing intimacy, freedom from parental influence, and capacity to care for others.	*Young adulthood.* Sense of identity is again tested by the challenge of achieving intimacy. Ability to form close relationships depends on having a clear sense of self. Core struggle: *intimacy* versus *isolation.* Theme: love.	The challenge of this period is to maintain one's separateness while becoming attached to others. Failing to strike a balance leads to self-centeredness or to exclusive focus on needs of others. Failure to achieve intimacy can lead to alienation and isolation.
Middle adulthood (ages 35–60)	*Genital stage* (continues).	*Middle age.* Individuals become more aware of their eventual death and begin to question whether they are living well. The crossroads of life; a time for reevaluation. Core struggle: *generativity* versus *stagnation.* Theme: care.	Failure to achieve a sense of productivity can lead to stagnation. Pain can result when individuals recognize the gap between their dreams and what they have achieved.
Late adulthood (age 60 onward)	*Genital stage* (continues).	*Later life.* Ego integrity is achieved by those who have few regrets, who see themselves as living a productive life, and who have coped with both successes and failures. Key tasks are to adjust to losses, death of others, maintaining outside interests, and adjusting to retirement. Core struggle: *integrity* versus *despair.* Theme: wisdom.	Failure to achieve ego integrity often leads to feelings of hopelessness, guilt, resentment, and self-rejection. Unfinished business from earlier years can lead to fears of death stemming from sense that life has been wasted.

Infancy

Developmental psychologists contend that a child's basic task in the first year of life is to develop a sense of trust in self, others, and the environment. Infants need to count on others; they need to sense that they are cared for and that the world is a secure place. They learn this sense of trust by being held, caressed, and loved.

Erikson asserted that infants form a basic conception of the social world. He saw their core struggle as *trust* versus *mistrust*. If the significant other persons in an infant's life provide the needed warmth, cuddling, and attention, the child develops a sense of trust. When these conditions are not present, the child becomes suspicious about interacting with others and acquires a general sense of mistrust toward human relationships. Although neither orientation is fixed in an infant's personality for life, it is clear that well-nurtured infants are in a more favorable position with respect to future personal growth than are their more neglected peers.

A sense of being loved is also the best safeguard against fear, insecurity, and inadequacy. Children who receive love from parents or parental substitutes generally have little difficulty accepting themselves, whereas children who feel unloved and unwanted may find it very hard to accept themselves. In addition, rejected children learn to mistrust the world and to view it primarily in terms of its ability to do them harm. Some of the effects of rejection in infancy include tendencies in later childhood to be fearful, insecure, jealous, aggressive, hostile, or isolated.

At times parents are unduly anxious about wanting to be the perfect mother and father. They spend much time worrying about "doing the right thing at the right time," and they hope to have the "perfectly well-adjusted child." The parents' chronic anxiety can be the very thing that causes difficulties, as their sons and daughters will soon sense that they must be "perfect children." Children can and do survive the "mistakes" that all parents make. When we talk about long-lasting negative effects, we are talking about the effects of chronic neglect or chronic overprotection.

According to the Freudian psychoanalytic view, the events of the first year of life (the oral stage) are extremely important for later development and adjustment. Infants whose basic needs for nurturing are not met during this time may develop greediness and acquisitiveness in later life as material things become substitutes for what the children really want—love and attention from parents. For instance, a person whose oral needs are unmet may become a compulsive eater, in which case food becomes a symbol for love. Other personality problems that might stem from this period include a mistrustful and suspicious view of the world, a tendency to reject affection from others, an inability to form intimate relationships, a fear of loving and trusting, and feelings of isolation.

The case of 9-year-old Joey, the "mechanical boy" described by Bettelheim in *The Empty Fortress* (1967), provides a dramatic illustration of how the pain of extreme rejection during infancy can affect us later on. When Joey first went to Bettelheim's school, he seemed devoid of any feeling. He thought of himself as functioning by remote control, with the help of an elaborate system of machines. He had to have his "carburetor" to breathe, "exhaust pipes" to exhale from, and a complex system of wires and motors in order to move. His delusion was so convincing that staff members at the school sometimes found themselves taking care to be sure that Joey was plugged in properly and that they didn't step on any of his wires.

Neither Joey's father nor his mother had been prepared for his birth, and they related to him as a thing, not a person. His mother simply ignored him, reporting that she had no feeling of dislike toward him but that "I simply did not want to take care of him." He was a difficult baby who cried most of the time, and he was kept on a rigid schedule. He wasn't touched unless necessary, and he wasn't cuddled or played with. Joey developed more and more unusual symptoms, such as head banging, rocking, and a morbid fascination with machines. Evidently, he discovered that machines were better than people; they didn't hurt you, and they could be shut off. During years of intense treatment with Bettelheim, Joey gradually learned how to trust, and he also learned that feelings are real and that it can be worth it to feel.

Another case that illustrates the possible effects of severe deprivation during the early developmental years is that of Sally, who is now in her forties. Sally was given up by her natural parents and spent the first decade of her life in orphanages and foster homes. She recalls pleading with one set of foster parents who had kept her for over a year and then said that they had to send her away. As a child Sally came to the conclusion that she was at fault; if her own parents didn't want her, who could? She spent years trying to figure out what she had done wrong and why so many people "sent her away."

As an adult Sally still yearns for what she missed during infancy and childhood. She has never really attained maturity; socially and emotionally, she is much like a child. She has never allowed herself to get close to anyone, for she fears that they will leave if she does. As a child she learned to isolate herself emotionally to survive, and she still operates on the assumptions she had as a child. Because of her fear of being deserted, she won't allow herself to venture out and take even minimal risks.

Sally is not unusual. We have worked with a number of individuals who suffer from the effects of early psychological deprivation, and we have observed that in most cases such deprivation has lingering adverse effects on a person's level of self-love and the ability to form meaningful relationships later in life. Many people, of all ages, struggle with the issue of trusting others in a loving relationship. They are unable to trust that another can or will love them, they fear being rejected, and they fear even more the possibility of closeness and being accepted and loved. Many of these people don't trust themselves or others sufficiently to make themselves vulnerable enough to experience love. We've all heard about children who were adopted, perhaps as infants, who are now striving to find their natural parents. Even if they love their adopted parents and view them as having done a splendid parenting job, these adult children often feel a void and wonder about the circumstances of their adoption. These adult children may feel that their biological mother and father did not want them, or that in some way they were at fault for what happened. Many people reexperience their childhood feelings of hurt and rejection through some form of counseling; in this way they come to understand that even though they did not feel loved by their parents, this doesn't mean that others find them unlovable now.

At this point, pause and ask yourself these questions:

- Am I able to trust others? myself?
- Am I willing to make myself known to a few selected people in my life?
- Do I basically accept myself as being OK, or do I seek confirmation outside of myself?
- Am I hungry for approval from others?
- How far will I go in my attempt to be liked? Do I need to be liked and approved of by everyone?
- Do I dare make enemies, or must I be "nice" to everyone?
- Am I in any way like Sally? Do I know of anyone who has had experiences similar to hers?
- How much do I really know about my early years? What have I heard from my parents and extended family about my infancy and early childhood?

Early Childhood

The tasks children must master in early childhood (ages 1 to 3) include learning independence, accepting personal power, and learning to cope with negative feelings such as rage and aggression. The critical task is to begin the journey toward autonomy by progressing from being taken care of by others to meeting some of their own physical needs.

In this second stage, children begin to communicate what they want from others. They also face continual parental demands. For instance, they are restricted somewhat from physically exploring their environment, they begin to be disciplined, and they have toilet training imposed on them. Freud labeled this developmental stage the anal stage and suggested that parental feelings and attitudes associated with toilet training would be highly significant for their children's later personality development. Thus, problems such as compulsive orderliness or messiness in adulthood may be due to parental attitudes during this early developmental stage. For instance, a father who insists that his son be unrealistically clean may find that the son develops into a sloppy person as a reaction—or that he becomes even more compulsively clean.

Erikson identified the core struggle of early childhood as *autonomy* versus *shame* and *doubt*. Children who fail to master the task of establishing some control over themselves and coping with the world around them develop a sense of shame, and they doubt their capabilities. Erikson emphasized that during this time children become aware of their emerging skills and have a drive to try them out. To illustrate this point, I (Marianne) remember when I was feeding one of our daughters during her infancy. Heidi had been a very agreeable child who swallowed all of the food I put into her mouth. One day, much to my surprise, she spit it right back at me! No matter how much I wanted her to continue eating, she refused. This was one way in which Heidi began asserting herself with me. As my children were growing up, I strove to establish a good balance between allowing them to develop their own identity and at the same time providing them with guidance and appropriate limits.

Parents who squelch any emerging individuality and who do too much for their children hamper their development. They are saying, however indirectly, "Let us do this for you, because you're too clumsy, too slow, or too inept to do things for yourself." Young children need to experiment; they need to be allowed to make mistakes and still feel that they are basically worthwhile. If parents insist on keeping their children dependent on them, the children will begin to doubt their own abilities. If parents don't appreciate their children's efforts, the children may feel ashamed of themselves or become insecure and fearful.

Sometimes children may want to do more than they are capable of doing at their age. For example, the 5-year-old son of a friend of ours went on a hike with his father. At one point the boy asked his father to let him carry a heavy backpack the way the "big people" do. Without saying a word, the father took his backpack off and handed it to his son, who immediately discovered that it was too heavy for him to carry. The boy simply exclaimed, "Dad, it's too heavy for me." He then went happily on his way up the trail. In a safe way the father had allowed his son to discover experientially that he was, indeed, too small. He had also avoided a potential argument with his son.

Young children also must learn to accept the full range of their feelings. They will surely experience anger, and it is important that they know and feel that anger is permissible. They need to feel loved and accepted with all of their feelings, otherwise they will tend to stifle their anger so as not to lose the love of their parents. When anger cannot be acknowledged or expressed, it becomes toxic and finds expression in indirect ways. One of the results of denying anger is that children begin to numb all of their feelings, including joy.

As adults, many of us have difficulty acknowledging our anger, even when it is fully justified. We swallow our anger and rationalize away other feelings, because we learned when we were 2 or 3 years old that we were unacceptable when we had such feelings. As children we might have shouted at our parents: "I hate you! I never want to see you again!" Then we may have heard an equally enraged parent reply: "How dare you say such a thing—after all I've done for you! I don't ever want to hear that from you again!" We soon take these messages to mean "Don't be angry! Never be angry with those you love! Keep control of yourself!" And we do just that, keeping many of our feelings to ourselves, stuffing them in the pit of our stomach and pretending we don't experience them. It is not surprising that so many of us suffer from migraine headaches, peptic ulcers, hypertension, and heart disease.

Again, take time out to reflect in a personal way on some of your current struggles toward autonomy and self-worth. You might ask yourself:

- Am I able to recognize my own feelings, particularly if they are "unacceptable" to others?
- How do I express my anger to those I love?
- Can I tolerate the ambivalence of feeling love and hate toward the same person?
- Have I established a good balance between depending on others and relying on myself?
- Am I able to let others know what I want? Can I be assertive without being aggressive?

The Preschool Years

The preschool years (ages 3 to 6) are characterized by play and by anticipation of roles. During this time, children try to find out how much they can do. They imitate others; they begin to develop a sense of right and wrong; they widen their circle of significant persons; they take more initiative; they learn to give and receive love and affection; they identify with their own gender; they begin to learn more complex social skills; they learn basic attitudes regarding sexuality; and they increase their capacity to understand and use language.

According to Erikson, the basic task of the preschool years is to establish a sense of competence and initiative. The core struggle is between *initiative* and *guilt*. Preschool children begin to initiate many of their own activities as they become physically and psychologically ready to engage in pursuits of their own choosing. If they are allowed realistic freedom to make some of their own decisions, they tend to develop a positive orientation characterized by confidence in their ability to initiate and follow through. If they are unduly restricted or if their choices are ridiculed, however, they tend to experience a sense of guilt and ultimately to withdraw from taking an active stance. For example, one middle-aged woman still finds herself extremely vulnerable to being seen as foolish. She recalls that during her childhood family members laughed at her attempts to perform certain tasks. Even now she very vividly carries these pictures in her head and allows them to have some control of her life.

In Freudian theory this is the phallic stage, during which children become increasingly interested in sexual matters and begin to acquire a clearer sense of gender-role identity. Before children enter school, they begin to decide how they feel about themselves in their roles as boys and girls. Children exhibit a natural curiosity about sexual matters, and very early in life they form attitudes toward their sexuality and sexual feelings, their bodies, and what they think is right and wrong. Many adults suffer from deep feelings of guilt concerning sexual pleasure or desires. Some have learned that their sexual organs are disgusting; others have traumatic memories associated with sexual intercourse. Much sexual dysfunctioning in adulthood has its roots in early conditioning and experiences.

Preschool children begin to pay attention to their genitals and experience pleasure from genital stimulation. They typically engage in both masturbatory and sex-play activities. They begin to show considerable curiosity about the differences between the sexes and the differences between adults and children. This is the time for questions such as "Where do babies come from?" and "Why are boys and girls different?" Parental attitudes toward these questions, which can be communicated nonverbally as well as verbally, are critical in helping children form a positive attitude toward their own sexuality. Since this is a time of conscience formation, one danger is that parents may instill rigid and unrealistic moral standards, which can lead to an overdeveloped conscience. Children who learn that their bodies and their impulses are evil soon begin to feel guilty about them. Carried into adult life, these attitudes can prevent people from appreciating and enjoying sexual intimacy. Another danger is that strict parental indoctrination, which can be accomplished in subtle, nonverbal ways, will lead to an infantile conscience. Children may develop a fear of questioning and thinking for themselves and blindly accept the dictates of their parents. Other effects of such indoctrination include rigidity, severe conflicts, guilt, remorse, and self-condemnation.

Children need adequate models if they are to accept their sexual feelings as natural and develop a healthy concept of their bodies and their gender-role identity. In addition to forming attitudes toward their bodies and sexuality, they begin to formulate their conceptions of what it means to be feminine or masculine. By simply being with their parents or other adults in their environment, they are getting some perspective on the way men and women relate to one another, and they are acquiring basic attitudes toward such relationships. They are also deciding how they feel about themselves in their roles as boys and girls. Their learning and decisions during the phallic stage pave the way for their ability to accept themselves as men or women in adulthood. Gender-role identity is discussed in depth in Chapter 4.

Pause and reflect on some of your own current struggles with these issues:

- What did you learn from your culture about the way to behave as a woman or a man?
- What are your standards of femininity or masculinity? Where did you get them?
- Are you comfortable with your own sexuality? with your body?
- Are there any unresolved conflicts from your childhood that get in the way of your enjoyment?
- Does your present behavior or current conflicts indicate areas of unfinished business?

Impact of the First Six Years of Life

In describing the events of the first six years of life, we have relied rather heavily on the psychoanalytic view of psychosexual and psychosocial development. You may be asking yourself why we are emphasizing the events of this period. In working with clients, we continue to realize the influence of these early years on their levels of integration and functioning as adults. Sometimes people ask: "Why look back into my past? I don't see any point in dredging up that painful period, especially since I've worked so hard to get that part of my life under control." Our point is that many of these childhood experiences have a profound impact on both the present and the future.

If you reached faulty conclusions based on your early life experience, you are likely to still be operating on the basis of them. If you told yourself as a child that "I can never do enough for my father," as an adult you may feel today that you can never do enough (or be enough) to meet the expectations of those who are significant in your life. Not only is our current functioning influenced by early interpretations, but our future is too. Our goals and purposes have some connection with the way we dealt with emerging issues during the first six years of life.

Consider Marty's case. People told Marty as a child that she couldn't do much and therefore shouldn't waste time striving. It would be best if she were simply to be satisfied with what she had. However, Marty challenged these messages and was intent on proving them wrong. In fact, much of what she does can be understood as attempts to prove that she can do what others were convinced she could never do.

In *Making Peace with Yourself*, Bloomfield (1985) writes about personal vulnerabilities and weaknesses originating during our early years, which he refers to as our *Achilles' heel*. Bloomfield believes that each of us has at least one Achilles' heel that regularly trips us up. If we ignore, suppress, or deny it, it will reappear unexpectedly. This idea parallels the powerful psychological principle: "What we resist persists." The *Achilles' syndrome* is the price we pay for resisting our Achilles' heel. For example, if your Achilles' heel is a fear of being rejected in love relationships and ending up a loner, you may avoid becoming intimate with others. The result is that you wind up alone. If Bloomfield's principle is correct, we do not gain in the long run by hiding and denying our personal vulnerabilities. By refusing to acknowledge our Achilles' heel, we actually remain controlled by past weaknesses and insecurities.

The Achilles' heel concept is similar to Jung's concept of the *shadow side* of personality, which is thought to contain the basic and primitive instincts. Known as our *dark side,* the shadow needs to be understood and restrained. Yet it is a mistake to view this only as our evil side, and even a greater mistake to deny this aspect of our being. In his workshops aimed at assisting people make a transformational journey, Brugh Joy (1979) talks about the importance of accepting the shadow. According to Joy, there is no self-realization until we acknowledge the disowned self. To realize our full being, it is essential to meet our shadow. Joy teaches that the shadow side is the source of spontaneity and vitality, and if it is not recognized, our personality becomes dull and lifeless. Furthermore, if we deny this facet, we become controlled by our unconscious. From Joy's perspective, if we strive to conquer something inside of us, that very thing conquers us. Simply understanding the many complexities within us, including our vulnerabilities, is a source of strength that can lead to wholeness. Joy would likely say, "Embrace your vulnerability, for it can be a path to integration."

In working in counseling groups with relatively well-functioning adults who have "normal" developmental issues, we find that a new understanding of their early years often entails a certain degree of emotional pain. Yet by understanding these painful events, they have a basis for transcending them and not being stuck replaying old self-defeating themes throughout their lifetime. We don't think healthy people are ever really "cured" of their Achilles' heel or their shadow. For example, if during your preschool years you felt abandoned by the divorce of your parents, you are still likely to have vestiges of fears and hesitations when forming close relationships. Yet you do not have to surrender to these traces of mistrust. Instead, you can gain control of your fears of loving and trusting.

In reviewing your childhood, you may well find some aspects that you like and do not want to change. You may also find a certain continuity in your life that gives you meaning. At the same time, if you are honest with yourself, you are likely to become aware of certain revisions you would like to make. This awareness is the first critical step toward changing.

When we consider typical problems and conflicts among people in our personal-growth groups, the following areas come to mind: inability to trust oneself and others; inability to freely accept and give love; difficulty in recognizing and expressing the full range of one's feelings; guilt over feelings of anger or hatred toward those one loves; inability or unwillingness to control one's own life; difficulties in fully accepting one's sexuality or in finding meaning in sexual intimacy; difficulty in accepting oneself as a woman or a man; and problems concerning a lack of meaning or purpose in life or a clear sense of personal identity and aspirations. Notice that most of these adult problems are directly related to the turning points and tasks of the early developmental years. The effects of early learning are reversible in most cases, but these experiences, whether favorable or unfavorable, clearly influence how we interpret future critical periods in our lives.

Some people learn new values, come to accept new feelings and attitudes, and overcome much of their past negative conditioning. In contrast, other people steadfastly hang on to the past as an excuse for not taking any action to change in the present. We can't change in a positive direction unless we stop blaming others for the way we are now. Statements that begin "If it hadn't been for . . ." are too often used to justify an immobile position. Blaming others for our present struggles ultimately keeps us trapped, waiting for "them out there" to change before we can change. Whenever you catch yourself pointing an accusing finger at someone else, it is a good idea to look at your other fingers—pointing back at you. Once we are able to see in ourselves the very traits that we accuse others of, and once we quit blaming others, we make it possible to take charge of our own lives.

A relevant case is that of Bryan, who used to blame his mother for everything. Because she had dominated his father, Bryan felt that he could not trust any woman now. If he couldn't trust his own mother, he reasoned, whom could he trust? At 25 Bryan saw himself as fearing independence, and he blamed his mother for his fear. He refused to date, and he tried to convince himself that he did so because his mother had "messed up my life by making me afraid." He continually wanted to use his therapy sessions to dwell on the past and blame his present problems on what his parents had and hadn't done. Through counseling Bryan became aware that dwelling on his past and focusing on others were ways he used to avoid assuming responsibility for his own life. After actively questioning some of his beliefs about women and about himself, Bryan decided that not all women were like his mother, that he didn't have to respond to women in the way his father had, and that he could change his life now if was willing to accept responsibility for doing so.

You may experience anger and hurt for having been cheated in the past, but it is imperative that you eventually claim the power you have been giving away to the people who were once significant in your life. Unless you recognize and exercise the power you now have to take care of yourself, you close the door to new choices and new growth.

➤ *Time Out for Personal Reflection*

1. Close your eyes and reflect for a moment on your memories of your first six years. Attempt to identify your earliest concrete single memory—something you actually remember that happened to you, not something you were told about. Spend a few minutes recalling the details and reexperiencing the feelings associated with this early event.

   a. Write down your earliest recollection: _____

   _____

   _____

   _____

   b. Do you have any hunches about how this early memory may still be having an impact on the way you think, feel, and behave today?

   _____

   _____

   _____

   _____

2. Reflect on the events that most stand out for you during your first six years of life. In particular, think about your place in your family, your family's reaction to you, and your reactions to each person in your family. What connections do you see between how it felt to be in your family as a child and how you now feel in various social situations? What speculations do you have concerning the impact your family had then and the effect that these experiences continue to have on your current personality?

   _____

   _____

   _____

   _____

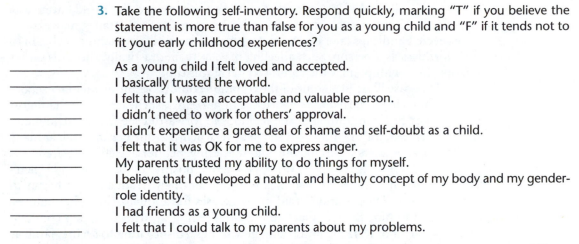

3. Take the following self-inventory. Respond quickly, marking "T" if you believe the statement is more true than false for you as a young child and "F" if it tends not to fit your early childhood experiences?

_____ As a young child I felt loved and accepted.
_____ I basically trusted the world.
_____ I felt that I was an acceptable and valuable person.
_____ I didn't need to work for others' approval.
_____ I didn't experience a great deal of shame and self-doubt as a child.
_____ I felt that it was OK for me to express anger.
_____ My parents trusted my ability to do things for myself.
I believe that I developed a natural and healthy concept of my body and my gender-
_____ role identity.
_____ I had friends as a young child.
_____ I felt that I could talk to my parents about my problems.

Look over your responses. What do they tell you about the person you now are? If you could live your childhood over again, how would you like it to be? Record some of your impressions in your journal.

Middle Childhood

During middle childhood (ages 6 to 12), children face these key developmental tasks: engage in social activities; expand their knowledge and understanding of the physical and social worlds; continue to learn and expand their concepts of an appropriate feminine or masculine role; develop a sense of values; learn new communication skills; learn how to read, write, and calculate; learn to give and take; learn how to accept people who are culturally different; learn to tolerate ambiguity; and learn physical skills.

For Freudians this period is the *latency stage*, characterized by a relative decline in sexual interests and the emergence of new interests, activities, and attitudes. With the events of the hectic phallic period behind them, children take a long breathing spell and consolidate their positions. Their attention turns to new fields, such as school playmates and books. They begin to reach out for friendly relationships with others in the environment.

Erikson, however, disagreed with the Freudian view of this period as a time of emotional latency and neutrality. He argued that the middle childhood years present unique psychosocial demands that children must meet successfully if their development is to proceed. According to Erikson, the major struggle of middle childhood is between *industry* and *inferiority*. The central task of this period is to achieve a sense of industry; failure to do so results in a sense of inadequacy and inferiority. Development of a sense of industry includes focusing on creating and producing and on attaining goals. Of course, starting school is a critical event of this time. The first four years of school are vital to successful completion of a healthy outcome of this stage. The child's self-concept is especially fragile before the 4th grade; if teachers are critical of a child's performance, this could have a lasting impact. Children who encounter failure during the early grades may experience severe handicaps later on. A child with early learning problems may begin to feel worthless as a person. Such a feeling may, in turn, drastically affect his or her relationships with peers, which are also vital at this time.

Helen's case illustrates some of the common conflicts of the elementary school years. When Helen started kindergarten, a bit too early, she was smaller than most of the other children. Although she had looked forward to beginning school and tried to succeed, for the most part she felt overwhelmed. She began to fail at many of the tasks her peers were enjoying and mastering. School-age children are in the process of developing their self-concepts, whether positive or negative, and Helen's view of her capacity to succeed was growing dimmer. Gradually, she began to avoid even simple tasks and to find many excuses to rationalize away her failures. She wanted to hide the fact that she was not keeping up with the other children. She was fearful of learning and trying new things, so she clung to secure, familiar ways. She grew increasingly afraid of making mistakes, for she believed that everything she did had to be perfect. If she did some art work, for instance, she would soon become frustrated and rip up the piece of paper because her picture wasn't coming out exactly as she wanted it to. Basically, Helen was afraid of putting her potential to the test, and she would generally freeze up when she had to be accountable for anything she produced. Her teachers' consistent evaluation of her was: "Helen is a sensitive child who needs a lot of encouragement and direction. She could do much more than she does, but she quits too soon, because she feels that what she does isn't good enough."

Helen grew to resent the fact that some of her teachers were not demanding much of her because they didn't want to push her. She then felt even more different from her peers, completing the vicious circle. Despite her will to try and her desire to succeed, she was prevented from venturing out by her fears of gambling and making mistakes. When she was in the 3rd grade, she was at least a grade level behind in reading, despite the fact that she had repeated kindergarten. As she began to feel stupid and embarrassed because she couldn't read as well as the other children, she shied away from reading aloud. Eventually, she received instruction in remedial reading, and this attention seemed to help. She was also given an intelligence test at the clinic, and the results were "low average." The reading staff and those who tested Helen were surprised, for they saw her as creative, insightful, and much brighter than the results showed. Again, she had frozen up when she felt she had to perform on a test.

Helen is now in college. She is still anxious about taking tests. Often she does poorly on an examination, not because she does not know the material but because she allows her anxiety to get the best of her. Helen could long ago have given up on school, yet being in a supportive environment, she has been able to continue her education in spite of her fears. Although she is not "cured" of her feelings of inadequacy and self-doubt, she has not allowed these feelings to control her. Instead, she is learning to manage her self-doubts by arguing back to those old voices that tell her she is basically inadequate.

Helen's case indicates that the first few years of school can have a powerful impact on a child's life and future adjustment to school. Her school experiences col-

ored her view of her self-worth and affected her relationships with other children. At this point ask yourself:

- Can I identify in any ways with Helen's case?
- What struggles did I experience in forming my self-concept?
- Does Helen remind me of anyone I know?

Forming a self-concept is a major task of middle childhood. Let's take a closer look at what this entails.

■ Developing a Self-Concept

The term *self-concept* refers to your cognitive awareness about yourself. It is your private mental image of yourself and a collection of beliefs about the kind of person you are (Hamachek, 1988, 1990). This picture includes your view of your worth, value, and possibilities; the way you see yourself in relation to others; the way you'd ideally like to be; and the degree to which you accept yourself as you are. From ages 6 to 12 the view you have of yourself is influenced greatly by the quality of your school experiences, by contact with your peer group and with teachers, and by your interactions with your family. To a large extent your self-concept is formed by what others tell you about yourself, especially during the formative years of childhood. Whether you develop a positive or negative outlook on your-self has a good deal to do with what people close to you have expected of you.

This view of yourself influences how you present yourself to others and how you act and feel when you are with them. For example, you may feel inadequate around authority figures. Perhaps you tell yourself that you have nothing to say or that whatever you might say would be stupid. Since you have this view of yourself, you behave in ways that persuade people to adopt your view of yourself. More of-ten than not, others will see and respond to you in the way you "tell" them you are. For this reason, it can be a most useful exercise for you to monitor the messages you are sending to others about yourself and become aware of the patterns you might be perpetuating. It is difficult for those who are close to you to treat you in a positive way when you consistently discount yourself. Why should others treat you better than you treat yourself? In contrast, people with a positive self-concept are likely to behave confidently, which causes others to react to them positively.

Once we have established our self-concept, there are a variety of strategies available to help us maintain and protect it from outside threats. We will explore these defense mechanisms next.

■ Protecting Our Self-Concept: Ego-Defense Mechanisms

Ego-defense mechanisms can be thought of as psychological strategies, such as self-deception and distortion of reality, that we use to protect our self-concept against unpleasant emotions. We use these protective devices at various stages of life to soften the blows of harsh reality. Ego defenses typically originate during our childhood years, and later experiences during adolescence and adulthood rein-force some of these styles of self-defense.

Freud conceived of ego-defense mechanisms as an unconscious process that prevented a person from becoming consciously aware of threatening feelings, thoughts, and impulses. Erikson's psychosocial theory, built around the idea that emotional and social growth progresses through a series of stages, each with its own unique ego accomplishments, provides a natural conceptual framework for understanding the defense of the self (Hamachek, 1988, 1990).

To illustrate the nature and functioning of these ego defenses, we will use the case of Helen discussed earlier. For the most part Helen made poor adjustments to her school and social life during her childhood years. Other children stayed away from her because of her aggressive and unfriendly behavior. She did not like her el-ementary school experience, and her teachers were not overly fond of her. Helen's behavioral style in coping with the pressures of school included blaming the out-side world for her difficulties. In the face of these failures in life, she might have made use of any one or a combination of the following ego-defense mechanisms.

Repression.   The mechanism of repression is one of the most important processes in psychoanalytic theory, and it is the basis of many other ego defenses. By using it, we exclude threatening or painful thoughts and feelings from aware-ness. By pushing them into the unconscious, we sometimes manage the anxiety that grows out of situations involving guilt and conflict. Repression may block out

stressful experiences that could be met by realistically facing and working through a situation. Helen was unaware of her dependence/independence struggles with her parents; she was also unaware of how her painful experiences of failure were contributing to her feelings of inferiority and insecurity. She had unconsciously excluded most of her failures and had not allowed them to come to the surface of awareness.

Denial.   Denial plays a defensive role similar to that of repression, but it generally operates at a preconscious or conscious level. In denial there is a conscious effort to suppress unpleasant reality. It is a way of distorting what the individual thinks, feels, or perceives to be a stressful situation. Helen simply "closed her eyes" to her failures in school. Even though she had evidence that she was not performing well academically, she refused to acknowledge this reality.

Displacement.   Displacement involves redirecting emotional impulses (usually hostility) from the real object to a substitute person or object. In essence, anxiety is coped with by discharging impulses onto a "safer target." For example, Helen's sister Joan was baffled by the hostility she received from Helen. Joan did not understand why Helen was so critical of her every action. Helen used Joan as the target of her aggression because Joan did exceptionally well at school and was very popular with her peers.

Projection.   Another mechanism of self-deception is projection, which consists of attributing to others our own unacceptable desires and impulses. We are able to clearly see in others the very traits that we disown in ourselves, which serves the purpose of keeping a certain view of ourselves intact. Typically, projection involves seeing clearly in others actions that would lead to guilt feelings in ourselves. Helen tended to blame everyone but herself for her difficulties in school and in social relationships. She complained that her teachers were unfairly picking on her, that she could never do anything right for them, and that other children were mean to her.

Reaction Formation.   One defense against a threatening impulse is to actively express the opposite impulse. This involves behaving in a manner that is contrary to one's real feelings. A characteristic of this defense is the excessive quality of a particular attitude or behavior. For example, Helen bristled when her teachers or parents offered to give her help. She was convinced that she did not need anyone's help. Accepting their offers would have indicated that she really was stupid.

Rationalization.   Rationalization involves manufacturing a false but "good" excuse to justify unacceptable behavior and explain away failures or losses. Such excuses help restore a bruised ego. Helen was quick to find many reasons for the difficulties she encountered, a few of which included sickness, which caused her to fall behind in her classes; teachers who went over the lessons too fast; other children who did not let her play with them; and siblings who kept her awake at night.

Compensation.   Another defense reaction is compensation, which consists of masking perceived weaknesses or developing certain positive traits to make up for limitations. The adjustive value in this mechanism lies in keeping one's self-esteem intact by excelling in one area to distract attention from an area in which the person is inferior. The more Helen experienced difficulties at school and with her peers, the more she withdrew from others and became absorbed in artwork that she did by herself at home.

Regression.   Faced with stress, some people revert to a form of immature behavior that they have outgrown. In regression, they attempt to cope with their anxiety by clinging to such inappropriate behaviors. Faced with failure in both her social and school life, Helen had a tendency to engage in emotional tirades, crying a lot, storming into her room, and refusing to come out for hours.

Fantasy.   Fantasy involves gratifying frustrated desires by imaginary achievements. When achievement in the real world seems remote, some people resort to screening out unpleasant aspects of reality and living in their world of dreams. During her childhood Helen developed a rich fantasy in which she imagined herself to be an actress. She played with her dolls for hours and talked to herself. In her daydreams she saw herself in the movies, surrounded by famous people.

Although ego-defense mechanisms have some adaptive value, their overuse can be problematic. While it is true that self-deception can soften harsh reality, the fact is that reality does not change through the process of distorting those aspects of it that produce anxiety. When these defensive strategies do not work, the long-term result is an even greater degree of anxiety. Overreliance on these defenses leads to a vicious circle—as the defenses lose their value in holding anxiety in check, people step up the use of other defenses.

All defenses are not self-defeating, however, and there is a proper place for them, especially when stresses are great. In the face of certain crises, for example, defenses can enable people to cope at least temporarily until they can build up other resources, both from their environment and from within themselves.

Before moving on to the section on adolescence, spend some time reflecting on the defense mechanisms you used during your childhood years. Do you see any analogies between the defenses you employed as a child and those you sometimes use at this time in your life? Think about some of the defenses you use and how they might serve you. Imagine how your life might be different if you gave up all your defenses.

Adolescence

The years from 12 to 18 constitute a stage of transition between childhood and adulthood. For most people this is a particularly difficult period. It is a paradoxical time. Adolescents are not treated as mature adults, yet they are often expected to act as though they had gained complete maturity. Continually testing the limits, adolescents have a strong urge to break away from dependent ties that restrict their freedom. It is not uncommon for adolescents to be frightened and lonely, but they may mask their fears with rebellion and cover up their need to be dependent by exaggerating their independence. It seems extremely important for adolescents to declare their uniqueness and establish a separate identity. Much of adolescents' rebellion, then, is an attempt to determine the course of their own lives and to assert that they are who and what they want to be, not what others expect them to be.

■ Developing an Identity

As infants we must learn to trust ourselves and others; as adolescents we need to find a meaning in life and adult role models in whom we believe. As toddlers we begin to assert our rights as independent people by struggling for autonomy; as adolescents we make choices that will shape our future. As preschoolers we try to achieve a sense of competence; as adolescents we explore choices about what we want from life, what we can succeed in, what kind of education we want, and what career may suit us.

Adolescence is a critical period in the development of personal identity. For Erikson, the major developmental conflicts of adolescents center on clarification of who they are, where they are going, and how they are going to get there. He sees the core struggle of adolescence as *identity* versus *role confusion*. Failure to achieve a sense of identity results in role confusion. Adolescents may feel overwhelmed by

the pressures placed on them and find the development of a clear identity a difficult task. They may feel pressured to make an occupational choice, to compete in the job market or in college, to become financially independent, or to commit themselves to physically and emotionally intimate relationships. In addition, they may feel pressured to live up to the standards of their peer group. Peer group pressure is a potent force, and some adolescents lose their focus on their own identities and conform to the expectations of their friends and classmates. If the need to be accepted and liked is stronger than the need for self-respect, adolescents will most likely find themselves behaving in nongenuine ways and increasingly looking to others to tell them what and who they should be.

A crucial part of the identity-formation process during adolescence is *individuation,* separating from our family system and establishing an identity based on our own experiences. This process of psychological separation from parental ties is the most agonizing part of the adolescent struggle and lays the foundation for future development. This view of achieving psychological separation from one's family is common in Western cultures. But in some other cultures, the wishes of parents have a major influence on the behavior of adult children. Furthermore, becoming psychologically separate from one's family may not be seen as a guiding value. Instead, the collective good is given far more weight than individual fulfillment. Many Third World developing cultures have no adolescent phase. At puberty boys and girls are initiated into adult roles for which they have long been prepared. Adolescence is a luxury these cultures cannot afford. The cultural conflict can be enormous when such families emigrate to the West and their children want to become "teens."

A strain on adolescents' sense of identity is imposed by the conflict between their awareness of expanding possibilities and society's narrowing of their options for action. Adolescents confront dilemmas similar to those faced by old people in our society. Both age groups must deal with finding a meaning in living and must cope with feelings of uselessness. Older people may be forced to retire and may encounter difficulty replacing work activities; young people have not completed their education or acquired the skills necessary for many occupations. Instead, they are in a constant process of preparation for the future. Even in their families adolescents may feel unneeded. Although they may be given chores to do, many adolescents do not experience much opportunity to be productive.

The question of options is made even more urgent by the myth that the choices we make during adolescence bind us for the rest of our lives. Adolescents who believe this myth will be hesitant to experiment and test out many options. Too many young people yield to pressures to decide too early what they will be and what serious commitments they will make. Thus, they may never realize the range of possibilities open to them. To deal with this problem, Erikson suggested a *psychological moratorium*—a period during which society would give permission to adolescents to experiment with different roles and values so they could sample life before making major commitments.

Adolescents are also faced with choices concerning what beliefs and values will guide their actions; indeed, forming a philosophy of life is a central task of adolescence. In meeting this challenge young people need adequate models, for a sense of moral living is largely learned by example. Adolescents are especially sensitive to duplicity, and they are quick to spot phony people who tell adolescents how they *ought* to live while themselves living in very different ways. They learn values by observing and interacting with adults who are positive examples rather than by being preached to. Of course, not all role models are positive. In some cases, adolescents adopt drug dealers or other criminals as role models. Many adolescents look for an identity by affiliation with a gang, and they may find role models within a gang.

A particular problem adolescents face in the area of values pertains to sexual behavior. Adolescents are easily aroused sexually, and they are inundated with sexual stimuli. Yet they are expected to make decisions regarding the expression of their sexuality in ways that are congruent with their value system. Sexual conflicts can produce much frustration, anxiety, and guilt. And unintended pregnancies are still very much a part of many adolescent sexual encounters. Adolescent sexuality is compounded by the threat of AIDS and other sexually transmitted diseases. Sexual experimentation can be life-threatening. Yet adolescents feel that they are invincible and take lightly any cautions about safe sex. A recent news report stated that 50 percent of gay men between the ages of 18 and 22 claimed they were not practicing safe sex, yet the majority of them had knowledge of the potentially devastating consequences of this behavior. Wrestling with these difficult issues is part of the struggle of being an adolescent.

■ The Crisis of Adolescence

In *All Grown Up and No Place to Go,* David Elkind (1984) writes about teenagers in crisis. Elkind believes that in the 1960s teenagers had a clearly defined position in the social structure; they were the "future leaders" and the "next generation." Society recognized that the transition from childhood to adulthood was challenging and that adolescents needed time, support, and guidance while striving for maturity. Today, says Elkind, young people have lost their once privileged position. Premature adulthood has been thrust on them. Today's youth are expected to meet the challenges that life imposes on them with the same degree of maturity once expected only of middle-aged people — but without adequate preparation time. To complicate the situation, many adolescents lack positive adult role models. Their parents are struggling with the demands of work and home and are attempting to find meaning in their own lives. Many parents are too preoccupied with their own lives to give young people the time and attention they need. Adolescents are expected to be grown up yet to behave like obedient children on demand. Elkind has captured a central dilemma of today's adolescents when he refers to them as being "all grown up with no place to go."

Today's adolescents also have to cope with violence at school. At one time children and young people were relatively safe in school, but the scene has changed drastically in recent years. It is not uncommon for adolescents, and even children, to bring guns or knives to school. News reports of an adolescent injuring fellow classmates or a teacher are not uncommon. Not only do today's teens have to contend with peer pressure, parental pressure, and the confusion and pain that accompanies finding their identities, they also have to worry about being shot by a schoolmate or being the victim of some other form of violence or intimidation.

Adolescence is typically a turbulent and fast-moving period of life, often marked by feelings of powerlessness, confusion, and loneliness. It is a time for making critical choices, even the ultimate choice of living fully or bringing about one's own death. Decisions are being made in almost every area of life, and these decisions to a large extent define our identity. The following "Time Out" is a chance for you to spend some time reflecting on the choices you made during your adolescent years, as well as clarifying the impact that these experiences continue to exert on you today.

➤ *Time Out for Personal Reflection*

At this point it could be useful to review the choices open to adolescents, and especially to think of the choices you remember having made at this time in your life. How do you think those choices have influenced the person you are today?

1. What major choices did you struggle with during your adolescent years?

_____

_____

_____

_____

2. How do you think your adolescence affected the person you are today?

_____

_____

_____

_____

Chapter Summary

A road map of the developmental tasks of the life span reveals that each stage presents certain dangers and offers particular opportunities. Crises can be seen as challenges to be met rather than as catastrophic events that happen to us. In normal development critical turning points and choices appear at each developmental stage. Our early experiences influence the choices we make at a later time in our development. No neat delineation exists between one stage and another. Instead, stages blend into one another. We all experience each period of life in our own unique ways.

The struggle toward autonomy, or psychological independence, begins in early childhood, takes on major proportions during adolescence and young adulthood, and extends into later adulthood. The process of individuation, and the value attached to it, are greatly influenced by culture. Actualizing our full potential as a person and learning to stand alone in life, as well as to stand beside others, is a task that is never really finished. Although major life events during childhood and adolescence have an impact on the way that we think, feel, and behave in adult life, we are not helplessly molded and hopelessly determined by such events. Instead, we can choose to change our attitudes toward these events, which in turn will affect how we behave today.

Freud's psychoanalytic view of human development during the first six years of life emphasizes the importance of acquiring a sense of trust toward the world, of learning how to recognize and express the full range of feelings, and of acquiring a healthy attitude toward sexuality and a clear sense of our gender-role identity. His psychosexual perspective shows how our later personality development hinges on the degree to which we have successfully met the demands and conflicts during early childhood.

Erikson built on Freud's basic ideas, and his psychosocial theory offers a more complete and comprehensive perspective of the unique tasks of the entire life span. In his eight stages of development, Erikson emphasizes the critical turning points facing us during each transition in our lives. At these points we can either successfully resolve the basic conflict or get stuck on the road to development. Again, early choices affect the range of choices open to us later in life.

From infancy through adolescence we are faced with developmental challenges at each stage of life. The basic task of *infancy* is to develop a sense of trust in others and our environment, so we can trust ourselves. Later personality problems that can stem from a failure to develop trust include fearing intimate relationships, low self-esteem, and isolation. *Early childhood* presents the challenge of beginning to function independently and acquiring a sense of self-control. If we do not master this task, becoming autonomous is extremely difficult. During the *preschool years* we are forming our gender-role identity, and ideally we experience a sense of competence that comes with making some decisions for ourselves. Parental attitudes during this period are very powerful, and these attitudes are communicated both verbally and nonverbally. Our school experiences during *middle childhood* play a significant role in our socialization. At this time the world is opening up to us, and we are expanding our interests outside of the home. Problems that typically begin at this phase include a negative self-concept, conflicts over values, confused gender-role identity, a fear of new challenges, and disturbed interpersonal relationships. *Adolescence* is the period when we are forming an identity as well as establishing goals and values that give our lives meaning. A danger of this time of life is that we can follow the crowd out of a fear of being rejected and fail to discover what it is that we want for ourselves.

Each of these developmental phases helps lay the foundation on which we build our adult personality. As you will see in the next chapter, mastery of these earlier challenges is essential if we are to cope with the problems of adult living.

Activities and Exercises

1. Write an account in your journal of the first six years of your life. Although you may think that you can't remember much about this time, the following guidelines should help in your recall:
   a. Write down a few key questions that you would like answered about your early years.
   b. Seek out your relatives, and ask them some questions about your early years.
   c. Collect any reminders of your early years, particularly pictures.
   d. If possible, visit the place or places where you lived and went to school.

2. Choose from among the many exercises in this chapter any that you'd be willing to integrate into a self-help program during your time in this course. What

things are you willing to do to bring about some of the changes you want in your life?

3. Pictures often say more about you than words. What do your pictures tell about you? Look through any pictures of yourself as a child and as an adolescent, and see if there are any themes. What do most of your pictures reveal about the way you felt about yourself? Bring some of these pictures to class. Have other members look at them and tell you what they think you were like then. Pictures can also be used to tap forgotten memories.

4. Select one or more books for further reading on the topics explored in this chapter. For a full bibliographic reference for each book, consult the "References and Suggested Readings" at the end of this book. For this chapter we highly recommend: *Making Peace with Yourself: Transforming Your Weaknesses into Strengths* (Bloomfield, 1985); *The Seven Habits of Highly Effective People* (Covey, 1990); *The Measure of Our Success: A Letter to My Children and Yours* (Edelman, 1992); *All Grown Up and No Place To Go* (Elkind, 1984).

3

Adulthood and Autonomy

Independence means not being lonely even when you are alone.
— BERNIE SIEGEL

✔ *Prechapter Self-Inventory*

Use the following scale to respond: 4 = this statement is true of me *most* of the time; 3 = this statement is true of me *much* of the time; 2 = this statement is true of me *some* of the time; 1 = this statement is true of me *almost none* of the time.

_____ 1. For the most part, my values and beliefs are very much like my parents'.
_____ 2. I'm an independent person more than I'm a dependent person.
_____ 3. I think about early messages I received from my parents.
_____ 4. I would say that I have psychologically divorced my parents and become my own parent.
_____ 5. As I get older, I feel an urgency about living.
_____ 6. Much of my life is spent in doing things that I do not enjoy.
_____ 7. I look forward with optimism and enthusiasm to the challenges that lie ahead of me.
_____ 8. I expect to experience a meaningful and rich life when I reach old age.
_____ 9. There are many things I can't do now that I expect to do when I retire.
_____ 10. I have fears of aging.

Introduction

In this chapter we continue our discussion of the life-span perspective by focusing on the transitions and turning points in adulthood. Our childhood and adolescent experiences lay the foundation for our ability to meet the developmental challenges of the various phases of adulthood. But throughout adulthood many choices are still open to us. Before taking up early, middle, and late adulthood, we will examine how you can become more autonomous. One facet of the struggle toward autonomy involves recognizing the early life decisions you made and realizing that you can change them if they are no longer appropriate or useful. This change entails questioning some of the messages that you received and accepted during your early childhood. You can also learn to argue with your self-defeating thoughts and beliefs and acquire a more rational, positive, and constructive set of beliefs.

We will describe some typical developmental patterns, but everybody does not go through these stages in the same way at the same time. Your family and your culture influence the manner in which you confront developmental tasks. It is important that you understand the ways your culture and family-of-origin experiences have contributed to influencing the person you are. Your passage through adulthood is characterized by the choices you make in response to the demands made on you. It would be a good idea to look for a pattern of choices in your life. You may see that you are primarily adapting yourself to others. Or you may discover a pattern of choosing the path of security rather than risking new adventures. On the other hand, you may be pleased with many of the decisions that you have made. As you think about these choices at critical turning points in your adulthood, look for a unifying theme beginning in childhood. Once you become aware of patterns in your life, you can work to change those patterns that you determine are not serving you well. If you understand earlier experiences and any self-defeating decisions that have influenced you, it is possible to create a different future.

If you are a young adult, you may wonder why you should be concerned about middle age and later life. We invite you to look at the choices you are making now that will have a direct influence on the quality of a later adulthood phase. As you read this chapter, reflect on what you hope to be able to say about your life when you reach later adulthood.

The Struggle toward Autonomy

As we leave adolescence and enter young adulthood, our central task is to assume increased responsibility and independence. Although most of us have moved away from our parents physically, not all of us have done so psychologically. To a greater or lesser degree, our parents will have a continuing influence on our lives. Cultural factors play a significant role in determining the degree to which our parents influence our lives. For example, in some cultures developing a spirit of independence is not given priority. Instead, value is placed on cooperation with others and on a spirit of interdependence. Within some cultures, parents continue to have a significant influence on their children even when they reach adulthood. Respect and honor for parents may be values that are extolled above individual freedom by the adult children.

Regardless of your cultural background, the challenge we face as mature adults is to be aware of the present influence that our parents have on our decisions and behavior. Having reviewed your own childhood and adolescent years in the last chapter, you can probably recognize more clearly the impact of your parents on your life. The struggle toward autonomy entails choosing for yourself and working for your own approval rather than living your life primarily by your parents' designs and to earn their approval. Being an autonomous person does not mean that you will not share many of your parents' values. Rebellion against whatever your parents stand for is not a sign of being autonomous.

Making decisions about the quality of life you want for yourself and affirming these choices is partly what autonomy is about. Autonomy also entails your willingness to accept responsibility for the consequences of your choices rather than looking for others to blame if you are not satisfied with the way your life is going. Furthermore, separating from your family and finding your own identity is not something you do at a given time once and for all. The struggle toward autonomy begins in early childhood and continues throughout life.

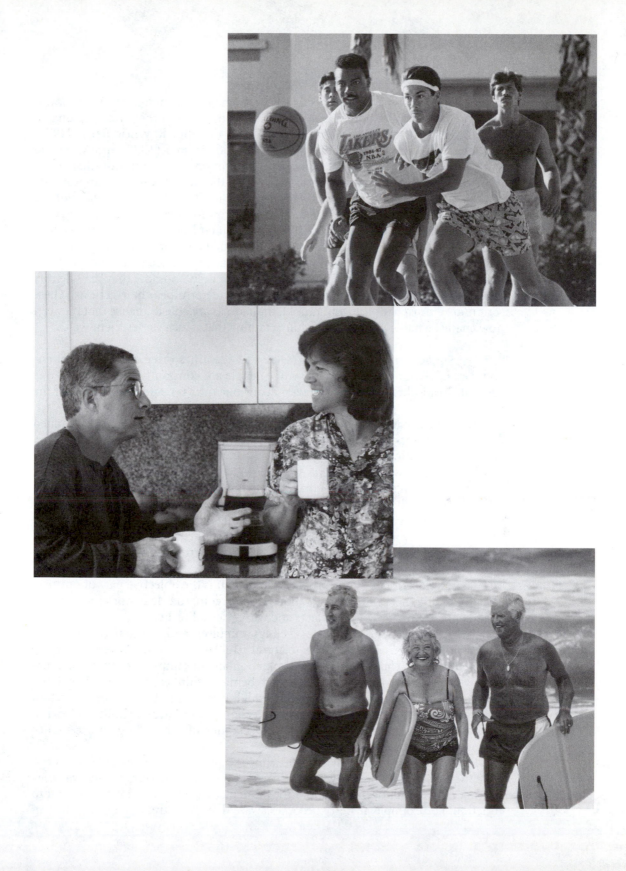

■ Recognizing Early Learning and Decisions

Transactional analysis (TA) offers a useful framework for understanding how our learning during childhood extends into adulthood. TA is a theory of personality and a method of counseling that was originally developed by Eric Berne (1975) and later extended by practitioners such as Claude Steiner (1975) and Mary and Robert Goulding (1978, 1979). The theory is built on the assumption that adults make decisions based on past premises, premises that were at one time appropriate to their survival needs but may no longer be valid. It stresses the capacity of the person to change early decisions and is oriented toward increasing awareness, with the goal of enabling people to alter the course of their lives. TA teaches people how to recognize the three ego states (Parent, Adult, and Child) in which they function. Through TA, people learn how their current behavior is affected by the rules and regulations they received and incorporated as children and how they can identify the "life script," and also the family script, that determines their actions. These scripts are almost like plots that unfold. Individuals are able to realize that they can now change what is *not* working while retaining that which serves them well.

Ego States: Parent, Adult, and Child.   TA identifies three ego states that encompass important facets of personality. People are constantly shifting from one ego state to another, and their behavior at any one time is related to the state of the moment.

The *Parent* part of personality represents that which has been incorporated from one's parents and parental substitutes. When we are in the Parent ego state, we react to situations as we imagine our parents might have reacted, or we act toward others the way our parents acted toward us. The Parent contains all the "shoulds" and "oughts" and other rules for living. When we are in that ego state, we may act in ways that are strikingly similar to those of our parents. We are likely to use some of their very words and phrases, and our posture, gestures, tone and quality of voice, and mannerisms may replicate theirs. Such behavior occurs whether the Parent in us is a positive ego state (a Nurturing Parent) or a negative one (a Critical Parent).

The *Adult* ego state is our processor of data. It is the objective part of our personality and gathers information about what is going on. It is not emotional or judgmental but works with the facts and with external reality.

The *Child* ego state consists of feelings, impulses, and spontaneous acts. The Child in each of us is either the "Natural Child," the "Little Professor," or the "Adapted Child." The Natural Child is the spontaneous, impulsive, open, alive, expressive, often charming but untrained being within each of us. The Little Professor is the unschooled wisdom of a child. It is manipulative, egocentric, and creative. The Adapted Child is the tamed version of the Natural Child, the part of us that learns to accommodate to the expectations of others to gain acceptance and approval.

People who participate in TA counseling are taught how to recognize what ego state they are functioning in when they are faced with a problem. In this way they can make conscious decisions about the particular ego state in which they want to function. For example, if Betty becomes aware that she is treating her children in the same critical way her own mother responded to her, she is in a position to change her behavior. As Betty becomes more aware of her ego states in various situations, she also becomes more aware of her adaptive behavior (both to her internal Parent and to the outside world). With this awareness she can knowingly choose other options.

The Life Script.   The concept of the life script is an important contribution of TA. A life script is made up of both parental teachings and the early decisions we make as a child. Often, we continue to follow our script as an adult.

Scripting begins in infancy with subtle, nonverbal messages from our parents. During our earliest years we learn much about our worth as a person and our place in life. Later, scripting occurs in both subtle and direct ways. Some of the messages we might "hear" include: "Always listen to authority." "Don't act like a child." "We know that you can perform well, and we expect the best from you, so be sure you don't let us down." "Never trust people; rely on yourself." "You're really stupid, and we're convinced that you'll never amount to much." These messages are often sent in disguised ways. For example, our parents may never have told us directly that sexual feelings are bad or that touching is inappropriate. However, their behavior with each other and with us may have taught us to think in this way. Moreover, what parents *don't* say or do is just as important as what they say directly. If no mention is ever made of sexuality, for instance, that very fact communicates significant attitudes.

On a broader level than the messages we receive from our parents are the life scripts that are a part of our cultural context. Each culture has a set of values that are transmitted in many ways in the family circle. A few examples of cultural messages pertaining to the family are listed below:

- "Older people are to be revered and respected."
- "Don't bring shame to the family."
- "Don't talk about family matters outside the family circle."
- "Don't demonstrate affection in public."
- "Always obey your parents and grandparents."
- "The mother is the heart of the family."
- "The father is the head of the family."
- "Avoid conflict and strive for harmony within the family."
- "Never get a divorce."

Our life script, including the messages from both our family of origin and our culture, forms the core of our personal identity. Our experiences may lead us to such conclusions as "I really don't have any right to exist." "I can only be loved if I'm productive and successful." "I'd better not trust my feelings, because they'll only get me in trouble." These basic themes running through our lives tend to determine our behavior, and very often they are difficult to unlearn. In many subtle ways these early decisions about ourselves can come back to haunt us in later life. Our beliefs about ourselves can even influence how long and how well we live. After his liver transplant, the late Mickey Mantle looked back on his life with a number of regrets. He thought that he would die very young because both his father and

grandfather died at an early age, leading to his famous line: "If I had known I was going to live so long, I'd have taken better care of myself."

Life scripts seem to operate on physical diseases such as cancer. In *Love, Medicine, and Miracles,* Siegel (1988) writes about personality programming as a significant factor in disease. For example, he finds that many of his patients with cancer are convinced that the only way they can receive love is by dying. They have made a "Don't exist" or "Don't be well" decision. Siegel finds that his patients tend to get the same diseases as their parents and to die at the same age. They appear doomed to reenact their parents' scripts. He contends that one's psychological conditioning is at least as critical as genetic predisposition in leading to disease. He arrived at this conclusion by observing people who changed their negative conditioning once they became aware of it. A good illustration of this fatalistic life script is given by a nurse who said to Siegel after one of his lectures: "I think you may have saved my life. I've been waiting to die of cancer, since my mother has it and my father had it. It never occurred to me that I didn't have to have it" (Siegel, 1988, p. 88). Understanding one's life script is a significant factor in why some people seem to need an illness such as cancer. Siegel believes that sickness gives people "permission" to do things they would otherwise be inhibited doing. For example, illness allows them to take time to reflect, meditate, and chart a new course of life.

Illness serves as one example of how one's life script unfolds and influences the quality of one's life, unless new decisions are made. Here is another example that may help clarify how early messages and the decisions we make about them influence us in day-to-day living. In my (Jerry's) own case, even though I now experience myself as successful, for many years of my life I felt unsuccessful and unworthy. I haven't erased my old script completely, and I still experience self-doubts and struggle with insecurities. I don't think I can change such long-lasting feelings by simply telling myself "OK, now that I'm meeting with success, I'm the person I was meant to be." I continue to deal with feelings of insecurity. It could be that my striving for success is part of the picture of coping with basic feelings of inadequacy.

I am convinced that part of the dynamics motivating me toward success are linked to the acceptance I wanted from my parents, especially from my father. In many important ways my father did not feel successful, and I believe that on some level my own strivings have been not only to prove my own worth but also to make up for some of the successes that could have been his. Even though he died 30 years ago, on a psychological plane I am still making some attempt to win his acceptance and make him proud of my accomplishments. As a child I did not feel that I was able to do much of anything very well. Although my external reality has certainly changed from the time I was a child to now, I continue to play out some of the underlying patterns. For me this does not mean that I need to put an end to my projects, yet I do want to be aware of who I am in service to and not spend the rest of my life living up to parental expectations.

In short, although I believe that I can change some of my basic attitudes about myself, I don't think I can ever get rid of all vestiges of the effects of my early learning and decisions. In general, although we need not be determined by old decisions, it's wise to be continually aware of manifestations of our old ways that interfere with our attempts to develop new ways of thinking and being.

Injunctions.   Let's look more closely at the nature of the early messages (often called injunctions) that we incorporate into our lives. First of all, these injunctions aren't just planted in our heads while we sit by passively. By making decisions in response to real or imagined injunctions, we assume some of the responsibility for indoctrinating ourselves. Thus, if we hope to free ourselves, we must become aware of what these "oughts" and "shoulds" are and of how we allow them to operate in our lives.

The following list, based on the Gouldings' work (1978, 1979), includes common injunctions and some possible decisions that could be made in response to them.

1. *"Don't make mistakes."* Children who hear and accept this message often fear taking risks that may make them look foolish. They tend to equate making mistakes with being a failure.
   - *Possible decisions:* "I'm scared of making the wrong decision, so I simply won't decide." "Because I made a dumb choice, I won't decide on anything important again!" "I'd better be perfect if I hope to be accepted."

2. *"Don't be."* This lethal message is often given nonverbally by the way parents hold (or don't hold) the child. The basic message is "I wish you hadn't been born."
   - *Possible decisions:* "I'll keep trying until I get you to love me." "If things get terrible, I'll kill myself."

3. *"Don't be close."* Related to this injunction are the messages "Don't trust" and "Don't love."
   - *Possible decisions:* "I let myself love once, and it backfired. Never again!" "Because it's scary to get close, I'll keep myself distant."

4. *"Don't be important."* If you are constantly discounted when you speak, you are likely to believe that you are unimportant.
   - *Possible decisions:* "If, by chance, I ever do become important, I'll play down my accomplishments."

5. *"Don't be a child."* This message says: "Always act adult!" "Don't be childish and make a fool of yourself." "Keep control of yourself."
   - *Possible decisions:* "I'll take care of others and won't ask for much myself." "I won't let myself have fun."

6. *"Don't grow."* This message is given by the frightened parent who discourages the child from growing up in many ways.
   - *Possible decisions:* "I'll stay a child, and that way I'll get my parents to approve of me." "I won't be sexual, and that way my father won't push me away."

7. *"Don't succeed."* If children are positively reinforced for failing, they may accept the message not to seek success.
   - *Possible decisions:* "I'll never do anything perfect enough, so why try?" "I'll succeed, even it kills me." "If I don't succeed, then I'll not have to live up to high expectations others have of me."

8. *"Don't be you."* This involves suggesting to children that they are the wrong sex, shape, size, color, or have ideas or feelings that are unacceptable to parental figures.
   - *Possible decisions:* "They'd love me only if I were a boy (girl), so it's impossible to get their love." "I'll pretend I'm a boy (girl)."

9. *"Don't be sane"* and *"Don't be well."* Some children get attention only when they are physically sick or acting crazy.
   - *Possible decisions:* "I'll get sick, and then I'll be included." "I am crazy."

10. *"Don't belong."* This injunction may indicate that the family feels that the child does not belong anywhere.
    - *Possible decisions:* "I'll be a loner forever." "I'll never belong anywhere."

Injunctions in Alcoholic Families.   In our work with both undergraduate and graduate students in human services and counseling, we are surprised by the large number whose parents are alcoholics. Certain patterns of injunctions, roles that are learned, and decisions about life often characterize adult children from alcoholic families.

In *It Will Never Happen to Me,* Claudia Black (1987) vividly portrays the life histories of adult children of alcoholics (ACAs), and we have adapted much of the material in this section from her book. Black discusses three central injunctions that she detects over and over in her work with these clients: "Don't talk." "Don't trust." "Don't feel."

- *"Don't talk."* The family injunction is not to discuss real issues in the family. Children are conditioned to ignore these issues in the hope that the hurt will go away. Children learn not to rock the boat. The key dynamic is denial of the family secret of alcoholism.
- *"Don't trust."* Adult children of alcoholics learn to always be on guard, to rely on themselves and not to trust others with their feelings. In alcoholic homes children learn that their parents are not consistently available and cannot be relied on for safety. Unfortunately, they carry this pattern of not trusting from their childhood into their adulthood.
- *"Don't feel."* Children develop a denial system to numb their feelings. They learn not to share what they feel, because they are convinced that their feelings will not be validated within their family. Gradually, they build walls for self-protection as a way of coping with a feared world. They learn to deny and discount their feelings, they hide their pain, and they do not express what is inside of them. This process of denial interferes in their emotional life when they reach adulthood.

Children raised in alcoholic families enter adulthood with strategies for survival that worked to some degree in their childhood and adolescent years. Over the years they have refined behaviors such as being responsible, adjusting, or placating, as well as not talking, not trusting, and not feeling. On reaching adulthood, most ACAs continue to struggle with problems related to trust, dependency, control, identification, and expression of feelings.

Children tend to adopt certain roles for survival in alcoholic families. In her research and therapeutic work with ACAs, Black has found that later, as adults, they play out these same roles. She writes that the majority of ACAs adopt one or a combination of these roles: the responsible person, the adjuster, or the placater.

- *The responsible person.* Children who miss their childhood by having to mature very early often take on household and parenting responsibilities for other siblings. When structure and consistency are not provided, these children provide it for themselves. They rely completely on themselves, for they have learned many times over that they cannot count on their parents.
- *The adjuster.* Some children make an early decision that "since I can't do anything about the family situation, I'll adjust to it." As children, adjusters become detached; as adults they have no sense of self, they are not autonomous, and they typically feel that they have few choices.
- *The placater.* Some children become skilled at listening and providing empathy and tend to deny their own feelings in the hopes that adapting will bring peace to the family. Placaters have a difficult time dealing with their own feelings. For example, if they cry, they tend to cry alone.

These roles are often found in other people besides ACAs. Many students who read about these roles question why they find so many similarities to ACAs, even though they did not grow up in alcoholic homes. There are many other forms of dysfunctional behavior in families besides alcoholic patterns. For example, incest victims get the message that what is going on is secret, which can be reinforced with the threat of violence if the child informs. People who experienced incest frequently learn to deny what is taking place, both outside of them and in their inner world as well. They are likely to incorporate shame, guilt, and feelings of self-blame. All of these are manifestations of accepting injunctions on either a verbal or a nonverbal level.

As you can see, these are not rigid categories that box people in but general patterns of learned behavior. The roles that children play in a dysfunctional family tend to evolve from childhood to adulthood. As children, individuals may busy themselves by taking care of others and pleasing others; as adults, they often become professional helpers and strive to please their clients. They become carriers of the pain of others. Yet if they don't attend to their own needs and feelings, eventually they burn out. These adults have a difficult time asking for what they need for themselves, and in their personal relationships they tend to seek out others who are takers.

Overcoming Injunctions.   I (Marianne) want to share some messages I heard growing up, as a personal example of a struggle with listening to injunctions from both parents and society. I was born and spent my childhood and adolescence in a farming village in Germany. Some of the messages I received, though they were not typically verbalized, were "You can't do anything about it." "Things could be worse, so don't talk so much about how bad things are." "Accept what you have, and don't complain about what you don't have." "Don't be different. Fit in with the community. Do what everybody else does." "Be satisfied with your life."

Although my childhood was very good in many respects and I was satisfied with part of my life, I still wanted more than I felt I could get by remaining in the village and becoming what was expected of me. It was a continuing struggle not to surrender to these expectations, but having some adult role models who themselves had challenged such injunctions inspired me to resist these messages. As early as age 8 I felt a sense of daring to be different and hoping someday to go to America. Although I doubted myself at times, I still began saving every penny I could lay my hands on. Finally, at the age of 19 I asked my father for permission to take a ship to the United States and surprised him when I told him that I had saved enough money to buy a ticket.

Even though there were many obstacles, I seemed to be driven to follow a dream and a decision that I made when I was only 8. When I did come to America, I eventually fulfilled another dream, and consequently challenged another injunction, by furthering my education. The theme of my struggles during my earlier years is that I was not willing to surrender to obstacles. I argued with myself about simply accepting what seemed like limited choices for a life's design, and in doing so I began writing a new life script for myself. It was important to me not to feel like a victim of circumstances. I was willing to do what was necessary to challenge barriers to what I wanted and to pursue my dreams and goals. Although I fought against these injunctions at an early age, it does not mean that they have gone away forever. I continue to have to be aware of them and not allow them to control me as an adult.

At this point, think about some of the childhood decisions you made about yourself and about life. For example, you might have made any one of these early decisions:

- "I will be loved only when I live up to what others expect of me."
- "I'd better listen to authorities outside of myself, because I can't trust myself to make decent decisions."
- "I won't let myself trust people, and that way they won't ever let me down again."

Themes like these that run through your life determine not only your self-image but also your behavior. It is a difficult matter to discard these self-defeating assumptions and learn new and constructive ones in their place. This is one reason for learning how to critically evaluate these questions:

- What messages have I listened to and "bought"?
- How valid are the sources of these messages?
- In what ways do I now continue to say self-defeating sentences to myself?
- How can I challenge some of the decisions I made about myself and make new ones that will lead to a positive orientation?

■ Learning to Dispute Self-Defeating Thinking

As children and adolescents we uncritically incorporate certain assumptions about life and about our worth as a person. Rational emotive behavior therapy and other cognitive-behavioral therapies are based on the premise that emotional and behavioral problems are originally learned from significant others during childhood.

Others gave us faulty beliefs, which we accept unthinkingly. We actively keep alive false beliefs by the processes of self-suggestion and self-repetition (Ellis, 1988). It is largely our own repetition of early-indoctrinated faulty beliefs that keeps dysfunctional attitudes operational within us. Self-defeating beliefs are supported and maintained by negative and dysfunctional statements that we make to ourselves over and over again: "If I don't win universal love and approval, then I'll never be happy." "If I make a mistake, that would prove that I am an utter failure."

Albert Ellis (1988, 1994), the developer of rational emotive behavior therapy (REBT), describes some of the most common ways people make themselves miserable by remaining wedded to their irrational beliefs. Ellis has devised an A-B-C theory of personality that explains how people develop negative evaluations of themselves. He holds that it is our faulty thinking, not actual life events, that creates emotional upsets and that leads to our misery. He contends that we have the power to control our emotional destiny and suggests that when we are upset it is a good idea to look to our hidden dogmatic "musts," "oughts," and absolutistic "shoulds." For Ellis, practically all human misery and serious emotional turmoil is unnecessary.

An example will clarify this A-B-C concept. Assume that Sally's parents abandoned her when she was a child (A, the activating event). Sally's emotional reaction may be feelings of depression, worthlessness, rejection, and unlovability (C, the emotional consequence). However, Ellis asserts, it is not A (her parents' abandonment of her) that caused her feelings of rejection and unlovability; rather, it is her belief system (B) that is causing her low self-esteem. She made her mistake when she told herself that there must have been something terrible about herself for her parents not to want her. Her faulty beliefs are reflected through self-talk such as: "I am to blame for what my parents did." "If I were more lovable, they would have wanted to keep me."

According to Ellis (1988, p. 60), most of our irrational ideas can be reduced to three main forms of what he refers to as *must*urbation. The three basic "musts" that create emotional problems are:

- "I *must* perform well and win the approval of important people, or else I am an inadequate person!"
- "Others *must* treat me fairly and considerately!"
- "My life *must* be easy and pleasant. I need and *must* have the things I want, or life is unbearable!"

REBT is designed to teach people how to dispute irrational beliefs such as these. Let's apply REBT to our example. Sally does not need to continue believing that she is basically unlovable. Instead of clinging to the belief that something must have been wrong with her for her parents to have rejected her, she can begin to dispute this self-defeating statement and think along different lines: "It hurts that my parents didn't want me, but perhaps *they* had problems that kept them from being good parents." "Maybe my parents didn't love me, but that doesn't mean that nobody could love me." "While it's unfortunate that I didn't have parents in growing up, it's not devastating, and I no longer have to be a little girl waiting for their protection."

One member of a therapeutic group of ours had major struggles in believing he was a worthwhile person. Bob learned how to pay attention to his internal dia-

logue and realized how his thoughts influenced what he did and how he felt about himself. Bob reported the following about how his self-talk got in his way.

What I am noticing and changing are my internal dialogues that I carry on within myself. I see how I have always judged myself critically. I have somehow made a major breakthrough on giving myself a break from the negative chatter that has always gone on in my thoughts. It finally dawned on me that I am my own worst critic.

I am noticing that I am countering my self-talk more comfortably, and almost automatically. I seem to finally be in the process of forgiving myself and getting down to some more reasonable expectations for myself. I keep coming back to the lesson that anything worth learning is worth failing at. I am attempting to allow myself the many small failures in my life. The part that is different is that I am asking myself what I could do different next time. I want to focus on the lesson that allows me to learn, not the mistakes.

Bob is a good example of a person who can change his life by challenging and changing his self-destructive beliefs about himself. Ellis stresses that your feelings about yourself are largely the result of the way you think. Thus, if you hope to change a negative self-image, it is essential to learn how to dispute the illogical sentences you now continue to feed yourself and to challenge faulty premises that you have accepted uncritically. Further, you also need to work and practice replacing these self-sabotaging beliefs with constructive ones. If you wish to study common ways of combating the negative self-indoctrination process, we highly recommend *How to Stubbornly Refuse to Make Yourself Miserable about Anything—Yes, Anything!* (Ellis, 1988). Two other excellent books in this area are: *Feeling Good: The New Mood Therapy* (Burns, 1981) and *How You Feel Is up to You* (McKay & Dinkmeyer, 1994).

■ Learning to Challenge Your Inner Parents

We'd like to expand a bit on the general concepts of transactional analysis and rational emotive behavior therapy and discuss some related ideas about challenging early messages and working toward autonomy. The term *inner parent* refers to the attitudes and beliefs we have about ourselves and others that are a direct result of things we've learned from our parents or parental substitutes. The willingness to challenge this inner parent is a mark of autonomy. Since being autonomous means that we are in control of the direction of our lives, it implies that we have discovered an identity that is separate and distinct from the identities of our parents and of others.

It should be noted that many of the values we incorporated from our parents may be healthy standards for guiding our behavior. No doubt our past has contributed in many respects to the good qualities we possess, and many of the things that we like about ourselves may be largely due to the influence of the people who were important to us in our early years. What is essential is that we look for the subtle ways in which we have psychologically incorporated our parents' values in our lives without a deliberate choice.

How do we learn to recognize the influence that our parents continue to have on us? One way to begin is by talking back to our inner parent. In other words, we can begin to notice some of the things we do and avoid doing, and then ask ourselves why. For instance, suppose you avoid enrolling in a college course because you'd long ago branded yourself "stupid." You may tell yourself that you'd never be able to pass the class, so why even try? In this case an early decision you made about your intellectual capabilities prevents you from branching out to new endeavors. Rather than stopping at this first obstacle, however, you could challenge yourself by asking: "Who says I'm too stupid? Even if my father or my teachers have told me that I'm slow, is it really true? Why have I accepted this view of myself uncritically? Let me check it out and see for myself."

In carrying out this kind of dialogue, we can talk to the different selves we have within us. You may be struggling to open yourself to people and trust them, for example, while at the same time you hear the inner injunction "Never trust anybody." In this case you can carry on a two-way discussion between your trusting side and your suspicious side. The important point is that we don't have to passively accept as truth the messages we learned when we were children. As adults we can now put these messages to the test.

In his excellent book *Making Peace with Your Parents*, psychiatrist Harold Bloomfield (1983) makes the point that many of us suffer from psychological wounds as a result of unfinished business with our parents. We often keep the past alive by insisting on blaming them for all our problems. Instead of pointing the blaming finger at our parents, we can look at ways we can give ourselves some of the things that we may still expect or hope for from our parents. If we don't get past the blaming, we end up wedded to resentment. As long as we cling to our resentments, expect our parents to be different from who they are, or wait for their approval, we are keeping painful memories and experiences alive. If we harbor grudges against our parents and focus all our energies on changing them, we have little constructive energy left over to assume control of our own lives. Instead of trying to change them, we can approach them in the very ways that we'd like them to treat us. According to Bloomfield, before we can resolve any conflicts with our actual parents, we first must make peace with our inner parent.

To be at peace with yourself, you need to let go of festering resentments, to work through unresolved anger, and to cease blaming others. These factors not only poison relationships but also take a toll on the way you feel about yourself. It is only when you find a sense of inner peace that you can ever hope to make peace with the significant people in your life. You do have a choice. Even though your family situation may have been far from ideal, you now can choose the attitude you take toward your past circumstances. If you choose to assume responsibility for the person you are now, you are moving in the direction of becoming your own parent.

■ Becoming Your Own Parent

Achieving emotional maturity involves divorcing ourselves from our inner parent and becoming our own "parent." But maturity is not some fixed destination at which we finally arrive; it is, rather, a direction in which we can choose to travel. In writing about the real meaning of independence, which is a core ingredient of maturity, Siegel (1993) emphasizes that being independent doesn't mean that we don't need others.

> Independence means knowing your ability to deal with adversity as well as expressing feelings, asking for help when appropriate, learning to share your needs. It means not being lonely even when you are alone. It means developing into a full and complete human being, in the healthiest sense of the word. (p. 5)

What are some of the characteristics of the person who is moving toward becoming his or her own parent? There is no authoritative list of the qualities of an autonomous person, but the following characteristics may stimulate you to come up with your own view of what kind of parent you want to be for yourself and what criteria make sense to you in evaluating your own degree of psychological maturity. For each of these characteristics, ask yourself whether it applies to you and whether you agree that it is a mark of one who is becoming independent. We encourage you to add to or modify this list as you see fit.

1. People moving in the direction of autonomy recognize the ways in which their inner parent controls them. They see how they are controlled by guilt or by the promise of love and how they have cooperated in giving parents and parent substitutes undue power in their lives.

2. Autonomous individuals have a desire to become both free and responsible and to do for themselves what they are capable of doing.

3. People moving in the direction of autonomy have a sense of identity and uniqueness. Rather than only looking outside of themselves, they also find answers within. Instead of looking primarily to what others expect of them and seeking their approval, they ask: "Who is it that I want to become? What seems like the right thing to do? What do I expect of myself?"

4. Autonomous people do not have a need to prove their autonomy. They are willing to consider the opinions of their parents or other significant people in the framework of their decision-making process.

5. People moving in the direction of autonomy have a sense of commitment and responsibility. They are committed to some ideals and personal goals that make sense to them. Their sense of commitment includes a willingness to accept responsibility for their actions rather than blaming circumstances or other people for the way their lives are going.

6. The discovery of a meaning or purpose in life is an important mark of independent people. Being concerned about making a difference and taking actions to bring about social change are often routes to a meaningful life.

7. In addition to pursuing self-interests, autonomous individuals are also concerned with reaching out to others, sharing with them, and giving something of themselves to make society a better place.

In writing about "becoming your own best parent," Bloomfield (1983) challenges us as *adults* to recognize that we are responsible for satisfying our psychological needs for maintenance, encouragement, and affection. His message is that rather than getting stuck whining about all the ways our parents did not live up to our expectations, we can learn to give to ourselves what we missed from our parents.

Recall that we have emphasized that you do not find yourself in isolation; rather, the process of self-discovery is bound up with the quality of your relationships to others. Autonomy does not mean being completely independent or not needing others. Becoming your own person does not imply "doing your own thing" irrespective of your impact on those with whom you come in contact. Instead, being autonomous implies that you have questioned the values you live by and made them your own; part of this process includes concern for the welfare of those people you love and associate with. Consider these questions as a way of clarifying the meaning autonomy has for you:

- Is it important to you to feel that you are your own person?
- To what degree do you think you can live by your own standards and still be sensitive to the needs and wants of others?
- Are you satisfied with living by the expectations that others have for you?
- Do you want to become more independent, even though there are risks involved?

➤ *Time Out for Personal Reflection*

The following self-inventory is designed to increase your awareness of the injunctions you have incorporated as a part of your self-system and to help you challenge the validity of messages you may not have critically examined.

1. Place a check (√) in the space provided for each of the following "don't" injunctions that you think applies to you.

_____	Don't be you.
_____	Don't think.
_____	Don't feel.
_____	Don't be close.
_____	Don't trust.
_____	Don't be sexy.
_____	Don't fail.
_____	Don't be foolish.
_____	Don't be important.
_____	Don't brag.

_____   Don't let us down.
_____   Don't grow or change.

2. Check the following ways that you sometimes badger yourself with "do" messages.

_____   Be perfect.
_____   Say only kind things.
_____   Be more than you are.
_____   Be obedient.
_____   Work up to your potential.
_____   Be practical at all times.
_____   Listen to authority figures.
_____   Always put your best foot forward.
_____   Put others before yourself.
_____   Be seen but not heard.

List any other injunctions you can think of that apply to you:

_____

_____

_____

_____

3. What are some messages you've received concerning

your self-worth? _____

your potential to succeed? _____

your gender role? _____

your intelligence? _____

your trust in yourself? _____

trusting others? _____

making yourself vulnerable? _____

your security? _____

your aliveness as a person? _____

your creativity? _____

your ability to be loved? _____

your capacity to give love? _____

4. Because your view of yourself has a great influence on the quality of your interpersonal relationships, we invite you to look carefully at some of the views you have of yourself and also to consider how you arrived at these views. To do this, reflect on these questions:

a. How do you see yourself now? To what degree do you see yourself as confident? secure? worthwhile? accomplished? caring? open? accepting?

_____

_____

_____

_____

b. Do others generally see you as you see yourself? What are some ways others view you differently from how you view yourself?

_____

_____

_____

_____

c. Who in your life has been most influential in shaping your self-concept, and how has he or she (they) affected your view of yourself? (father? mother? friend? teacher? grandparents?)

_____

_____

_____

_____

Early Adulthood

In the previous chapter we discussed the developmental process from infancy through adolescence based on Freud's psychosexual stages and Erikson's psychosocial stages. Inasmuch as Freud deemphasized development in adulthood, this chapter will rely on Erikson's perspective on the core struggles and choices from early adulthood through late adulthood.

■ Stages of Adulthood

In *New Passages,* Gail Sheehy (1995) describes a new map of adult life. Contending that we need new markers for life transitions, she states that "the old demarcation points we may still carry around—an adulthood that begins at 21 and ends at 65—are hopelessly out of date" (p. 7). People who are today in their twenties, thirties, and early forties are confronted with a different set of conditions than was the case 20 years ago. Middle age has been pushed ahead to the fifties. Today, people at 50 are dealing with transitions that were characteristic of people at 40 just a couple of decades ago. Sheehy's most recent research, based on a collection of life histories of people facing the challenges of "second adulthood" (age 45 and beyond), leads her to one overriding conclusion: "There is no longer a standard life cycle. People are increasingly able to customize their life cycles" (p. 16). Sheehy has provided a revised map of adult life, with the following overarching periods: provisional adulthood (18 to 30), first adulthood (30 to 45), and second adulthood (45 to 85+).

■ Provisional Adulthood

The period of provisional adulthood encompasses people age 18 to 20. According to Sheehy (1995), contemporary young adults live at an accelerated pace, even though many of the responsibilities of full adulthood are delayed. This is a time when we begin detaching from the family and search for a personal identity. Some of the tasks of this period involve locating ourselves in a peer group role, establishing a gender identity, finding an occupation, and developing a personal world view. According to Erikson, we enter adulthood after we master the adolescent conflicts over *identity* versus *role confusion.* Our sense of identity is tested anew in adulthood, however, by the challenge of *intimacy* versus *isolation.*

One characteristic of the psychologically mature person is the ability to form intimate relationships. Before we can form such relationships, we must be sure of our own identity. Intimacy involves sharing, giving of ourselves, and relating to another out of strength and a desire to grow with the other person. Failure to achieve intimacy can result in isolation from others and a sense of alienation. The fact that alienation is a problem for many people in our society is evidenced by the widespread use of drugs and by other ways in which we try to numb a sense of isolation. If we attempt to escape isolation by clinging to another person, however, we rarely find success in the relationship.

Erikson's concept of intimacy can be applied to any kind of close relationship between two adults. Relationships involving emotional commitments may be between close friends of the same or the opposite sex, and they may or may not have a sexual dimension. Some of the characteristics of people who have achieved a sense of intimacy include: having a clear sense of personal identity; being tolerant of differences in others; trusting others and themselves in relationships; establishing cooperative, affiliative relationships with others; being willing to give in relationships; believing in the value of mutual interdependence as a way to work through difficulties; being willing to commit to relationships that demand some degree of sacrifice; and being able to form close emotional bonds without fearing the loss of personal identity (Hamachek, 1990).

■ Entering the Twenties

During their twenties young people are faced with a variety of profound choices. In their early twenties young adults move away from the safe shelter of the family and confront insecurity about the future as they attempt to establish independence. This time is often characterized by considerable agitation and change.

If you are in this age group, you are no doubt facing decisions about how you will live. Your choices probably include questions such as "Will I choose the security of staying at home, or will I struggle financially and psychologically to live on my own?" "Will I stay single, or will I get involved in some committed relationship?" "Will I stay in college full time, or will I begin a career?" "If I choose a career, what will it be, and how will I go about deciding what I might do in the work world?" "If I marry, will I be a parent or not?" "What are some of my dreams, and how might I make them become reality?" "What do I most want to do with my life at this time, and how might I find meaning?"

Choices pertaining to work, education, marriage, family life, and lifestyle are complex and deeply personal, and it is common to struggle over what it is we really want. There is the temptation to let others decide for us or to be overly influenced by the standards of others. But if we choose that path, we remain psychological adolescents at best. We have the choice whether to live by parental rules or to leave home psychologically and decide for ourselves what our future will be. The following personal statements of individuals in their twenties illustrate the struggles of this period. A young man says:

I want to live on my own, but it's very difficult to support myself and go to college at the same time. The support and approval of my parents is surely something I want, yet I am working hard at finding a balance between how much I am willing to do to get their approval and how much I will live by my values. I love my parents, yet at the same time I resent them for the hold they have on me.

Another person in her twenties expresses her desire for intimacy, along with her reservations and doubts:

While I realize that I want to be in a close relationship with a man, I know that I am also afraid of getting involved. I wonder if I want to spend the rest of my life with the same person. At other times I'm afraid I'll never find someone I can love who really loves me. I don't want to give up my freedom, nor do I want to be dependent on someone.

Steven, age 24, is worried about the prospects of employment:

Now that I'm out of college, will I have an opportunity to use what I studied for all these years? Will I be able to get the kind of job I want in these difficult economic times?

Martha, age 23, typifies young people who are willing to allow themselves to dream and remain open about what they want in life. Martha works for a savings and loan association, and she is about to begin full-time graduate study toward a counseling degree. Here is what she is looking forward to:

At this time in my life I think I have a thousand choices open to me. I don't like my job as a loan officer that much, but it does provide me with security. I never want to stop learning, and I'm sure I want to be a vital person. At some time, though not yet, I'd like to be married. Eventually I'd like kids. I'd like to write books someday, as well as having a counseling practice.

When Martha was asked what she'd like to be able to say in her old age, she replied:

I have a friend whose grandmother was 63 and she rode a pogo stick. I'd like to be as energetic in my old age as I am now. I never want to get bogged down with old ideas. Some people get set in their values, and they just won't change. I always want to evaluate and to be in the process of integrating new values in my life.

When Martha was asked if she saw herself as typical of those her age, her answer was:

Most people between 18 and 23 don't look inward that much. I think they look to other people to make choices for them. I hope I can do what feels right to me at the time. I'm uncertain now about many of my specific goals. I like taking life as it comes, but by that I'm not talking about being passive. I hope to be open to the possibilities that might eventually open up to me. I don't want to lose myself in someone else, but I would like to share my life with someone else.

Bret is 21, and he is struggling hard to get through college. He is a part of a single-parent family and has little financial help. In fact his mother depends on him to contribute some of his earnings to the family. While he is attempting to carve out a life for himself, he feels burdened with the responsibility of providing both emotional and financial support for his mother and his siblings. At times, taking care of both himself and his family seems overwhelming, and he feels like giving up.

■ Transition from the Twenties to the Thirties

The transition from the late twenties to the early thirties is a time of changing values and beliefs. Inner turmoil increases for many during this period. However, many others delay making a commitment about relationships and careers. It used to be quite common for young people in their late twenties and early thirties to have a family and to be firmly established in a career. Now, taking on these responsibilities has been delayed for various reasons. It is not uncommon now for couples to delay having children until their later thirties.

During this transition, people often take another look at the dreams they had earlier. They may reevaluate their life plans and make significant shifts. Some become aware that their dreams may not have materialized, which causes them to wonder what kind of future they want for themselves and others in their lives. Although this recognition often brings anxiety, it can be the catalyst for making new plans and working hard to attain them.

Consider Pam's evolution in her process of striving to make her dreams turn to reality:

When I was growing up, a college education was not considered essential for a female. The belief in my family was that as a female I would grow up, get married, have children, live in a home with a white picket fence and be financially supported by my husband. The most I might have expected of myself was to become a part-time secretary.

When I turned 17 I attended college for a couple of years, but I did not take my studies seriously, which showed in my grades. I was just biding my time until Mr. Right came along to carry me away. I got married, and in the next few years reality set in. My husband and I had marital problems, the economy took a severe downturn, and I eventually ended up getting a divorce. Reality turned out to be very different from the dreams I had while growing up.

In my late twenties I began taking inventory of my life. I began to think about my life goals and what it was that I truly wanted for myself. I realized that I wanted a career that I found meaningful, one that I felt would make a difference. I wanted financial security and a nice home in which to raise my children. Although I had remarried by this time, I did not want to make the same mistake again of depending on someone else to fulfill my goals and secure my future. For me, education seemed to be the key to achieve these goals. At 30, I returned to college and completed my last two years with a 4.0 grade point average. What I learned and what I am continuing to learn is that you don't achieve goals by dreaming about them, wishing for them, or depending on someone else to fulfill them. Instead, dreams become reality by working hard. I did not understand the value of an education and how having a college education could change my life and help me achieve my goals. I see things very differently now. I see how life is not about meeting Prince Charming and being swept away, or about luck. Life is about choices, personal responsibility, and hard work.

➤ *Time Out for Personal Reflection*

1. Think about a few of the major turning points in your young adulthood. Write down not more than two turning points, and then state how you think they were important in your life. What difference did your decision at these critical times make in your life?

Turning point: _____

Impact of the decision on my life: _____

_____

_____

_____

_____

Turning point: _____

Impact of the decision on my life: _____

_____

_____

_____

_____

2. Complete the following sentences by giving the first response that comes to mind:

a. To me, being an independent person means _____

_____

b. The things I received from my parents that I most value are _____

_____

c. The things I received from my parents that I least like and most want to change
are _____

_____

d. If I could change one thing about my past, it would be _____

_____

e. My fears of being independent are these: _____

_____

f. One thing I most want for my children is _____

_____

g. I find it difficult to be my own person when _____

_____

h. I feel the freest when _____

_____

Middle Adulthood

The time between the ages of 30 and 65 is characterized by a "going outside of ourselves." It is a time for learning how to live creatively with ourselves and with others, and it can be the time of greatest productivity in our lives. In middle age we reach the top of the mountain yet at the same time realize that we eventually will begin the downhill journey. In addition, we may painfully experience the discrepancy between the dreams of our twenties and thirties and the hard reality of what we have achieved.

Sheehy (1995) compares life to a three-act play: "It's as though when we are young, we have seen only the first act of the play. By our forties we have reached the climactic second-act curtain. Only as we approach fifty does the shape an meaning of the whole play become clear. We move into the third act with the intention of a resolution and tremendous curiosity about how it will all come out" (p. 150).

■ The Late Thirties

People in their thirties often experience doubts and reevaluate significant aspects of their lives. Both Gould (1978) and Levinson (1978) found signs of increased turmoil during the thirties, and it is not uncommon for people to experience a crisis at this time in their lives. These crises center on doubts about their earlier commitments and on concerns over getting locked into choices that make it difficult for them to move in new directions. During this period of unrest, disillusionment, and questioning, people often modify the rules and standards that governed their lives earlier. They also realize that their dreams do not materialize if they simply wish for things to happen; that there is no magic in the world; that life is not simple but, in fact, is complicated and bewildering; and that we get what we want not by waiting and wishing passively but by working actively to attain our goals. As we open up in our thirties, a crisis can be precipitated when we discover that life is not as uncomplicated as we had envisioned it to be.

Sheehy (1976) contends that we become impatient with living a life based on "shoulds" when we enter our thirties. Both men and women speak of feeling restricted at this time and may complain that life is narrow and dull. Sheehy asserts that these restrictions are related to the outcomes of the choices we made during our twenties. Even if these personal and career choices have served us well to date, in our thirties we become ready for some changes. That is a time for making new choices and perhaps for modifying or deepening old commitments. We are likely to review our commitments to career, marriage, children, friends, and life's priorities. Because we realize that time is passing, we make a major reappraisal of how we are spending our time and energy. We begin to realize that we don't have forever to reach our goals.

This process of self-examination may involve considerable turmoil and crisis. We may find ourselves asking: "Is this all there is to life?" "What do I want for the rest of my life?" "What is missing from my life now?" A woman who has primarily been engaged in a career may now want to spend more time at home and with the children. A woman who has devoted most of her life to being a homemaker may want to begin a new career outside the home. Men may do a lot of questioning about their work and wonder how they can make it more meaningful. It is likely that they will struggle with defining the meaning of success. They may be exteriorly focused in measuring success, which puts the source of the meaning of life on quicksand. They are likely to begin to question the price of success. Single people may consider finding a partner, and those who are married may experience a real crisis in their marriage, which may be a sign that they cannot continue with old patterns.

■ Life during the Forties

Sheehy (1976) used to consider the mid-thirties as the halfway mark and the prime of life. She referred to the period between 35 and 45 as the "Decline Decade," as if people had only until their mid-forties to resolve the crisis of midlife. Now Sheehy (1995) claims that it is a mistake to view the early forties as a time when people drop off the edge of a cliff. Although many people believe that when they reach forty their time is running out, more and more people are finding ways to avoid the restrictive identity that used to define middle age. In Sheehy's recent life history interviews with people in middle life, she found a new theme of rebirths permeating their stories. She writes: "More and more people were beginning to see there was the possibility of a new life to live, one in which we could concentrate on becoming better, stronger, deeper, wiser, funnier, freer, sexier, and more attentive to living the privileged moments, even as we were getting older, lumpier, slower, and closer to the end" (p. xiii). Indeed, we are retaining some of our youth for a longer period of time. The second half of life enlarges the boundaries of vital living, and it offers new opportunities for growth and change.

Sheehy's views on middle life are supported by Erikson's psychosocial developmental theory. For Erikson, the stimulus for continued growth in middle age is the core struggle between *generativity* and *stagnation*. Generativity is not restricted to just fostering children but includes being productive in a broad sense — for example, through creative pursuits in a career, in leisure-time activities, in teaching or caring for others, or in some meaningful volunteer work. Two basic qualities of the productive adult are the ability to love well and the ability to work well. Adults who fail to achieve a sense of productivity begin to stagnate, a form of psychological death.

According to Hamachek (1990), people who have a sense of generativity tend to focus more on what they can give to others than on what they can get. They are absorbed in a variety of activities outside of themselves, such as contributing to society or in other ways reflecting a concern for others. They display other-centered values and attitudes. They feel a strong inclination to express their talents. In short, they enjoy being productive and creative. In contrast, people who are not able to achieve a sense of generativity become stagnant. This stagnation is manifested by attitudes such as focusing on what they can get from others, displaying self-centered attitudes and values, avoiding risks and choosing the security provided by a routine existence, and showing little interest in making the world a better place.

Sheehy (1995) refers to middle life as the "most unrevealed" portion of adult life. When we reach middle age, we come to a crossroads. During our late thirties and into our mid-forties, we are likely to question what we want to do with the rest of our lives. We face both dangers and opportunities — the danger of slipping into a deadening rut and the opportunity to choose to rework the narrow identity of the first half of our life.

During middle age we realize the uncertainty of life, and we discover more clearly that we are alone. We stumble on masculine and feminine aspects of ourselves that had been masked. We may also go through a grieving process, because many parts of our old self are dying. This process allows us to reevaluate and reintegrate an emerging identity that is not the sum of others' expectations. A few of the events that might contribute to a midlife transformation are:

- We may come to realize that some of our youthful dreams will never materialize.
- We may begin to experience the pressure of time, realizing that now is the time to accomplish our goals.
- We may realize that life is not necessarily just and fair and that we often do not get what we had expected.

- There are marital crises and challenges to old patterns. A spouse may have an affair or seek a divorce.
- Coping with growing older is difficult for many; the loss of some of our youthful physical qualities can be hard to face.
- Our children grow up and leave home at this time. People who have lived largely for their children now may face emptiness.
- We may be confronted with taking care of our elderly parents, just about the time as taking care of our children was coming to an end.
- The death of our parents drives home a truth that is difficult for many to accept; ultimately, we are alone in this life.
- We may lose a job or be demoted, or we may grow increasingly disenchanted with our work.
- A woman may leave the home to enter the world of work and make this her primary interest.
- Women may be confronted with menopause, which can be a crisis for some.

Along with these factors that can precipitate a crisis, the following choices are available to us at this time:

- We can decide to go back for further schooling and gear up for a new career.
- We can choose to develop new talents and embark on novel hobbies, and we can even take steps to change our lifestyle.
- We can look increasingly inward to find out what we most want to do with the rest of our life and begin doing what we say we want to do.

According to Carl Jung, we are confronted with major changes and possibilities for transformation when we begin the second half of life between 35 and 40. Jung's therapy clients consistently revealed signs of experiencing a pivotal middle-age life crisis. Although they may have achieved worldly success, they typically were challenged with finding meaning in projects that had lost meaning. Many of his clients struggled to overcome feelings of emptiness and flatness in life.

Jung believed that major life transformations are an inevitable and universal part of the human condition at this juncture in life. He maintained that when the zest for living sags, it can be a catalyst for necessary and beneficial changes. To undergo such a transformation requires the death of some aspect of our psychological being, so new growth can occur that will open us to far deeper and richer ranges of existence. To strive for what Jung called *individuation* — integration of the unconscious with the conscious and psychological balance — people during their middle-age years must be willing to let go of preconceived notions and patterns that have dominated the first part of their lives. Their task now is to be open to the unconscious forces that have been influencing them all of their lives and to deepen the meaning of their lives.

For Jung, people can bring unconscious material into awareness by paying attention to their dreams and fantasies and by expressing themselves through poetry, writing, music, and art. Individuals need to recognize that the rational thought patterns that drove them during the first half of life represent merely one way of being. At this time in life, you must be willing to be guided by the spontaneous flow of the unconscious if you hope to achieve an integration of all facets of your being, which is part of psychological health (Schultz & Schultz, 1994).

You may be some distance away from middle age, but we hope you don't stop reading at this point, determined that this will never happen to you! Now may be a good time for you to reflect on the way your life is shaping up and to think about the person you'd like to be when you reach middle age. To help you in making this projection, consider the lives of people you know who are over 40. Do you have any models available in determining what direction you will pursue? Are there some ways you'd not want to live? Also, consider the following brief statements made by middle-aged people:

Roger says that it's difficult to always be striving for success, and he shares some of his loneliness:

So much of my life has been bound up in becoming a success. While I am successful, I continually demand more of myself. I'm never quite satisfied with anything I accomplish, and I continually look ahead and see what has to be done. It's lonely when I think of always swimming against the tide, and I fear getting dragged into deep water that I can't get out of. At the same time, I don't seem to be able to slow down.

Brenda says that she has stayed in a miserable marriage for 23 years. She finally recognizes that she has run out of excuses for staying. She must decide whether to maintain a marriage that is not likely to change much or decide on ending it:

I'm petrified by the idea that I have to support myself and that I'm responsible for my own happiness—totally. All these years I've told myself that if he were different, I'd feel much more fulfilled than I do in life. I also had many reasons that prevented me from taking action, even when it became very clear to me that he wasn't even slightly interested in seeing things change. I'm not afraid to go out and meet people on a social basis, but I'm terrified of getting intimately involved with a man on a sexual or emotional basis. When I think of all those years in an oppressive marriage, I want to scream. I know I've kept most of these screams inside of me, for I feared that if I allowed myself to scream I'd never stop—that I might go crazy. Yet keeping my pain and tears inside of me has made my whole body ache, and I'm tired of hurting all the time. I want something else from life besides hurt!

A 49-year-old re-entry student described going back to college as "a wonderful adventure that has opened new doors for me, and created a few obstacles." Although Linda had self-doubts and was intimidated over even the thought of becoming a student again, she cast her doubts aside and pursued her dream of attending university. She challenged the expectations of remaining in old roles and made choices to do something different with her life.

As a young woman I tried too hard to be superwife, mother, daughter, and friend. I had the role of peacemaker, was very quiet, stayed in the background, and desired to help a star to shine. I had always been there for others, sometimes to the neglect of my own needs and wants. I put too much effort into doing and little into just being. As a result of my personal therapy and other learning, I knew I wanted to change. I started to embrace being genuine and took more risks. I became more verbal and enjoyed participating in class. I began to notice where I could shine. I let go of the self-talk that kept me feeling stupid. I saw hope.

My Life Began at 40.   Joan Lunden, the anchorwoman on "Good Morning America," said that the reality of being 40 was a catalyst that helped her confront the truth about herself. Although she was successful and in the prime of her life, she was exhausted, unhappy, and weighed 50 pounds more than she now does at age 44. Joan admits that she caved in under the pressure of living a lie, attempting to present herself to 5 million television viewers as a contented and fulfilled woman. Her 39th birthday was somewhat of a wake-up call in that she admitted to herself that she was close to the breaking point. She made strides in changing once she courageously faced the truth about her life. Realizing that she was not living the way she wanted to and that all was not well in her life, Joan took steps toward rebuilding her life. At age 44, Joan reports that people tell her that she looks better than ever and she feels stronger, happier, and calmer. She admits that for her, life *did* begin at 40 (Lunden, 1995).

■ The Fifties

People begin the process of preparing for older age in their fifties. Many are at their peak in terms of status and personal power, and this can be a satisfying time of life. They do not have to work as hard as they did in the past, nor do they have to meet others' expectations. They can enjoy the benefits of their long struggle and dedication rather than striving to continually prove themselves. It is likely that rearing children and work are moving toward a culmination. Adults at this stage often do a lot of reflecting, contemplating, refocusing, and evaluating, so they can continue to discover new directions. Sheehy (1995) captures this period as a time of new opportunity: "Millions of people entering their forties and fifties today are able to make dramatic changes in their lives and habits, to look forward to living decades more in smoothly functioning bodies with agile minds — so long as they remain open to new vistas of learning and imagination and anticipate experiences yet to be conquered and savored" (p. xvii).

Rather than focusing on the fifties as a time of decline, we can enhance our lives by looking for what is going right for us. Instead of concentrating research on retirement, widowhood, meaninglessness, and impoverishment, Sheehy (1995) suggests that we look at the positive and creative dimensions of middle life — sources of love, meaning, fun, spiritual companionship, sexuality, and sustained well-being. Sheehy reports that this is an exciting time for women: "As family obligations fade away, many become motivated to stretch their independence, learn new skills, return to school, plunge into new careers, rediscover the creativity and adventurousness of their youth, and, at last, listen to their own needs" (p. 140). Although many women may experience this as an exciting time, they are often challenged to cope with both the physical and psychological adjustments surrounding menopause. Some women, fearing that menopause means losing their youthful looks, sink into depression. For many, menopause represents a crisis. In *The Silent*

Passage, Gail Sheehy (1992) tells us that far from being a marker that signifies the beginning of the end, menopause is better seen as a gateway to a second adulthood. Sheehy's book breaks the silence of menopause that is caused by shame, fear, misinformation, and the stigma of aging in a youth-obsessed society.

For men, the fifties can be a time to awaken their creative side. Instead of being consumed with achievement strivings, many men reveal human facets of themselves beyond rational thinking that can result in a richer existence. But men, too, are challenged to find new meaning in their lives. Projects that once were highly satisfying may now lack luster. Some men become depressed when they realize that they have been pursuing empty dreams. They may have met goals they set for themselves only to find that they are still longing for a different kind of life. For both women and men in their fifties, examining priorities often leads to new decisions about how they want to spend their time.

At the time of this writing, I (Jerry) am 58, and I am finding it an optimal time to renew my priorities. For the past 34 years, I have devoted most of my time to accomplishing professional goals. I have experienced a culmination of many of these goals, and now I am being challenged to discover other ways of defining and expressing myself. Although I could continue on the path I've been pursuing, there may be other callings that I have not really allowed myself to consider. A part of me is willing to settle for what I have, but another part of me wonders who and what I can become if I remain open to possibilities. Increasingly, I am aware of untapped inner resources; at the same time, I am devoting most of my energy to achieving goals in the outer world.

➤ *Time Out for Personal Reflection*

If you have reached middle age, think about how the following questions apply to you. In your journal you might write down your reactions to a few of the questions that have the most meaning for you. If you haven't reached middle age, think about how you'd like to be able to answer these questions when you reach that stage in your life. What do you need to do now to meet your expectations? Do you know a middle-aged person who serves as a role model for you?

- Is this a time of "generativity" or of "stagnation" for you? Think about some of the things you've done during this time of life that you feel the best about.
- Do you feel productive? If so, in what ways?
- Are there some things that you'd definitely like to change in your life right now? What prevents you from making these changes?
- What questions have you raised about your life during this time?
- Have you experienced a midlife crisis? If so, how has it affected you?
- What losses have you experienced?
- What are some of the most important decisions you have made during this time of your life?

- Are you developing new interests and talents?
- What do you look forward to in the remaining years?
- If you were to review the major successes of your life to this point, what would they be?

Late Adulthood

During what Sheehy (1995) refers to as the "age of integrity" (ages 65 to 85+), our central developmental tasks include adjusting to decreased physical and sensory capacities, adjusting to retirement, finding a meaning in life, being able to relate to the past without regrets, adjusting to the death of a spouse or friends, accepting inevitable losses, maintaining outside interests, and enjoying grandchildren. Late adulthood is a time for reflection and integration. Many physical and psychological changes occur as we approach old age. How we adapt to these changes is influenced by our past experiences, coping skills, beliefs about changing, and personality traits. At this time, work, leisure, and family relationships are major dimensions of life.

The sixties have changed just as dramatically as the earlier stages of middle life. The vast majority of over-sixties are quite able, both physically and mentally, to function independently. Most people in their sixties have reached a stage where maximum freedom coexists with a minimum of physical limitations. Indeed, only 10 percent of Americans 65 and over have a chronic health problem that interferes with their daily living (Sheehy, 1995, pp. 350–352).

As is the case for each of these developmental stages, there is a great deal of individual variance. Many 70-year-old people have the energy that many middle-aged people have. How people look and feel during late adulthood is more than a matter of physical age; it is largely a matter of attitude. To a great degree, vitality is influenced by your state of mind more than by chronological years lived.

Prevalent themes for people in late adulthood include: loss; loneliness and social isolation; feelings of rejection; the struggle to find meaning in life; dependency; feelings of uselessness, hopelessness, and despair; fears of death and dying; grief over others' deaths; sadness over physical and mental deterioration; and regrets over past events. Today, many of these themes characterize people in their mid-eighties more than people in their sixties and even seventies.

According to Erikson, the central issue of this age period is *integrity* versus *despair.* Those who succeed in achieving ego integrity feel that their lives have been productive and worthwhile and that they have managed to cope with failures as well as successes. They can accept the course of their lives and are not obsessed with thoughts of what might have been and what they could or should have done. They can look back without resentment and regret and can see their lives in a perspective of completeness and satisfaction. They accept themselves for who and what they are, and they also accept others as they are. They believe that who they are and what they have become are to a great extent the result of their choices. They approach the final stage of their lives with a sense of integration, balance, and wholeness. Finally, they can view death as natural, even while living rich and meaningful lives until the day they die.

Unfortunately, some elderly people fail to achieve ego integration. Typically, such people fear death. They may develop a sense of hopelessness and feelings of self-disgust. They approach the final stage of their lives with a sense of personal fragmentation. They often feel that they have little control over what happens to them. They cannot accept their life's cycle, for they see whatever they have done as "not enough" and feel that they have a lot of unfinished business. They yearn for another chance, even though they realize that they cannot have it. They feel inadequate and have a hard time accepting themselves, for they think that they have wasted their lives and let valuable time slip by. These are the people who die unhappy and unfulfilled.

We often imagine that people in their eighties and nineties live in rest homes and convalescent homes. We forget that many people of advanced age live by themselves and take care of themselves quite well. For instance, I (Marianne) occasionally visit with one of Jerry's aunts who is 94 years old. We always have good discussions about the past as well as the present. She has an incredible memory and shows interest in what is happening in the world. She remains active by gardening, sewing, and taking care of her household. During each visit, she proudly displays the fruits from her garden. She follows a daily routine that she seems to enjoy. At times she resists fully accepting her limitations, but eventually she is willing to receive the help needed to make her life more comfortable. For example, at one time she fought her family when they wanted to give her a lifeline system (a system the elderly use to signal a need for help). Eventually she did accept the offer, and she recently enthusiastically explained how the system works as well as telling me with a smile that this gives her adult children peace of mind. She has a deep religious faith, which has given her the strength to cope with many of the hardships she has had to endure. Another source of vitality is her involvement with her children, grandchildren, and great grandchildren. She now has a caretaker stay at her house to help her during the week, and on the weekends her adult children take turns being with her. I always walk away from these visits feeling uplifted, positive about aging, and saying to myself "I hope I will feel as positive about life should I be fortunate enough to reach 94."

Old age does not have to be something we look forward to with horror or resignation; nor must it be associated with bitterness. However, many elderly people in our society do feel resentment, because we have generally neglected them. Many of them are treated as members of an undesirable minority and are merely tolerated or put out to pasture in a convalescent home. Their loss is doubly sad, because the elderly can make definite contributions to society.

Elderly people have a wealth of life experiences and coping skills, and they are likely to share this wisdom if they sense that others have a genuine interest in them. Many elderly persons are still very capable, yet the prejudice of younger adults often keeps us from acknowledging the value of the contributions the elderly offer us. Perhaps because we are afraid of aging and confronting our own mortality, we "put away" the elderly so they won't remind us of our future.

■ Stereotypes of Aging

Ageism predisposes us to discriminate against old people by avoiding them or in some way victimizing them because of their age alone. Some of the stereotypes associated with older people that need to be challenged are:

- All elderly eventually become senile.
- Old people are nonproductive and cannot contribute to society.
- Retirement is just a step away from death.
- It's disgraceful for an old person to remarry.
- Old people are not creative.
- Growing old always entails having a host of serious physical and emotional problems.
- Older people are set in their ways, stuck on following rigid patterns of thinking and behaving, and are not open to change.
- When people grow old, they are no longer capable of learning or contributing.
- Old people are no longer beautiful.

- An elderly person will die soon after his or her mate dies.
- Most elderly persons are lonely.
- Old people are no longer interested in sex.
- Most old people live in institutional settings.
- Depression is a natural consequence of aging.
- Preoccupation with death and dying is typical of older adults.

These are just some of the negative perceptions and stereotypes of older people that are common in our society. These myths can render older people helpless if they accept them.

The attitude an older person has about aging is extremely important. Like adolescents, the aged may feel a sense of uselessness because of others' views of them. It is easy to accept the myths of others and turn them into self-fulfilling prophecies.

Again, although you may not have reached old age, we hope you won't brush aside thinking about your eventual aging. Your observations of the old people you know can provide you with insights about what it is like to grow older. From these observations, you can begin to formulate a picture of the life you'd like to have as you get older.

➤ *Time Out for Personal Reflection*

1. If you haven't yet reached old age, imagine yourself doing so. Think about your fears and about what you'd like to be able to say about your life—your joys, your accomplishments, and your regrets. To facilitate this reflection, you might consider the following questions:

   - What do you most hope to accomplish by the time you reach old age?
   - What are some of your greatest fears of growing old?
   - What kind of old age do you expect? What are you doing now that might have an effect on the kind of person you'll be as you grow older?
   - Do you know some elderly person who is a role model for you?
   - What are some things you hope to do during the later years of your life? How do you expect that you will adjust to retirement? What meaning do you expect your life to have when you reach old age?
   - How would you like to be able to respond to your body's aging? How do you think you'll respond to failing health or to physical limitations on your lifestyle?
   - Assume that you will have enough money to live comfortably and to do many of the things that you haven't had time for earlier. What do you think you'd most like to do with whom?
   - What would you most want to be able to say about yourself and your life when you become elderly?

   In your journal you might write down some impressions of the kind of old age you hope for, as well as the fears you have about growing older.

Chapter Summary

Adulthood involves the struggle for autonomy. One part of this quest is learning to challenge our inner parent and doing what is necessary to become our own parent in a psychological sense.

Transactional analysis can help us recognize early learning and decisions. Our life script is made up of both parental messages and decisions we make in response to these injunctions. The events of childhood and, to some extent, adolescence contribute to the formation of our life script, which we tend to follow into adulthood. By becoming increasingly aware of our life script, we are in a position to revise it. Instead of being hopelessly "scripted" by childhood influences, we can use our past to change our future. In short, we can shape our destiny rather than being passively shaped by earlier events.

Our quest for autonomy and maturity is truly a lifelong endeavor. Each stage of adulthood presents us with different tasks. Meeting the developmental tasks of later life hinges on successfully working through earlier issues.

During early adulthood it is important to learn how to form intimate relation-ships. To develop intimacy we must move beyond the self-preoccupation that is characteristic of adolescence. This is also a time when we are at our peak in terms of physical and psychological powers and can direct these resources to establish ourselves in all dimensions of life. Choices that we make pertaining to education, work, and lifestyle will have a profound impact later in life.

As we approach middle age, we come to a crossroads. Midlife is filled with a potential for danger and for new opportunities. At this phase we can assume a stance that "it's too late to change," or we can make significant revisions. There are opportunities to change careers, to find new ways to spend leisure time, and to find other ways of making a new life.

Later life can be a time of real enjoyment, or it can be a time of looking back in regret to all that we have not accomplished and experienced. It is important to recognize that the quality of life in later years often depends on the choices we made at earlier turning points in life.

To review the tasks and the choices of each period of the entire life span, we recommend that you review the developmental stages table presented in Chapter 2 and think about the continuity of the life cycle. Now that you have studied each stage of life, reflect on the meaning of these stages to you. If you have not yet ar-rived at a particular stage, think about what you can do at this time to assure the quality of life you'd like in a future phase.

The experiences and events that occur during each developmental stage are crucial in helping to determine our attitudes, beliefs, values, and actions regarding the important areas of our lives that will be discussed in the chapters to come: gen-der-role identity, work, the body, love, sexuality, intimate relationships, loneliness and solitude, death and loss, and meaning and values. For this reason we've de-voted considerable attention to the foundations of life choices. Understanding how we got where we are now is a critical first step in deciding where we want to go from here.

Activities and Exercises

1. Do you believe that you're able to make new decisions? Do you think you're in control of your destiny? In your journal write down some examples of new de-cisions — or renewals of old decisions — that have made a significant difference in your life.
2. Mention some critical turning points in your life. Draw in your journal a chart showing the age periods you've experienced so far and indicate your key suc-cesses, failures, conflicts, and memories for each stage.
3. After you've described some of the significant events in your life, list some of the decisions you have made in response to these events. How were you affected by some of these milestones in your life? Then think about what you've learned

about yourself from doing these exercises. What does all of this tell you about the person you are today?

4. Many students readily assert that they are psychologically independent. If this applies to you, think about some specific examples that show that you have questioned and challenged your parents' values and that you have modified your own value system.

5. To broaden your perspective on human development in various cultural or ethnic groups, talk to someone you know who grew up in a very different environment from the one you knew as a child. You could find out how his or her life experiences have differed from yours by sharing some aspects of your own life. Try to discover whether there are significant differences in values that seem to be related to the differences in your life experiences. This could help you reassess many of your own values.

6. Talk with some people who are significantly older than you. For instance, if you're in your twenties, you could interview a middle-aged person and an elderly person. Try to get them to take the lead and tell you about their lives. What do they like about their lives? What have been some key turning points for them? What do they most remember of the past? You might even suggest that they read the section of the chapter that pertains to their present age group and react to the ideas presented there.

7. Select one or more of the following books for further reading on the topics explored in this chapter: *Making Peace with Your Parents* (Bloomfield, 1983); *Feeling Good: The New Mood Therapy* (Burns, 1981); *How to Stubbornly Refuse to Make Yourself Miserable About Anything — Yes, Anything!* (Ellis, 1988); *New Passages* (Sheehy, 1995).

4

Becoming the Woman or Man You Want to Be

When gender transcendence occurs, people can be just people.
— *BASOW*

✔ *Prechapter Self-Inventory*

Use the following scale to respond: 4 = this statement is true of me *most* of the time; 3 = this statement is true of me *much* of the time; 2 = this statement is true of me *some* of the time; 1 = this statement is true of me *almost none* of the time.

_____ 1. It is important to me to be perceived as feminine (masculine).

_____ 2. I have a clear sense of what it means to be a man (woman).

_____ 3. It is relatively easy for me to be both logical and emotional, tough and tender, objective and subjective.

_____ 4. I have trouble accepting both women who show masculine qualities and men who show feminine qualities.

_____ 5. It is difficult for me to accept in myself traits that are often associated with the other sex.

_____ 6. I welcome the change toward more flexibility in gender roles.

_____ 7. I think I'm becoming the kind of woman (man) I want to become, regardless of anyone else's ideas about what is expected of my sex.

_____ 8. I'm glad that I'm the gender that I am.

_____ 9. I feel discriminated against because of my sex.

_____ 10. My parents provided good models of what it means to be a woman and a man.

Introduction

Kevin was a client in one of our therapeutic groups. His view of himself as a man stemmed from years of traditional child-rearing practices, which were continued in school and reinforced by his culture. For a long time Kevin did not even realize he was being restricted psychologically by the expectations for his gender. This dawning awareness came to him mainly because of a crisis he faced in midlife. He was shocked when his father had a heart attack, and he realized the toll that living by traditional roles had taken on his father.

This crisis was the impetus that helped Kevin make some choices about changing his future. He began to look at the impact his definition of maleness was having on all aspects of his life. He realized that he had never questioned his attitudes about gender-role behavior and that he was behaving unconsciously and automatically rather than by choice. To become a more expressive man, Kevin had to struggle against years of conditioning that restricted the range of emotional responses that were acceptable. Although he increased his level of consciousness intellectually through reading and personal counseling, Kevin had trouble catching up emotionally and behaviorally with what he knew. In other words, his intellectual enlightenment did not easily lead to his feeling and acting differently.

All of us are partially the product of our cultural conditioning. Behavior depends not on sex but on prior experience, learned attitudes, cultural expectations, sanctions, opportunities for practice, and situational demands. We learn behavior that is appropriate for our sex by interacting in society. Socialization or enculturation is a process of learning those behaviors that are appropriate to a sex, an age, or a class. Learning about gender differences does not cease with childhood; rather, it is a lifelong process. We never stop acquiring cultural meaning and directions (Lott, 1994).

Many men and women in our society live a restricted and deadening life because they have accepted certain cultural judgments about what it means to be male or female. Basow (1992) points out how inaccurate gender stereotypes are when it comes to individuals:

> (1) people cannot be viewed simply as collections of consistent traits, because situations also are important; (2) males and females specifically cannot be viewed as having unique traits that are opposite each other; and (3) whatever attributes are thought of as distinctly masculine or feminine are also possessed by at least some members of the other sex. (p. 9)

Unfortunately, too many people are caught in rigid roles and expect sanctions when they deviate from those roles. People often become so involved in their roles that they become alienated from themselves. They no longer know what they are like inside, because they put so much energy into maintaining an acceptable image.

In this chapter we invite you to examine the experiences that have directly and indirectly shaped your gender-role identity. With this increased awareness, you will be able to assess both the positive and negative effects your gender-role socialization is having on all aspects of your life. Then you can decide what changes, if any, you want to make. We encourage you to think critically about gender-role stereotypes and to form your own standards of what it means to be a woman or a man. This assessment requires patience and an appreciation of the difficulties involved in overcoming ingrained attitudes. The real challenge is to translate your new attitudes into new ways of behaving.

Male Roles

Many men are now questioning the values and expectations that were a basic part of their socialization. Increasingly, men are unwilling to be cast in a rigid role; rather, they are giving more expression to both the masculine and feminine dimensions of their personalities. However, far too many men in our society still live a restricted and deadening life, accepting the cultural myths about what it means to be "manly." These men are so involved in the many roles they play that they no longer know what they are like inside. They have put all their energy into maintaining an acceptable male image.

■ The All-American Male

What is the stereotype of the all-American male, and what aspects of themselves do many men feel they must hide to conform to it? In general, the stereotypical male is cool, detached, objective, rational, worldly, competitive, and strong. A man who attempts to fit the stereotype will suppress most of his feelings, for he sees the subjective world of feelings as being essentially feminine. A number of writers have identified the characteristics of a man living by the stereotype and the feelings he may attempt to suppress or deny (Basow, 1992; Goldberg, 1976, 1979, 1987; Jourard, 1971; Keen, 1991; Kimmel, 1987a, 1987b; Lerner, 1985, 1989; Lott, 1994, Mornell, 1979; Rabinowitz & Cochran, 1994; Witkin, 1994). Keep in mind that the following discussion is about the *stereotypical* view of males, and certainly many men do not fit this narrow characterization. It would be a mistake to conclude that this picture is an accurate portrayal of the way most men are. But these characteristics outline the limited view of the male role that many men have accepted, to a greater or lesser degree:

■ *Emotional unavailability.* A man tends to show his affection by being a "good provider." Frequently, he is not emotionally available to his female partner. Because of this, she may complain that she feels shut out by him. He also has a difficult time dealing with her feelings. If she cries, he becomes uncomfortable and quickly wants to "fix her" so she will stop crying.

■ *Independence.* Rather than admitting that he needs anything from anyone, he may lead a life of exaggerated independence. He feels that he should be able to do by himself whatever needs to be done, and he finds it hard to reach out to others by asking for emotional support or nurturing.

■ *Aggressiveness.* He feels that he must be continually active, aggressive, assertive, and striving. He views the opposites of these traits as signs of weakness, and he fears being seen as soft.

■ *Denial of fears.* He won't recognize his fears, much less express them. He has the distorted notion that to be afraid means that he lacks courage, so he hides his fears from himself and from others. He lacks the courage to risk being seen as frightened.

■ *Protection of his inner self.* With other men he keeps himself hidden because they are competitors and in this sense potential enemies. With women, he doesn't disclose himself because he is afraid they will think him unmanly if they see his inner core. A woman may complain that a man hides his feelings from her, yet it is probably more accurate to say that he is hiding his feelings from himself. Because he would find the range of feelings to be terrifying, he has unconsciously sealed off most of his feelings.

■ *Invulnerability.* He cannot make himself vulnerable, as is evidenced by his general unwillingness to disclose much of his inner experience. He won't let himself feel and express sadness, nor will he cry. He interprets any expression of emotional vulnerability as a sign of weakness. To protect himself, he becomes emotionally in-sulated and puts on a mask of toughness, competence, and decisiveness.

■ *Lack of bodily self-awareness.* Common physical stress signals that men identify include headaches, nausea, heartburn, muscle aches, backaches, and high blood pressure. However, a man often ignores these stress symptoms, denies their potential consequences, and avoids addressing their causes. He doesn't recognize bodily cues that may signal danger. For example, heart disease rates and cardiovas-cular disease death rates are twice as high in men as in women (Witkin, 1994). He drives himself unmercifully and views his body as some kind of machine that won't break down or wear out. He may not pay attention to his exhaustion until he collapses from it.

■ *Remoteness with other men.* Although he may have plenty of acquaintances, he doesn't have very many male friends he confides in. It is not uncommon for men to state that they don't have a single male friend with whom they can be inti-mate. He can talk to other men about things but finds it hard to be personal.

■ *Driven to succeed.* He has been socialized to believe that success at work is the measure of his value as a man. He hides from failure and thinks he must at all times put on the facade of the successful man. He feels he's expected to succeed and produce, to be "the best," and to get ahead and stay ahead. He measures his worth by the money he makes. Based on his feelings of inferiority and insecurity, he is driven to prove his superiority. He has to win at all times, regardless of the costs, which means that someone else has to lose.

■ *Denial of "feminine" qualities.* Because he plays a rigid male role, he doesn't see how he can be a man and at the same time possess (or reveal) traits usually at-tributed to women. Therefore, he is highly controlled, cool, detached, and shuts out much of what he could experience, which results in an impoverished life. He finds it difficult to express warmth and tenderness, especially public displays of tenderness or compassion. Because he won't allow the feminine experience to be a part of his life, he disowns any aspects within himself that he does not perceive to be manly.

■ *Avoidance of physical contact.* He has a difficult time touching freely or ex-pressing affection and caring to other men. He thinks he should touch a woman only if it will lead to sex, and he fears touching other men because he doesn't want to be perceived as a homosexual.

■ *Rigid perceptions.* He sees men and women in rigid categories. Woman should be weak, emotional, and submissive; men are expected to be tough, logical, and aggressive. He does not give himself much latitude to deviate from a narrow band of expression.

■ *Devotion to work.* He puts much of his energy into external signs of success. Thus, little is left over for his wife and children, or even for leisure pursuits. A man's obsession with defining himself mainly through work provides an accept-able outlet for pent-up energy. The result of getting lost in his work is forgetting to make contact with his inner spiritual self and intimate contact with others (Rabinowitz & Cochran, 1994).

■ *Loss of the male spirit.* Because he is cut off from his inner self, he has lost a way to make intuitive sense of the world. Relying on society's definitions and rules about masculinity rather than his own leaves him feeling empty, and he experiences guilt, shame, anxiety, and depression (Keen, 1991).

In our work with men we find that many of them show a variety of these characteristics. In the safe environment that group therapy can provide, we also see a strong desire in these men to modify some of the ways in which they feel they must live. They are willing to take the risk of expressing and exploring feelings on a range of topics. For instance, they are willing to let the other group members know that they do not always feel strong and that they are scared at times. As trust builds within the therapeutic group, the men become increasingly willing to share deep personal pain and longings. They struggle a great deal not only in showing to others their tender side but also in accepting this dimension of themselves. It takes some time for them to get beyond their embarrassment at owning feelings such as love, compassion, rejection, sadness, fear, joy, and anger. As these men become more honest with women, they typically discover that women are more able to accept, respect, and love them. The very traits that men fear to reveal to women are the characteristics that draw others closer to them. This often results in removing some of the barriers that prevent intimacy between the sexes.

Men often hide their feelings of vulnerability and are ever watchful of others' reactions, looking for indications that they might be exposed to ridicule. This theme of men hiding their true nature is characteristic of many men, regardless of their racial, ethnic, and cultural background. Audrey Chapman (1993), a therapist with a good deal of experience working with black men, claims that black men have a desire to connect with someone after years of frustration at not "getting it right." She says that black men are skilled at hiding feelings. They see crying as the ultimate affront to manhood, and they test the waters to determine the level of safety. Underneath their surface bravado is likely to be a scared and lonely person. Chapman emphasizes how important it is to learn to listen and be patient when these men do express what they are feeling or thinking. Chapman writes: "If I could stress only one issue with black women, it would be the necessity of understanding and accepting the fragility of our men's psyche. They desire and need bonding as much as we do, but they need a road map to get where they long to be" (p. 225).

■ The Price Men Pay for Remaining in Traditional Roles

What price must a man pay for denying most of his inner self and putting on a false front? First, he loses a sense of himself because of his concern with being the way he thinks he should be as a male. Writing on the "lethal aspects of the male role," Sidney Jourard (1971) contends that men typically find it difficult to love and be loved. They won't reveal themselves enough to be loved. They hide their loneliness, anxiety, and hunger for affection, making it difficult for anyone to love them as they really are. Part of the price these guarded males pay for their seclusion is that they must always be vigilant for fear that someone might discover what is beneath their armor.

Another price men pay for living by stereotypical standards is the susceptibility to stress-related disorders. Although men have recently been paying more

attention to their physical health, evidence continues to show that they have higher rates of stress and ailments related to stress than do women. For example, this year 8 men out of every 100 will die from heart problems, compared to only 4 women out of 100 (Witkin, 1994). (An exception is women who are striving to compete in heretofore "male" arenas.) This point reaffirms a key idea we will explore further in Chapter 6: The truth is in your body. Stress takes a toll on the body, as evidenced by a wide range of psychosomatic disorders. When denial and stress are chronic, the body will not lie but will show signs of wear and tear. Unfortunately, many men do not respect these messages until the damage to their bodies is severe.

In *The New Male,* Herb Goldberg (1979) develops the idea that if men continue to cling to the traditional masculine blueprint they will end their lives as pathetic throwaways. He describes such men as alive at 20, machines at 30, and burned out by 40. During their twenties, most of their energies are directed toward "making it" while denying important needs and feelings. At 20 these men are typically urgently sexual, restless and passionate about converting their ideas into reality, eager to push themselves to their limits (if they recognize any), curious and adventurous, and optimistic about the possibilities for living. In his early twenties the traditional male is driven by societal pressures to prove his manliness, long before he is aware of who he is and what it is he really wants for himself. He locks himself in a cage of expectations. At 30 he has convinced himself that he is not a person but a machine that has to function so the job can get done. By his forties he may experience a "male menopause" as his functioning begins to break down. Goldberg sees this decline as the result of years of repression and emotional denial, which make him a danger to both himself and others.

In their excellent book, *Man Alive: A Primer of Men's Issues,* Rabinowitz and Cochran (1994) write about the price men pay for hiding their fears and attempting to live by a rigid traditional model of masculinity. They state that adhering to a rigid model of what it means to be a man keeps men looking for the perfect job, house, and partner to make them happy. Yet in the process, they avoid knowing themselves and appreciating the richness of life. According to Weiten and Lloyd (1994), the principal costs to men of remaining tied to traditional gender roles are excessive pressure to succeed, an inability to express emotions, and sexual difficulties.

If you are a man, ask yourself to what degree you are tied into your socialization regarding expected male patterns. The chances are good that you have been an active agent in your own gender-role socialization. Now might be a good time to reevaluate the costs associated with your gender-role identity and to consider in what ways, if any, you may want to alter your picture of what it means to be a man.

■ The Danger of Emotional Denial

How might emotional denial make a man dangerous to others? One way is in domestic violence and spousal abuse. Rape is another way men exert power over and try to control women. In our view, much of the violence by men toward the women in their lives is a result of faulty beliefs, injunctions, and assumptions about what it means to be a man. These men believe they are destined to use power to control women. But a man who resorts to violence is acting out of fear, not strength. He cannot accept any hint of his being weak, and he sees his inability to control a woman as a weakness. Thus, he overcompensates by dominating and using force to exert his will. Because he hates what he fears in himself and because it is mirrored by the woman, he attempts to destroy and conquer her. This physically abusive behavior is not a sign of strength but is grounded in the weakness that he disowns.

Men who have difficulty expressing their anger in constructive ways often deny their role in contributing to the problematic situation; instead, they tend to view the problem externally and blame others for what they are feeling. Those who psychologically and physically abuse a spouse are venting their feelings on a target they see as being the source of their misery. Because of the international attention of the O. J. Simpson trial, there has been a great deal of media attention drawn to the incidences, causes, and prevention of spouse abuse. But long before this trial, the mental health professions had designed programs to offer help to both the victims and the perpetrators of physical violence.

Groups have been designed to help men who are physically violent. In their group for the treatment of men who batter, Grusznski and Bankovics (1990) found that for many of these men violence has been their only way to deal with stressful situations. The group experience teaches men to recognize how their behavior and attitudes, such as the need for power and control over women at all costs, result in problems for both them and their partners. These groups allow men to challenge and change some of their destructive ways and to incorporate alternatives to violent behavior.

Unless men who are prone to physical violence accept responsibility for their actions, treatment will not be successful. One of our colleagues conducts a group for men who are violent, and he observes a good deal of resistance on their part in seeing that they have a problem expressing their anger. Men who batter often begin group counseling in a state of denial. They typically externalize the source of their problems, and they rarely attribute their problems to their violent behavior. However, if they do not eventually recognize and accept their own problematic behavior, it is unlikely that they will change — or that they will understand the impact of this violence on their partners, their relationships, and themselves (Edleson & Tolman, 1994).

■ Challenging Traditional Male Roles

In his book, *The Inner Male,* Goldberg (1987) acknowledges that the option of behaving in less traditional ways has increased. Yet he adds that new pressures are pushing men to move back into traditional role-playing behavior and that men pay a steep price for moving too far beyond society's expectations for them. Overall, however, there is a new social atmosphere that makes it easier for men to let go of ritualistic, self-destructive behavior patterns.

In his discussion of the challenges facing contemporary males, Goldberg predicts that the psychological growth and evolution of males will involve a lessening of the rigid defensiveness that filters and distorts their experience. As men discard their self-destructive notions and behaviors, they will be able to reconnect with themselves and others. In mapping the territory for the journey toward becoming a freer male, Goldberg maintains that psychological evolution will alter the traditional ways men relate to one another. They will no longer need to be guarded, self-protective, and distrustful.

More and more men are challenging the conditioning that directs them to fall passively into a rigid role (Goldberg, 1987). Leroy, who participated in one of our personal-growth groups, is an example of an individual who is willing to break out of rigid patterns of behavior adopted to conform to society's view of a real man. Leroy told us the following story.

> *I was a driving and driven man who was too busy to smell the flowers. My single goal in life was to prove myself and become a financial and business success. I was on my way to becoming the president of a corporation, and I was thinking that I had it made. When I got my W-2 form, I became aware that I had made more money than was in my plan for success, yet I had had a miserable year. I decided that I wanted to experience life, to smell more flowers, and to not kill myself with a program I had never consciously chosen for myself.*

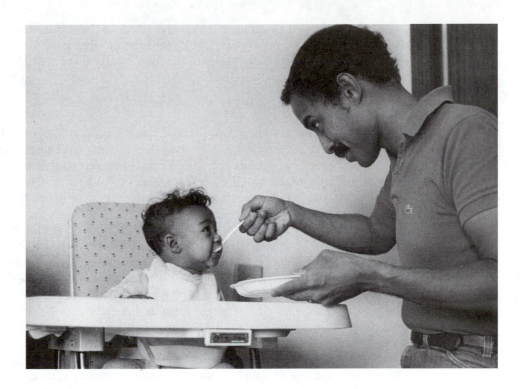

Leroy's decision did not come easy. It was, and continues to be, a real struggle for him to admit that he is only human. It is not easy for him to allow himself to experience and express feelings, yet he is making fine strides at becoming a sensitive, caring, and expressive man. He is actively talking back to inner voices that tell him he *must* keep driving himself, that he *must* constantly set and achieve new goals and that he does not have time to enjoy and savor life. For him a turning point was landing in the hospital and almost dying. This jarred him into accepting that he was not an indestructible machine. Leroy has changed his priorities and is working hard at changing his behavior.

To me, life was a constant struggle, and I could never let down. Life was a series of performances that involved me pleasing others and then waiting for the applause to come. The applause was never enough, because I prostituted myself. I was always disappointed by the applause, because I felt empty when the applause would die down. So I continued to push myself to give more performances. But out of my illness I began to look at my life and slow down, and I realized there is a world out there that does not solely involve my work. I decided to work no more than 50 hours a week; before getting sick I was working 70 to 90 hours a week. With that extra time, I decided to smell life — there are a lot of roses in life, and the scent is enticing and exciting to me. I'll thrive on it as long as I can breathe.

At 54, Leroy showed the courage to reverse some of the self-destructive patterns that were killing him. He began deciding for himself what kind of man he wanted to be rather than living by an image of the man others thought he should be.

■ Are Men Changing?

How much are the traditional notions of what a man is supposed to be really changing? Are different models now available to men that allow them a wider range of feelings and behavioral traits? We see some trends that seem to support the idea of an evolution of male consciousness. And some researchers (Sleek, 1994) suggest that men are struggling to overcome stereotypes and to redefine what it takes to be a man.

The Society for the Psychological Study of Men and Masculinity (SPSMM), founded in 1990 by a group of psychologists, serves as a platform for understanding men. SPSMM is concerned with teaching men how to transcend societal standards on manhood, helping them learn to show their emotions and find personal identity beyond their jobs. SPSMM emphasizes empathy for men, recognizing that much of what men have been taught to value since childhood is now being challenged or has been discredited. Members of SPSMM have indicated that men should take pride in some traditional male characteristics, such as protecting the family. However, men would be better off if they relinquished some of their obsolete behaviors, a few of which include sex without intimacy, rage in place of sadness, and pursuing their careers instead of spending time with their children. If men are able to be more emotionally aware and connected, they will become the fathers they wanted for themselves.

Men are showing a clear interest in men's consciousness-raising workshops. There is a great increase in the number of conferences, workshops, retreats, and gatherings for men. Three key books have provided impetus for the men's movement. One is the poet Robert Bly's best-selling book, *Iron John* (1990). According to Bly, men suffer from "father hunger," which results in unhappiness, emotional immaturity, and search for substitute father figures. Bly writes and talks about the ways that having an absent, abusive, or alcoholic father results in the wounding of the sons. Bly says that many mothers look to their sons to meet their own emotional needs, which are often denied to them by their husbands. The boy feels ashamed when he is not able to psychologically fill his mother's longing.

Writers have emphasized that love has often failed men because they have expected the women in their lives to heal their boyhood wounds caused by their fathers. Those who do the wounding must be the ones who do the healing. One of the bases of men's gatherings is to share common struggles, reveal their stories, and find healing in the men's collective. The fact that men from all walks of life are becoming interested in talking about their socialization from boyhood to manhood indicates that many men are rebelling against the steep price they have paid for subscribing to traditional role behavior.

Many men lack adequate male models who demonstrate healthy male behavior. Sam Keen's (1991) *Fire in the Belly: On Being a Man* describes what men lack.

Keen talks about the importance of men writing their autobiographies in ways that can help them become aware of their family scripts and move away from the myths that formed their socialization.

In *Man Alive: A Primer of Men's Issues,* Fredric Rabinowitz and Sam Cochran (1994) believe that men are about to enter a renaissance of awareness and growth, extending past the roles they play as workers and providers and allowing them to know themselves more deeply. Rabinowitz and Cochran make the point that men are frequently shut off from their emotional selves as a way to survive the demands society places on them as men. Men are expected to be focused and task-oriented. From infancy through adulthood, men are socialized to give short shrift to their emotions.

Some of the goal-oriented behavior men learn does have benefits. Men have the challenge of learning to balance their adaptive strengths with respect for their emotions, for emotions provide the foundation for friendships, relationships, and life choices (Gaylin, 1992). Matthew's case illustrates his journey in acquiring this balance.

> *Most of my masculine training came from my experiences at elementary, junior high, and high school. I remember the locker room being filled with threatening words like "pussy," "wimp," "fag," and "girl." Physically I was tall and thin. I remember looking at the big strong kids in my class and thinking I "should" be like them, and anything less was considered unmanly. I also remember how my one and only year of playing football was a complete disaster. The coaches would yell at us, calling us names like "wimp." I often felt very belittled in front of my peers.*
>
> *In junior high school there was no room for me to be emotional, caring, or sensitive. I remember feeling different and weird because my feelings, behaviors, and thoughts were different from others. I had difficulty connecting with others because I preferred to talk about serious and meaningful things rather than superficial "guy" stuff. I learned indirectly from my dad that being a man meant holding in your feelings and working things out on your own. Asking for help was a sign of weakness and meant that you couldn't stand on your own two feet. The messages from my father, along with the messages from coaches and peers, created a lot of pressure for me to be tough and hard. I still feel as though my masculinity is in question in some areas of my personal relationships. Because I was culturally and socially conditioned to be in control and to be strong, "wishy-washy" behavior and fear of conflict are in my mind "unmanly." Men are supposed to be aggressive and take control. Thus, I have often felt weak and wimpy in my relationships. This adds to the pressures I place on myself as to how I "should" be with others.*
>
> *I felt as though I could not be myself but rather had to be the tough, unemotional person called "a man." The truth of it all is that I am a sensitive and emotional person who likes to ask people for help and who likes to talk about real and meaningful "things" in my life. I am learning that expressing feelings and telling others what I want and need are strengths. I believe doing so is a sign of strength.*

➤ *Time Out for Personal Reflection*

1. The following characteristics have been identified as part of the stereotype of the all-American male. On the line following each trait, write either a potential benefit or a potential liability associated with that trait:

Emotional unavailability _____

_____

Independence _____

_____

Aggressiveness _____

_____

Denial of fears _____

_____

Protection of inner self _____

_____

Invulnerability _____

_____

Lack of bodily awareness _____

_____

Remoteness with other men _____

_____

Drivenness to succeed _____

_____

Denial of "feminine" qualities _____

_____

Avoidance of physical contact _____

_____

Rigid perceptions _____

_____

Devotion to work _____

_____

Loss of male spirit _____

_____

2. What are your thoughts about the price men pay for accepting traditional roles?

_____

_____

_____

_____

3. What are some specific qualities you most respect in men?

_____

_____

_____

_____

Female Roles

Like men, women in our society have also suffered from gender stereotypes. Gender roles and stereotypes lead to a variety of negative outcomes with respect to self-concept, psychological well-being, and physical health (Basow, 1992). People tend to adapt their behavior to fit gender-role expectations, and women have been encouraged to lower their aspirations for achievement in the competitive world. Many women are concerned that they will be perceived as unfeminine if they strive for success with too much zeal. But this rigid viewpoint is changing as women actively fight the stereotype of the passive, dependent, and unaccomplished female. Like men, women pay a price for living by narrowly defined rules of what women should be. Typically, women who achieve career success continue to carry the major responsibilities of parent and spouse (Weiten & Lloyd, 1994). In addition to assuming the responsibilities of parent, spouse, and career, an increasing number of women are expected to become caretakers of their own and their spouse's aging parents.

■ Traditional Roles for Women

Traditional gender stereotypes of women are still prevalent in our culture. The following characteristics fit the traditional portrait of femininity, but women in increasing numbers are beginning to risk operating outside these narrow limits.

■ *Women are warm, expressive, and nurturing.* In their relationships with other women and with men, women are expected to be kind, thoughtful, and caring. This can put an unrealistic burden on women, because many times women may not feel like displaying warmth and caring. With the focus on these roles, many women have difficulty asking for these very qualities from others. Women are so attuned to giving that they often do not allow themselves to receive nurturance.

■ *Women are not aggressive or independent.* If women are even assertive, they might well be viewed as being hard and aggressive. If they display independence, men may accuse them of trying to "prove themselves" by taking on masculine roles. Those women who are independent may struggle within themselves over being too powerful or not needing others.

■ *Women are emotional and intuitive.* women who defy their socialization may have trouble getting their emotional needs recognized. But women can be emotional and rational at the same time. Having an intuitive nature does not rule out being able to think and reason logically.

■ *Women are passive and submissive.* A home orientation, being prone to tears and excitability in minor crises, indecisiveness, religiosity, and tactfulness are expected of the female role. If women deviate from these behavior patterns, they run the risk of being "unfeminine."

■ *Women are more interested in relationships than in professional accomplishments.* Rather than competing or striving to get ahead, women are expected to maintain relationships. Many women are concerned about the quality of their relationships, but at the same time they are also interested in accomplishing goals they set for themselves.

The costs to women who maintain traditional gender roles are diminished aspirations, frustration associated with the housewife role, and ambivalence about sexuality (Weiten & Lloyd, 1994). Just as subscribing to traditional male roles stifles creativity in men, unthinkingly accepting traditional roles can result in greatly restricting the range of women. Indeed, if they choose to, women can experience mutual behavioral characteristics such as being both dependent and independent, giving to others and being open to receiving, thinking and feeling, and being tender and being firm. Rather than being cemented to a single behavioral style, women who are rejecting traditional roles are saying that they are entitled to express the complex range of characteristics that are appropriate for different situations. Many women are resisting being narrowly defined.

If you are a woman, ask yourself to what degree you are tied to your socialization regarding expected female patterns. As is the case with men, you have likely been an active agent in your own gender-role socialization. Now might be a good time to reevaluate the costs associated with your gender-role identity and to consider whether you want to alter your picture of what it means to be a woman.

If you are a man, reflect on how you have been affected by female roles and ways you may want to change in relation to women. Consider the flexibility you might gain if women had a wider range of traits and behaviors available to them.

■ Challenging Traditional Female Roles

Basow (1992) cites considerable research evidence supporting the existence of gender stereotypes, but there are signs that women are increasingly recognizing the price they have been paying for staying within the limited boundaries set for

them by their culture. We are realizing that gender stereotypes influence societal practices, discrimination, individual beliefs, and sexual behavior itself. Basow emphasizes that gender stereotypes are powerful forces of social control but that women can choose either to be socially acceptable and conform or to rebel and deal with the consequences of being socially unacceptable. Sensitizing ourselves to the process of gender-role development can help us make choices about modifying the results of our socialization. Women are beginning to take actions that grow out of their awareness.

The changing structure of gender relations has altered what women expect of men and the role men play in women's lives. According to Kathleen Gerson (1987), the so-called traditional family has given way to a variety of family and household forms, and it becomes difficult to argue that the traditional division of labor between the sexes is natural, inevitable, or morally superior. There is no single standard of family life. Among the new options are equity in parenting and freedom from family commitments. Gerson writes that the larger social changes are promising women new sources of power but also bringing about new insecurities. In *Composing a Life*, Mary Catherine Bateson (1990) claims that the guidelines for composing a life are no longer clear for either sex. Especially for women, previous generations can no longer be used as a model. For women, some of the basic concepts used to design a life — work, home, love, commitment — have different meanings today.

It is clear that despite the staying power of gender stereotypes increasing numbers of women are rejecting limited views of what a woman can be. Without discarding many of the traits traditionally attributed to them, women are reinventing

themselves. Today's women are pursuing careers that in earlier times were closed to them. They are demanding equal pay for equal work. Many women are making the choice to postpone marriage and child rearing until they have established themselves in careers, and some are deciding not to have children. Choosing a single life is now an acceptable option. In dual-career marriages, responsibilities previously allocated to one sex or the other are now shared. Women are assuming positions of leadership in government and business. They are questioning many of the attitudes they have incorporated and are resisting the pressures to conform to traditional gender-role behaviors. In particular, many women are challenging the pressures put on them to find satisfaction exclusively or primarily in marriage and family life.

These choices are not easy for women to make. Indeed, many barriers still stand in the way of gender equity. The process of becoming a fulfilled women entails challenging both societal and internal barriers. Julie's story reveals a woman who fought traditional socialization.

> *I grew up in a family where my parents' gender roles were at times reversed, and at other times mixed and ambiguous, but never traditional. This affected me in several ways. I developed into a girl whose behavior and dress was nontraditional. I experienced conflict within myself relating to the nontraditional roles my parents played. There was anger at times at both my mother and my father for not being like "other" parents.*
>
> *I wasn't raised as a little boy or as a little girl. This was not deliberate or conscious, it was just how two adults whose own roles were mixed would raise*

children. I ended up being a tom boy—wearing a baseball cap and pants under my dresses. I climbed trees and played for hours in my self-made mud pools. Fortunately, I was never criticized or discouraged. It seemed that the way I was acting out my gender role was not an issue for my parents. I don't ever remember being told to "act like a young lady" or "girls shouldn't do that," although one time my mother reprimanded me for taking such wide strides when I walk. I remember it being a bit of a shock to me because I had never noticed my stride before. To this day, I'm conscious at times of my stride.

It wasn't until around the age of 12 that I began to feel the discomfort of not behaving like all the other girls. The discomfort was internal. I don't remember it ever being noticed or brought up by other kids. I felt different because the other girls seemed different. I just didn't ever feel "girly."

I didn't experience any external pressures until I had my first boyfriend. These pressures were limited to my sister's macho boyfriend who would state that I "was the one who wore the pants" and I was "the boss." These comments would feed into my own insecurities and conflicts about not being the type of girl I was "supposed" to be—and about having a boyfriend who was not being the type of man he was "supposed" to be. I often feel too strong, and my boyfriends seem too weak. I'm embarrassed sometimes because I "control" the relationship. And I'm embarrassed because the woman is not supposed to be in control. I don't choose this position; it just happens naturally, or so it seems.

I feel this internal conflict in my workplace also. I feel like I'm supposed to be wearing skirts, dresses, and heels. But I don't wear these things, and at times I feel like I'm somehow less of a woman. I sometimes feel bad that I'm not as chatty as most of the women I work with. I've heard that people think I'm arrogant—and I assume it's because I don't stop and talk to everyone who walks across my path. I think that a good percentage of men would not like me because I'm not feminine enough. I'm too strong and too opinionated. I'm not passive. And I doubt that I'd ever be described as a "sweet girl/woman."

I have bouts of hating that I am all these things. Society seems to be whispering that I am a bitch if I am not sweet and selfless. My bouts of disliking that I am who I am are closely matched by my strength, which says: Who cares! I am who I am. I'm proud that I am strong and able and smart and opinionated. As I surround myself with more and more women who are like me, I am calmed. I'm proud of these women and continually try to remind myself that I should be proud of myself too.

■ Women and Work Choices

The number and proportion of women employed in the workplace is increasing, and more than 60 percent of all adult females are expected to participate in the labor force by the year 2000. More and more women are now looking to an occupation outside the home as a major source of their identity (Lock, 1996a). Many women work not only out of choice but also out of necessity. Some feel the pressure of taking care of the home and holding down an outside job to help support the family. And many single parents must work. Consider the case of Deborah, who after her divorce said, "I know I can survive, but it's scary for me to face the world alone. Before, my job was an additional source of income and something I did strictly out of choice. Now a job is my livelihood and the means to support my children."

Seventy-nine percent of women with no children under age 18 are currently working outside the home. Women are now exploring a wide variety of options — they are joining the labor force, going back to college, and entering professional schools. Women are studying medicine, business, and law. More women are assuming leadership roles. They work in two thirds of all new jobs created (Naisbitt & Aburdene, 1991).

Naisbitt and Aburdene (1991) have predicted that the 1990s will be the decade of women's leadership in the world of work. Here are some of their findings and specific predictions:

- Women are starting new businesses twice as often as men are.
- In the 1990s it will be increasingly recognized that women and men function equally well as business leaders; consequently, women will take on leadership roles denied to them in the past.
- In the 1990s the numbers of female physicians and attorneys will increase substantially, as will their influence.
- In the not-too-distant future, people will look back with some wonderment on the days when women were excluded from the higher echelons of business and political leadership, much as we now look back on the days when women were not permitted to vote.

Although women are found working in virtually all areas of the economy, their numbers are still small in jobs traditionally performed by men. And although some progress has been made with respect to gender equity in the world of work, many challenges must still be met before women achieve equality with men in the work force. In *Backlash*, Susan Faludi (1991) points out that about a third of the new jobs for women were at or below the poverty level — jobs that men turned down. In addition, the average woman earns considerably less than the average man in the same occupational category, receives fewer benefits, and works under poorer conditions (Lott, 1994).

According to Carney and Wells (1995), surveys indicate that social change is accelerating as different options are becoming available to women who want to combine a career with marriage and a family. The challenge for these women is learning how to balance the difficult demands of a two-career family. Increasingly, couples are postponing having children so the woman can get established in her career. Many women who have made the personal and financial investment of preparing for a career are open to taking a maternity leave and returning to work.

Other women are making the choice to find their fulfillment primarily through the roles of wife, mother, and homemaker. These women are not assuming these roles because they feel that they *must* or because they feel that they cannot enter the world of work; they *want* to devote most of their time to their family. These women often struggle with feeling that they *should* want a career outside the home, because they have heard so much about finding satisfaction in that way. But they do not feel incomplete without an outside career, and they need to learn how to feel comfortable with their choice.

One woman we know, Valerie, talks about the importance of accepting her choice, despite reactions from others that she should not settle for being "merely" a mother. Valerie and her husband, Pheng, had agreed that after they had children both would continue working.

> When our first child was born, I continued to work as planned. What I had not foreseen was the amount of energy and time it took to care for our son, Dustin. Most important, I hadn't realized how emotionally attached I would become to him. My work schedule was extremely demanding, and I was only able to see Dustin awake for one hour a day. Pheng was being Mr. Mom in the evening until I returned home, which eventually strained our marriage. I felt torn. When I was working, I felt I should be at home. I began to feel jealous of the babysitter, who had more time with Dustin than I did.
>
> When our second son, Vernon, was born, I quit my job. Since we primarily depended on Pheng's income, we thought it best that I stay home with our children. Some of my friends are pursuing a career while they take care of a family. For me, it was too difficult to manage both to my satisfaction. It means a lot to me to be involved in my sons' activities and have an influence on their lives. I have been active as a volunteer in their school, which I find very rewarding. Some of my friends cannot understand why I stay home, but I know I'm in the place where I need to be—for them and for me.
>
> I do intend to return to my career once Vernon and Dustin begin high school, and at times I miss the stimulation my job provided. But overall I have no regrets about our decision.

■ Women in Dual-Career Families

One of the realities of our time is that more married women now have full-time jobs outside the home. Although a career meets the needs of many women who want something more than taking care of their families, it dramatically increases their responsibilities. Unless their husbands are willing to share in the day-to-day tasks of maintaining a home and rearing children, these women often experience fragmentation. Some women burden themselves with the expectation that they should perform perfectly as workers, mothers, and wives. The "superwoman syndrome" is described by Carol Orsborn (1986) in her book *Enough Is Enough*. Orsborn herself became one of these superwomen. She describes herself at age 37 as an unqualified success on every front, a woman of the 1980s who had proven that she could have it all. Yet her life was being ruined. Like other superwomen, she could point to her accomplishments, which were many. She was the president of her own company, a published journalist, a brown belt in karate, a devoted wife, and mother of two. In her struggle for perfection in all areas of her life, however, she became aware that she was losing her own sense of identity. Such women need to reevaluate their priorities and decide how they want to live. Eventually, many

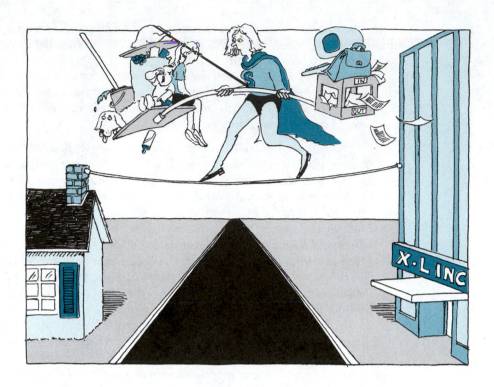

women realize that they simply cannot continue to balance career and home responsibilities, and they finally exclaim that enough is enough! For women who are trying to do it all, Betty Friedan's advice is worth considering: Yes, women can have it all, but just not all at once.

Marsha, a physician, is another woman facing the challenge of a dual career. She holds a teaching position at a hospital. In addition to practicing medicine, she must teach interns, keep current in her field, and publish.

> *I enjoy pretty much everything I'm doing, but I do feel a lot of pressure in doing all that needs to be done. Much of the pressure I feel is over my conviction that I have to be an outstanding practitioner, teacher, and researcher and must also be fully available as a mother and a wife. There is also pressure from my husband, Daniel, to assume the bulk of the responsibility for taking care of our son and for maintaining the household. With some difficulty Daniel could arrange his schedule to take an increased share of the responsibility, but he expects me to consider his professional career above my own. I need to leave my job early each day to pick up our son from the day-care center. I fight traffic and get myself worked up as I try to get to the center before it closes. I put myself under a great deal of stress holding up all my roles. I feel the toll balancing family and work responsibilities is taking on my physical and emotional well-being.*

Some women experience a lack of support and an actual resistance from the men in their lives when they do step outside traditional roles and exercise their options. Although Marsha did not get much resistance from her husband about maintaining her career, she received very little active support to make balancing her double life possible. The power resided with her husband, and she was expected to make decisions that would not inconvenience him greatly. Basow (1992) notes that since men typically have been the dominant sex, with most of the power, it is difficult for them to share this power with women. Those husbands who see themselves as liberated are put to the test when they are expected to assume increased responsibilities at home. They may say that they want their wives to "emerge and become fulfilled persons" but also send messages such as: "Don't go too far! If you want, have a life outside of the home, but don't give up any of what you are doing at home." A woman who has to fight her husband's resistance may have an even more difficult fight with herself. Both husband and wife may need to reevaluate how realistic it is to expect that she can have a career and also assume the primary responsibility for the children, along with doing all the tasks to keep a home going. Both parties need to redefine and renegotiate what each is willing to do and what each considers essential. Ideally, women and men should be free to choose which, if either, spouse stays at home. But we have yet to reach this ideal state.

Dual-career couples are often challenged to renegotiate the rules that governed the early phase of their relationship. Such is the case with Lucy and Bud. Lucy, a re-entry college student who also works, reports that she generally likes most aspects of her life, yet her relationship with her husband is strained because of the direction in which she is moving.

> *Where I struggle is with my husband, who would prefer a traditional stay-at-home wife and mother. Now that I am older, I want to discover who I am. What is sad and painful for me is that Bud doesn't seem to appreciate the woman I am becoming. He prefers the old "doer" that I was. But I won't go back to the compliant person I was, and I will not sacrifice my true feelings and thoughts to please others.*
>
> *I appreciate the importance of negotiation and listening to my husband. I still love and care for him, but I am grieving because I don't have the relationship I long for. I desire a good and honest relationship where both of us are willing to be challenged and are open to change. I will be disappointed if we never get to that place.*

In both of the cases just described, the husbands are resisting the growth of their wives. They do not see their wives as equal partners. In dual-career families, both partners must be willing to renegotiate their relationship.

Belinda is a professional woman with a husband and three young children. Her husband, Burt, shows a great deal of interest in Belinda's personal and professional advancement. She often tells her colleagues at work how much support she gets from him. When Bert was offered a higher paying job that entailed a move to another state, he declined the offer after a full discussion with his wife and children. They decided that the move would be too disruptive for all concerned. During the times when Belinda is experiencing the most pressure at work, Bert is especially sensitive and takes on more responsibility for household chores and for taking care of their children. This is an example of a dual-career couple who have created a more equitable division of responsibilities.

■ Difficulties and Fears

Many women hear "inner voices" that get in the way of them enjoying their work and striving for success. What they tell themselves is a reflection of the messages they were given as children. They simply were not reinforced for professional achievements when they first began their careers, and now they have difficulty recognizing their own merits as professional persons. For these women to enjoy their successes, they must change their self-talk.

Just as a woman can question the traditional female stereotype, she can also question the myth that a successful and independent woman doesn't need anyone and can make it entirely on her own. This trap is very much like the trap that many males fall into and may even represent an assimilation of traditional male values. Ideally, a woman will learn that she can achieve independence, exhibit strength, and succeed while at times being dependent and in need of nurturing. Real strength allows either a woman or a man to be needy and to ask for help without feeling personally inadequate.

We have experienced the particular difficulties a woman has while working in a husband and wife team. We often present workshops at professional conventions. We are comfortable with the way we work together, and each of us can appreciate and enjoy the other's style. In fact, we often get very positive feedback about the way we work with each other. Yet we have noticed that Marianne must work harder for the recognition she gets than does Jerry. We often find that people refer to our mutual projects, such as books that we co-author, as "Jerry's books." This response comes not only from men but also from women. When we begin a workshop, people tend to look at Jerry as the "expert" and "authority" on our subject. It is only as we have more contact with our audience that many of them are willing to include Marianne as an equal professional and recognize her contributions. In situations such as this, as difficult as they might be, Marianne tries to avoid a defensive stance yet find ways to assert herself professionally. It is interesting that even among well-educated mental-health professionals, gender biases do exist.

■ One Woman's Struggle

Susan is one of the many women struggling to break out of rigid traditional roles and move toward greater independence. She describes the nature of her struggle.

> *In high school I was an exceptional student and had aspirations to go to college, but I was discouraged by my family. Instead, they encouraged me to marry the "nice guy" I had been dating through high school, letting me know that I would risk losing David if I went off to college. My parents told me that David could provide a good future for me and that it was not necessary for me to pursue college or a career. Without much questioning of what I was told, I got married and had two children. Others thought I had a good life,*

that I was well provided for and that my husband David and I were getting along well. For me, I remember first feeling restless and dissatisfied with my life when my children went to school. David was advancing in his career and was getting most of his satisfaction from his work. Around him, I felt rather dull and had a vague feeling that something was missing from my life. I had never forgotten my aspiration to attend college, and I eventually enrolled. Although David was not supportive initially, he later encouraged me to complete my education. But he made it perfectly clear that he expected me not to neglect my primary responsibilities to the family.

As I was pursuing my college education, I often had to make difficult choices among multiple and sometimes conflicting roles. Sometimes I felt guilty about how much I enjoyed being away from my family. For the first time in my life I was being known as Susan and not as someone's daughter or wife. Although at times David felt threatened by my increasing independence from him, he did like and respect the person I was becoming.

Susan's situation illustrates that women who for many years have followed traditional roles can successfully shed them and define new roles for themselves. Some of the themes that she and many women like her struggle with are dependence versus independence, fear of success, looking outside of yourself for support and direction, expecting to be taken care of, and questioning the expectations of others.

➤ *Time Out for Personal Reflection*

1. In the blank, write "A" if you agree and "D" if you disagree with the statement.

_____   Women's socialization has encouraged them to lower their aspirations for achievement in the competitive world.

_____   Like men, women pay a price for living by narrowly defined rules of what women should be.

_____   Many women are concerned that they will appear unfeminine if they strive for success.

_____   Most women are passive, dependent, and unassertive.

_____   By nature, women are more nurturing than men.

_____   Women have a tendency to be emotional and not rational.

_____   Women are still subject to discrimination in our society.

_____   Today, women have attained equality with men in the workplace.

_____   Most women need a career outside the home to satisfy themselves.

_____   Many women today reject the societal standard of what it means to be feminine and are discarding traditional roles.

2. What challenges must women face in dual-career families?

_____

_____

_____

_____

3. What are your thoughts about the price women must pay for accepting traditional roles?

_____

_____

_____

_____

4. What specific qualities do you most respect in women?

_____

_____

_____

_____

Liberation for Both Women and Men

Some forces in contemporary society contribute to keeping women isolated, either in a nuclear family or alone in an apartment. The women's movement has been instrumental in showing women how to deal with this isolation and to see through the myths that reduce their personal power (Lott, 1994). *Power* is a word now used by more women with less self-consciousness and apology. Lott asserts that women are less constrained by gender ideology and freer to choose other options largely because of the feminist movement. The main tenet of the movement is that women must be respected and allowed to develop as full human beings. According to Lerner (1985), women can be pioneers in the process of personal and social change. They can use their anger to create new and more functional relationships. It is especially important that women avoid getting trapped in blaming and focusing on others. To do this, it is helpful to have support from other women. "Our challenge is to listen carefully to our own anger and to use it in the service of change" (p. 224).

The increasing liberation of women has also stimulated some degree of liberation for men. This trend is underscored by Basow's (1992) contention that a goal worth striving for is allowing people to be fully human and to bring about changes in our society that will reflect that humanity. She states: "Eliminating gender stereotypes and redefining gender in terms of equality does not mean simply liberating women, but liberating men and our society as well" (p. 359).

Gerson (1987) contends that men cannot remain insulated from the changes taking place in women's lives and will be forced to adjust to new social circumstances. Men have also begun to realize the steep price of gender expectations, and men are now exploring the idea of a nonpatriarchal society (Lott, 1994).

In his lectures on the men's movement and in his book *Iron John,* the poet Robert Bly (1990) addresses the subject of men learning to experience and express their feelings. He believes that the time is ripe for a new vision of masculinity. In the preface to *Iron John,* he writes:

> We are living at an important and fruitful moment now, for it is clear to men that the images of adult manhood given by the popular culture are worn out; a man can no longer depend on them. By the time a man is thirty-five he knows that the images of the right man, the tough man, the true man which he received in high school do not work in life. Such a man is open to new visions of what a man is or could be. (p. ix)

Women and men need to remain open to each other and be willing to change their attitudes if they are interested in releasing themselves from stereotyped roles. We are in a transitional period in which men and women are redefining themselves and ridding themselves of old stereotypes; yet too often we needlessly fight with each other when we could be helping each other be patient as we learn new patterns of thought and behavior. As men and women alike pay closer attention to deeply ingrained attitudes, they may find that they haven't caught up emotionally with their intellectual level of awareness. Although we might well be "liberated" intellectually and *know* what we want, many of us have difficulty *feeling* OK about what we want. The challenge is getting the two together.

Alternatives to Rigid Gender-Role Expectations

The prevalence of certain male and female stereotypes in our culture doesn't mean that all men and women live within these narrow confines. The alternative to living according to a stereotype is to realize that we can actively define our own standards of what we want to be like as women or as men. We don't have to blindly accept roles and expectations that have been imposed on us or remain victims of our early conditioning, or of our own self-socialization. We can begin to achieve autonomy in our sexual identity by looking at how we have formed our ideals and standards and who our models have been; then we can decide whether these are the standards we want to use in defining our gender-role identity now.

■ Androgyny as an Alternative

One appealing alternative to rigid gender stereotypes is the concept of *androgyny,* the coexistence of male and female personality traits and characteristics in the same person. Androgyny refers to the flexible integration of strong "masculine" and "feminine" traits in unique ways: Androgynous people are able to recognize and express both "feminine" and "masculine" dimensions. To understand androgyny it is essential to remember that both biological characteristics and learned behavior play a part in how this gender role is actualized. We all secrete both male and female hormones, and we all have both feminine and masculine psychological characteristics, which Carl Jung labeled the *animus* and the *anima*. Taken together, the animus and the anima reflect Jung's conception of humans as androgynous (see Harris, 1996, for a more complete discussion of Jung's theory of personality).

Since women share some of the psychological characteristics of men (through their animus), and since men possess some feminine aspects (through their anima), both can better understand the opposite sex. Jung was very insistent that women and men must express both dimensions of their personality. Failure to do so means that part of our nature is denied, which results in one-sided development. Becoming fully human implies accepting the full range of our personality characteristics. Androgyny does not mean being neuter or imply anything about one's sexual orientation (Basow, 1992). Instead, the concept describes the degree of flexibility a person has regarding stereotypic gender role behaviors.

Androgynous individuals are able to adjust their behavior to what the situation requires in integrated and flexible ways. They are not bound by rigid, stereotyped behavior. Androgynous people have a wider range of capacities than those who are entrapped by gender-typed expectations and can give expression to a rich range of behaviors. Thus, they may perceive themselves as being both understanding, affectionate, and considerate *and* self-reliant, independent, and firm. The same person has the capacity to be an empathic listener to a friend with a problem, a forceful leader when a project needs to be moved into action, and an assertive supervisor.

Because *masculine* and *feminine* imply a false dichotomy, Lott (1994) urges discontinuing use of these terms. Masculinity and femininity continue to be regarded as distinctive ways of behaving, yet such a dualistic view of human personality is rooted in sex-role stereotypes that are not supported by evidence. Both genders show wide individual differences along all behavioral dimensions. In reality, we are multidimensional beings, and polarities of behavioral traits are rare.

Some of you may feel threatened by our presentation of androgyny as an alternative to traditional gender roles. If so, we urge you to consider the notion that people do have both feminine and masculine aspects within them. To become fully human, we need to realize the rich and complex dimensions of our being.

■ Gender-Role Transcendence

According to Basow (1992), androgyny may be one step on the path to transcending gender roles, but it is not the only nor necessarily the best way for personal change to occur. Basow suggests that we need to define healthy human functioning independently of gender-related characteristics. She believes that the ultimate goal is to move beyond gender roles by transcending traditional gender-role polarities to reach a new level of synthesis. In this view the world is not divided into polarities of masculinity and femininity; rather, people have a range of potentials that can be adapted to various situations. As Basow puts it: "When gender transcendence occurs, people can be just people — individuals in their own right, accepted and evaluated on their own terms" (p. 327). When individuals go beyond the restrictions imposed by gender roles and stereotypes, they experience a sense of uniqueness because each person has different capabilities and interests. The transcendence model implies that personality traits should be divorced from biological sex. Those who advocate gender-role transcendence claim that this practice will enable individuals to free themselves from linking specific behavior patterns with a gender. They argue that if there were less emphasis on gender as a means of categorizing traits, individuals would be freer to develop their own unique potentials (Weiten & Lloyd, 1994).

➤ *Time Out for Personal Reflection*

1. The following statements may help you assess how you see yourself in relation to gender roles. Place a "T" before each statement that generally applies to you and an "F" before each one that generally doesn't apply to you. Be sure to respond as you are now rather than as you'd like to be.

_____ I am more rational than emotional.
_____ I'm more an active person than a passive person.
_____ I'm more cooperative than I am competitive.
_____ I tend to express my feelings rather than keeping them hidden.
_____ I tend to live by what is expected of my sex.
_____ I see myself as possessing both masculine and feminine characteristics.
_____ I'm afraid of deviating very much from the customary gender-role norms.
_____ I'm adventurous in most situations.
_____ I feel OK about expressing both negative and positive feelings.
_____ I'm continually striving for success.
_____ I fear success as much as I fear failure.

Now look over your responses. Which characteristics, if any, would you like to change in yourself?

_____

_____

_____

_____

2. What are your reactions to the changes in women's views of their gender role? What impact do you think the feminist movement has had on women? on men?

_____

_____

_____

_____

_____

3. What do you think of the concept of androgyny? Would you like to possess more of the qualities you associate with the other sex? If so, what are they? Are there any ways in which you feel limited or restricted by rigid gender-role definitions and expectations?

_____

_____

_____

_____

_____

Chapter Summary

The gender-role standard of our culture has encouraged a static notion of clear roles into which all biological males and females must fit. Masculinity has become associated with traits that imply power, authority, and mastery; femininity has become associated with traits that suggest passivity and subordination. These concepts of masculinity and femininity are historically and socially conditioned. They are not part of a woman's or a man's basic nature.

Many men have become prisoners of a stereotypical role that they feel they must live by. Writers who address the problems of traditional male roles have focused on characteristics such as independence, aggressiveness, worldliness, directness, objectivity, activity, logic, denial of fears, self-protection, lack of emotional expressiveness, lack of bodily awareness, denial of "feminine" qualities, rigidity, obsession with work, and fear of intimacy. Fortunately, an increasing number of men are challenging the restrictions of these traditional roles. Books on men's issues have recently appeared that describe the challenges men face in breaking out of rigid roles and defining themselves in new ways.

Women, too, have been restricted by their cultural conditioning and by accepting gender-role stereotypes that keep them in an inferior position. Adjectives often associated with women include gentle, tactful, neat, sensitive, talkative, emotional, unassertive, indirect, and caring. Too often women have defined their own preferences as being the same as those of their partners, and they have had to gain their identity by protecting, helping, nurturing, and comforting. Despite the staying power of these traditional female role expectations, more and more women are rejecting the limited vision of what a woman is "expected" to be. Like men, they are gaining increased intellectual awareness of alternative roles, yet they often struggle emotionally to *feel* and *act* in ways that differ from their upbringing. The challenge for both sexes is to keep pace on an emotional level with what they know intellectually about living more freely.

We described androgyny as one path toward uprooting gender-role stereotypes. However, it is not the only way, or even the best way, to bring about this change. Ideally, you will be able to transcend rigid categories of "femininity" and "masculinity" and achieve a personal synthesis whereby you can behave responsively as a function of the situation. The real challenge is for you to choose the kind of woman or man you want to be rather than passively accepting a cultural stereotype or blindly identifying with some form of rebellion. When you examine the basis of your gender-role identity and your concept of what constitutes a woman or a man, you can decide for yourself what kind of person you want to be instead of conforming to the expectations of others.

In this chapter we've encouraged you to think about your attitudes and values concerning gender roles and to take a close look at how you developed them. Even though cultural pressures are strong toward adopting given roles as a woman or a man, you are not hopelessly cemented into a rigid way of being. You can challenge role expectations that restrict you and determine whether the costs of having adopted certain roles are worth the potential gains.

Activities and Exercises

1. Write down the characteristics you associate with being a woman (or feminine) and being a man (or masculine). Then think about how you acquired these views and to what degree you're satisfied with them.
2. Men and women are challenging traditional roles. Based on your own observations, to what extent do you find this to be true? Do your friends typically accept traditional roles, or do they tend to challenge society's expectations?
3. Interview some people from a cultural group different from your own. Describe some of the common gender stereotypes mentioned in this chapter and determine if such stereotypes are true of the other cultural group.
4. Make a list of gender-role stereotypes that apply to men and a list of those that apply to women. Then select people of various ages and ask them to say how much they agree or disagree with each of these stereotypes. If several people bring their results to class, you might have the basis of an interesting panel discussion.
5. For a week or two, pay close attention to the messages you see on television, both in programs and in commercials, regarding gender roles and expectations of women and men. Record your impressions in your journal.
6. Select one or more of the following books for further reading on the topics explored in this chapter: *Gender: Stereotypes and Roles* (Basow, 1992); *Iron John: A Book About Men* (Bly, 1990); *The Hazards of Being Male* (Goldberg, 1976); *The New Male* (Goldberg, 1979); *The Inner Male* (Goldberg, 1987); *Prisoners of Men's Dreams* (Gordon, 1991; *The Book of Guys* (Keillor, 1993); *Fire in the Belly: On Being a Man* (Keen, 1991); *Women's Lives: Themes and Variations in Gender Learning* (Lott, 1994); *Man Alive: A Primer of Men's Issues* (Rabinowitz & Cochran, 1994); *The Mismeasure of Women* (Tauris, 1992); *To Be a Man: In Search of the Deep Masculine* (Thompson, 1991); *The Male Stress Syndrome: How to Survive Stress in the '90s* (Witkin, 1994).

5

Work and Leisure

Working to live — living to work.

✔ *Prechapter Self-Inventory*

Use the following scale to respond: 4 = this statement is true of me *most* of the time; 3 = this statement is true of me *much* of the time; 2 = this statement is true of me *some* of the time; 1 = this statement is true of me *almost none* of the time.

_____   1. I'm in college because it's necessary for the career I want.

_____   2. My primary reason for being in college is to grow as a person and fulfill my potential.

_____   3. I'm attending college to give me time to decide what to do with my life.

_____   4. I wouldn't work if I didn't need the money.

_____   5. Work is a very important means of expressing myself.

_____   6. I expect to change jobs several times during my life.

_____   7. A secure job is more important to me than an exciting one.

_____   8. If I'm unhappy in my job, it's probably my fault, not the job's.

_____   9. I expect my work to fulfill many of my needs and to be an important source of meaning in my life.

_____   10. I want work to allow me the leisure time that I require.

Introduction

Freud identified *lieben und arbeiten,* "to love and to work," as core characteristics of the healthy person. Deriving satisfaction from loving and working are of paramount importance. As you will see, work has an impact in many areas of our lives; and the balance we find between work and leisure can contribute to our personal vitality or be a stressful experience that ultimately results in burnout.

Work is a good deal more than an activity that takes up a certain number of hours each week. If you feel good about your work, the quality of your life will improve. If you don't like your job and dread the hours you spend on it, your relationships and your feelings about yourself are bound to be affected. In the *Wellness Workbook,* John Travis and Regina Sara Ryan (1994) suggest that work and play "are the stuff of our lives," as we are generally doing one or the other for most of our waking hours. They advocate that it is more important to become aware of what we are doing and perhaps to change our attitudes toward work and play rather than to change *what* we do for work or play. It is certainly worth the effort to think about ways to improve the quality of the many hours you devote to work and to leisure in your daily life.

If you are a re-entry student, you may already have a career. You may be working at a job, carrying out responsibilities in the home, and also being either a part-time or a full-time college student. Your college work may be preparing you for a career change or a job promotion. If you have not yet begun a career, you can use this chapter to examine your expectations about work. Make an assessment of your personal interests, needs, values, and abilities, and begin the process of matching these personal characteristics with occupational information and trends in the world of work. In *Taking Charge of Your Career Direction,* Lock (1996a) acknowledges that choosing an occupation is not easy. Externally, the working world is constantly changing; internally, your expectations, needs, motivations, values, and interests may change. Deciding on a career involves integrating the realities of these two worlds. Lock emphasizes the importance of *actively choosing* a career.

> You must accept the responsibility of choosing an occupation for yourself and then be willing to live with the consequences of that decision. These words are easily said but difficult to practice. There will be times when you want to escape the responsibility that freedom of choice brings, but no good counselor, parent, friend, or test interpreter will allow you to abdicate that responsibility. (p. 4)

One way to assume an active role in deciding on a career is to talk to other people about their job satisfaction. But don't let others' expectations or attitudes determine how you feel about your work, or you'll surrender some of your autonomy. It's important to sort out your own attitudes about a career. One of the major factors that might prevent you from becoming active in planning for a career is the temptation to put off doing what needs to be done to *choose* your work. If you merely "fall into" a job, you will probably be disappointed with the outcome.

It could well be a mistake to think about selecting *one* occupation that will last a lifetime. It may be more fruitful to choose a general type of work or a broad field of endeavor that appeals to you. You can consider your present job or field of study as a means of gaining experience and opening doors to new possibilities, and you can focus on what you want to learn from this experience. It can be liberating to realize that your decisions about work can be part of a developmental process and that your jobs can change as you change or can lead to related occupations within your chosen field.

The fast pace of social and technological change in today's world is forcing people to adapt to a changing world of work. The average American entering the work force today will change careers, not just jobs, three times (Bolles, 1995; Naisbitt & Aburdene, 1991). Some experts tell people that they can expect to have five different careers during their working years. This means that people entering the work force in the 1990s need to have more than specific knowledge and skills; they need to be able to adapt to change. One career may pave the way to another.

Before continuing with this chapter, let's clarify the terms *career, occupation, job,* and *work.* A *career* can be thought of as your life's work. A career spans a period of time and may involve one or several occupations; it is the sequence of a person's work experience over time. An *occupation* is your vocation, profession, business, or trade, and you may change your occupation several times during your lifetime. A *job* is your position of employment within an occupation. Over a period of time you may have several jobs within the same occupation. A job is what you do to earn money to survive and to do the things you'd like to do. *Work* is a broad concept that refers to something you do because you want to, and we hope, because you enjoy it. Ideally, your job and your work involve similar activities.

Work is fulfilling when you feel you are being compensated adequately and when you like what you are doing.

Your College Education as Your Work

You may already have made several vocational decisions and held a number of different jobs, you may be changing careers, or you may be in the process of exploring career options and preparing yourself for a career. If you are in the midst of considering what occupations might best suit you, it would be helpful to review the meaning that going to college has for you now. There is doubtless some relationship between how you approach your college experience and how you will someday approach your career.

School may be your primary line of work for the present, but for those of you who are engaged in a career and have families, school is not likely to be your main source of work. Regardless of your commitments outside of college, it is a good idea to reflect on why you are in college. Ask yourself these questions: Why am I in college? Is it my choice or someone else's choice for me? Do I enjoy most of my time as a student? Is my work as a student satisfying and meaningful? Would I rather be somewhere else or doing something other than being a student? If so, why am I staying in college?

The reasons for attending college are many and varied, but studies suggest that student motivations can be summarized under the following three categories (Herr & Cramer, 1988):

- *Self-fulfillers.* If you are in this category, your primary concern is searching for a personal identity and using your college experience as a means of self-fulfillment. You expect school to provide a supportive environment for self-expansion through academic pursuits.
- *Careerists.* If you are in this category, you are attending college mainly for vocational reasons. School is a means to an end rather than an end in itself. Although you may have other motivations, they are secondary to your major goal of adequately preparing yourself for a selected occupation.
- *Avoiders.* The decision to go to college is sometimes more an avoidance maneuver than a conscious striving for a career goal or for self-development. You may be in college largely as a result of pressure from parents or peers. You also may not be quite certain what you want to do with your life and may hope that you can clarify your thoughts. Some attend college as a delaying tactic. Others are interested primarily in the social life.

Herr and Cramer maintain that many students in each of these categories can benefit from career counseling. Self-fulfillers may eventually realize that even though personal growth is a laudable goal they will have to work. Careerists may discover that their original career choice is inappropriate and that they need to search out alternatives. Avoiders eventually realize that they cannot endlessly put off their career choice. Whatever your motivation for going to college, career-development assistance can provide you with the tools you need to make good career decisions.

Brandi's story illustrates how motivations for going to college can change. Brandi, now age 21, initially enrolled in college on a scholarship to participate in the gymnastics team. Brandi made choices to broaden her life beyond gymnastics, as you can see from her account.

> *I had been a gymnast since I was 4 years old, and I didn't know any kind of life without it. My body was consistently failing me though, and going to practice every day was becoming harder and harder. It was frustrating not to be able to do what I was once capable of, and I found I was becoming very un-happy as a gymnast. I had been a gymnast all my life, and I wanted the chance to be a normal student for a while.*
>
> *Knowing that I was not going to be able to continue as a gymnast much longer, I decided it was important to end my gymnastics career while I still liked my sport. My coach expected a lot from me, and I expected a lot from myself. However, I felt as though I was not going to be able to reach these ex-pectations. I was also tired of waking up and wondering how much I was go-ing to be hurting physically every day. There were many pressures on me, such as struggles to be thin, get good grades, and practice at a level that was equiv-alent to what my coach wanted.*
>
> *Gymnastics took an enormous amount of time and energy. I found myself wanting to put my time and energy into my college education as I began to set new goals for myself. It was the first time in my life that I really wanted to ac-complish something that did not involve gymnastics. My choice to leave the team was very difficult and scary. I was so used to gymnastics being such a large part of my life, and such a large part of who I was. I am very happy with the choice I made, and even though I miss gymnastics at times, I now have my education and other things in my life to accomplish and look forward to.*

In Chapter 1 we asked you to review the impact of your experiences in ele-mentary school and secondary school on yourself as a learner. If you saw yourself as a passive learner, you were encouraged to take steps to become an active and in-volved one. This would be a good time to review the goals you set and determine how well you are progressing toward them. If you established a contract to take in-creased responsibility for your own learning and to get personally involved in this book and the course, reevaluate how you are doing. Perhaps this is an ideal time to set new goals, to modify your original goals, or to try new behavior in reaching your goals.

If you like the meaning your college experience has for you as well as your part in creating this meaning, you are likely to assume responsibility for making your job satisfying. If you typically do more than is required as a student, you are likely to be willing to go beyond doing what is expected of you in your job. If you are the kind of student who fears making mistakes and will not risk saying what you think in class, you may carry this behavior into a job. You may be afraid of jeopardizing your grades by being assertive, and someday you may very well be unassertive in the work world out of fear of losing your job or not advancing. If you have taken on too many courses and other projects, planned poorly, procrastinated, and fallen behind, you may feel utter frustration and exhaustion by semester's end. Might you not display this same behavior in your work?

Make an honest inventory of your role as a student. If you are not satisfied with yourself as a student, the situation is far from being hopeless. If you decide that your present major is not what really interests you, you are no more wedded to your course of study than you are to one particular job in the future. Determine for yourself why you are in college and what you are getting from and giving to this project.

Choosing an Occupation or a Career

What do you expect from work? What factors do you stress in selecting a career or an occupation? In working with college students, we find that many of you haven't thought seriously about why you are choosing a given vocation. For some, parental pressure or encouragement is the major reason for being in college. Others have idealized views of what it would be like to be a lawyer, an engineer, or a doctor. Many college students haven't looked at what they value the most and whether these values can be attained in their chosen vocation. John Holland's (1992) theory of career decision making is based on the assumption that career choices are an expression of personality. Holland believes that the choice of an occupation reflects the person's motivation, knowledge, personality, and ability. Occupations represent a way of life. Dave's personal story illustrates this search for a satisfying career. Dave chose college without knowing what he wanted. Eventually he found a direction by pursuing what interested him.

I went to college right out of high school even though I wasn't sure that college was for me. I went because I thought I needed a college degree to get a good job and to succeed.

My first year was a bit rough because of the new surroundings. In my classes I felt like a number, and it didn't seem to matter if I attended classes or not. College provided a wide range of freedom. I was the one who was responsible to show up for class. It was hard for me to handle this freedom. I found it easier to go off with my friends. Needless to say, my grades took a nose dive. I was placed on academic disqualification. As a result, I decided to go to a community college. But my pattern of not taking school seriously remained the same.

Although I wanted to eventually finish college, I knew that university life was not right for me at this time. I decided to move out of my parents' home and worked full time. Although I was working, I managed to take a few night classes at a community college. I knew that if I left college completely it would be harder to ever return.

Eventually I accepted a job with a promotional marketing firm. It was a fun job sampling different consumer goods targeted toward people participating in various sporting events (10K races, tournaments, bike races). I was given more responsible assignments, and I really enjoyed what I was doing. I asked myself: "How could I apply what I enjoyed doing and make it a career?" This question led me to doing research on the sports entertainment field to discover a career path.

My research convinced me of the importance of returning to college full time. Now I was focused and determined to receive my degree and to pursue a career in the sports entertainment industry. Knowing what I wanted as a career made selecting a major relatively easy. I majored in business with a marketing emphasis and did extremely well. My journey took me from academic disqualification to graduating with honors.

After graduation I accepted a job from the same marketing firm where I had worked earlier, only this time it was a higher level job that included travel. After many interviews I accepted a job with a professional baseball team. After working there for more than two years, I was offered a job with Disney Sports Enterprises (for the Mighty Ducks Hockey Team) in the sales and marketing department, where I am currently employed. I sell advertising, sponsorships, and various ticket packages. My work involves implementing much of what I learned in my major. This position is ideal because it allows me to do what I enjoy and use what I learned in college.

Following my interests has led to an exciting career. I look forward to getting up and going to work, which is both fun and challenging. I am able to combine my sports hobbies with my profession. This work is personally rewarding, and I feel energized and motivated on the job. My work doesn't seem like "work." To me, this is one of the keys to a meaningful life.

■ The Disadvantages of Choosing an Occupation Too Soon

So much emphasis is placed on what you will do "for a living" that you may feel compelled to choose an occupation or a career before you are really ready to do so. In our society, we are pressured from an early age to grow up and encouraged to identify with some occupation. Children are often asked: "What are you going to be when you grow up?" Embedded in this question is the implication that we're not grown up until we've decided to *be* something. Our society expects young people to identify their values, choose a vocation and a lifestyle, and then settle down (Carney & Wells, 1995). The implication is that once young people make the "right decision," they should be set for life. Yet deciding on a career is not that simple.

One of the disadvantages of focusing on a particular occupation too soon is that students' interest patterns are often not sufficiently reliable or stable in high school or sometimes even in the college years to predict job success and satisfaction. Furthermore, the typical student does not have enough self-knowledge or knowledge of educational offerings and vocational opportunities to make realistic decisions. The pressure to make premature vocational decisions often results in choosing an occupation in which one does not have the interests and abilities required for success. At the other extreme, however, are those who engage in delay, defensive avoidance, and procrastination. An individual on this end of the scale drifts endlessly and aimlessly, and life may be pretty well over when he or she asks,

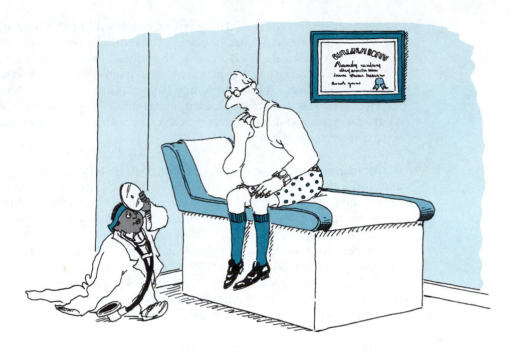

"Where am I going?" It is clear that either extreme is dangerous. We need to be cautious in resisting pressures from the outside to decide too quickly on a life's vocation, yet we also need to be alert to the tendencies within ourselves to expect that what we want will come to us easily.

■ Factors in Vocational Decision Making

Career development researchers have found that most people go through a series of stages when choosing an occupation or, more typically, several occupations to pursue. As with life span stages, different factors emerge or become influential at different times throughout this process. Factors that have been shown to be important in the occupational decision-making process include: self-concept; motivation and achievement; attitudes about occupations; abilities; interests; values; temperament and personality styles; socioeconomic level; parental influence; ethnic identity; gender; and physical, mental, emotional, and social handicaps. In choosing your vocation (or evaluating the choices you've made previously), consider which factors really mean the most to you. Let's take a closer look at how some of these factors may influence your vocational choice, keeping in mind that vocational choice is a process, not an event.

Self-Concept.   People with a poor self-concept are not likely to envision themselves in a meaningful or important job. They are likely to keep their aspirations low, and thus their achievements will probably be low. They may select and remain in a job they do not enjoy or derive satisfaction from because they are convinced this is all they are worthy of. Choosing a vocation can be thought of as a public declaration of the kind of person we see ourselves as being. Casey and Vanceburg (1985) capture the notion that how we view ourselves has a great deal to do with how others perceive and treat us: "Our self-perception determines how we present ourselves. The posture we've assumed invites others' praise, interest, or criticism. What others think of us accurately reflects our personal self-assessment, a message we've conveyed directly or subtly."

Motivation and Achievement.   Setting goals is at the core of the process of deciding on a vocation. If you have goals but do not have the energy and persistence to pursue them, your goals will not be met. Your need to achieve along with your achievements to date are related to your motivation to translate goals into action plans. In thinking about your career choices, identify those areas where your drive is the greatest. Also, reflect on specific achievements. What have you accomplished that you feel particularly proud of? What are you doing now that moves you in the direction of achieving what is important to you? What are some of the things you dream about doing in the future? Thinking about your goals, needs, motivations, and achievements is a good way to get a clearer focus on your career direction.

Attitudes about Occupations.   We develop our attitudes toward the status of occupations by learning from the people in our environment. Typical first graders are not aware of the differential status of occupations, yet in a few years these children begin to rank occupations in a manner similar to that of adults. As students advance to higher grades, they reject more and more occupations as unacceptable. Unfortunately, they rule out some of the very jobs from which they may have to choose if they are to find employment as adults. It is difficult for people to feel positive about themselves if they have to accept an occupation they perceive as low in status.

Abilities.   Ability or aptitude has received a great deal of attention in the career decision-making process, and it is probably used more often than any other factor to evaluate potential for success. *Ability* refers to your competence in an activity; *aptitude* is your ability to learn. Both general and specific abilities should be considered in making career choices, but scholastic aptitude or IQ—a general ability typically considered to consist of both verbal and numerical aptitudes—is particularly significant because it largely determines who will be able to obtain the level of education required for entrance into higher status occupations. You can measure and compare your abilities with the skills required for various professions and academic areas of interest to you.

Interests.   Your interests reflect your experiences or ideas pertaining to work-related activities that you like or dislike. Interest measurement has become increasingly popular and is used extensively in career planning. Vocational planning should give primary consideration to interests. First, determine your areas of vocational interest. Next, identify occupations in your interest areas. Then, determine which occupations correspond to your abilities.

Occupational interest surveys can be used to compare your interests with those of others who have found job satisfaction in a given area (Carney & Wells, 1995). Researchers have shown that a significant relationship exists between interests and abilities. Abilities and interests are two integral components of career decision making, and understanding how these factors are related is essential (Randahl, 1991). But remember that interest alone does not necessarily mean that you have the ability to succeed in a particular occupation.

Several interest inventories are available to help you assess your vocational interests. If you were going to select just one instrument, we recommend Holland's Self-Directed Search (SDS) Interest Inventory, which is probably the most widely used interest inventory. Other interest and personality inventories you may want to consider taking are the Vocational Preference Inventory, the Strong Interest Inventory, the Kuder Occupational Interest Inventory, and the Myers-Briggs Type Indicator. This last instrument assesses types of human personality. For further information about such inventories, contact the counseling center at your college.

Values.   Your values indicate who you are as a person, and they influence what you want from life. It is important to assess, identify, and clarify your values so you will be able to match them with your career choices. An inventory of your values can reveal the pattern behind aspects of life that you prize and will also enable you to see how your values have emerged, taken shape, and changed over time.

Your *work values* pertain to what you hope to accomplish through your role in an occupation. Work values are an important aspect of your total value system, and knowing those things that bring meaning to your life is crucial if you hope to find a career that has personal value for you. A few examples of work values include: helping others, influencing people, finding meaning, prestige, status, competition, friendships, creativity, stability, recognition, adventure, physical challenge, change and variety, opportunity for travel, moral fulfillment, and independence. Because specific work values are often related to particular occupations, they can be the basis of a good match between you and a position.

■ Personality Types and Choosing a Career

People who exhibit certain values and particular personality traits are a good match with certain career areas. John Holland (1992) has identified six worker personality types, and his topology is widely used as the basis for books on career development, vocational tests used in career counseling centers, and self-help approaches for making career decisions.* Because his work has been so influential in vocational theory, it is worth going into some detail about it here. As you read the descriptions of Holland's six personality types, take the time to think about the patterns that fit you best.

*Holland's (1992) six personality types are realistic, investigative, artistic, social, enterprising, or conventional. Our discussion of these six types is based on Holland's work as refined by Jim Morrow (retired professor of counseling, Western Carolina University, North Carolina). For more information about Holland's personality types and implications for selecting a career, we highly recommend John Holland's (1994) *Self-Directed Search (Form R)*. For further information contact: Psychological Assessment Resources, Inc., P. O. Box 998, Odessa, FL 33556 or telephone (1-800-331-TEST).

As you read about these six personality types, remember that most people do not fall neatly into one category but have characteristics from several types. When you come across a phrase that describes you, put a check mark in the space provided. Then look again at the six personality types and select the three types (in rank order) that best describe the way you see yourself. As you become more aware of the type of person you are, you can apply these insights in your own career decision-making process.

Realistic Types

_____ are attracted to outdoor, mechanical, and physical activities, hobbies, and occupations

_____ like to work with things, objects, and animals rather than with ideas, data, and people

_____ tend to have mechanical and athletic abilities

_____ like to construct, shape, and restructure and repair things around them

_____ like to use equipment and machinery and to see tangible results

_____ are persistent and industrious builders but seldom creative and original, preferring familiar methods and established patterns

_____ tend to think in terms of absolutes, dislike ambiguity, and prefer not to deal with abstract, theoretical, and philosophical issues

_____ are materialistic, traditional, and conservative

_____ do not have strong interpersonal and verbal skills and are often uncomfortable in situations in which attention is centered on them
_____ tend to find it difficult to express their feelings and may be regarded as shy

Investigative Types

_____ are naturally curious and inquisitive
_____ need to understand, explain, and predict what goes on around them
_____ are scholarly and scientific and tend to be pessimistic and critical about non-scientific, simplistic, or supernatural explanations
_____ tend to become engrossed in whatever they are doing and may appear to be oblivious to everything else
_____ are independent and like to work alone
_____ prefer neither to supervise others nor to be supervised
_____ are theoretical and analytic in outlook and find abstract and ambiguous problems and situations challenging
_____ are original and creative and often find it difficult to accept traditional attitudes and values
_____ avoid highly structured situations with externally imposed rules but are themselves internally well-disciplined, precise, and systematic
_____ have confidence in their intellectual abilities but often feel inadequate in social situations
_____ tend to lack leadership and persuasive skills
_____ tend to be reserved and formal in interpersonal relationships
_____ are not typically expressive emotionally and may not be considered friendly

Artistic Types

_____ are creative, expressive, original, intuitive, and individualistic
_____ like to be different and strive to stand out from the crowd
_____ like to express their personalities by creating new and different things with words, music, materials, and physical expression like acting and dancing
_____ want attention and praise but are sensitive to criticism
_____ tend to be uninhibited and nonconforming in dress, speech, and action
_____ prefer to work without supervision
_____ are impulsive in outlook
_____ place great value on beauty and esthetic qualities
_____ tend to be emotional and complicated
_____ prefer abstract tasks and unstructured situations
_____ find it difficult to function well in highly ordered and systematic situations
_____ seek acceptance and approval from others but often find close interpersonal relationships so stressful that they avoid them
_____ compensate for their resulting feelings of estrangement or alienation by relating to others primarily indirectly through art
_____ tend to be introspective

Social Types

_____ are friendly, enthusiastic, outgoing, and cooperative
_____ enjoy the company of other people

_____ are understanding and insightful about others' feelings and problems
_____ like helping and facilitating roles like teacher, mediator, adviser, or counselor
_____ express themselves well and are persuasive in interpersonal relationships
_____ like attention and enjoy being at or near the center of the group
_____ are idealistic, sensitive, and conscientious about life and in dealings with others
_____ like to deal with philosophical issues such as the nature and purpose of life, religion, and morality
_____ dislike working with machines or data and at highly organized, routine, and repetitive tasks
_____ get along well with others and find it natural to express their emotions
_____ are tactful in relating to others and are considered to be kind, supportive, and caring

Enterprising Types

_____ are outgoing, self-confident, persuasive, and optimistic
_____ like to organize, direct, manage, and control the activities of groups toward personal or organizational goals
_____ are ambitious and like to be in charge
_____ place a high value on status, power, money, and material possessions
_____ like to feel in control and responsible for making things happen
_____ are energetic and enthusiastic in initiating and supervising activities
_____ like to influence others
_____ are adventurous, impulsive, assertive, and verbally persuasive
_____ enjoy social gatherings and like to associate with well-known and influential people
_____ like to travel and explore and often have exciting and expensive hobbies
_____ see themselves as popular
_____ tend to dislike activities requiring scientific abilities and systematic and theoretical thinking
_____ avoid activities that require attention to detail and a set routine

Conventional Types

_____ are well-organized, persistent, and practical
_____ enjoy clerical and computational activities that follow set procedures
_____ are dependable, efficient, and conscientious
_____ enjoy the security of belonging to groups and organizations and make good team members
_____ are status-conscious but usually do not aspire to high positions of leadership
_____ are most comfortable when they know what is expected of them
_____ tend to be conservative and traditional
_____ usually conform to expected standards and follow the lead of those in positions of authority, with whom they identify
_____ like to work indoors in pleasant surroundings and place value on material comforts and possessions
_____ are self-controlled and low-key in expressing their feelings
_____ avoid intense personal relationships in favor of more casual ones

_____   are most comfortable among people they know well
_____   like for things to go as planned and prefer not to change routines

Relationships among the Personality Types.   As you were reading the descriptions of the six personality types, you probably noticed that each type shares some characteristics with some other types and also is quite different from some of the others. To help you compare and contrast the six types, Holland's "hexagon" illustrates the order of the relationships among the types.

Each type shares some characteristics with those types adjacent to it on the hexagon. Each type has only a little in common with those types two positions removed from it, and it is quite unlike the type opposite it on the hexagon. For example, the investigative type shares some characteristics with the realistic and artistic types, has little in common with the conventional and social types, and is quite different from the enterprising type. If you read the descriptions of the six types once more with the hexagon in mind, the relationships among the types will become clearer.

People who feel that they resemble two or three types that are not adjacent on the hexagon may find it difficult to reconcile the conflicting elements in those type descriptions. It is important to remember that the descriptions provided are for "pure" types and that very few people resemble a single type to the exclusion of all others. This is why we ask you to select the three types that you think best describe you.

Once you have compared your personal traits with the characteristics of each of the six types, it is possible to find a general area of work that most matches your personal qualities, interests, and values. This topic is addressed in the next section. The following "Time Out" will assist you in assessing your personality type. It will also encourage you to have someone you know assess you.

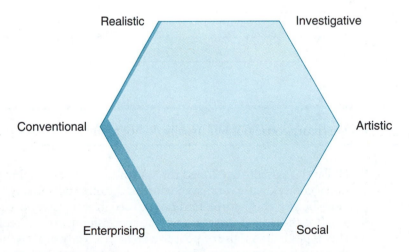

Holland's Hexagon

➤ *Time Out for Personal Reflection*

This exercise will help you become familiar with Holland's personality types.

1. Read the descriptions and other information furnished about Holland's six personality types at least two or three times.
2. Which of the six personality types best describes you? No one type will be completely "right" for you, but one of them will probably sound more like you than the others. Consider the overall descriptions of the types, and don't concentrate on just one or two characteristics of a type. As soon as you are satisfied that one type describes you better than the others, write that type down on the space for number 1 at the end of this exercise.
3. Which of the six types next best describes you? Write that type down in the space for number 2. Write down the type that next best describes you in the space for number 3.
4. Next, give the descriptions of the six types to someone who knows you very well. Ask them to read the descriptions carefully and order them in terms of their resemblance to you, just as you have done. Do not show or tell them how you rated yourself.
5. After the other person finishes rating you, compare your own rating with theirs. If there is not close agreement among the three types on both lists, ask the other person to give examples of your behaviors that prompted his or her ratings. The other person may not have rated you very accurately, or your behavior may not portray you to others as you see yourself. The purpose of this exercise is to familiarize you with Holland's personality types. It may have a "bonus" effect of better familiarizing you with yourself.

Your rating of yourself:

1. _____

2. _____

3. _____

Rating by someone who knows you well:

1. _____

2. _____

3. _____

The Process of Deciding on a Career

Holland originally developed his system as a way of helping people make occupational choices. After you have identified the three personality types that most closely describe you, this information can be used in your career decision-making process.

It is more likely that you will be successful in your career if your own personality types match those of people who have already proven themselves in the career that you hope to pursue. Holland has developed elaborate materials that can help you assess your personality type and compare it with the dominant types in various occupations. Here is a list of possible occupations associated with each personality type.

Realistic Type: carpenter, electronics engineer, emergency medical technology, mechanical engineering, industrial design, sculpture, law enforcement, photography, wildlife conservation management, orthodontics assistant, culinary arts, locomotive engineer, camera repair, cement masonry, jewelry repair, diesel mechanics, optician, floral design, marine surveying, automotive technology.

Investigative Type: economics, marketing, linguistics, biology, dentistry, food technology, optometry, medicine, physician's assistant, pollution control and technology, surveying, quality control management, meteorology, public health administration, highway engineering, veterinary medicine, biochemistry, cardiology, chemistry.

Artistic Type: acting/theater, creative writing, dance, journalism, commercial art, music, technical writing, fashion illustration, art education, graphic arts and design, cosmetology, fashion design, audiovisual technology, furniture design, interior decorating and design, photography, architecture, landscape architecture, stage design.

Social Type: education, motion pictures/cinema, probation and parole, recreation education/leadership, social work, hospital administration, rehabilitation counseling, nursing, psychology, school administration, labor relations, religious education, television production, library assistant, air traffic control, real estate, physical therapy, home economics, beautician, dental assistant.

Enterprising Type: accounting, travel agency management, park administration, dietetics, laboratory science, banking and finance, industrial engineering, international engineering, fire science management, records management, fashion merchandising, business administration, travel administration, marketing, law, international relations, marketing, outdoor recreation.

Conventional Type: computer and data processing, office machine technology, bookkeeping, building inspection, computer operator, court reporter, library assistant, medical records technology, personnel clerk, secretarial science, quality control technology, orthodontics assistant, electrical technology, medical secretary.

This process of selecting a career is more than a simple matter of matching information about the world of work with your personality type. You will find it useful to go through the following steps, or at least some of these steps, several times. For example, gathering and assessing information is a continual process rather than a step to be completed.

■ *Begin by focusing on yourself.* Continue to identify your interests, abilities, values, beliefs, wants, and preferences. Keep these questions in mind: Who am I? How do I want to live? Where do I want to live? What kind of environment do I envision in my occupation? Whom will I spend my time with? The awareness that comes from focusing on yourself can arouse anxiety because gaining a clear perspective takes time.

- *Generate alternative solutions.* This stage is closely related to the next two. Rather than first narrowing down your options, consider a number of alternatives or different potential occupations that you are drawn to. In this step it is wise to consider your work values and interests, especially as they apply to Holland's six personality types.

- *Gather and assess information about the alternatives generated.* Ask yourself, "Where do I best fit?" You'll need to find a career that matches your interests, values, and talents. Be willing to research the occupations that attract you. Read about their educational requirements and their positive and negative characteristics. Talk to as many people as you can who are involved in them. Ask them how their occupation may be changing in the years to come. Examine the social, political, economic, and geographic environment as a basis for assessing factors that influence your career choice.

- *Weigh and order your alternatives.* After you arrive at a list of alternatives, spend adequate time prioritizing them. Consider the practical aspects of your decisions, such as: Where do I most want to live? What values do I place on money and material goods? What are my values pertaining to family and time with friends? How much leisure is available to me in this job? What do I most want the outcome of my decision to be? Integrate occupational information and the wishes and views of others with your knowledge of yourself.

- *Make the decision and formulate a plan.* It is best to think of a series of many decisions at various turning points. In formulating a plan, read about the preparation required for your chosen alternative. Ask, "How can I best get to where I want to go?" This involves knowing your skills and having a clear plan that will help you attain your objectives. Remember, although you are ultimately responsible for deciding what path to follow, you are not riveted to your decision forever.

- *Carry out the decision.* After deciding, take practical steps to make your vision become a reality. Realize that committing yourself to implementing your decision does not mean that you will have no fears. The important thing is not to allow these fears to keep you frozen. You will never know if you are ready to meet a challenge unless you put your plan into action. Part of the way you can carry out a decision is to learn how to sell yourself. To market your skills to employers, you need to learn how to identify employment sources, prepare resumes, and meet the challenges of job interviews. One excellent way to acquire these marketing skills is by reading books; another resource is specific courses and workshops on job marketing skills available through the career guidance office at your college.

- *Get feedback.* After taking practical steps to carry out your decision, you will need to determine whether your choices are viable for you. Both the world of work and you will change over time, and what may look appealing to you now may not seem appropriate at some future time. Remember that career development is an ongoing process, and it will be important to commit yourself to repeating at least part of the process as your needs change or as occupational opportunities open up or decline. You stand a greater chance of being satisfied with your work if you put time and thought into your choice and if you actively take steps to find a career or an occupation that will bring enrichment.

For a more detailed discussion of the steps we have outlined here, see *Taking Charge of Your Career Direction* (Lock, 1996a). Lock emphasizes the following key components of the career-planning process: awareness and commitment, knowledge of the environment, self-knowledge, occupational alternatives, information about occupational prospects, decision making, implementation, and feedback or reevaluation.

➤ *Time Out for Personal Reflection*

This is a survey of your basic attitudes, values, abilities, and interests in regard to occupational choice.

1. Rate each item, using the following code: 1 = this is a *most important* consideration; 2 = this is *important* to me, but not a top priority; 3 = this is *slightly important*; 4 = this is of *little* or *no importance* to me.

_____	financial rewards
_____	security
_____	challenge
_____	prestige and status
_____	the opportunity to express my creativity
_____	autonomy—freedom to direct my project
_____	opportunity for advancement
_____	variety within the job
_____	recognition
_____	friendship and relations with co-workers
_____	serving people
_____	a source of meaning
_____	the chance to continue learning
_____	structure and routine

Once you've finished the assessment, review the list and write down the three most important values you associate with selecting a career or occupation.

_____

_____

_____

_____

2. In what area(s) do you see your strongest abilities?

_____

_____

_____

_____

3. What are a few of your major interests?

_____

_____

_____

_____

4. Which one value of yours do you see as having some bearing on your choice of a vocation?

_____

_____

_____

_____

5. At this point, what jobs do you see as most suitable to your interests, abilities, and values?

_____

_____

_____

_____

Choices at Work

Just as choosing a career is a process, so is creating meaning in our work. If we grow stale in our jobs or do not find avenues of self-expression through the work we do, we eventually lose our vitality. In this section we look at ways to find meaning in work and at approaches to keeping our options open.

■ The Dynamics of Discontent in Work

It is certainly true that if you're dissatisfied with your job one recourse is to look for a new one. Change alone, however, might not produce different results. In general, it's a mistake to assume that change necessarily cures dissatisfactions, and this very much applies to changing jobs. To know whether a new job would be helpful, you need to understand as clearly as you can why your present job isn't satisfactory to you. Consequently, it's important to consider some of the external factors that

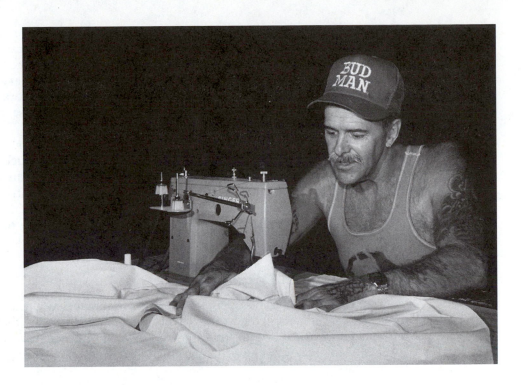

can devitalize you in your job and the very real pressures your job often creates. It is also critical to deal with those factors *within yourself* that lead to discontent at work. The emphasis of our discussion will be on what you can do to change some of these factors in the job and in yourself.

You may like your work and derive satisfaction from it yet at the same time feel drained because of irritations produced by factors that aren't intrinsic to the work itself. Such factors may include low morale or actual conflict and disharmony among fellow workers; authoritarian supervisors who make it difficult for you to feel any sense of freedom on the job; or organizational blocks to your creativity. Countless pressures and demands can sap your energy and lead you to feel dissatisfied with your job. These include having to meet deadlines and quotas; having to compete with others instead of simply doing your best; facing the threat of losing your job; feeling stuck in a job that offers little opportunity for growth or that you deem dehumanizing; dealing with difficult customers or clients; and having to work long hours or perform exhausting or tedious work. A stress that is particularly insidious — because it can compound all the other dissatisfactions you might feel — is the threat of cutbacks or layoffs, an anxiety that becomes more acute when you think of your commitments and responsibilities. In addition to the strains you may experience on the job, you may also have the daily stress of commuting to and from work. You may be tense before you even get to work, and the trip home may only increase the level of tension or anxiety you bring home with you. One real problem for many is that relationships with others are negatively affected by this kind of pressure. In one suburb, a new train route carries workers from their homes to downtown. This scenic ride gives them a chance to read, look out the window, or just reflect instead of having to endure a solitary battle with traffic. This train ride provides for more personal time. If your work is draining and deenergizing, you may have little to give your children, spouse, and friends, and you may not be receptive to their efforts to give to you.

All these factors can contribute to a general discontent that robs your work of whatever positive benefits it might otherwise have. In the face of such discontent, you might just plod along, hating your job and spoiling much of the rest of your life as well. The alternative is to look at the specific things that contribute to your unhappiness or tension and to ask yourself what you can do about them. You can also ask what you can do about your own attitudes toward those pressures and sources of tension.

■ Self-Esteem and Work

With downsizing and layoffs, people sometimes find themselves out of work due to circumstances beyond their control. Unemployment is a reality that can erode self-esteem. Maria's story illustrates how self-esteem and identity are often anchored to your ability to engage in meaningful work, and how losing your job can be devastating.

> *Two years ago I had an accident at work that forever changed who I was and required that I modify my future goals and plans. After hurting my back, I was told that I was no longer able to continue in the job that I had been engaged in for 16 years. I didn't want to believe this, and for a time I was in denial. When this harsh reality eventually hit me, I became depressed.*
>
> *I didn't know who I was anymore. Working had been my life. It was my identity. I felt lost and very empty inside, and my self-esteem plummeted. I found myself making very little money, and at my age this was a failure. Being on worker's compensation, I was required to get training in a different line of work. Changing careers at this point in my life was a most difficult task. I was both angry and scared.*
>
> *As the emptiness inside me deepened, I realized the hardest part for me was that I had very little control over what I was going through. I had to rely on the decisions of my doctors and the insurance company. I felt as though I had lost all control over my life. To make matters even worse, I had to live at home with my parents. This felt like another loss of identity, because I ceased to be the head of my own household. Instead, I was the child of my parents again. I was no longer in charge of my own life.*
>
> *Coping with these circumstances was difficult, yet not impossible. The first thing I did was pray that God would help me through this crisis, making me stronger and restoring my self-esteem. I also relied on my friends, who gave me support and encouragement. Most importantly, I tried to keep on talking to myself daily. I told myself that I was a good person, no matter what the circumstances, and no matter what anyone thought. In the end, it just*

took hard work, help from others, and positive thinking to keep sane and keep my self-esteem afloat.

Maria's story demonstrates how losing a job had a negative impact on her life. But she learned a crucial lesson. Maria learned to separate her worth as a person from her job performance. She realized that she was a good person even though her options had been limited by losing her job.

■ Creating Meaning in Work

Work can be a major part of your quest for meaning, but it can also be a source of meaninglessness. Work can be an expression of yourself; it can be "love made visible" (Gibran, 1923, p. 27). It can be a way for you to be productive and to find enjoyment in daily life. Through your work you may be making a significant difference in the quality of your life or the lives of others, and this may give you real satisfaction. But work can also be devoid of any self-expressive value. It can be merely a means to survival and a drain on your energy. Instead of giving life meaning, it can actually be a destructive force that contributes to burnout and even an early death. Ask yourself: Is my work life-giving? Does it bring meaning to my life? If not, what can I do about it? Is my most meaningful activity — my true work — something I do away from the job?

If you find your work meaningless, what can you do about it? What can you do if, instead of energizing you, your job drains you physically and emotionally? What are your options if you feel stuck in a dead-end job? Are there some ways that you can constructively deal with the sources of dissatisfaction within your job? When might it be time for you to change jobs as a way of finding meaning?

One way to examine the issue of meaninglessness and dissatisfaction in work is to look at how you really spend your time. It would be useful to keep a running account for a week to a month of what you do and how you relate to each of your activities. Which of them are draining you, and which are energizing you? While you may not be able to change everything about your job that you don't like, you might be surprised by the significant changes you can make to increase your satisfaction. People often adopt a passive and victimlike position in which they complain about everything and dwell on those aspects that they cannot change. Instead, a more constructive approach is to focus on those factors within your job that you can change.

Perhaps you can redefine the hopes you have for the job. Of course, you may also be able to think of the satisfactions you'd most like to aim for in a job and then consider whether another job more clearly meets your needs and what steps you must take to obtain it. You might be able to find ways of advancing within your present job, making new contacts, or acquiring the skills that eventually will enable you to move on.

Although making changes in your present job might increase your satisfaction in the short term, the time may come when these resources no longer work and you find yourself stuck in a dead-end job that leads toward frustration. Changing jobs as a way to create meaning is possible, but you have to be prepared to pay the price. Changing jobs might increase your satisfaction with work, but changing jobs after a period of years can entail even more risk and uncertainty than making your first job selection.

You may be enthusiastic about some type of work for years and yet eventually become dissatisfied because of the changes that occur within you. With these changes comes the possibility that a once-fulfilling job will become monotonous and draining. If you outgrow your job, you can learn new skills and in other ways increase your options. Because your own attitudes are crucial, when a feeling of dissatisfaction sets in, it's wise to spend time rethinking what you want from a job and how you can most productively use your talents. Look carefully at how much the initiative rests with you—your expectations, your attitudes, and your sense of purpose and perspective.

Changing Careers in Midlife

Being aware of options can be an important asset at midlife. Most of the people we know have changed their jobs several times; you might think about whether this pattern fits any people you know. And whether or not you've reached middle age, ask yourself about your own beliefs and attitudes toward changing careers. Although making large changes in our lives is rarely easy, it can be a good deal harder if our own attitudes and fears are left unquestioned and unexamined.

A common example of midlife change is the woman who decides to return to college or the job market after her children reach high school age. Many community colleges and state universities are enrolling women who realize that they would like to develop new facets of themselves. This phenomenon is not unique to women. Many middle-age men are re-entry students pursuing an advanced degree or a new degree. Some men quit a job they've had for years, even if they're successful, because they want new challenges. Men often define themselves by the work they do, and work thus becomes a major source of the purpose in their lives. If they feel successful in their work, they may feel successful as persons. If they become stagnant in work, they may feel that they are ineffectual in other areas. People sometimes decide on a career change even as they approach late adulthood.

Thomas Bonacum was drafted into the army at age 21 and became a drill instructor. After leaving the army, Tom completed his degree in engineering, which led to a job as an industrial engineer. A few years later he was laid off and then joined the police department. During the time he was a police officer, he returned to college to get another degree in criminal justice. He became a police sergeant and eventually taught criminal justice for four years in the police academy during his 22 years in police work.

After the death of his wife of 35 years, "Father Tom" made a significant change of careers. With the support and encouragement of his four grown children, he entered the seminary in his late fifties and was ordained as a Catholic priest at age 60.

At age 77, Father Tom is now retired, yet he still keeps active in the church and conducts services on weekends at an Indian reservation. Because of his varied and rich life experiences, people find it easy to relate to him. He is able to empathize with both the joys and the struggles of his parishioners.

Father Tom is an example of a person who was able to translate a dream into reality. When he graduated from high school, he tried to become a priest but discovered that he wasn't ready for some of the people in church, and they were not ready for him. He exemplifies a man who was willing to make career changes throughout his life and who dared to pursue what might have seemed like an impossible career choice. Many of us would not even conceive of such a drastic career change, yet Father Tom not only entertained this vision but also realized his dream.

For many it may be extremely risky and seemingly unrealistic to give up their job, even if they hate it, because it provides them with a measure of financial security. This is especially true during economically difficult times. The costs involved in achieving optimal job satisfaction may be too high. People might choose to stay with a less-than-desirable career yet at the same time discover other avenues for satisfaction. People who feel stuck in their jobs would do well to ask themselves these questions: Does the personal dissatisfaction outweigh the financial rewards? Is the price of mental anguish, which may have resulted in physical symptoms, worth the price of keeping this job?

Retirement

Many people look forward to retirement as a time for them to take up new projects. Others fear this prospect and wonder how they will spend their time if they are not working. The real challenge of this period, especially for those who retire early, is to find a way to remain active in a meaningful way. Some people consciously choose early retirement because they have found more significant and valuable pursuits. For other people, however, retirement does not turn out as expected, and it can be traumatic. Some questions to raise are: How can people who have relied largely on their job for meaning or structure in their lives deal with having much time and little to do? Must they lose their sense of purpose and value apart from their occupation?

Ray, a 73-year-old retired person, worked for 32 years as a salesman for a large dairy company. Here is Ray's description of his experience with work and retirement.

I loved my work. My job was my life. I looked forward to going to work, I liked helping people, and I thrived on the challenges of my career. I worked for 50 hours a week, and at age 57 I stopped very abruptly. While I had made some plans for my financial retirement, I was not prepared for the emotional toll that not working would take on me. My work was my identity, and it helped me to feel worthwhile. For at least two years, I did not know what to do with myself. I sat around and began feeling depressed. It took me some time to adjust to this new phase in my life, but eventually I began to feel that I mattered. With the help of some friends I began to take on small jobs outside the home. I managed rentals, did repair work, and did some volunteer work

at my church. Simply getting out of the house every day gave me another opportunity to contribute, which changed my attitude.

Today, at 73, I can honestly say that I like my life. Leisure is something I value now, rather than fearing it, which was the case in my younger years. There are plenty of work projects to keep me busy. There are always things to fix, work to be done in my shop, and plenty of chores. I don't seem to run out of things to do. Fortunately, I love fishing and golfing. Each year I go on several fishing trips, and my wife and I do a lot of traveling. By being active in the church, I've learned the value of fellowship and sharing with friends. I've found that I don't have to work 50 hours a week to be a productive human being. Just because I'm retired doesn't mean that I want to sit in a rocking chair most of the day. While I retired from my career, I have not retired from life.

Although many people take early retirement in their fifties, retirement generally comes later in life than was the case a couple of decades ago. Most people who are over 65 will continue to find some form of work, even if they decide to retire from a full-time job. They may work part time, serve as community volunteers, become consultants, or become self-employed. People in their sixties and seventies may seek work not only because they want to feel a sense of purpose but because they want to support themselves for greatly elongated later lives (Sheehy, 1995).

Retirement can usher in new opportunities to redesign your life and tap unused potentials, or it can be a coasting period where people simply mark time until their end. While some people thrive on retirement and find ways to be productive and enjoy their leisure, others feel threatened by it and see retirement as being "put out to pasture," which was true for Ray when he first retired.

A couple who did not deal well with retirement are Leona and Marvin. Both had very active careers and retired relatively early. They began to spend most of their time with each other. After about two years they grew to dislike each other's company. They both began to have physical symptoms and became overly preoccupied with their health. Leona chronically complained that Marvin did not talk to her, to which he usually retorted, "I have nothing to say, and you should leave me alone." They were referred by their physician for marital counseling. One of the outcomes of this counseling was that they both secured part-time work. They found that by spending time apart they had a greater interest in talking to each other about their experiences at work. They also began to increase their social activities and started to develop some friendships, both separately and together. Marvin and Leona recognized that they had retired too early from life as well as from work.

Just because people no longer work at a job does not mean that they have to cease being active. Many options are open to retired people who would like to stay active in meaningful ways. This is the time for them to get involved with the projects they have so often put on the back burner due to their busy schedules. A high school teacher who retired at 55 is now making wooden toys for underprivileged children with a group of men. This offers both companionship and doing something productive for those in need. What is essential is for retirees to keep themselves vital as physical, psychological, and social beings. Some other ways retired people can stay active involve:

- going back to school to take classes simply for interest or to prepare themselves for a new career
- becoming an integral part of community activities
- sharing their expertise, experiences, and wisdom with others
- becoming more interested in and caring for their grandchildren
- taking trips to places that they have wanted to see
- visiting relatives and friends
- taking time for more physical activity
- cultivating hobbies that they have neglected
- joining a senior citizens' center

This list is not exhaustive, and you can probably add to it.

Retirees do have choices and can create meaning in their lives. They may discover that retirement is not an end but rather a new beginning. One 93-year-old woman, who had lived alone since her husband died until a year ago when she found it necessary to have a live-in caretaker assist her and do routine chores in the house, has a routine that involves talking with friends, watching her favorite shows on television, and doing crossword puzzles. When her grandchildren ask her if she isn't lonely, she quickly responds by letting them know that she enjoys her solitude and that her days are full. She likes not having to answer to anyone but herself, and she looks forward to each day. She doesn't brood over the past, nor does she wish that things had been different. Instead, she accepts both her accomplishments and her mistakes, and she still finds life meaningful.

The Place of Work and Leisure in Your Life

One way to look at the place that work and leisure occupy in your life is to consider how you divide up your time. In an average day, most people spend about eight hours sleeping, another eight hours working, and the other eight hours in routines such as eating, traveling to work, and leisure. If your work is something that you enjoy, then at least half of your waking existence is spent in meaningful activities. Yet if you dread getting up and hate going to work, those eight hours can easily have a negative impact on the other eight hours you are awake.

■ Work and the Meaning of Your Life

If you expect your work to be a primary source of meaning but feel that your life isn't as rich with meaning as you'd like, you may be saying, "If only I had a job that I liked, *then* I'd be fulfilled." This type of thinking can lead you to believe that somehow the secret of finding purpose in your life depends on something outside yourself.

If you decide that you must remain in a job that allows little scope for personal effort and satisfaction, you may need to accept the fact that you won't find much meaning in the hours you spend on the job. It's important, then, to be aware of the effects that your time spent on the job have on the rest of your life and to minimize them. More positively, it's crucial to find something outside your job that fulfills your need for recognition, significance, productivity, and excitement. By doing so, you may develop a sense of your true work as something different from what you're paid to do.

Your job may provide you with the means for the productive activities you engage in away from the job, whether they take the form of hobbies, creative pursuits, volunteer work, or spending time with friends and family. One high school teacher we know finds himself discouraged over how little his students are interested in learning. Rather than expecting to get all his rewards from teaching, he finds meaning in making things and remodeling his house. He loves to travel, work on antiques, and read. Although he enjoys aspects of his teaching profession, he finds many of his rewards outside the classroom. If this person didn't find his own rewards, many that are beyond his job, he would soon feel trapped in an unfulfilling job. The point is to turn things around so that you are the master rather than the victim of your job. Too many people are so negatively affected by their job that their frustration and sense of emptiness spoil their eating, leisure time, family life, sex life, and relationships with friends. For some, job dissatisfaction can be so great that it results in physical or psychological illness. If you can re-assume control of your own attitudes toward your job and find dignity and pride elsewhere in your life, you may be able to lessen these negative effects. Seeking counseling is one means to achieve greater control of your life. It can be an excellent way for you to deal with the frustrating and negative effects that work has on you and those around you. Counseling often helps people recognize the stagnant roles they are

caught up in both at work and in their personal relationships — and then assists them in creating more satisfying ways of being.

■ Leisure and the Meaning of Your Life

Work alone does not generally result in fulfillment. Even rewarding work takes energy, and most people need some break from it. Leisure is "free time," the time that we control and can use for ourselves. Whereas work requires a certain degree of perseverance and drive, play requires the ability to let go, to be spontaneous, and to avoid getting caught in the trap of being obsessed with what we "should" be doing. Leisure implies flowing with the river rather than pushing against it and making something happen. Compulsiveness dampens the enjoyment of leisure time, and planned spontaneity is almost a contradiction in terms.

The balance between work and leisure depends on the needs of the individual. Some people schedule leisure activities in such a manner that they actually miss the point of recreation. There are those people who "work hard at having a good time." Others become quickly bored when they are not doing something. For Bob and Jill, leisure is more of a burden than a joy. He is a laborer, she is a hairstylist, and both of them work hard all week. They say they like a weekend trip to the river, but their "vacation" includes driving in a car with two whiny children who constantly ask when they will get there. After coping with traffic, they often feel more stressed once they return home from the river. They need to assess whether their leisure is providing them with what they want.

As a couple, we attribute different meanings to our leisure time. I (Jerry) tend to plan most of the things in my life, including my leisure time. I often combine work and leisure. Until recently, I seemed to require less leisure than some people, because most of my satisfactions in life came from my work. Many of my "hobbies" are still work-related, and although my scope tends to be somewhat narrow, this has been largely by choice. I am aware that I have had trouble with unstructured time. I am quite certain that leisure has represented a personal threat; as if any time unaccounted for is not being put to the best and most productive use. However, I am learning how to appreciate the reality that time is not simply to be used in doing, producing, accomplishing, and moving mountains. Although it is a lesson that I am learning relatively late in life, I am increasingly relishing times of being and experiencing, as well as time spent on accomplishing tasks. Experiencing sunsets, watching the beauty in nature, and being open to what moments can teach me are ways of using time that I am coming to cherish. Although work is still a very important part of my life, I am realizing that this is only a *part* of my life, not the totality of it. In essence, I am learning the importance of making time for leisure pursuits, which are essential for revitalization.

Marianne, on the other hand, wants and needs unstructured and spontaneous time for unwinding. I (Marianne) am uncomfortable when schedules are imposed on me. I don't particularly like to make detailed life plans, for this gets in the way of my relaxing. Although I plan for trips and times of recreation, I don't like to have everything I am going to do on the trip planned in advance. I like the element of surprise. It feels good to flow with moments and let things happen rather than working hard at making things happen. Also, I don't particularly like to combine work and leisure. For me, work involves considerable responsibility, and it is hard for me to enjoy leisure if it is tainted with the demands of work, or if I know that I will soon have to function in a professional role.

The objectives of planning for a career and planning for creative use of leisure time are basically the same: to help us develop feelings of self-esteem, reach our potential, and improve the quality of our lives. If we do not learn how to pursue interests apart from work, we may well face a crisis when we retire. In fact, some writers have cited evidence that many people die soon after their retirement (Joy, 1990; Siegel, 1988, 1989). If we do plan for creative ways to use leisure, we can experience both joy and continued personal growth.

■ A Couple Who Are Able to Balance Work and Leisure

Judy and Frank have found a good balance between work and leisure. Although they both enjoy their work, they have also arranged their lives to make time for leisure.

Judy and Frank were married when she was 16 and he was 20. They now have two grown sons and a couple of grandchildren. At 59 Frank works for an electrical company as a lineman, a job he has held for close to 35 years. Judy, who is now 55, delivers meals to schools.

Judy went to work when her two sons were in elementary school. Although she felt no financial pressure to do so, she took the job because she liked the extras their family could afford with her salary. Because she was efficient as a homemaker, she felt that her days would not be filled with housework alone. She was interested in doing something away from home. Judy continues her work primarily because she likes the contact with both her co-workers and the children and adolescents whom she meets daily. She has a good way with children, and they respond well to her. She values the influence she has on them and the affection she receives from them. If she had her preference, Judy would work only three days a week instead of the five she now does. She would like more time to enjoy her grandchildren and would like a longer weekend.

Frank is satisfied with his work, and he looks forward to going to the job. Considering that he stopped his education at high school, he feels he has a good job that both pays well and offers many fringe benefits. Although he is a bright person, he expresses no ambition to increase his formal education. A few of the things Frank likes about his work are the companionship with his co-workers, the physical aspects of his job, the security it affords, and the routine. As a mechanically inclined person, he is both curious about and challenged by how things work, what makes them malfunction, and how to repair them. He fixes things not only on his job but also at home and for his neighbors.

Judy and Frank have separate interests and hobbies, yet they also spend time together. Both of them are hardworking, and they have achieved success financially and personally. They feel pleased about their success, since they can see the fruits of their labor. They spend most of their weekends at their mountain cabin, which both of them helped build. He fishes, hikes, jogs, rides his motorcycle, cuts wood, fixes the house, visits with friends, and watches ball games on TV. She is talented in arts and crafts, repairing the cars, housepainting, and preparing delicious meals. Together they enjoy their grandchildren, their friends, and themselves.

Judy and Frank enjoy their work life and their leisure life, both as individuals and as a couple. A challenge that many of us will face is finding ways of using our leisure as well as they do. In a high-technology age, the question of how we can creatively use our increased leisure time must be addressed. Just as our work can have either a positive or a negative influence on our life, so, too, can leisure.

➤ *Time Out for Personal Reflection*

1. List a few of the most important benefits that you get (or expect to get) from work or college.

   _____

   _____

   _____

   _____

2. How do you typically spend your leisure time?

   _____

   _____

   _____

   _____

3. Are there any ways that you'd like to spend your leisure time differently?

   _____

   _____

   _____

   _____

4. What nonwork activities have made you feel creative, happy, or energetic?

   _____

   _____

   _____

   _____

5. Could you obtain a job that would incorporate some of the activities you've just listed? Or does your job already account for them?

   _____

   _____

_____

_____

6. What do you think would happen to you if you couldn't work? Write what first comes to mind.

_____

_____

_____

_____

Chapter Summary

Some people are motivated to go to college because it offers opportunities for personal development and the pursuit of knowledge; others are in college primarily to attain their career objectives; and some go because they are avoiding making other choices in their lives. Clarifying your own reasons for being in college can be useful in the process of long-range career planning.

Choosing a career is best thought of as a process, not a one-time event. The term *career decision* is misleading, because it implies that we make one choice that we stay with permanently. Most of us will probably have several occupations over our lifetimes, which is a good argument for a general education. If we prepare too narrowly for a specialization, that job may become obsolete, as will our training. In selecting a career or an occupation, it is important to first assess our attitudes, abilities, interests, and values. The next step is to explore a wide range of occupational options to see what jobs would best fit our personality. Becoming familiar with Holland's six personality types is an excellent way to consider the match between your personality style and the work alternatives you are considering. Choosing an occupation too soon can be risky, because our interests change as we move into adulthood. Passively falling into a job rather than carefully considering where we might best find meaning and satisfaction can lead to dissatisfaction and frustration.

Because we devote about half of our waking hours to our work, it behooves us to actively choose a form of work that can express who we are as a person. Much of the other half of our waking time can be used for leisure. With the trend toward increased leisure time, cultivating interests apart from work becomes a real challenge. Just as our work can profoundly affect all aspects of our lives, so, too, can leisure have a positive or negative influence on our existence. Our leisure time can be a source of boredom that drains us, or it can be a source of replenishment that energizes us and enriches our lives.

Although work is seen as an important source of meaning in our lives, it is not the job itself that provides this meaning. The satisfaction we derive depends to a great extent on the way we relate to our job, the manner in which we do it, and the meaning that we attribute to it. Perhaps the most important idea in this chapter is that we must look to ourselves if we're dissatisfied with our work. We can increase our power to change unfavorable circumstances by recognizing that we are mainly responsible for making our lives and our work meaningful. This theme is illustrated by the Serenity Prayer, which is certainly worth reflecting on to determine the sphere of our responsibility: "God grant me the serenity to accept the things I cannot change, the courage to change the things I can, and the wisdom to know the difference."

Activities and Exercises

1. Interview a person you know who dislikes his or her career or occupation. You might ask questions such as the following:

   - "If you don't find your job satisfying, why do you stay in it?"
   - "Do you feel that you have much of a choice about whether you'll stay with the job or take a new one?"
   - "What aspects of your job bother you the most?"
   - "How does your attitude toward your job affect the other areas of your life?"

2. Interview a person you know who feels fulfilled and excited by his or her work. Some questions you might ask are:

   - "What does your work do for you? What meaning does your work have for the other aspects of your life?"
   - "What are the main satisfactions for you in your work?"
   - "How do you think you would be affected if you could no longer pursue your career?"

3. You might interview your parents and determine what meaning their work has for them. How satisfied are they with the work aspects of their lives? How much choice do they feel they have in selecting their work? In what ways do they think the other aspects of their lives are affected by their attitudes toward work? After you've talked with them, determine how your attitudes and beliefs about work have been influenced by your parents. Are you pursuing a career that your parents can understand and respect? Is their reaction to your career choice important to you? Are your attitudes and values concerning work like or unlike those of your parents?

4. If your college has a vocational counseling program available to you, consider talking with a counselor about your plans. You might want to explore taking vocational interest and aptitude tests. If you're deciding on a career, consider discussing how realistic your vocational plans are. For example,

   - What are your interests?
   - Do your interests match the careers you're thinking about pursuing?
   - Do you have the knowledge you need to make a career choice?

- Do you have the aptitude and skills for the careers you have in mind?
- What are the future possibilities in the careers you're considering?

5. If you're leaning toward a particular occupation or career, seek out a person who is actively engaged in that type of work and arrange for a time to talk with him or her. Ask questions concerning the changes of gaining employment, the experience necessary, the satisfactions and drawbacks of the position, and so on. In this way, you can make the process of deciding on a type of work more realistic and perhaps avoid disappointment if your expectations don't match reality.

6. Most career guidance centers in colleges and universities now offer one or more computer-based programs to help students decide on a career. One popular program is known as the System of Interactive Guidance and Information, more commonly referred to as SIGI. This program assesses and categorizes your work values in these ten areas: income, prestige, independence, helping others, security, variety, leadership, leisure, working in one's field of interest, and early entry. Taking the SIGI will aid you in identifying specific occupations you might want to explore. SIGI Plus is an updated version of the original SIGI.

    Consider scheduling an appointment in the career counseling center at your college to participate in a computer-based occupational guidance program. In addition to SIGI, other programs are the Career Information System (CIS), the Guidance Information System (GIS), Choices, and Discover. Each of these programs develops lists of occupations to explore. Other instruments assess values. One is the Allport, Vernon, and Lindzey Study of Values. Another is Super's Work Values Inventory. Consider taking the Myers-Briggs Type Indicator, which is an inventory that indicates your temperament style. It may well be worthwhile to meet with a career counselor to discuss the value assessment instruments and the follow-up counseling that could be of use to you.

7. The abbreviated description of Holland's six personality types and the exercise in this chapter should not be thought of as a complete and accurate way to assess your personality. If you are interested in a more complete self-assessment method that also describes the relationship between your type and possible occupations or fields of study, we strongly recommend that you take Form R of the *Self-Directed Search* (Holland, 1994). The *Self-Directed Search* consists of a test as well as these booklets designed to accompany this test: (1) You and Your Career, (2) The Occupations Finder, (3) The Educational Opportunities Finder, (4) The Leisure Activities Finder, and (5) Assessment Booklet: A Guide to Educational and Career Planning. All of these resources are available from Psychological Assessment Resources, P. O. Box 998, Odessa, FL 33556 or telephone (1-800-331-8378).

8. Here are some steps you can take when exploring the choice of a major and a career. Place a check before each item you are willing to seriously consider. I am willing to:

_____   talk to an adviser about my intended major
_____   interview at least one instructor regarding selecting a major
_____   interview at least one person I know in a career that I am interested in

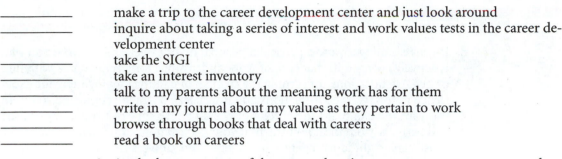

make a trip to the career development center and just look around

inquire about taking a series of interest and work values tests in the career development center

take the SIGI

take an interest inventory

talk to my parents about the meaning work has for them

write in my journal about my values as they pertain to work

browse through books that deal with careers

read a book on careers

9. Apply the seven steps of the career planning process to your own career planning. Set realistic goals to do one or more of the following or some other appropriate activity:

- Choose a major that most fully taps your interests and abilities.
- Take time to investigate a career by gathering further information.
- Develop contacts with people who can help you meet your goals.
- Take steps that will enable you to increase your exposure to a field of interest.

In your journal, write down at least a tentative plan for action. Begin by identifying some of the key factors associated with selecting a career. Write down the steps you are willing to take at this time. (Your plan will be most useful if you identify specific steps you are willing to take. Include seeking the help of others somewhere in your plan.)

10. In addition to visiting your counseling center for information about testing and counseling for career development, we strongly advise that you do some reading about the career decision-making process. Six books we highly recommend are: *What Color Is Your Parachute?* (Bolles, 1995); *Discover the Career within You* (Carney & Wells, 1995); three by Robert Lock (1996a, 1996b, & 1996c): *Taking Charge of Your Career Direction, Job Search,* and *Student Activities for Taking Charge of Your Career Direction and Job Search;* and *Occupational Information Overview* (Sharf, 1993). Lock describes a systematic, rational approach to the process of career decision making, and Carney and Wells focus on specific skills needed for career planning. Bolles provides many practical suggestions on ways to decide on a vocation. Besides books, you will find some useful information in the following three resource guides put out by the U.S. Department of Labor: *Guide for Occupational Exploration* (1979), *Dictionary of Occupational Titles* (4th ed., revised, 1991), and *Occupational Outlook Handbook, 1994–1995* (1994).

6

Your Body and Wellness

Wellness stresses positive health rather than merely the absence of disabling symptoms.

✔ *Prechapter Self-Inventory*

Use the following scale to respond: 4 = this statement is true of me *most* of the time; 3 = this statement is true of me *much* of the time; 2 = this statement is true of me *some* of the time; 1 = this statement is true of me *almost none* of the time.

_____ 1. Touching and being touched are important to me.
_____ 2. The way I take care of my body expresses the way I feel about myself.
_____ 3. When I look in the mirror, I feel comfortable with my physical appearance.
_____ 4. When something ails me, I tend to want to treat the symptom rather than looking for the cause.
_____ 5. Making basic changes in my lifestyle to improve my health is not something I often think about.
_____ 6. My diet consists mainly of junk food.
_____ 7. Exercise is a priority in my life.
_____ 8. I dream a lot and am able to remember many of my dreams.
_____ 9. I see dreaming as a way to understand myself and to remain psychologically healthy.
_____ 10. If I had a personal problem I could not resolve by myself, I'd seek professional assistance.

Introduction

Your body is the primary subject of this chapter, but emotional and interpersonal factors play a role in maintaining physical well-being. Therefore, we take a holistic approach to wellness.

We begin the chapter by exploring the topic of accepting responsibility for your general state of wellness. We look at the ways your self-image is influenced by your perception of your body. We will explore how your bodily identity, which includes the way you experience yourself and express yourself through your body, affects your beliefs, decisions, and feelings about yourself. If you look at your body, you'll see that it reflects some significant choices. Do you take care of the physical you? How comfortable are you with your body? How do your feelings and attitudes about it affect your choices in areas such as self-worth, sexuality, and love? How aware are you of the impact your emotional state has on your physical state? How does the quality of your relationships affect your physical health?

Next, we explore the goal of wellness as a lifestyle choice that enhances body and mind. We take up subjects such as making decisions about diet, exercise, and rest and ultimately accepting responsibility for your body. Although you might readily say that you desire the state of wellness as a personal goal, many of us have experienced frustrations and discouragement in attaining this goal. Wellness is not something that merely happens to you. It is the result of being consciously aware of what your physical and psychological well-being entails and making a commitment to wellness. Wellness is more than the absence of illness. In many ways, the medical model ignores wellness and focuses on the removal of symptoms, which results in a negative view of health. Relatively few physicians ask their patients questions about aspects of their lifestyles that may have contributed to their health problems.

An honest examination of the choices you are making about your body and your overall wellness can reveal a great deal concerning your feelings about your life. If you aren't taking care of your body, what beliefs and attitudes may be getting in the way? What resources do you require to begin modifying those parts of your lifestyle that affect your bodily well-being?

We look at the role of rest and sleep, exercise, diet and nutrition, and spirituality in holistic health. Because we see dreams as a path to self-understanding and to wellness, dreaming is a topic in this chapter. At times coping effectively with personal problems calls for professional help. Counseling can help you understand yourself. This too is a path to both psychological and physical wellness. In this chapter we invite you to look at the full range of choices available to you to help you stay healthy.

Wellness and Life Choices

The concept of wellness fits into a holistic view of health. Traditional medicine focuses on identifying symptoms of illness and curing disease. By contrast, *holistic health* focuses on all facets of human functioning. It emphasizes the intimate relationship between our body and all the other aspects of ourselves — psychological, social, intellectual, and spiritual. Wellness is an active process consisting of conscious choices we make in fashioning a lifestyle where these human dimensions are integrated. And it stresses positive health rather than merely the absence of disabling symptoms. Just as there are many degrees of being ill, there are degrees of wellness.

Donatelle, Snow-Harter, and Wilcox (1995) state that if you are living a wellness lifestyle you are moving toward more deliberate, conscious actions to create the best self possible within the limitations of your situation. They emphasize three aspects that characterize a wellness lifestyle:

- assuming personal responsibility for your actions and the quality of your health
- having a genuine concern for others and being tolerant of imperfections in others
- being willing to devote time and energy to developing a sound basis for making good decisions about health

And what are the benefits of adopting a wellness lifestyle? Donatelle and her colleagues (1995) list these important long-term benefits:

- improved cardiovascular efficiency
- increased muscular tone, strength, flexibility, and endurance
- reduced risk for injuries

- improved sense of self-control, self-efficacy, and self-esteem
- improved management and control of stress
- improved outlook on life
- improved interpersonal relationships
- decreased mortality (death) and morbidity (illness) from infections and chronic diseases

It is clear that wellness is a lifestyle choice rather than a one-time decision. Wellness is a process that involves identifying personal goals, prioritizing your goals and values, identifying any barriers that might prevent you from reaching your goals, making an action plan, and then committing yourself to following through on your plans to reach your goals.

In their *Wellness Workbook,* Travis and Ryan (1994) describe wellness as a bridge supported by two piers — self-responsibility and love. They write that self-responsibility and love flow from the appreciation that we are not merely separate individuals, nor are we simply the sum of separate parts. Instead, we are integrated beings, and we are united in one energy system with everything else in creation. For them, health is best conceived of on an illness-wellness continuum that ranges from premature death on one side to high-level wellness on the other side. The essence of wellness is captured in these brief statements:

- Wellness is a choice — a decision you make to move toward optimal health.
- Wellness is a way of life — a lifestyle you design to achieve your highest potential for well-being.
- Wellness is a process — a developing awareness that there is no end point but that health and happiness are possible in each moment, here and now.
- Wellness is an efficient channeling of energy — energy received from the environment, transformed within you, and sent on to affect the world outside.
- Wellness is the integration of body, mind, and spirit — the appreciation that everything you do and think and feel and believe has an impact on your state of health.
- Wellness is the loving acceptance of yourself. (p. xiv)

Schafer (1992) describes wellness as living at your highest possible level as a whole person. People who are functioning at an optimal level are characterized by the absence of illness and low illness risk, maximum energy, full enjoyment of life, the capacity to make the most of their abilities, satisfying relationships, and commitment to the common good. According to Schafer, behavioral-medicine studies clearly demonstrate that wellness is acquired and maintained by healthful daily habits, some of which are sleep, exercise, ways of dealing with anger and tension, work satisfaction, and the presence of energizing visions for yourself and the world. His guiding philosophy about wellness can be summarized in these four suggestions:

- Allow yourself to have visions and dreams, some of which have social significance or will benefit others in significant ways.
- Be willing to work hard, sometimes with others, to make these dreams and visions a reality.
- Balance hard work and play, care of the body and spirit, and intimate relationships.
- Enjoy the process of living. (p. 511)

■ Wellness as an Active Choice

Wellness entails a lifelong process of taking care of our needs on all levels of functioning, and it implies that we see ourselves as constantly growing and developing. Well people are committed to creating a lifestyle that contributes to taking care of their physical selves, challenging themselves intellectually, expressing the full range of their emotions, finding rewarding interpersonal relationships, and searching for a meaning that will give direction to their lives.

A combination of factors contributes to our sense of well-being. Thus, a holistic approach must pay attention to specific aspects of our lifestyle, including: how we work and play, how we relax, how and what we eat, how we think and feel, how we keep physically fit, our relationships with others, and our spiritual needs. One of our friends, Ron Coley, captures the essence of living a balanced life when he talks about the importance of REDS (rest, exercise, diet, and spirituality) as the keys to health. When something is amiss in our lives, we are generally failing to take proper care of one of these basic human dimensions. Maintaining a balanced life involves attending to our physical, emotional, social, mental, and spiritual needs. To the degree that we ignore or neglect one of these areas, we pay a price in terms of optimal functioning. We agree with Ron's assertion that if you pay attention to the balance among these four critical areas the general result is wellness.

Dr. Bernie Siegel, a psychologically and spiritually oriented physician, promotes a similar viewpoint. Siegel (1988) believes that illness serves some function and makes sense if we look at what is going on with people who become physically sick. He investigates the quality of their psychological and spiritual lives as the key to understanding the mystery of illness and fostering health. From Siegel's perspective, when we are not meeting our emotional and spiritual needs, we are setting ourselves up for physical illness. Happy people don't get sick. In his work with cancer patients, Siegel finds that one of the most common precursors of cancer is a traumatic loss or a feeling of emptiness in one's life. He also finds that depressed people — those "going on strike from life" — are at much greater risk for contracting cancer than are nondepressed people. One of his patients who developed cancer shortly after her children left home wrote to him, "I had an empty place in me, and cancer grew to fill it" (p. 81). As a physician, Siegel views his role not simply as finding the right treatments for a disease but also as helping his patients resolve emotional conflicts, find an inner reason for living, and release the healing resources within.

The popularity of Siegel's books and videotapes points to the power within us to keep ourselves well and heal ourselves. Scores of self-help books and home videos address the subjects of stress management, exercise, meditation, diet, nutrition, weight control, control of smoking and drinking, and wellness medicine. We are beginning to realize the value of preventive medicine, and wellness clinics, nutrition centers, and exercise clubs are becoming increasingly popular.

It is beyond the scope of this book to prescribe a lifestyle that will lead to wellness. Our purpose is to introduce you to the issues involved in wellness, to encourage you to think about the priority you are placing on physical and psychological well-being, and to invite you to consider whether you want to make any changes in your lifestyle to promote wellness.

■ One Man's Wellness Program

To make this discussion of wellness more concrete, we'll provide a case illustration of a client, whom we'll call Kevin, who was in one of our therapeutic groups. We mentioned Kevin earlier in the chapter on gender roles (Chapter 4). When we first met Kevin in the group, he struck us as being closed off emotionally, rigid, stoic, and defensive. For many years he had thrown himself completely into his work as an attorney. Although his family life was marked by tension and bickering with his wife, he attempted to block out the stress at home by burying himself in his law cases and by excelling in his career. Here is his own account of his life.

> When I reached middle age, I began to question how I wanted to continue living. My father suffered a series of heart attacks. I watched my father decline physically, and this jolted me into the realization that both my father's time and my own time were limited. I finally went for a long-overdue physical examination and discovered that I had high blood pressure, that my cholesterol level was abnormally high, and that I was at relatively high risk of having a heart attack. I also learned that several of my relatives had died of heart attacks. I decided that I wanted to reverse what I saw as a self-destructive path. After talking with a physician, I decided to change my patterns of living in several ways. I was overeating, my diet was not balanced, I was consuming a great deal of alcohol to relax, I didn't get enough sleep, and I was "too busy" to do any physical exercise. My new decision involved making contacts with friends. I learned to enjoy playing tennis and racquetball on a regular basis. I took up jogging. If I didn't run in the morning, I felt somewhat sluggish during the day. I radically changed my diet in line with suggestions from my physician. As a result, I lowered both my cholesterol level and my blood pressure without the use of medication; I also lost 20 pounds and worked myself into excellent physical shape. Getting into personal counseling was extremely helpful, because my sessions with a counselor helped me make some basic changes in the way I approach life and also helped me put things into perspective.

Let's underscore a few key points in Kevin's case. First of all, he took the time to seriously reflect on the direction he was going in life. He did not engage in self-deception; rather, he admitted that the way he was living was not healthy. On finding out that heart disease was a part of his family history, he did not shrug his shoulders and assume an indifferent attitude. Instead, he made a decision to take an active part in changing his life on many levels. He cut down on drinking and relied less on alcohol as an escape. He changed his patterns of eating, sleeping, and exercise, which resulted in his feeling better physically and psychologically. Although he was still committed to his law practice, he pursued it less compulsively. He realized that he had missed play in his life, and he sought a better balance between work and play.

With the help of counseling, Kevin realized the high price he was paying for bottling up emotions of hurt, sadness, anger, guilt, and joy. Although he did not give up his logical and analytical dimensions, he added to his range as a person by allowing himself to express what he was feeling. He learned that unexpressed emotions would find expression in some form of physical illness or symptom. Kevin learned the value of taking his emotions seriously rather than denying them. He continued to question the value of living exclusively by logic and calculation, in both his professional and personal life. As a consequence, he cultivated friendships and let others who were significant to him know that he wanted to be closer to them. Kevin could have asked his physician for a prescription and could have assumed a passive stance toward curing his illness. Instead, he was challenged to review his life to determine what steps he could take to get more from the time he had to live. A person who knew him only casually commented one day that he seemed so much different than he had a year before. She remembered him as being uptight, unfriendly, uncommunicative, angry-looking, and detached. She was surprised at his changes, and she used adjectives such as *warm, open, relaxed, talkative,* and *outgoing* to describe him.

■ Accepting Responsibility for Your Body

The American public is becoming increasingly informed about exercise programs, dietary habits, and ways to manage stress. More health insurance companies are providing payment for preventive medicine as well as remediation; one does not need to look far to find a preventive health clinic. Many communities provide a wide variety of programs aimed at helping people improve the quality of their lives by finding a form of exercise that suits them.

Major health insurance companies take surveys of their clients' lifestyles to identify positive and negative habits that affect their overall health. One of our daughters signed up for health insurance with a major company. She was asked to fill out a series of surveys at regular intervals to monitor her health practices. This company also presented her with a book describing many common health problems and ways to prevent them. This move is certainly motivated by the company's desire to reduce payments to subscribers. However, another motivation might well be a desire to assist people in developing sound health habits that will lead to prevention of serious health problems.

Doctors often find that people they see are more interested in getting pills and in removing their symptoms than in changing a stressful lifestyle. Some of these patients see themselves as victims of their ailments rather than as being responsible for them. Some physicians resist prescribing pills to alleviate the symptoms of what they see as a problematic lifestyle. Psychologically oriented physicians emphasize the role of *choice* and *responsibility* as critical determinants of our physical and psychological well-being. In their practice these doctors challenge their patients to look at what they are doing to their bodies through lack of exercise, the substances they take in, and other damaging behavior. While they may prescribe medication to lower a person's extremely high blood pressure, they inform the patient that medications can do only so much and that what is needed is a radical change in lifestyle. The patient is encouraged to share with the physician the responsibility for maintaining wellness.

Many popular books on the market today reveal an interest among the general public in natural methods of healing. Increasingly, people are showing concern over the possible side effects of drugs and medications, and they are taking steps to educating themselves about prescription drugs. *Prescription for Nutritional Healing* (Balch & Balch, 1990) is a self-help guide that educates people on the value of drug-free remedies such as vitamins, minerals, herbs, and food supplements. Other books that deal with drug side effects and warnings include: *Complete Guide to Prescription and Non-Prescription Drugs* (Griffith, 1990), *The PDR Family Guide to Women's Health and Prescription Drugs* (Physicians' Desk Reference, 1994), and *Worst Pills, Best Pills* (Wolfe, Fugate, Hulstrand, & Kamimoto, 1988). These books offer information to consumers about the uses and potentially harmful side effects of medications and allow consumers to share with their physicians the responsibility for the proper use of medicine. Consumers are encouraged to question physicians about the medications they prescribe. While many people prefer to turn over complete authority for health care to their physicians, the books on the market give signs that many people are taking a more active role and assuming more responsibility in their health care.

Whether you see yourself as a passive victim or an active agent in maintaining your health can make a world of difference. If you believe you simply catch colds or are ill-fated enough to get sick, and if you don't see what you can do to prevent bodily illnesses, your body is controlling you. But if you recognize that the way you lead your life (including accepting responsibility for what you consume, how you exercise, and the stresses you put yourself under) has a direct bearing on your physical and psychological well-being, you can be in control of your body. If you listen to yourself, you will be able to make choices about your health care that enhance the quality of your life. Take a moment to answer this question: "Do I control my body, or does my body control me?"

► *Time Out for Personal Reflection*

1. Here are some common rationalizations people use for not changing patterns of behavior that affect their bodies. Look over these statements and decide what ones, if any, you use. What others do you sometimes use that are not on this list?

_____	I don't have time to exercise every day.
_____	No matter how I try to lose weight, nothing seems to work.
_____	I sabotage myself, and others sabotage me, in my attempts to lose weight.
_____	I'll stop smoking as soon as my life becomes less stressful.
_____	When I have a vacation, I'll relax.
_____	Even though I drink a lot (or use other drugs), it calms me down and has never interfered with my life.
_____	I need a drink (or a marijuana cigarette) to relax.
_____	Food isn't important to me; I eat anything I can grab fast.
_____	I simply don't have time to eat three balanced meals a day.
_____	Food has gotten so expensive, I just can't afford to eat decent meals anymore.

_____ If I stop smoking, I'll surely gain weight.

_____ I simply cannot function without several cups of coffee.

_____ If I don't stop smoking I might get lung cancer or die a little sooner, but we all have to go sometime.

What other statements could you add to this list?

_____

_____

_____

_____

2. Complete the following sentences with the first word or phrase that comes to mind:

   a. One way I abuse my body is _____

   b. One way I neglect my body is _____

   c. When people notice my physical appearance, I think that _____

   _____

   d. When I look at my body in the mirror, I _____

   e. I could be healthier if only _____

   f. One way I could cut down the stress in my life is _____

   _____

   g. If I could change one aspect of my body it would be my _____

   h. One way that I relax is _____

   i. I'd describe my diet as _____

   j. For me, exercising is _____

   _____

Your Bodily Identity

We are limited in how much we can actually change our body, but there is much we can do to work with the material we have. First, however, we must pay attention to what we are expressing about ourselves through our body, so we can determine whether we *want* to change our bodily identity. This involves increasing our awareness of how we experience our body through touch and movement. As you read this section, reflect on how well you know your body and how comfortable you are with it. Then you can decide about changing your body image—for example, by losing weight or gaining weight.

■ Experiencing and Expressing Yourself through Your Body

Some of us are divorced from our bodies; the body is simply a vehicle that carries us around. If someone asks you what you are thinking, you are likely to come up with a quick answer. If asked what you are experiencing and sensing in your body, however, you may be at a loss for words. Yet your body can be eloquent in its expression of who you are. Much of our life history is revealed through our bodies. We can see evidence of stress and strain in people's faces. Some people speak with a tight jaw and seem to literally choke off their feelings. Others typically walk with a slouch and shuffle their feet, expressing their hesitation in presenting themselves to the world. Their bodies may be communicating their low self-esteem and their fear of interacting with others. As you look at your body, what feelings do you have? What story does your body tell about you?

Here are some ways that our bodies express our selves:

- The eyes can express life or emptiness.
- The mouth can be too tight or too loose.
- The neck can hold back expressions of anger or crying, as well as holding onto tensions.
- The chest can develop armor that inhibits the free flow of crying, laughing, and breathing.
- The diaphragm can restrict the expression of rage and pain.
- The abdomen can develop armor that is related to fear of attack.
- The pelvis can be rigid and asexual, or it can become a source of intense pleasure.

Unexpressed emotions do not simply disappear. The chronic practice of "swallowing" emotions can take a physical toll on your body and manifest itself in physical symptoms such as severe headaches, ulcers, digestive problems, and a range of other bodily dysfunctions. In counseling clients, we often see a direct relationship between a person's physical constipation and his or her emotional constipation. When people are successful in expressing feelings of hurt and anger, they often comment that they are finally no longer physically constipated. If we seal off certain emotions, such as grief and anger, we also keep ourselves from experiencing intense joy. Let's take a closer look at what it means to experience ourselves through our bodies.

Experiencing Your Body.   One way of experiencing your own body is by paying attention to your senses of touch, taste, smell, seeing, and hearing. Simply pausing and taking a few moments to be aware of how your body is interacting with the environment is a helpful way of learning to make better contact. For example, how often do you allow yourself to really taste and smell your food? How often are you aware of the tension in your body? How many times do you pause to smell and touch a flower? How often do you listen to the chirping of birds or the other sounds of nature? If these simple pleasures are important to us, we can increase our sensory experience by pausing more frequently to fully use all of our senses.

Enjoying our physical selves is something we often fail to make time for. Treating ourselves to a massage, for example, can be exhilarating and can give us clues to how alive we are physically. Dancing is yet another avenue through which we can enjoy our physical selves and express ourselves spontaneously. Dance is a popular way to teach people through movement to "own" all parts of their bodies and to express themselves more harmoniously. These are a few ways to become more of a friend and less of a stranger to your body. You can express your feelings through your body if you allow yourself to be in tune with your physical being.

The Importance of Touch.   Some people are very comfortable with touching themselves, with touching others, and with being touched by others. They require a degree of touching to maintain a sense of physical and emotional well-being. Other people show a great deal of discomfort in touching themselves or allowing others to be physical with them. They may bristle and quickly move away if they are touched accidentally. If such a person is embraced by another, he or she is likely to become rigid and unresponsive. For instance, in Jerry's family of origin there was very little touching among members. He found that he had to recondition himself to feel comfortable being touched by others and touching others. In contrast, Marianne grew up in a German family characterized by much more spontaneous touching. Between the two of us there are differences in the amount of touching that we seek and require.

Another example of attitudes toward touching is that of Marisa, a college student. She came from a family that freely touched, and she liked to touch and be touched. Marisa found out the hard way that not all people were as comfortable with touching as she was. When she spontaneously touched her female roommates, she noticed their discomfort and felt rebuffed. When they finally discussed the issue, she discovered that her roommates had misinterpreted her touching as a sign of sexual advances.

Some time ago I (Marianne) was teaching in Hong Kong and became friends with a college counselor. One day while we were walking, she spontaneously interlocked her arm with mine. Then she quickly pulled it back, looked embarrassed, and apologized profusely. Her apology went something like this: "I am very sorry. I know that you in America do not touch like this." I let her know that I, too, came from a culture where touching between females was acceptable and that I had felt very comfortable with her touching me. We discovered that we had had similar experiences of feeling rejected by American women who misunderstood our spontaneous touching.

In many cultures touching is a natural mode of expression; in others, touching is minimal and is regulated by clearly defined boundaries. Some cultures have taboos against touching strangers, against touching people of the same sex, against touching people of the opposite sex, or against touching in certain social situations. In spite of these individual and cultural differences, studies have demonstrated that physical contact is essential for healthy development of body and mind.

Harlow and Harlow (1966) studied the effects of maternal deprivation on monkeys. In these experiments the monkeys were separated from their mothers at birth and raised in isolation with artificial mothers. When young monkeys were raised under conditions of relatively complete social deprivation, they manifested a

range of symptoms of disturbed behavior. Infant monkeys reared in isolation during the first six months after birth showed serious inadequacies in their social and sexual behavior later in life. There are critical periods in development when physical stimulation is essential for normal development. Touching is important for developing in healthy ways physically, psychologically, socially, and intellectually.

In writing about touch deprivation, Travis and Ryan (1994) contend that it leads to a sense of alienation from ourselves and isolation from others. They point out that such deprivation results in boredom and lack of energy for life in general, sexual dysfunction, and unsatisfying relationships.

■ Your Body Image

We rarely come across people who are really satisfied with their physical appearance. Even when people receive compliments about the way they look, they may be quick to respond with "Thank you, but I need to lose some weight." Or, "I need to gain some weight." "I could be in better shape." "I need to exercise some more." "I feel a little flabby right now." It seems as though everyone is striving for the "perfect body," yet few people achieve it.

Your view of your body and the decisions you have made about it have much to do with the choices we will study in the rest of this book. In our view people are affected in a very fundamental way by how they perceive their body and how they think others perceive it. If you feel basically unattractive, unappealing, or physically inferior, these self-perceptions are likely to have a powerful effect on other areas of your life.

For example, you may be very critical of some of your physical characteristics; you may think that your ears are too big, that you're too short, or that you're not muscular enough. Or you may have some of these common self-defeating thoughts:

- "If I had a beautiful body, then I'd like myself."
- "Unless I have the ideal body, people won't like me."
- "There's really nothing nice about my body."
- "There's nothing I can do to change anything about my body."

Perhaps some part of you believes that others will not want to approach you because of your appearance. If you *feel* that you are basically unattractive, you may well tell yourself that others will see your defects and will not want to be with you. In this way you contribute to the reactions others have toward you by the messages you send them. You may be perceived by others as aloof, distant, or judgmental. Even though you may want to get close to people, you may also be frightened of the possibility of meeting with their rejection.

If something like this is true of you, we challenge you to look at the part you may be playing in contributing to the reactions you get from others. How does your state of mind influence both your view of yourself and the view others have of you? Do you take even less care of your body because you're unhappy with it? Why should others approach you if you continue to tell them that you are not worth approaching? Will others think more of you than you think of yourself?

You may say that there is little you can do to change certain aspects of your physical being such as your height or basic build. Yet you *can* look at the attitudes you have formed about these physical characteristics. How important are they to who you are? How has your culture influenced your beliefs about what constitutes the ideal body?

We are also prone to develop feelings of shame if we unquestioningly accept certain cultural messages about our bodies. As children and, even more so, as adolescents, many of us learn to associate parts of our body with shame. Small children may be oblivious to nudity and to their bodies, but as they run around nude and are made the objects of laughter and jokes by other children and by adults they gradually become more self-conscious. Sometimes the sense of shame remains with people into adulthood. The following brief case descriptions represent some typical difficulties:

- Donna painfully recalls that during her preadolescence she was much taller and more physically developed than her peers. She was often the butt of jokes by both boys and girls in her class. While she is no longer taller than most people around her, she still walks stoop-shouldered, for she still feels self-conscious and embarrassed over her body.
- In a group-counseling session, Tim finally shares his concern over the size of his penis, which he thinks is small. His anxiety about this has caused him extreme embarrassment when he has showered with other men, and it has inhibited him in

his sexual relations. He is convinced that women will laugh at him and find him sexually inadequate. He is very surprised and relieved when several other male members let him know that they also have had these concerns.

■ Herbert, a physically attractive young man, is highly self-conscious about his body, much to the surprise of those who know him. He seems to be in good physical condition, yet he gets very anxious when he gains even a pound. As a child he was overweight, and he developed a self-concept of being the "fat kid." Even though he changed his physique years ago, the fear of being considered fat still lurks around the corner.

Consider whether you, too, made some decisions about your body early in life or during adolescence that still affect you. Did you feel embarrassed about certain of your physical characteristics? As you matured physically, these characteristics might have changed — or become less important to others — yet you may still be stuck with some old perceptions and feelings. Even though others may think of you as an attractive person, you may react with suspicion and disbelief. If you continue to tell yourself that you are in some way inferior, your struggle to change your self-concept may be similar to that of Donna, Tim, or Herbert.

■ Weight and Your Body Image

From years of experience in reading student journals and counseling clients, we have concluded that many people are preoccupied with maintaining their "ideal weight." Although some people view themselves as too skinny and strive to gain weight, many more are looking for effective ways to lose weight. You may be one of these people and may find that your weight significantly affects the way you feel about your body. Perhaps you have said:

■ "I've tried every diet program there is, and I just can't seem to stick to one."
■ "I've lost extra pounds many times, only to put them on again."
■ "I'm too occupied with school to think about losing weight."
■ "I love to eat, and I hate to exercise."
■ "I don't particularly like the way I look, but it takes too much effort to change it."

We have noticed in our travels to Germany how the standard of ideal weight can differ from culture to culture. The same thin person who is viewed as attractive in the United States might well be seen as undernourished, skinny as a rail, and even somewhat sickly in Germany. A person with a certain amount of weight is generally considered attractive and healthy looking in Germany. Toward the end of a visit to her hometown, Marianne knows that it is time for her to lose weight when people there tell her, "You look good and well-nourished."

It may also help to examine how unrealistic societal standards regarding the ideal body can lead to the perpetual feeling that you are never physically adequate. For example, our society places tremendous pressure on women to be thin. Messages from the media reveal that thinness and beauty are often equated. For the many women who accept these cultural norms, the price they often pay is depression and loss of self-esteem. Some women are driven by perfectionistic standards that result in eating disorders. Anorexia and bulimia are frequently linked to the internalization of unrealistic standards that lead to negative self-perceptions and negative body images. Michelle's first-person account describing her struggle with *anorexia nervosa* illustrates how self-destructive striving for psychological and physical perfection can be.

> *I struggled with my eating disorder for quite a long time. When I was around 11 years old, I gradually began to lose weight for reasons that were a mystery even to me. I knew I was not slimming down to win the approval and acceptance of my peers at school, and I was not losing weight to feel fit and healthy. On the contrary, when my parents finally took me to the doctor to be examined for my weight loss, I was secretly hoping I would be diagnosed with some strange disease so I would receive everyone's attention and concern. I was consumed with guilt over the fact that I wanted my parents to worry about me, yet I continued to shed pounds. I vividly recall the moment my doctor explained that I had a disorder called* anorexia nervosa. *It was relatively unheard of at that time, and all I could think of was, "I hope I have this problem for a long time." Sounds pretty sick, huh? Well, I was sick, and just as a physical pain is the body's way of alerting one to a more serious problem, my anorexia was my psyche's way of alerting me to my deep emotional pain.*
>
> *For most of my life, I felt completely empty and emotionally dead inside. In retrospect, I am certain that the loss of my birthmother (who decided to relinquish me for adoption when I was an infant) laid the foundation for subsequent losses in my life to be internalized very deeply. Although I was not equipped as an infant with the verbal skills necessary to express my anguish and grief over this profound loss, I must have justified my mother's departure with the excruciating message that "I was not enough." This theme of loss and abandonment in my life undoubtedly contributed to my emotional emptiness. I proceeded through life feeling grossly inadequate as a human being and attempted to remedy this by transforming myself into a "perfect" child—a parent's dream come true! I strived to excel in virtually everything I attempted to ensure that I would be acceptable in the eyes of my parents. I couldn't risk losing my parent's affection and love, and my self-esteem was then so low that I believed that I had to accomplish extraordinary feats to be deemed as worthy as the average child. So I did. At home, not only did I clean my own room but I thoroughly cleaned the entire house. In school I was just as tenacious to please! My compulsion to overachieve got way out of hand. I had teachers apologizing to my parents that the best they could give me was an A+. At that time, my ego was so fragile that receiving a B would have probably pushed me over the edge. I would have most likely attempted suicide. It is no wonder that I developed anorexia at such a young age. I was a time bomb, long overdue to explode. I unconsciously, and perhaps even consciously, welcomed the onset of my eating disorder. Paradoxically, nearly starving myself to death, which might ordinarily be construed as a slow form of suicide, was in reality my only hope of saving my life and my soul. At a very basic level I felt emotionally and spiritually bankrupt, and my starved,*

emaciated body was truly a reflection of my starved, malnourished soul. I previously mentioned that I wanted to be sick for long time when I was initially diagnosed. As dysfunctional as that may sound, it now makes so much sense to me. I had such a deflated sense of myself that my anorexia gave me an identity; it gave me someone to be. It gave me one more "label" to wear, which I misinterpreted as dimension.

I started to make the most progress in my recovery when I could finally let go of the false security of these labels I had clung to for so many years. After a great deal of work in therapy, I was able to let go of some control and allow myself to experience just being an ordinary person.

I have accomplished a lot of things in my life that I am extremely proud of, but the one thing I am most proud of is that I have learned to be a real person who is comfortable making mistakes and being human. People often ask me if I fear becoming anorexic again. To that I respond, "No! I have no need to be anorexic anymore." Years ago I had no self-esteem. Hell! I had no "self" to even have esteem for! Today is a much different story. I don't need to self-destruct to be heard. I care too much about myself. I have developed a self that is worth caring about.

As the case of Michelle illustrates, it is easy to get trapped in self-destructive patterns of critical self-judgment. Being and feeling healthy — and choosing what that entails for yourself — are the real challenges to wellness.

Although weight is a significant health factor, your nutritional and exercise habits are also crucial to your overall well-being. Rather than too quickly deciding that you need to either gain or lose weight or to change your nutritional habits, it is a good idea to consult your physician or one of the nutrition centers in your area. If you decide you want to change your weight, there are many excellent support groups designed for this purpose, as well as self-help programs. The counseling centers at many colleges offer groups for weight control and for people with eating disorders.

A basic change in attitude and lifestyle is important in successfully dealing with a weight problem. Overweight people do not eat simply because they are hungry. They are typically more responsive to external cues in their environment. One of these is the acquiescence of well-meaning friends, who may joke with them by saying: "Oh, don't worry about those extra pounds. What's life without the enjoyment of eating? Besides, there's more of you to love this way!" This kind of "friendship" can make it even more difficult to discipline ourselves and to watch what and how much we eat.

In our counseling groups we often encourage people who view themselves as having a weight problem to begin to pay more attention to their body and to increase their awareness about what their body communicates to them and to others. A useful exercise has been to ask them, "If your body had a voice, what would it be saying?" The following are examples of what their bodies might communicate:

- "I don't like myself."
- "My weight will keep me at a distance."
- "I'm making myself ill."

- "I'm burdened."
- "I don't get around much anymore!"
- "I'm basically lazy and self-indulging."
- "I work very hard, and I don't have time to take care of myself."

If you don't like what your body is saying, it is up to you to decide what, if anything, you want to change. Should you decide that you don't want to change, this is a choice that you need not be defensive about. There is no injunction that you *must* change.

If you have not liked your physical being for some time but have not been able to change it, there may be some subtle reasons for your difficulty. Being overweight may have certain "payoffs," even if they are negative. Here are some possible reasons people become and stay overweight.

- An overweight son or daughter may keep weight on as a way of getting constant parental attention, even if that attention consists of nagging over what he or she is eating.
- A girl may gain weight during adolescence because her father is threatened by her physical attractiveness.
- Overweight people may convince themselves that they are being rejected for their obesity and thus not have to look at other dimensions of themselves.
- Some who are afraid of getting close to others may use their weight as a barrier.
- Those who are afraid of their sexuality and where it might lead them often gain weight as a way to keep themselves safe from sexual involvement.

Are there people you know, including yourself, overweight for these reasons? Others may nag you to do something about your weight. They may be well-intentioned, yet you may resist their efforts because of the payoffs you are receiving. Ultimately, it is you who must decide what you want to do about your body.

➤ *Time Out for Personal Reflection*

1. What are your attitudes toward your body? Take some time to study your body and become aware of how you look to yourself and what your body feels like to you. Try standing naked in front of a full-length mirror, and reflect on some of these questions:

   - Is your body generally tight or relaxed? What parts tend to be the most unrelaxed?
   - What does your face tell you about yourself? What kind of expression do you convey through your eyes? Are there lines on your face? What parts are tight? Do you force a smile?
   - Are there any parts of your body that you feel ashamed of or try to hide? What aspects of your body would you most like to change? What are the parts of your body that you like the best? the least?

2. After you've done the exercise just described (perhaps several times over a period of a few days), record a few of your impressions below, or keep an extended account of your reactions in your journal.

   a. How do you view your body, and how do you feel about it?

   _____

   _____

   _____

   b. What messages do you convey to others about yourself through your body?

   _____

   _____

   _____

   c. Are you willing to make any decisions about changing your body?

   _____

   _____

   _____

3. If you decide to stand naked in front of a mirror, go through each of your body parts and "become each part," letting it "speak." For example, give your nose a personality, and pretend that your nose could speak. What might it say? If your legs were to speak, what do you imagine they'd say? (Do this for every part of your body, even if you find yourself wanting to bypass certain parts. In that case you might say: "I'm an ugly nose that doesn't want any recognition. I'd just like to hide, but I'm too big to be inconspicuous!")

4. If you are overweight, is your weight a barrier and a burden? For example, consider whether your weight is keeping you from doing what you want to do. Does it keep certain people away from you? You might pick up some object that is equivalent to the extra pounds you carry with you, let yourself hold this object, and then put it down and begin to experience the excess weight of your body.

5. Imagine yourself looking more the way you'd like to. Let yourself think about how you might be different, as well as how your life would be different.

Dreams as a Path to Self-Understanding and Wellness

Dreams contribute significantly to health and well-being. Dreaming helps us deal with stress, work through loss and grief, resolve anger, and bring closure to painful life situations. Dreams can be healing, but you must learn to pay attention to the wisdom of your unconscious.

In our work as counselors, we've learned that there is a relationship between remembering your dreams and your readiness to deal with problems and internal conflicts. Indeed, many clients report that they dream more frequently as they progress in their counseling.

■ Dreams as an Indicator of Psychological Health

Dreams can reveal significant clues to events that have meaning for us. If we train ourselves to recall our dreams (and this can indeed be learned) and discipline ourselves to explore their meanings, we can get a good sense of our struggles, wants, goals, purposes, conflicts, and interests. Dreams can shed a powerful light on our past, present, and future dynamics and on our attempt to identify meaning. They are messages that deserve to be listened to and respected. Dreams can provide a pathway to a better understanding of yourself and the choices open to you.

As much as we believe in the healing capacity of dreams, we have some concerns in writing about this topic. Indeed, a little knowledge can be a dangerous thing. Sometimes people attempt to analyze their dreams (and the dreams of their friends and family members) without a full understanding of the complexity of dream interpretation. We caution you to avoid analyzing and interpreting dreams of others unless you have the necessary education and training in dream work.

However, you can learn about yourself by simply paying more attention to your dreams to see what they might be telling you about yourself. There is considerable value in simply writing down your dreams in your journal, and sharing a dream with someone you trust can be self-revealing and helpful, even though neither of you attempts to analyze the dream. The late Carl Whitaker, one of the pioneers in family therapy, recommended that family members share their dreams with one another. He was not suggesting that they attempt to analyze their dreams; rather, he felt that family members could get to know one another more intimately by revealing and talking about their dreams.

Until recently, I (Jerry) rarely had dreams that I could remember. But a few years ago I attended a conference focused on exploring our dreams. I began to record whatever fragments of dreams I could recall, and interestingly, during this conference I started to recall some vivid and rich dreams. I have made it a practice to record in my journal any dreams upon awakening, along with my impressions and reactions to the dreams. It helps me to share my dreams with Marianne or other friends; especially useful is comparing impressions others have of my dreams.

All the images in my dreams are manifestations of some dimension within me. In Gestalt fashion, I typically allow myself to reflect on the ways the people in my dreams represent parts of myself. "Becoming the various images" in the dream is one way for me to bring unconscious themes forward. I am finding that my dreams have a pattern and that they are shorthand ways of understanding conflicts in my life, decisions to be made at crossroads, and themes that recur from time to time. Even a short segment of a dream often contains layers of messages that make sense when I look at what is going on in my waking state.

■ Exploring the Meaning of Dreams

People have been fascinated with dreams and have regarded them as significant since ancient times. But dreams have been the subject of scientific investigation only since the mid-19th century. Dreams are not mysterious; they are avenues to self-understanding. Rosalind Cartwright considers dreams as opportunities to work through everyday problems. According to her cognitive problem-solving view, there is considerable continuity between waking and sleeping time. Dreams allow us to think creatively about our problems, because when we dream we are not restricted by rational thought (Cartwright & Lamberg, 1992). Cartwright believes that dreams function to restore our sense of competence. When we are under severe stress, dreams can help us resolve our problems. Cartwright (1991) found that women who were experiencing a divorce tended to dream about problems related to their stressful situation. In addition, those women who dealt with their divorce in their dreams made a better waking adjustment to the divorce than those who did not. Cartwright has also worked with depressed women who were instructed to alter the plots in their dreams. Some of these women were able to change the plots of their dreams toward happier endings. Happier dream endings can carry over and influence waking thoughts, feelings, and actions and, thus, have therapeutic value (Cartwright, 1991; Cartwright & Lamberg, 1992).

The process of dream work is far more complex than this brief discussion suggests. Freud, Jung, Adler, and Perls all have contributed to our understanding of dreams and dream work. Let's look at some of these different ways of understanding dreams.

Freud's Approach to Dreams.   Freud pioneered the scientific study of dreams and made significant discoveries about their meaning and functioning. His classic book on this subject, *The Interpretation of Dreams,* was first published in 1900 (Freud, 1900/1965). Freud wrote that dreams represent repressed desires, fears, conflicts, and wishes in disguised or symbolic form. Dreams can be understood as repressed wishes that are buried in the unconscious because they are sometimes intolerably painful. Freud stressed the wish-fulfilling function of dreams and viewed them as attempts to satisfy unconscious needs.

In Freud's view dreams are the "royal road to the unconscious" — expressing unconscious wishes, needs, and fears. Dreams have both a *manifest* (or conscious) content and a *latent* (or hidden) content. The manifest content is the dream as it appears to the dreamer; the latent content consists of the disguised, unconscious motives that represent the hidden symbolic meaning of the dream. According to Freud, consistent symbols in dreams allow interpretation of their meaning. Although dream symbols have an apparent universality, dreams must be interpreted in an individual context. Symbols are specific to each dreamer, they reveal conflicts in a condensed and intensified form, and they derive their meaning from what is going on in the dreamer's life.

Jung's Approach to Dreams.   Carl Jung was greatly influenced by Freud's dream work, and Jung's theory assigned great value to dreams. Some dreams deal with an individual's relationship to a larger whole, such as the family, universal humanity, and generations over time.

Jung (1961) proposed that the contents of the collective unconscious are *archetypes,* images inherited from past generations. The *shadow* is one of the most important of these archetypes. It has the deepest roots and is the most dangerous and powerful of the archetypes. It represents our "dark side" — our socially reprehensible thoughts, feelings, and actions, which we disown by projecting them outward. In a dream all of these parts can be considered a manifestation of who and what we are.

To identify the expression of an archetype in a dream, Jung would ask dreamers to say what each part of the dream reminded them of. A certain element of a dream could then be amplified by the dreamer and also by the therapist through references to mythology, art, religion, and literature (Hall, 1984).

Brugh Joy (1990) draws heavily from Jungian concepts in his work with dreams. Exploration of dream material is such a fundamental, honest, and candid revelation about people that Joy says he cannot imagine working with individuals interested in psychological and spiritual development without focusing on dreams. "Dreams are like looking at an incredibly detailed and often complex blueprint of one's individual makeup. . . . Dreams are a threshold to understanding universal principles of Life in general, and they have collective as well as individual significance" (p. 185).

Adler's Approach to Dreams.   Adler viewed dreams as an expression of an individual's unique strivings toward goals and purposes. Adlerians view dreams as rehearsals for possible future courses of action. If we want to postpone action, we tend to forget our dreams (Mosak, 1989).

Adlerians pay particular attention to childhood dreams, recurrent dreams, and recent dreams. Dreams are weather vanes for counseling, bringing problems to the surface and pointing to the person's goals (Mosak, 1989). They are reminders of what the person is about and what the person expects and is planning to do. Dreams clarify our views of self and the world. They remind us of our life goals and guide us toward accomplishing these goals. Thus, there is no fixed symbolism to interpret dreams; one cannot understand dreams without considering the dreamer.

Perls's Gestalt Approach to Dreams.   Fritz Perls, the father of Gestalt therapy, discovered some ingenious methods to assist people in better understanding themselves. He suggested that we become friends with our dreams. According to Perls (1970), the dream is the most spontaneous expression of the existence of the human being; it is a piece of art that individuals chisel out of their lives. It represents an unfinished situation, but it is more than an incomplete situation, an unfulfilled wish, or a prophecy. Every dream contains an existential message about oneself and one's current struggle. Everything can be found in dreams if all the parts are understood and assimilated. Perls maintained that if dreams are properly worked with the existential message becomes clearer.

Gestalt therapy aims at bringing a dream to life by having the dreamer relive it as though it were happening now. The suggested format includes making a list of all the details of the dream, remembering each person, event, and mood in it, and then becoming each of these parts by acting and inventing dialogue. Perls saw dreams as "the royal road to integration." By avoiding analysis and interpretation and focusing instead on becoming and experiencing the dream in all its aspects, the dreamer gets closer to the existential message of the dream. Rainwater (1979) offers some useful guidelines for dreamers to follow in exploring their dreams:

- Be the landscape or the environment.
- Become all the people in the dream. Are any of them significant people?
- Be any object that links and joins, such as telephone lines and highways.
- Identify with any mysterious objects, such as an unopened letter or an unread book.
- Assume the identify of any powerful force, such as a tidal wave.
- Become any two contrasting objects, such as a younger person and an older person.
- Be anything that is missing in the dream. If you don't remember your dreams, then speak to your missing dreams.
- Be alert for any numbers that appear in the dream, become these numbers and explore associations with them.

When working with a dream, notice how you feel when you wake up (Rainwater, 1979). Is your feeling state one of fear, joy, sadness, frustration, surprise, or anger? Identifying the feeling tone may be the key to finding the meaning of the dream. As you play out the various parts of your dream, pay attention to what you say and look for patterns. By identifying your feeling tone and the themes that emerge, you will get a clearer sense of what your dreams are telling you. In Gestalt style dream work, you can focus on questions such as these:

- What am I doing in the dream?
- What am I feeling?
- What do I want in the dream?
- What is my relationship to other people in the dream?
- What kind of action can I take now? What is my dream telling me?

Dreams are full of symbols. Freud and Jung made contributions to universal symbols in understanding the meaning of dreams. Gestalt therapists contribute to dream work by emphasizing the individual meaning of symbols. The person assigns meaning to his or her own dream. For example, an unopened letter could represent a person who is clinging to secrets. An unread book might symbolize an individual's fear of not being noticed or of being insignificant. A Gestalt therapist might ask the person, "What is the first thing that comes to you when you think about an unopened letter?" One person replies, "I want to hide. I don't want anyone to know me." Another individual says, "I wish somebody would open me up." To understand the personal meaning of a dream, a therapist often asks, "What might be going on in your life now where what you just said would make sense?" In Gestalt therapy no established meaning fits everyone; rather, meaning is deciphered by each individual.

■ Examples of the Meaning of Dreams

Cynthia, a member in one of our therapy groups, shares how she works with dreams in her personal therapy. She makes many excellent points in learning how to use dreams to further self-understanding.

I was introduced to dream work by a therapist who insisted I keep a journal of my dreams and include them as part of our sessions. In addition, she had me join a group that focused on dreams. We gave each other feedback on the possible interpretation and meaning of our dreams. I soon learned that dreams can offer significant insight, direction, and growth in the process of therapy.

I find it helpful to write in my journal just before going to sleep at night; it helps me quiet down and center on what happened during the day. I keep a notebook by the side of my bed and jot down a few words if I wake up from a dream during the night or when I first wake up in the morning. I write down even a couple of words, if that is all I can recall, because this helps me bring back an entire dream.

Over the years, I have received many gifts from my dreams, and I now appreciate how much value they hold. Sometimes my dreams are consoling, and I get a sense of peace and security from them. I have dreamed many special scenes, such as my mother holding me or my first counselor talking to me in her office. I believe that I am still connected through my dreams to people who have had a strong impact on me, even though they may have died. Sometimes a dream places me in a circle of people, and I am given instruction about something. Some dreams bring up long-forgotten incidences from the past that are of value to me in my process of therapy.

Other dreams help me look at areas that need to be explored but that I am resistant to working on consciously. One such dream brought a childhood experience of having been molested to my attention. Another brought up sexual issues with my first husband that left long-term damage and needed to be looked at. Dreams such as these help guide my therapy. Sometimes I even dream about being in a session with my therapist, or in group. At times this is inspirational, but at other times it can be most stirring and upsetting.

Recently, I dreamed that I was a female goat following along a trail behind a male mountain goat that was extremely strong and skilled and had no fear in his ability to climb to the peak of this mountain. I was not as strong or nearly as skilled and realized that he was always looking up because he was so sure of his footing, whereas I was looking at my feet and the path right in front of me. My leader was wise and concerned about my journey, and he would stop at times and look back to see how I was managing. I saw that I was holding him back and told him that I wanted him to be free to reach his destination. He looked back at me, and through his eyes he told me that this is what love is. It is patient, and it is caring. It is protective and guiding. When I woke up, I wrote down the dream, and I felt a sense of hope for the direction of my path. I realized that not all males are alike. Some may leave you in the dust, but they don't have a clue about what love is. Dreams such as these keep me going!

Sometimes dreams provide clues to our concerns. In one of her therapy sessions, Julie reported this dream.

There is a well-dressed wheezing baby. I forget to feed the baby. I do everything for the baby. It is a very beautiful baby.

This dream illustrates how dreamers select unconscious symbols that powerfully represent core struggles in their lives. In the context of Julie's life struggle, the dream had a powerful meaning.

What Julie realized as she explored the possible meanings of her dream was that she was doing everything right, she was giving a lot to others, yet she was forgetting to take care of herself. The "wheezing baby" was a significant detail in Julie's dream, especially in light of the fact that she suffered from asthma, particularly when she became anxious. She discovered that she was the baby who went unfed. She had not been taking time to nurture herself. As she "became" the baby and took on its personality, she became aware — and was horrified — that she was doing everything for the baby except feeding it. By paying attention to what her dreams were telling her, Julie was able to express more and more of her pain and buried feelings. She became aware of a great deal of repressed pain in her life and of the many ways she was neglecting herself. "I haven't been able to breathe so freely in a long time," she said at one point.

Ruby explored the following dream during a therapy session.

A monkey is sitting on top of a horse. The monkey is bent over, holding on desperately. The horse is galloping with great speed along the beach. On top of the monkey are three monkeys weighing the first monkey down.

When the therapist asked Ruby what her mood had been when she awakened, she replied that she had felt scared and burdened. As the therapist worked with Ruby's dream, she was asked if the number 3 had any particular significance for her. She quickly said "No, it doesn't." Later she admitted that she had a husband and two children. She was asked to associate with and play out various parts of her dream, including the following:

- "I am the speeding horse. I'm running out of control, and I can't stop." The galloping horse had some meaning in terms of her fears that her life was getting away from her. She had fears that she was aging and that if she didn't do what she most wanted to do, she would soon have no time left.
- "I am the sand, and I'm being stomped on." Ruby's pattern was to allow people to walk all over her and not to assert herself with them.
- "I'm the monkey, holding on desperately. I have three monkeys on my back that are holding me down." She identified the three monkeys as her husband, son, and daughter, all of whom could be "monkeys on her back."

As part of her therapeutic work, Ruby symbolically talked to each of the monkeys in terms that she had never used with her husband and children. She told them that she wanted to be involved in their lives and give to them, but not to the extent of denying herself in the process. She also decided that she would periodically let them know how they were affecting her and would not allow herself to store up resentments. Since all three of them were adults, she wanted them to take on increased responsibility for themselves. Toward the end of one of her therapy sessions, after she had done considerable work with her dream, Ruby shared the following imagery. She had the image of a horse gracefully galloping along the beach. The monkey was sitting up, and there were no monkeys on its back. She felt very serene and at peace with herself.

As you can see, dreams are a rich source of meaning. If you listen closely to them, they will challenge you to look at ways in which you may want to change your life. I (Marianne) recently had a dream that challenged me to examine the way I was living. The dream occurred during a time when I was feeling personally and professionally overextended. I was giving out more than I was taking for myself. I make it a practice to write down and do Gestalt work with most of my dreams. Here is my dream, which occurred while I was in Germany.

My mother has cooked me a very special meal, and I am looking forward to eating it. There are many people there. By the time I go to get my food, everyone else has eaten the meal and none is left for me! I am very angry, resentful, and hurt that there is no more food.

The meaning of this dream was obvious to me. The overriding message was that I was not taking care of myself or nurturing myself. I was consciously aware that

I was working hard and not relaxing enough, but the dream made me confront my choices.

The examples we have presented here illustrate the breadth and value of dream work as an aid to self-understanding. If you listen to your dreams, you will learn something more about yourself. You can use this knowledge to make better choices and to live your life more fully.

➤ *Time Out for Personal Reflection*

1. Dreams have been described as a path to self-understanding and wellness. Consider these questions:

   - How often do you dream?
   - Can you remember your dreams when you waken?
   - Do you write your dreams down?
   - Do you reflect on your dreams and attempt to understand what they might be telling you?

2. Do you generally share your dreams with others? If so, what do you learn from this?

   _____

   _____

   _____

   Write your thoughts on the value you place on your dreams. To what extent do you use your dreams to better understand yourself?

   _____

   _____

   _____

3. The next section deals with counseling. Before reading the counseling section, take this brief inventory. If you generally agree with the statement, write "A" in the space; if you generally disagree with the statement, write "D" in the space.

   _____ Counseling is only for people who have serious mental or emotional problems.
   _____ Counseling generally aims at a major revamping of your personality.
   _____ A good counselor is able to solve any problems you bring to counseling.
   _____ The main function of an effective counselor is to give you good advice.
   _____ Most counselors are interested in changing your beliefs and values to conform to what they think is the desirable way to think.
   _____ If you go to a counselor, you can expect him or her to do most of the talking while you do most of the listening.
   _____ If you decide to see a counselor, this probably means that you are a weak person.

_____   If you are in counseling, you can expect rapid progress and major changes quickly, with little effort on your part.

_____   Counselors will be quick to make choices for you if you ask them for this direction.

Look over your answers to determine your attitudes toward counseling. All of the above are misconceptions about counseling and how it works. Thus, the more statements you agreed with, the more misconceptions you have bought into. As you read about counseling, consider how counseling might be of value to you in dealing with your problems and in staying psychologically healthy. Write down your thoughts on how open you are to considering counseling for yourself.

_____

_____

_____

Counseling as a Path to Self-Understanding and Wellness

We hope you'll keep the option open for yourself to seek professional counseling as one way to deal with any psychological problems that may arise. You don't have to be in a crisis to benefit from either individual or group counseling. You may find that you can only do so much by yourself in effectively dealing with problems at hand and in making the changes you desire. In our view, it is essential to attend to both your physical and your psychological health, because psychological pain often affects physical well-being.

When you find that you cannot give yourself the help you need or get needed assistance from your friends and family, you may want to seek out a professional counselor. When people are physically ill, they generally seek a physician's help. Yet when people are "psychologically ill," they often hesitate to ask for help. You would not put yourself down for going to a medical doctor for a physical ailment. Neither should you belittle yourself for recognizing that you need outside intervention for a psychological ailment.

You can also benefit from counseling without being psychologically impaired. Counselors can help their clients move ahead when they feel stuck in some aspect of living. Counseling can be instrumental in helping you get through a crisis, and it can also mobilize you in making decisions about your life. You might consider seeking counseling when you:

- feel out of control of your life
- are unhappy with where you are heading
- feel stuck in terms of making constructive choices
- are the victim of a crime or some form of abuse
- have no purpose or direction in life
- experience chronic depression

- are alienated from yourself and others
- experience a significant loss
- are having problems related to work or school
- are under chronic stress or have stress-related ailments
- are the victim of discrimination and oppression
- are divorcing or ending a significant relationship
- feel that you are using only a fraction of your potential

Counseling does not necessarily involve a major revamping of your personality. Instead of getting a major overhaul, you might need only a minor tune-up! Of course, many people don't take their car to a mechanic unless it breaks down—they don't want to take the time for preventive maintenance. Some won't go to a dentist until they are in excruciating pain with a toothache. Likewise, many people wait until they are unable to function at home, at work, or at school before they reach out for professional help.

Professional counselors are like mentors; they guide you to make use of your inner resources. Good counselors don't attempt to solve your problems for you. Instead, they teach you how to cope with your problems more effectively. In many respects, counselors are psychological educators, teaching you ways to get the most from living. They draw out the answers within you. They also have an investment in teaching you how to create more joy in your life, use your own strengths, and become the person you were meant to be and want to be. If you decide to get involved in counseling, you will generally be a collaborator with your counselor. Your counselor will ask what you want from counseling and is likely to explore your expectations about the kind of help you can get from him or her.

If counselors don't give advice, what do they do? Counselors are trained to listen to deeper messages and to assist you in listening to your inner voice. Their job is far more complex than dispensing advice on what to do about your problems. A counselor's function is to teach you how to eventually become your own therapist. A counselor can serve as a guide to help you find resources within yourself that you may not have known you had for resolving your problems.

Counselors do not change your beliefs through brainwashing; rather, they assist you in examining how your thinking affects the way you feel and act. A counselor will help you identify specific beliefs that may be getting in the way of your living effectively. You'll learn how to critically evaluate your values, beliefs, thoughts, and assumptions. Counseling can teach you how to substitute constructive thinking for self-destructive thinking. If you find it hard to identify and express feelings such as joy, anger, fear, or guilt, counseling can help you learn to do so. If you present behavior prevents you from getting where you want to go, most counselors will help you explore alternative ways of acting.

Not only do you explore and learn new behaviors during the therapeutic hour but most counselors assist their clients in carrying out in everyday life what they are learning in the counseling session. Counselors are likely to collaborate with you in designing homework assignments that will help you apply new skills.

Therapeutic work can be difficult for you *and* for the counselor. Self-honesty isn't easy. Confronting and dealing with your problems takes courage. By simply going in for counseling, you have taken the first step in the healing process. Recognizing the need for help is itself significant in moving forward. Being willing to look at all sides of your self presupposes high self-motivation. Self-exploration requires discipline, patience, and persistence. There may be times when progress seems slow, for counseling does not work wonders. Indeed, at times you may feel worse before you get better because old wounds are brought to the surface and explored.

Selecting the counselor who is right for you is of the utmost importance. Unfortunately, some people just pick a counselor from the phone book and barely check the person's qualifications. Just as it is important to go to a physician you trust, it is critical that you find a counselor whom you can trust. You are unlikely to bare your soul to a counselor in whom you do not have confidence. It's OK for you to ask questions about the counselor's training and background. In fact, ethical therapists feel a responsibility to inform their clients about the way counseling works.

A good way to find an effective therapist is to ask others who have been in counseling. A personal referral to a specific person can be useful. However you select a counselor, do some research and make a thoughtful decision. Counseling is a highly personal matter, and you stand a greater chance of doing the hard work self-learning demands if you trust your counselor.

Remember, counseling is a process of self-discovery aimed at empowerment. If your counseling is successful, you will learn far more than merely how to solve a specific problem. You will acquire skills you can use to confront new problems and challenges as they arise. Ultimately, you'll be better equipped to make your own choices about how you want to live.

Chapter Summary

The purpose of this chapter has been to encourage you to think about how you are treating your body and how you can take control of your physical and psychological well-being. Even if you are not presently concerned with health problems, you may have discovered that you hold some self-defeating attitudes about your body. A theme of this chapter has been to examine what might be keeping you from really caring about your body or acting on the caring that you say you have. It is not a matter of smoking or not smoking, of exercising or not exercising; the basic choice concerns how you feel about yourself and about your life. When you accept responsibility for the feelings and attitudes you have developed about your body, you begin to free yourself from feeling victimized by your body.

You can enhance your experience of the world around you by seeing, hearing, smelling, tasting, and touching. You can become less of a stranger to your body through relaxation, dance, and movement. Touch is particularly important. For healthy development, both physical and emotional, you need both physical and psychological contact.

Your body presents an image, both to you and to others, of how you view yourself. Your body image is not something you are born with. You acquire your attitudes about your body in the context of your culture. You can challenge some of the attitudes you have picked up, especially if they are self-critical. This may be a good time for you to think about how your perceptions of your body affect other areas of your life. Your ability to love others, to form nourishing sexual and emotional relationships with others, to work well, to play with joy, and to fully savor each day depends a great deal on both your physical and psychological health. You may be keeping yourself imprisoned if you are unwilling to initiate positive contact with other people simply because you assume they won't like the way you look. Allow your body to express your feelings of tenderness, anger, and enthusiasm. If you tend to be rigid and under control, imagine how it would feel to be free of these restraints.

Remember that you are a whole being, integrated in your physical, emotional, social, mental, and spiritual dimensions. If you neglect any one of these aspects of your self, you will feel the impact on the other dimensions of your being. Take a moment to think again about how well you are taking care of yourself physically. Ask yourself how committed you are to a wellness perspective. Consider the value you place on taking good care of yourself through practices such as meditation, relaxation exercises, paying attention to your spiritual life, participating in meaningful religious activities, maintaining good nutritional habits, getting adequate sleep and rest, and participating in a regular exercise program. Ask yourself whether your daily behavior shows that you value your physical and psychological health.

Once you've made this assessment, decide on a few areas you'd like to improve. Then begin working on a plan to change one aspect at a time.

Activities and Exercises

1. Wellness means different things to different people. When you think of wellness, what aspects of your life do you most think of? Look at what you are doing to maintain a general state of wellness. How much of a priority do you place on wellness?

2. In your journal record for a week all of your activities that are healthy for your body as well as those that are unhealthy. You may want to list what you eat, whether you smoke or drink, your sleep patterns, and what you do for exercise and relaxation. Then look over your list and choose one or more areas that you'd be willing to work on during the next few months.

3. If you have trouble remembering your dreams, before you go to sleep (for about a month) tell yourself "I will have a dream tonight, and I will remember it." Keep a paper and a pen near your bed. Write down even brief fragments you may recall when you wake up and jot down anything you can remember. If you don't recall dreaming, at least write that down. This practice may increase your ability to remember your dreams.

4. If you are aware of dreaming fairly regularly, develop the practice of writing your dreams in your journal as soon as possible upon awakening. Look at the pattern of your dreams; become aware of the kinds of dreams you are having and what they might mean to you. Simply reading your descriptions of your dreams can be of value to you.

5. Make a list of all the reasons you would not want to seek out a counselor when you are in psychological pain. Consider some of the following:

   - I feel too embarrassed to seek out a counselor. What would people think?
   - I should be able to take care of my emotional problems by myself.
   - I can't afford to see a counselor

   Then apply this same list to answer the question why you would not seek out a physician when you are in physical pain. Review this list to determine your attitudes regarding psychological health and physical health.

6. Select one or more of the following books for further reading on the topics explored in this chapter: *A Guide to Psychotherapy* (Amada, 1995); *Creating Health* (Chopra, 1992); *Perfect Health* (Chopra, 1994); *You Can Heal Your Life* (Hay, 1987); *Instead of Therapy* (Rusk, 1991); *Love, Medicine, and Miracles* (Siegel, 1988); *Peace, Love, and Healing* (Siegel, 1989); *How to Live Between Office Visits: A Guide to Life, Love, and Health* (Siegel, 1993); *Wellness Workbook* (Travis & Ryan, 1994).

7

Managing Stress

Either you control your stress,
or stress controls you.

✔ *Prechapter Self-Inventory*

Use the following scale to respond: 4 = this statement is true of me *most* of the time; 3 = this statement is true of me *much* of the time; 2 = this statement is true of me *some* of the time; 1 = this statement is true of me *almost none* of the time.

_____   **1.** My lifestyle is stressful.

_____   **2.** I have relied on drugs or alcohol to help me through difficult times, but I don't abuse these substances.

_____   **3.** It is relatively easy for me to fully relax.

_____   **4.** The way I live, I sometimes worry about having a heart attack.

_____   **5.** I'm able to recognize some of my thoughts and beliefs that contribute to my stress level.

_____   **6.** Stress has sometimes made me physically ill.

_____   **7.** If I don't control stress, I believe that it will control me.

_____   **8.** Meditation is a practice I use to deal with stress.

_____   **9.** Burnout is a real concern of mine.

_____   **10.** I feel a need to learn more stress management techniques.

Introduction

Stress is an event or series of events that lead to strain, which often results in physical and psychological health problems. Therefore, learning to cope with stress is essential if we hope to maintain a sense of wellness. Everyday living involves dealing with frustrations, conflicts, pressures, and change. Moreover, at certain times in our lives most of us are confronted with severely stressful situations that are difficult to cope with — the death of a family member or a close friend, the loss of a job, a personal failure, or an injury. Even changes that we perceive to be positive, such as getting a promotion or moving to a new location, can be stressful and often require a period of adjustment. If stress is severe enough, it takes its toll on us physically and psychologically.

Siegel (1988) indicates that the level of stress is largely determined by cultural factors. Cultures that emphasize competition and individualism produce the most stress. Cultures that place a high value on cooperation and collectivism produce the least stress, and also have the lowest rates of cancer. In collectivist cultures, supportive relationships are the norm, the elderly are respected and given an active role, and religious faith is valued. Siegel is convinced that chronic patterns of intense stress lower the efficiency of the body's disease-fighting cells. His work with cancer patients has taught him that stresses resulting from traumatic loss and major life changes are in the background of most of those who get cancer. He adds, however, that not everyone who suffers stressful changes in lifestyle develops an illness. The deciding factor seems to be how people cope with the problems and stresses they face. It seems to be particularly important to be able to express your feelings about situations rather than denying that your feelings exist or swallowing them.

In most places in the modern world, stress is an inevitable part of life. We cannot eliminate stress. But we can learn how to monitor its physical and psychological impact, and we can manage stress. Recognizing ineffective or destructive reactions to stress is an essential step in dealing with stress. We don't have to allow ourselves to be victimized by the psychological and physiological effects of stress. It is true that many sources of stress are external, but how we perceive and react to stress is subjective and internal. By interpreting the events in our lives, we define what is and is not stressful—we determine our levels of stress adaptation. Therefore, the real challenge is to learn how to recognize and respond constructively to the sources of stress rather than trying to eliminate them. Some constructive paths to stress management addressed in this chapter include challenging self-defeating thinking and negative self-talk, developing a sense of humor, practicing meditation and other centering activities, and learning how to relax.

Sources of Stress

Because how we perceive events influences our stress level, and because stress tends to be self-imposed, we have more control over stress than we typically realize. Before we can exert control, however, we must identify the source of our stress. Two major sources of stress are environmental and personal factors.

■ Environmental Sources of Stress

Many of the stresses of daily life come from external sources. Consider some of the environmentally related stresses you face at the beginning of a semester. You are likely to encounter problems finding a parking place on campus. You may stand in long lines and have to cope with many other delays and frustrations. Some of the courses you need may be closed; simply putting together a decent schedule of classes may be next to impossible. You may have difficulty arranging your work schedule to fit your school schedule, and this can be compounded by the external demands of friends and family and other social commitments. Financial problems and the pressure to work to support yourself (and perhaps your family too) make being a student a demanding task.

Our minds and bodies are also profoundly affected by more direct physiological sources of stress. Illness, exposure to environmental pollutants, improper diet, lack of exercise, poor sleeping habits, abusing our bodies in any number of other ways—all of these take a toll on us. Listening to reports of violence on the streets and in homes on the news can also be stressful.

■ Psychological Sources of Stress

Stress is a subjective phenomenon. How we label, interpret, think about, and react to events in our lives has a lot to do with determining whether those events are stressful. Weiten and Lloyd (1994) identify frustration, conflict, change, and pressure as key elements of psychological stress. As we consider each of these sources of stress, think about how they apply to you and your situation.

Frustration results from something blocking attainment of your needs and goals. External sources of frustration, all of which have psychological components, include failures, losses, accidents, delays, hurtful interpersonal relationships, loneliness, and isolation. Additionally, internal factors can hinder you in attaining your goals. These include a lack of basic skills, physical handicaps, a lack of belief in yourself, and any self-imposed barriers you may create that block the pursuit of your goals. What are some of the major frustrations you experience, and how do you typically deal with them?

Conflict, another source of stress, occurs when two or more incompatible motivations or behavioral impulses compete for expression. Conflicts can be classified as approach/approach, avoidance/avoidance, and approach/avoidance (Weiten & Lloyd, 1994).

- *Approach/approach conflicts* occur when a choice must be made between two or more attractive or desirable alternatives. Such conflicts are inevitable because we have a limited time to do all the things we would like to do and be all the places we'd like to be. An example of this type of conflict is being forced to choose between two job offers, both of which have attractive features.

- *Avoidance/avoidance conflicts* arise when a choice must be made between two or more unattractive or undesirable goals. At times you may feel caught "between a rock and a hard place." These conflicts are the most unpleasant and the most stressful. You may have to choose between being unemployed and accepting a job you do not like, neither of which appeals to you.
- *Approach/avoidance conflicts* are produced when a choice must be made between two or more goals, each of which has attractive and unattractive elements. For example, you may be offered a challenging job that appeals to you but that entails much traveling, which you consider a real drawback.

How many times have you been faced with two or more desirable choices and forced to choose one path? And how many times have you had to choose between unpleasant realities? Perhaps your major conflicts involve your choice of a lifestyle. For example, have you wrestled with the issue of being independent or blindly following the crowd? of living a self-directed life or living by what others expect of you? Consider for a few minutes some of the major conflicts you've recently faced. How have these conflicts affected you? How do you typically deal with the stress you experience over value conflicts?

Change can be a source of stress, especially life changes that involve major adjustments in your living circumstances. Holmes and Rahe (1967) and their colleagues did a classic study on the relationship between stressful life events and physical illness. Their assumption is that changes in personal relationships, career changes, and financial changes are often stressful, even if these changes are positive. Disruptions in the routines of life can lead to stress. However, the demands for adjustment to these life changes are more important than the type of life changes alone.

Pressure, which involves expectations and demands for behaving in certain ways, is part of the "hurry sickness" of modern living. We may respond to the pressures placed on us by others at home, at school, at work, and in our social lives. Also, we continually place internally created pressures on ourselves. Many people are extremely demanding of themselves, driving themselves and never quite feeling satisfied that they've done all they could or should have. People face pressures in performing roles and responsibilities as well as in conforming to expectations. Striving to live up to the expectations of others, coupled with self-imposed perfectionistic demands, is a certain route to stress. If you find yourself in this situation, consider some of the irrational and unrealistic beliefs you hold. Are you overloading your circuits and heading for certain burnout? What ways do you push yourself to perform, and for whom? How do you experience and deal with pressure in your daily life?

Effects of Stress

Stress produces adverse physical effects. In our attempt to cope with everyday living, our bodies experience what is known as the "fight-or-flight" response. Our bodies go on constant alert status, ready for aggressive action to combat the many "enemies" we face. If we subject ourselves to too many stresses, the biochemical changes that occur during the fight-or-flight response may lead to chronic stress and anxiety. This causes bodily wear and tear, which can lead to a variety of what are known as *psychosomatic* or *psychophysiological* disorders. These are real bodily disorders manifested in disabling physical symptoms that are caused by emotional factors and the prolonged effects of stress. These symptoms range from minor discomfort to life-threatening conditions; most commonly they take the form of peptic ulcers, migraine and tension headaches, asthma and other respiratory disorders, high blood pressure, skin disorders, arthritis, digestive disorders, disturbed sleeping patterns, poor circulation, strokes, cancer, and heart disease. Explore how your physical symptoms may actually serve a purpose. Ask yourself how your life might be different if you weren't ill.

Allan Abbott (a family-practice doctor) and Colony Abbott (a nurse) spent some time treating indigenous people in Peru. This experience stimulated their interest in the ways in which stress affects the body. The Abbotts became especially interested in coronary-prone behavior, which is so characteristic of the North American way of life. While the leading causes of death in North America are cardiovascular diseases and cancer (diseases the Abbotts relate to stress), they rarely cause the death of Peruvian Indians, whose lives are relatively stress free.

In the Abbotts' view our bodies are paying a high price for the materialistic and stressful manner in which we live. Allan Abbott estimates that about 75 percent of the physical ailments he treats are psychologically and behaviorally related to stress. As an aside, he asserts that 90 percent of what he does as a physician that makes a significant difference is psychological in nature rather than medical. According to him, belief in the doctor and in the process and procedures a doctor employs has a great deal to do with curing patients. Taking a blood test, having an X ray done, getting a shot, and simple conversation with the physician all appear to help patients improve. Indeed, faith healers work on this very principle, embracing the role of belief and its effect on the body.

The psychiatrist and founder of reality therapy, William Glasser (1985), maintains that psychosomatic illness is a creative process. In a chronic illness for which there is no known physical cause, our bodies are involved in a creative struggle to satisfy our needs. Glasser's advice is that since there is no specific medical treatment for psychosomatic disorders, the best course of action is to attempt to regain effective control over whatever is out of control in the person's life. He does not like phrases such as *getting depressed, getting angry, having a headache,* and *feeling anxiety.* Instead, he substitutes words such as *depressing, angering, headaching,* and *anxietying.* He emphasizes that people choose these behaviors in an attempt to meet their needs and wants, and people have some control over what they continue to choose to do. Although it may be difficult to directly control your feelings and thoughts, Glasser maintains that you have control over your behavior. If you change your behavior, you increase the chances that your feelings and thoughts will also change.

In his book *Joy's Way,* Brugh Joy (1979) describes how a life-threatening illness was the catalyst for him to call an end to a prosperous and growing private practice as a physician and a position as a clinical professor of medicine. He dropped a role that had brought him a great deal of success and security but that had also sickened him in some key respects. After giving up traditional medicine, Joy traveled through Europe, Egypt, India and Nepal for nine months on his own pilgrimage toward spiritual reawakening, which led to his physical and psychological healing. Joy returned to California to open a center in the desert where he taught groups of people how to engage wider ranges of the consciousness, which could lead to major life transformations. Along with Bernie Siegel and other physicians, Joy believes that we become sick because of the stresses associated with psychological and spiritual anomalies. From Joy's perspective, people generally become sick for one of two reasons: either because their life is too restricted for the person they potentially could become, or because their life is too expansive and exceeds their potential.

In *Avalanche,* Joy (1990) elaborates further on the meaning of physical illness and death. For example, when their last child is leaving home, some mothers may develop a life-threatening illness, primarily because they have based their existence on their family and cannot view themselves as separate from this entity. Some men who face retirement, with the potential loss of power, may become ill. Joy and other physicians have observed "a tendency for spouses to die within a two-year period following the death of a husband or wife. In such cases the surviving partner is unable to engage a sense of self that can sustain life without the other person" (Joy, 1990, p. 65). It is clear that an intimate connection exists between the body and the mind and that emotional restriction can lead to sickness.

In our counseling practice we see evidence of this connection between stress and psychosomatic ailments. We continue to work with people who deal with their emotions by denying or repressing them or finding some other indirect channel of expression. Consider Lou's situation. He is a young man who suffered from occasional asthmatic attacks. He discovered during the process of therapy, that he became asthmatic whenever he was under emotional stress or was anxious. To his surprise he found that he could control his symptoms when he began to express his feelings and talk about what was upsetting him. While continuing to receive medical supervision for his asthma, he improved his physical condition as he learned to more fully explore his emotional difficulties. As he let out his anger, fear, and pain, he was able to breathe freely again.

Other examples can be found that illustrate how our bodies pay the price for not coping with stress adequately. Consider Sarah's account of how the stress of her perfectionistic strivings resulted in severe headaches.

> *I have often described myself as a perfectionist, yet this word implies that I am constantly striving for something I never reach. This is not accurate, as I almost always reach my goals. So I redefine myself as driven, ambitious, and focused. In today's world, these are assets associated with the highest powered executives in America.*
>
> *As a graduate student in a counseling program, I have had my share of stress and pressure. Over the past three semesters, I noticed that my monthly headaches were increasing in frequency and duration. What was once a minor inconvenience if the weather was hot or the sun was in my eyes became a*

daily occurrence. At first I believed it was stress. But the headaches would wake me up from a deep sleep, my head pounding and hammering, and the hypochondriac in me sought medical attention, which was to no avail. There was no blood clot in my brain, nor did I suffer from any other terminal illness.

So I pushed on, each semester getting closer and closer to graduating with a degree that would bring me my dream of counseling and teaching. Being the empirical researcher I am, I began systematically recording the time and date of each headache. When the last day of the semester arrived, I eagerly began my summer vacation. Weeks went by without so much as a twinge of pain in my head.

As the fall semester approaches, I am certain that my headaches will begin again. In anticipation, I have begun meditating and will try to learn to work with my pain, instead of against it, which often makes it worse. I hope to learn to play and relax with the same intensity that I bring to my work. Praising the side of me that works so hard by taking time for myself to meditate, watch soaps, shop, or lie in the sun, is a goal I have for myself. Life will inevitably feel out of control at times, and my body will cry out for a break when I push too hard.

Stories such as Sarah's are not uncommon. Physical symptoms often decrease or disappear when we learn to identify and appropriately express our feelings or challenge unrealistic goals of perfectionism.

■ High Stress and Your Heart

Coronary disease accounts for approximately 40 percent of the deaths in the United States annually. Faced with this challenging statistic, if behavioral characteristics contributing to heart disease could be isolated, individuals would be able to make different choices and change behaviors that might be killing them. Meyer Friedman and Ray Rosenman (1974) pioneered the study of a certain personality structure, which they called Type A, that leads to a stressful lifestyle and, in turn, to coronary disease. It seems clear that Type A people actually create much of the stress they experience by their beliefs, self-talk, and behavior.

What are the main characteristics of the Type A personality? The primary behavioral characteristics are *time urgency, preoccupation with productivity and achievement, chronic activation, aggressive and hostile behavior,* and *competitive drive.* Type A people are characterized by behaviors that seem to result from "hurry sickness." They are highly motivated and driven to perform. They tend to take on too many projects, and they are driven by deadlines. They are chronically harried, are constantly in competition with the clock, and strive to do more and more in less and less time. These individuals typically move, walk, talk, and eat rapidly. They overemphasize words in their speech and are often impatient in conversations. They tend to interrupt others and finish sentences for people who they think are speaking too slowly. Even the briefest delays are met with irritation and impatience. They typically change lanes on the freeway to make up a few car lengths. They are constantly trying to work and move faster than others. Their

general impatience is seen in their attempts to do two or more things at once, which is referred to as *multiphasia.* They may eat and read, eat lunch while walking from one place to the other, read while sitting on the toilet, or even think of work when they are having sex. Typically, people with Type A behavior patterns over-schedule activities and become tense when they don't complete the unrealistic tasks they have set for themselves. By assuming too many responsibilities, they become trapped in several stressful situations at once.

Type A people operate on the assumption that their personal worth depends largely on what they produce and that their success depends on being able to accomplish herculean feats. These beliefs often lead to behaviors such as hostility, aggressiveness, competitiveness, and impatience. They continually create new demands for themselves, and when anything blocks their striving toward their ambitions, they become irritated and overreact to the hassles of everyday life. Of course, along with these self-imposed demands comes increased stress. There is a pervasive sense of guilt when they are not being productive. Relaxation and vacations are difficult for them, because they are often thinking of all the work they could be doing instead of "wasting time" by nonproductively playing.

The destructive core of Type A characteristics, which increases the risk of heart attack, is the hostile behavior and cynical attitudes toward life. In *The Male Stress Syndrome,* Georgia Witkin (1994) writes: "Feeling hostile and cynical, the Type A man sets up a negative self-fulfilling prophecy for his work and play relationships. He often expects the same competitiveness and impatience that he feels—and therefore gets it" (p. 44). Type A individuals find stress in every situation. They seem to be wedded to the long-term stress that is killing them. Witkin states that the link between cardiovascular disease and stress shows up in study after study. People high in *cynical hostility* tend to be distrustful, moody and resentful. When these people become upset, which they frequently do, they manifest physiological reactions. Although the conclusions from research on specific Type A behavior patterns and coronary heart disease are not conclusive, it appears that cynical hostility is the most toxic element of the Type A syndrome (Rosenman, 1991).

Based on his research, Wright (1988) discusses some important conclusions about coronary-prone behaviors for the layperson. From his perspective, job involvement alone does not appear to cause coronary disease. In fact, genuine involvement in work can be a source of meaning in life. What is damaging is the desperate striving to accomplish too much in too short a time. Apparently, it is the hostile and aggressive behavior associated with fierce competitive striving that results in an early death from a heart attack, not simply having Type A characteristics. The key to reducing coronary risk lies not in working less but in changing attitudes that lead to hostility and aggression. Wright proposes that it would be well to find a way to keep "the baby" (drive, ambition, and the resulting accomplishments) while throwing out the "bath water" (urgency, chronic activation, and the resulting heart disease). He believes that the challenge is to examine our values and make some basic changes in our lifestyles. We need to learn to run the race of life like a marathon rather than a series of 100-yard dashes.

■ Stress and the Hardy Personality

Typical advice given to those who want to stay healthy is to reduce stress as much as possible. Maddi and Kobasa (1984) question whether this advice is realistic or even desirable. Their studies point to the importance of how individuals perceive stressful life events and how they respond to them. Maddi and Kobasa's study addressed the question of who stays well and why. They identified a personality pattern called hardiness that distinguished people who succeeded in coping with change without becoming ill. Hardiness is a personality style characterized by an appetite for challenge, a sense of commitment, and a strong sense of being in control of their lives (Kobasa, 1979; Kobasa, Maddi, & Kahn, 1982; Maddi & Kobasa, 1984).

Not only do hardy personalities seem to be able to survive stress and life changes but they actually appear to thrive under conditions of rapid and clustered changes. Based on their study of high-stress executives who remained healthy, Kobasa, Maddi, and Kahn (1982) identified these personality traits:

- *A liking for challenge.* Hardy executives tend to seek out and actively confront challenges. They thrive under conditions of challenge, difficulty, and adversity. Rather than viewing difficult situations as being catastrophic, they perceive them as an opportunity for growing and learning. For them, change is the norm of life. Instead of being riveted to the past, they welcome change and see it as a stimulus for creativity. Less hardy executives tend to view change as threatening.

- *A strong sense of commitment.* People who are committed have high self-esteem, a zest for life, and a meaning for living. Stress-resistant executives display a clear sense of values, well-defined goals, and a commitment to putting forth the maximum effort to achieve their goals. In contrast, less hardy executives lack direction and do not have a commitment to a value system.
- *An internal locus of control.* Individuals with an internal locus of control believe they can influence events and their reactions to events. Such individuals accept responsibility for their actions. They believe that their successes and failures are determined by internal factors, such as their abilities and the actions they take. People with an external locus of control believe that what happens to them is determined by factors external to themselves such as luck, fate, and chance. Hardy individuals tend to exhibit an internal locus of control, whereas less stress-resistant individuals feel powerless over events that happen to them.

The work of Kobasa and her colleagues has been a catalyst for research on the way personality affects health and the ability to tolerate stress. Their studies demonstrate that hardiness is a buffer against distress and illness in coping with the stresses associated with change.

➤ *Time Out for Personal Reflection*

1. What are the major stressors in your life today?

   _____

   _____

   _____

2. What steps can you take to reduce stress in your life? Select a specific action you are willing to take as a way to manage stress.

   _____

   _____

   _____

3. In this chapter we encourage you to assume personal responsibility for the way stress affects your body. For example, instead of saying "I have a headache," you are asked to say "I am headaching." How might your life be different if you accepted responsibility for your bodily symptoms (such as stomachaches, headaches, and muscular tension)?

   _____

   _____

_____

_____

4. Reflect on the characteristics of the Type A personality that may apply to you. List any of them that you see in yourself.

_____

_____

_____

5. Having a "hardy personality" can help you stay healthy as you cope with change and stress. What personality characteristics do you have that either help or hinder you in dealing with stressful situations?

_____

_____

_____

Destructive Reactions to Stress

Reactions to stress can be viewed on a continuum from being effective and adaptive, on one end, to being ineffective and maladaptive, on the other. If your reactions to stress are ineffective over a long period of time, physical and psychological harm is likely. Ineffective ways of dealing with stress include defensive behavior and abusing drugs or alcohol. Burnout is a common outcome of ineffectively coping with stress.

■ Defensive Behavior

If you experience stress associated with failure in school or work or in some aspect of your personal life, you may defend your self-concept by denying or distorting reality. Although defensive behavior does at times have adjustive value and can result in reducing the impact of stress, such behavior actually increases levels of stress in the long run. If you are more concerned with defending your bruised ego than with coping with reality, you are not taking the steps necessary to reduce the source of stress. In essence, you are denying that a problem situation exists or minimizing an unpleasant reality. One problem with relying too heavily on defensive behavior is that the more you use defense mechanisms the more you increase your anxiety. When this happens, your defenses become entrenched. This leads to a vicious cycle that is difficult to break and ultimately makes coping with stress most difficult. Take time to review the discussion on ego-defense mechanisms in

Chapter 2 and reflect on the degree to which you use defense mechanisms to cope with the stresses in your life.

■ Drugs and Alcohol

Many people are conditioned to take an aspirin for a headache, to take a tranquilizer when they are anxious, to rely on stimulants to keep them up all night at the end of a term, and to use a variety of drugs to reduce other physical symptoms and emotional stresses. Some time back, I (Jerry) took a vigorous bike ride on rough mountain trails. I returned home with a headache, a condition that afflicts me only occasionally. Instead of recognizing that I had overexerted myself and needed to take a rest, my immediate reaction was to take aspirin and proceed with my usual work for the day. My body was sending me an important signal, which I was ready to ignore by numbing. Perhaps many of you can identify with this tendency to quickly eliminate symptoms rather than recognizing them as a sign of the need to change certain behaviors. Americans rely heavily on drugs to alleviate symptoms of stress rather than looking at the lifestyle that produces this stress.

Most of us use drugs or alcohol in some form or another. We are especially vulnerable to relying on drugs when we feel out of control, for drugs offer the promise of helping us gain control. Consider some of the ways we attempt to control problems by relying on both legal and illegal drugs. If we are troubled with shyness, boredom, anxiety, depression, or stress, we may become chemically dependent to relieve these symptoms. A drawback to depending on these substances to gain control is that through them we numb ourselves physically and psychologically. Instead of paying attention to our bodily signals that all is not well, we deceive ourselves into believing we are something we are not.

When drugs or alcohol are used excessively to escape painful reality, it compounds our problems rather than solving them. As tolerance is built up for these substances, we tend to become increasingly dependent on them to anesthetize both physical and psychological pain and addiction can result. Alcohol is perhaps the most widely used and abused drug of all. It is also the most dangerous and debilitating. This is true not only because of its effects on us physically and psychologically but also because it is legal, accessible, and socially acceptable.

Once the effects of the drugs or alcohol wear off, we are still confronted by the painful reality we sought to avoid. Although drugs and alcohol can distort reality, at the same time these substances prevent us from finding direct and effective means of coping with stress. The problem here is that stress is now controlling us instead of our controlling stress.

Ask yourself whether you have a problem with using substances as a way of coping with stress. For example, you may be worried about the effects drinking has on you. Perhaps the most difficult aspect of making this self-assessment is simply being honest with yourself. In the final analysis, people who use any drug must honestly consider what they are getting from it as well as the price they are paying for their decision. You must determine for yourself whether the toll on your physical and psychological well-being is too high.

■ Burnout as a Result of Continual Stress

The phenomenon of burnout is receiving increasing attention. What is burnout? What are some of its causes? What can be done to prevent it? How can it be overcome?

Burnout is a state of physical, emotional, intellectual, and spiritual exhaustion characterized by feelings of helplessness and hopelessness. It is the result of repeated pressures, often associated with intense involvement with people over long periods of time. Striving for unrealistic goals can lead to a chronic state of feeling frustrated and let down. People who are burned out have depleted themselves on all levels of human functioning. Although they have been willing to give of themselves to others, they have forgotten to take care of themselves and generally feel negative about themselves and others.

Burnout is a problem for workers and for students as well. Students say that burnout often catches them by surprise. Often, students do not recognize the general hurry of their lifestyle, nor do they always notice the warning signs that they have pushed themselves to the breaking point. Many students devote the majority of their time to school and work while neglecting to maintain their friendships, make quality time for their family, or take time for their own leisure pursuits. Semester after semester they crowd in too many units, convincing themselves that they must push themselves to graduate so they can start making money. Sometimes they do not realize the price they are paying. Eventually they become apathetic, just waiting for the semester to end. They are physically and emotionally exhausted and often feel socially cut off.

In Chapter 5 we talked about the dynamics of discontent related to work. If we feel trapped by meaningless work, especially if we do not have a variety of leisure pursuits that give us meaning, there is a high potential for burnout. For example, doing the same routine, distasteful work eventually exacts a toll. If we are giving and extending ourselves but getting very little in return for our investment, our energy eventually dries up. Unless we replenish the well that we dip into for others, we will have very little to offer them.

So what can you do if you feel a general sense of psychological and physical exhaustion? Christina Maslach (1982), a psychologist who has studied burnout extensively, maintains that there are many constructive approaches. Once we recognize our state and seriously want to change it, the situation is not hopeless. Instead of working harder, we can "work smarter," which means changing the way we approach our jobs so we suffer less stress. Setting realistic goals is another coping skill. We can also work at conquering feelings of helplessness, since such feelings lead to frustration and anger, which in turn result in our becoming exhausted and cynical. We can learn to relax, even if such breaks are short. Instead of taking personally all the problems we encounter, we can condition ourselves to assume a more objective perspective. Most important, we can learn that caring for ourselves is every bit as important as caring for others. In the next section we will consider other constructive approaches to dealing with stress.

Although learning coping skills to deal with the effects of burnout is helpful, our energies are best directed toward preventing the condition. The real challenge is to learn ways to structure our lives so we can stay alive as a person as well as a worker (or student). Maslach (1982) asserts that the key to prevention is early action. She stresses using solutions before there is a problem. This includes becoming sensitive to the first signs of burnout creeping up on us. Finding ways to energize ourselves is critical as a preventive measure. This is where learning how to use leisure to nurture ourselves is so important. Each of us can find a different path to staying alive personally. The point is to slow down and monitor the way we are living so we can discover that path.

Constructive Responses to Stress

To cope with stress effectively you first need to face up to the causes of your problems, including your own part in creating them. Instead of adopting destructive reactions to stress, you can employ task-oriented constructive approaches aimed at realistically coping with stressful events. Weiten and Lloyd (1994) describe constructive coping as behavioral reactions to stress that tend to be relatively healthy or adaptive. Constructive coping:

- involves a direct confrontation with a problem
- entails staying in tune with reality
- is based on an accurate and realistic appraisal of a stressful situation rather than on a distortion of reality
- involves learning to recognize and inhibit harmful emotional reactions to stress
- entails a conscious and rational effort to evaluate alternative courses of action
- is not dominated by wishful or dysfunctional thinking

The following sections focus on a variety of stress buffers that are positive ways to deal with stress. These buffers include: maintaining sound health practices (adequate rest, exercise, and diet/nutrition; good time management; an ability to deal with self-defeating thoughts and messages; a sense of humor; a low-stress lifestyle; meditation; mindfulness and deep relaxation; and therapeutic massage). Take some time for quiet reflection and consider whether you might benefit from some of these practices.

■ Maintaining Sound Health Practices

Earlier we described REDS (rest, exercise, diet, and spirituality) as a formula for wellness. Developing sound habits pertaining to sleeping, eating, and exercising is basic to any stress management program. Getting adequate rest and sleep is a key element in a stress-buffering program; if you are rested, you are less prone to the negative impact of stress. Exercise not only makes you look and feel better but it fortifies you in dealing with stress. It is a natural means of reducing the negative effects of stress. Making healthy nutritional choices provides you with the necessary fuel to cope with stress more effectively.

Rest.   Sleep is a fundamental aspect of being healthy. Rest is restorative. It helps you recover from the stresses you experienced during the day, and it provides you with energy to cope effectively with challenges you'll face tomorrow. If you sleep between six and nine hours each night, you are in the normal range. Sleep deprivation leads to increased vulnerability to emotional upset and leaves you susceptible to the negative consequences of stress. Sleep disturbances tend to result in increased irritability, difficulty concentrating, memory loss, increased physical and emotional tension, and being overly sensitive to criticism. Insomnia can be caused by stress and is often the result of not being able to "turn off thinking" when you're trying to sleep. If you are interested in sleeping well, do what you can to take your mind off your problems. Ruminating about your difficulties is one of the key factors contributing to insomnia.

If you have problems sleeping, consider some of these tips for preventing and coping with insomnia (Schafer, 1992):

- Establish a regular sleep routine.
- Use relaxation methods.
- Exercise regularly.
- Minimize noise.

- Avoid eating heavy meals close to bedtime, and avoid caffeine for several hours before sleep.
- Quit smoking; nicotine, like caffeine, is a stimulant.
- If you can't sleep, get up and read or watch television or listen to soothing music.
- Maintain realistic self-talk about sleep.

Hales (1997) adds these suggestions for getting better sleep:

- Avoid long naps during the day.
- Avoid alcohol after dinner.
- Unwind in the evening.
- Don't go to bed starved or stuffed.
- Develop a bedtime sleep ritual.
- Remember that the quality of sleep matters more than the quantity.

Exercise. A central component to maintaining wellness in any stress-management program is regular exercise. Exercise is a natural means of reducing the negative effects of stress. It can prolong and enhance your life. Exercise has a number of benefits, a few of which include: releasing endorphins (which improve your mood and give you energy), slowing down the aging process, releasing anger and anxiety, releasing pent-up emotions, increasing feelings of well-being and self-esteem, preventing hypertension, alleviating and preventing depression, decreasing negative thinking, reducing the risk of illnesses, increasing physical strength and endurance, and providing you with a source of enjoyment. Weiten and Lloyd (1994) cite an array of benefits of exercise. An appropriate and regular exercise program can:

- enhance cardiovascular fitness, thereby reducing your susceptibility to coronary heart disease
- help you avoid obesity
- indirectly reduce your risk for diabetes, respiratory difficulties, arthritis, and back pain
- decrease risk for colon cancer in men and for breast and reproductive cancer in women
- reduce the potentially damaging physical effects of stress
- produce desirable personality changes that may promote physical wellness

Allan Abbott (personal communication, January 5, 1996) questions the advice of some physicians of exercising for 20 to 30 minutes, three times a week. He doesn't think this is enough. But how much exercise is enough? Based on his review of experts in this field who assessed the scientific evidence, Abbott suggests that every adult should accumulate 30 minutes or more of moderate-intensity physical activity on most, preferably all, days of the week. For most people, this moderate physical activity can be accomplished by brisk walking (about 3 to 4 miles an hour). Even short periods of intermittent activity accumulated over a day have value. The total amount of regularly performed physical activity seems to be more important than the manner in which the specific activity is performed.

Although brisk walking for 30 minutes a day will provide many health benefits, intermittent activity can be beneficial — walking rather than driving short distances, walking up stairs instead of taking the elevator, or operating an exercise machine while watching television.

Designing an adequate program of physical activity is difficult for many people. Not only is exercise time-consuming but if you're not physically fit your initial attempts can be painful and discouraging. Don't give up! The secret to developing and maintaining a successful exercise program is to select a form of exercise that you enjoy. It is a good idea to gradually increase your participation in your program. Although it is important to engage in your exercise program regularly, be careful not to overdo it. More is not always better. If you approach exercise compulsively, it might become another demand on you, which can increase stress in your life. Instead, exercise, like rest, can be a break from the grind of work and can refresh you — and it can be fun!

Diet and Nutrition.   Nutrition is the science that explores the relationship between your body and the food you eat. There is a lot of truth in the axiom "You are what you eat." Your daily diet affects your long-term health more than any other factor within your control. If your primary diet consists of junk food, you'll not have the energy you need to meet the demands of everyday life. Irregular and inconsistent eating patterns are a key nutritional problem for many. Coping with stress will be much more difficult if you do not have adequate nutritional habits. Most nutritional experts suggest a varied diet, consisting of foods from each of these groups daily: fruits, vegetables, breads and other grain products, meat or poultry or fish, and milk products. Variety is a critical part of nutrition.

In *Invitation to Health,* Dianne Hales (1997) makes the point that your health is basically up to you. By learning how to eat wisely and well, how to manage your weight, and how to become physically fit, you can begin a lifelong journey toward wellness — which is also an excellent route to managing stress. Making healthy choices about diet and nutrition entails having specific knowledge about what you eat, so it is well for you to become a smart nutrition consumer. Besides eating to live, eating can bring increased satisfaction to living. Hales offers the following guidelines for developing eating habits that will lead to physical and psychological wellness:

- Eat with people whom you like.
- Talk only of pleasant things while eating.
- Eat slowly and experience the taste of the food you're eating.
- When you eat avoid reading, writing, working, and talking on the phone.
- Eat because you're hungry, not to change how you feel.
- After eating, take time to be quiet and rest.

■ Time Management

You can learn to manage your time so you get what you want from your life. If you are committed to leading a balanced life, efficient time management skills are essential. There is no one best way to budget your time; you have to find the system that works for you.

One sure thing is that everyone has the same amount of time, yet how people use time varies greatly from individual to individual. The way you choose to use your time is a good indicator of what you value. If learning time management skills is important to you, a good place to begin is by monitoring your time. Once you have identified how you spend your time, you'll be able to make conscious choices of where you want to allocate your limited time.

Using your time wisely is related to living a balanced life and is thus a part of wellness. Ask yourself these questions:

- Am I making the time to eat properly, get adequate sleep, and maintain a regular exercise program?
- Do I take the time to balance fun with work? Do I tell myself I don't have time for fun?
- Do I make time for nurturing my significant relationships? If I tell myself that I don't have time for my friends, what is the message here?
- Is there time in my day for meeting my spiritual needs? Do I allow time for quiet reflection of my priorities in life?
- Do I generally like the way that I am spending my time? If so, what would I like to be doing more of? If not, what would I like to reduce or cut out in my daily activities?

Time management is a key strategy in managing stress. Indeed, much of the daily stress you experience is probably due to taking on too many projects at once, not using your time effectively, and procrastinating. Putting things off, especially if they need immediate attention, is a certain route to stress. Procrastination has some obvious short-term gains or so many would not be chronic procrastinators! But over the long term, procrastination typically leads to disappointment, feelings of failure, anxiety, and increased stress.

Learning time management skills will be worth the investment of your time and effort. If you are not in control of where your time is going, then time is in control of you. Here are some suggestions for ways to remain in charge of your time (Corey, Corey, & Corey, 1997):

- Reflect on your long-range goals, prioritizing the steps you will take in reaching them.
- Break down long-range goals into smaller goals. Develop a plan of action for reaching subgoals.
- Be realistic in deciding what you can accomplish in a given period of time. Think about Oprah Winfrey's saying: "You can do it all. You just can't do it all at once."
- Before accepting new projects, think about how realistic it is to fit one more thing into your schedule. Put yourself in the driver's seat and don't allow others to overload your circuits.
- Create a schedule that helps you get done what you want to accomplish. Make use of daily, weekly, monthly, and yearly planners. Use to-do lists once you've identified your priorities.

- Don't try to do everything yourself. Ask for help from others and learn to delegate.
- Don't try to be productive every moment. Make time in your schedule for fun, exercise, meditation, socializing, and down time.
- If you do too many things at once, you increase your stress level. Concentrate on doing one thing at a time as well as you can.
- Strive to live in the present moment and experience what is going on now as fully as possible. Avoid ruminating about what you could have done in the past or endlessly planning about the future. Living in the past or in the future makes it difficult to savor present experiences and tends to escalate stress.

Changing Self-Defeating Thoughts and Messages

Your thoughts and what you tell yourself can contribute to your experience of stress. For example, these thoughts about using time often bring about stress: "When I take time for fun, I feel guilty.," "I'm constantly feeling rushed, telling myself that I ought to be doing more and that I should be working faster." "If there were more hours in a day, I'd find more things to do in a day and feel even more stressed."

In Chapter 3 we discussed ways to challenge parental injunctions, cultural messages, and early decisions. Those same principles can be effectively applied to coping with the negative impact of stress. Most stress results from beliefs about the way life is or should be. For example, the pressures you experience to perform and to conform to external standards are greatly exacerbated by self-talk such as "I must do this job perfectly." The cognitive techniques we described in Chapter 3 can help you uproot certain faulty beliefs that are based on "shoulds," "oughts," and "musts." If you can change your self-defeating beliefs about living up to external expectations, you are in a position to behave in ways that produce less stress. Even if it is not always possible to change a difficult situation, you can modify your beliefs about the situation. Doing so can result in decreasing the stress you experience. By monitoring your self-talk, you can identify beliefs that create stress.

Acquiring a Sense of Humor

Workshops and conferences aimed at teaching people ways of having fun and learning to laugh are becoming popular. It is a sad commentary that we have to be taught how to laugh, but for many of us this no longer seems to come naturally. Too many of us take ourselves far too seriously and have a difficult time learning how to enjoy ourselves. If we are overly serious, there is very little room for expressing the child within us. Laughing at our own folly, our own inconsistencies, and at some of our pretentious ways can be highly therapeutic. Taking time for play can be the very medicine we need to combat the negative forces of stress. If we learn to "lighten up," the stresses that impinge upon us can seem far less pressing. Laughter is a healing force; humor can be a powerful antidote to physical illness and stress.

Humor not only acts as a buffer against stress but provides an outlet for frustration and anger. Studies exploring the physiological changes caused by laughter show that laughter can release endorphins, lower heart rate and blood pressure, stimulate respiratory activity and oxygen exchange, and enhance immune and endocrine functions (Vergeer, 1995). Vergeer states that humor can be considered a transformative agent of healing and an approach for putting stressful situations into a new perspective.

■ Developing a Type B Personality

Earlier we described how a high-stress lifestyle can contribute to heart disease. If you identified with the characteristics that described a Type A personality, you may need to make substantial changes in your way of living to reduce stress. Friedman and Ulmer (1985) talk about the Type B personality, which in many ways is the opposite of the Type A orientation. The Type B personality is characterized by relaxed, patient, and amicable behavior. Type B people are not slaves of time and are not preoccupied with achievements and aggressive competition. When they work, they do so in a calm and unhurried manner. They are able to relax and have fun without feeling guilty. They are able to play without having to win at any cost.

It's best to think of Type A and Type B behavior as existing on a continuum. Chances are you are not a "pure" type but have a blend of both elements. If you recognize that you have more Type A characteristics than you'd like, and if *you* think it's important to change your behavior and reduce your stress, you can take steps toward change. The first step is to realize that the Type A syndrome is not an "incurable disease." Schafer (1992) writes, "In short, Type A behavior does appear to be amenable to change. It is not locked into our thinking, feeling, and acting forever. Reducing it does appear to improve the quality of our life. Perhaps it can also improve the length of life" (p. 176).

Many people have succeeded in making drastic changes in their lifestyles and have greatly reduced Type A behaviors. However, it takes a great deal of effort to modify Type A behavior because Western culture reinforces values associated with this behavior, which become deeply entrenched as a way of life. Unfortunately, many people have to first be jolted by a heart attack to take a serious look at the price of their hard-driving, competitive, aggressive, and stressful lifestyle. But there is no need to wait until you become physically and psychologically debilitated. You can decide now that it is valuable to change your behavior.

Transforming yourself from a Type A person entails learning a balance in life, especially a balance between work and play. It involves changing your attitudes and beliefs so you don't react so intensely to situations that can lead to stress. Most of all, it demands that you accept full responsibility for how you are living. A place to begin would be Charlesworth and Nathan's (1984) comprehensive and useful book, *Stress Management,* which presents some fine strategies for changing. Another book to read is Friedman and Ulmer's (1985) *Treating Type A Behavior and Your Heart.* Both books make it clear that recognizing your Type A behaviors and learning to manage the resulting stress is not a one-time task but an ongoing effort.

From a personal perspective I (Jerry) know how difficult it is to make the transformation from Type A to Type B. Although I do not see myself as a cynical or hostile person, which appears to be the toxic core of the Type A syndrome, people who know me well see the following behavior patterns: being wedded to work, impatience, a loathing for waiting, doing several things at once, taking on more projects than there is time for, meeting self-imposed deadlines, and a desire to control the universe! Over the years I have realized that I can't cram my life with activities all year, fragmenting myself with many stressful situations, and then expect a "day off" to rejuvenate my system. Even though I'm a somewhat slow learner in this respect, a few years ago I recognized the need to find ways of reducing, if not eliminating, situations that cause stress and to deal differently with the stresses that are inevitable. It has been useful for me to identify through patterns, beliefs, and expectations that lead to stress. Furthermore, I am increasingly making conscious choices about ways of behaving that can result in either stress or inner peace. I continue to learn that changing my thinking and behavior is an ongoing process of self-monitoring and making choices.

■ Meditation

Meditation is another constructive response to stress. Meditation is a process of directing attention to a single, unchanging or repetitive stimulus as a way of quieting "internal noise" or "mind chatter." It may include repetition of a word, sound, phrase, or prayer. Its main purpose is to eliminate mental distractions and relax the body (Williams & Knight, 1994). In a little book on meditation, Sogyal Rinpoche (1994) writes:

> Generally we waste our lives, distracted from our true selves, in endless activity; meditation, on the other hand, is the way to bring us back to ourselves, where we can really experience and taste our full being, beyond all habitual patterns. Our lives are lived in intense and anxious struggle, in a swirl of speed and aggression, in competing, grasping, processing, and achieving, forever burdening ourselves with extraneous activities and preoccupations. Meditation is the exact opposite. (pp. 6–7)

Doesn't this sound like a concise description of Type A patterns? One answer to fragmented existence is the practice of "bringing the mind home" through meditation. Rinpoche says that the practice of mindfulness is a way to bring the scattered mind home.

Meditation is enjoying increased popularity among people of all ages. For some people it still has an aura of mysticism, and they may shy away from it because it seems intricately bound up with elaborate rituals, strange language, strange clothing, and abstract philosophical and spiritual notions. But you don't have to wear exotic garb and sit in a lotus position to meditate. Sitting quietly and letting your mind wander or looking within can be a simple form of meditation. Most books dealing with meditation recommend 10 to 20 minutes of practice once or twice each day.

In writing about meditation, Joy (1979) points out that meditation is an empowering process that we can learn if we are willing to allow time for the experience. He adds that there are as many different ways to meditate as there are meditators. Some people allow an hour each morning for silence and internal centering. Others find that they can enter meditative states while walking, jogging, bike riding, or doing T'ai Chi.

For much of our waking time, we are thinking and engaging in some form of verbalization or inner dialogue. In fact, many of us find it difficult to quiet the internal chatter that typically goes on inside our heads. We are not used to attending to one thing at a time or fully concentrating on a single action. Oftentimes we miss the present moment by thinking about what we did yesterday or what we will do tomorrow or next year. Meditation is a tool, a means to the end of increasing awareness, becoming centered, and achieving an internal focus. In meditation our attention is focused, and we engage in a single behavior. Our attention is cleansed of preconceptions and distracting input so that we can perceive reality more freshly. Although we narrow our focus of attention when we meditate, the result is an enlarged sense of being.

Meditation is effective in creating a deep state of relaxation in a fairly short time. The meditative state not only induces profound relaxation but also reduces physical and psychological fatigue. Its beneficial effects are numerous, and it has been shown to relieve anxiety and stress-related disease. People who consistently practice meditation show a substantial reduction in the frequency of stress-related symptoms.

Herbert Benson (1976) described a simple meditative technique that has helped many people cope with stress. In Benson's studies the subjects achieved a state of deep relaxation by repeating a mantra (a word used to focus attention, such as *om*). He described the following three factors as crucial to inducing this state:

- Find a quiet place with a minimum of external distractions. The quiet environment contributes to the effectiveness of the repeated word or phrase by making it easier to eliminate distracting thoughts.
- Find an object or mantra to focus your attention on and let thoughts simply pass by. What is important is to concentrate on one thing only and learn to eliminate internal mental distractions as well as external ones.
- Adopt a passive attitude, which includes letting go of thoughts and distractions and simply returning to the object you are dwelling on. A passive attitude implies a willingness to let go of evaluating yourself and to avoid the usual thinking and planning.

You may argue that you can't find the time for morning meditation. However, if you don't carve out time for this centering activity, it is likely that you will be bounced around by events that happen to you throughout the day. If you are interested in making meditation part of your daily pattern, discipline and consistent practice are required. Most writers on meditation recommend sessions before breakfast and before dinner, lasting for at least 20 minutes. They often suggest that a sitting position is more conducive than lying in bed. Some write that meditation on an empty stomach is the most conducive to deep meditative states. They also agree that these exercises must be practiced for at least a month for meditation's more profound effects to be experienced. One excellent guide to meditation is the small book, *Meditation,* written by Sogyal Rinpoche (1994).

■ Mindfulness

Living by the values of accomplishing and producing, we sometimes forget the importance of experiencing the precious moment. By emphasizing *doing,* we forget the importance of *being.* The idea of mindfulness is that we experience each moment fully. It is a state of active attention that involves focusing on here-and-now awareness. Mindfulness is like meditation in that the aim is to clear your mind and calm your body. Jon Kabat-Zinn (1990) describes the seven attitudes necessary to the practice of mindfulness:

- Don't judge. Become aware of automatic judging thoughts that pass through your mind.
- Be open to each moment, realizing that some things can't be hurried.
- See everything as if you are looking at it for the first time.
- Learn to trust your intuitions.
- Rather than striving for results, focus on accepting things as they are.
- Develop an accepting attitude.
- Let go. Turn your mind off and simply let go of thoughts.

If you are living in the present moment, you are not ruminating about the past or worrying about the future. Living in the present allows you to gain full awareness of whatever actions you are engaged in and to be fully present when you are with another person. Begin the practice of mindfulness by simply paying attention to your breathing. You can then extend this to other facets of your daily life, such as walking.

■ Deep Relaxation

You don't have to settle for a range of psychosomatic complaints such as indigestion, backaches, insomnia, and headaches as part of your life. If you can genuinely learn to relax and take care of yourself in positive and nurturing ways, the benefits will enhance your life and the lives of the people close to you.

Take a few moments right now to relax and to think about how you relax. Do you engage in certain forms of relaxation on a regular basis? What do you consider to be relaxing? Look over the following list and decide which forms of relaxation are for you. Think about the quality of each form of relaxation and how often you use it:

- sitting in a quiet place for as few as ten minutes a day and just letting your mind wander
- listening to music and fully hearing and feeling it (without making it the background of another activity)
- sleeping deeply and restfully

- being involved in a hobby that gives you pleasure
- engaging in sports that have the effect of calming you
- asking for and receiving a massage
- taking longer than usual in lovemaking
- walking in the woods or on the beach
- closing your eyes and listening to the sounds in nature
- listening to the sounds of your breathing
- practicing some form of meditation each day
- relaxing in a hot tub
- allowing yourself to have fun with friends
- regularly practicing muscle-relaxation exercises
- practicing some form of self-hypnosis to reduce stress and eliminate outside distractions

Williams and Knight (1994) describe a progressive muscular relaxation technique that they recommend be practiced for 10 to 20 minutes. This form of deep relaxation involves the following steps:

- Get comfortable, be quiet, and close your eyes.
- Pay attention to your breathing. Breathe slowly through your nose. And exhale slowly through your nose.
- Clench and release your muscles. Tense and relax each part of your body two or more times. Clench while inhaling; release while exhaling.
- Tense and relax, proceeding through each muscle group.

In the complex society most of you live in, you'll inevitably encounter obstacles to fully relaxing. Even if you take a few moments in a busy schedule to unwind, your mind may be reeling with thoughts of past or future events. Another problem is simply finding a quiet and private place where you can relax, and a time when you'll be free from interruptions. Learn how to let go for even a few minutes so you can unwind while waiting in a line or riding on a bus. Deep relaxation is a powerful positive response to stress.

■ Therapeutic Massage

In many European countries, and in Eastern cultures as well, massage is a well-known way to enhance health. In fact, physicians often prescribe therapeutic massage and mineral baths to counter the negative effects of stress. Unfortunately, massage has sometimes been linked to selling sex, especially through certain "massage parlors." Massage is a legitimate route to maintaining wellness and coping with stress, but use caution in selecting a reputable practitioner.

Earlier we talked of the need for touch to maintain the well-being of the body and mind, and we also mentioned how the body tells the truth. Massage is one way of meeting the need for touch; it is also a way to discover where and how you are holding onto the tension produced by stressful situations. Practitioners who have studied physical therapy and therapeutic massage say that the body is the place where changes need to be made if long-lasting psychological changes are to result.

Therapeutic massage is an excellent way to develop awareness of the differences between tension and relaxation states and to learn how to release the muscular tightness that so often results when you encounter stress. It is also a good way to learn how to receive the caring touch of another.

➤ *Time Out for Personal Reflection*

1. Self-inventory: What stresses me? Here is a list of some common stressors. Check off any of these stressors that frequently apply to you.

_____   trying to balance school with work
_____   attempting to do too much in too short a time
_____   illnesses
_____   problems with my relationships
_____   sexual difficulties
_____   job dissatisfaction
_____   unemployment
_____   discrimination
_____   academic demands at college
_____   serious illness or injury of close family member
_____   troubles with employers or with co-workers
_____   financial worries
_____   conflicts with my partner
_____   breakup of a relationship
_____   inability to sleep well
_____   problems with eating
_____   changes in my life situation
_____   meeting deadlines
_____   being on my own
_____   loneliness
_____   being on academic probation
_____   worries about what to do after graduation
_____   feeling depressed
_____   competition
_____   living up to the expectations of others
_____   critical self-talk
_____   concerns over body image
_____   driving in traffic
_____   poor time management
_____   fears of making mistakes and failing

other: _____

_____

_____

_____

Look over the items you've checked. Do you see any patterns in the factors that lead to your stress? If you had to select the top three stressors, which would they be? How might you better deal with them?

_____

_____

_____

_____

_____

_____

2. How well do you sleep? Are you getting adequate rest and sleep? What changes are you willing to make to help you get enough rest?

_____

_____

_____

_____

3. Do you value regular physical exercise? What kind of physical activity do you enjoy most? What gets in your way of exercising? What patterns are you willing to change?

_____

_____

_____

_____

4. Do you have a healthy diet? Are there any changes in your diet, nutrition, and eating habits you are willing to make?

_____

_____

_____

_____

5. This self-inventory is designed to assist you in pinpointing some specific ways you might better manage stress. Check all of the statements that express a goal that has meaning for you or describes a form of behavior you would like to acquire.

_____ I avoid using drugs and alcohol as a way to cope with stressful situations.

_____ I am interested in paying attention to the subtle signs of burnout, so I can take action before advanced stages of burnout set in.

_____ Learning time management skills is a priority for me.

_____ I am willing to make a schedule as a way to better organize my time.

_____ My negative self-talk often results in stressing me out. I would like to identify those thoughts that get in my way and challenge my thinking.

_____ Meditation is a practice I'd be willing to experiment with for at least a month as a way to center myself and as a way to better manage stress.

_____ Mindfulness implies experiencing each moment as fully as possible. I want to acquire the kind of attention that involves focusing on here-and-now awareness.

_____ Taking short relaxation breaks appeals to me, and I'm willing to do what it takes to learn relaxation methods.

6. This time management inventory can help you recognize your own time traps. Decide whether each statement is more true or more false as it applies to you and place a T for true or an F for false in the space provided.

_____ I often find myself taking on tasks because I'm the only one who can do them.

_____ I often feel overwhelmed because I try to do too much in too little time.

_____ No matter how much I do, I feel that I'm always behind and never quite caught up.

_____ I frequently miss deadlines.

_____ I simply have too many irons in the fire.

_____ I am a chronic procrastinator.

_____ I tend to be a perfectionist, and this leaves me never feeling satisfied with what I'm accomplishing.

_____ I'm bothered by many unscheduled interruptions when I'm trying to do important work.

_____ I'm aware of hurrying much of the time and feeling hassled.

_____ I have a hard time getting to important tasks and sticking to them.

What behaviors would you most like to improve with respect to managing your time?

_____

_____

_____

7. What beliefs or attitudes make it difficult for you to cope with stress? In other words, what do you sometimes tell yourself that increases your level of stress?

_____

_____

_____

8. What behaviors are you willing to work on to gain better control over the stressors in your life?

_____

_____

_____

_____

Chapter Summary

One enemy of your overall well-being is excessive stress. You have learned that the way you process the stress of daily living has a lot to do with your mental attitude, yet stress affects you physically as well as psychologically. You cannot realistically expect to eliminate stress from your life, but you can modify your way of thinking and your behavior patterns to reduce stressful situations and manage stress more effectively.

Conquering stress requires a willingness to accept responsibility for what you are doing to your body. A central message is to listen to your body and respect what you hear. If you are feeling the effects of stress in your body, this is a signal to pay attention and change what you are thinking and doing. If you fail to heed the warning of your body, you may suffer a heart attack or some other form of illness. It is a shame that some people will not choose to slow down until they do become ill.

Remember that you are a whole being, which implies an integration of your physical, emotional, social, mental, and spiritual dimensions. If you neglect any one of these aspects of your self, you will feel the impact on the other dimensions of your being. Think again about how well you are taking care of yourself physically, emotionally, socially, and spiritually. Ask yourself the degree to which you know your priorities and are acting on them.

In this chapter we have described a number of strategies for effectively managing stress. There is no one right way to cope with stress, which means you are challenged to devise your own personal approach to handle the stresses of daily life. While you may not be able to eliminate certain stressors in your life, there is a lot that you can do. By focusing on constructive reactions to stress and taking action, you gain personal power that enables you to manage stress—instead of letting stress control you. You can apply tools of time management to attain your goals. You can identify and change your self-defeating thoughts that lead to stress. Acquiring a sense of humor will allow you to put many of your difficulties into perspective. Take time to reflect on the ways you can manage the stresses you face, and you'll find a way to turn stressors into challenges. Consider the value you place on taking good care of yourself through practices such as meditation, relaxation exercises, paying attention to your spiritual life, participating in meaningful religious activities, maintaining good nutritional habits, getting adequate sleep and rest, and participating in a regular exercise program. Ask yourself whether your daily behavior provides evidence that you value your physical, psychological, social, and spiritual health. Once you've made this assessment, decide on a few areas you'd like to improve. Then begin working on a plan to change one aspect at a time. Even small changes can lead to significant improvements for yourself and those close to you.

Activities and Exercises

1. How are you coping with stress? Keep an account in your journal for one week of the stressful situations you encounter. After each entry, note these items: To what degree was the situation stressful because of your thoughts, beliefs, and assumptions about the events? How were you affected? Do you see any ways of dealing with these stresses more effectively?

2. How are you using your time? Take an inventory of how you use your time. Be consistent in recording what you do. Keep a log of your activities for at least a week (two weeks would be better) to see where your time is going. Carry a pocket notebook. A couple of times each hour write down what you have done. After a week add up the hours you're spending on personal, social, job, and academic activities. Then ask yourself these questions:

   - Am I spending my time the way I want to?
   - Am I accomplishing what I have set out to do each day? Is it what I wanted to do?
   - Am I feeling rushed?
   - Am I spending too much time watching television?
   - Am I balancing activities that I need to do with ones that I enjoy?
   - How would I like to use time differently than I did last week?
   - How well am I currently managing time?

3. List three to five things you can do to feel better when you are experiencing stress (meditate, engage in deep breathing, exercise, talk to a friend, and so forth). Put this list where you can see it easily, and use it as a reminder that you have some ways to reduce stress.

4. Identify some environmental sources of stress or other stresses that are external to you. Finding a parking spot, navigating in rush hour traffic, and noise are all external factors that can put a strain on you. Once you've identified external stressors, write in your journal about how you might deal with them differently. What ways could a change in your thinking or adopting a new attitude change the impact of these external sources of stress?

5. How does stress affect your body? For at least a week, or better for two weeks, record how daily stresses show up in bodily symptoms. Do you have headaches? Are your troubled with muscular aches? Do you have trouble sleeping? Does stress affect your appetite?

6. Consider the constructive ways to cope with stress presented in this chapter. Might some of these stress management strategies help you keep stress from getting the best of you? If you can select even two or three new stress management strategies and begin to practice them regularly (such as relaxation exercises, meditation, or humor), your ability to effectively curb the effects of stress are likely to be significantly improved. Write out a plan for practicing these techniques and make a commitment to a friend on what you are willing to do to better deal with your stress.

7. If you sometimes have trouble sleeping, try some of the suggestions listed in this chapter to determine if they might work for you. If you do not get adequate rest and sleep, what steps can you take to make changes?

8. Assess how exercise (or the lack of exercise) is affecting how you feel physically and psychologically and how it influences your ability to deal with stress. If you are interested in engaging in some form of regular physical activity, decide on some exercise that you would enjoy doing. Start small so you don't get overwhelmed, but stick with your physical activity for at least two to four weeks to see if you begin to feel a difference.

9. Select one or more of the following books for further reading on the topics explored in this chapter: *Beyond the Relaxation Response* (Benson, 1984); *Burnout: The Cost of Caring* (Maslach, 1982); *Stress and Health* (Rice, 1992); *Stress Management for Wellness* (Schafer, 1992); *The Male Stress Syndrome* (Witkin, 1994).

8 *Love*

✔ *Prechapter Self-Inventory*

Use the following scale to respond: 4 = this statement is true of me *most* of the time; 3 = this statement is true of me *much* of the time; 2 = this statement is true of me *some* of the time; 1 = this statement is true of me *almost none* of the time.

_____ 1. Loving more than one person of the opposite sex diminishes my capacity to be deeply involved with another person.

_____ 2. I have a fear of losing others' love.

_____ 3. When I experience hurt or frustration in love, I find it more difficult to trust and love again.

_____ 4. I make myself known in significant ways to those I love.

_____ 5. I find it difficult to express loving feelings toward members of the same sex.

_____ 6. I am as afraid of being accepted by those I love as I am of being rejected.

_____ 7. I have to take some risks if I'm to open myself to loving.

_____ 8. In my loving relationships there is complete trust and an absence of fear.

_____ 9. I accept those whom I love as they are, without expecting them to be different.

_____ 10. I need constant closeness and intimacy with those I love.

Introduction

In this chapter we invite you to look carefully at your style of loving by examining your choices and decisions when giving and receiving love. People often say that either they have love in their lives or they don't. We believe that you have the capacity to become better at loving. You can look at the situations you create for yourself and consider how conductive these are to sharing love. You can also look at your attitudes toward love. Some of the questions we examine are: How are love, sexuality, and intimacy interrelated? What is the difference between authentic love and inauthentic love? Is love active or passive? Do we fall in and out of love? How much are we responsible for creating a climate in which we can love others and receive love from them? Do we have romantic and unrealistic ideals of what love should be? If so, how can we challenge them? In what ways does love change as we change? What are the myths surrounding love? Is it worth it to love?

Freud defined the healthy person as one who can work well and love well. Like work, love can make living worthwhile, even during bleak times. We can find meaning in actively caring for others and in helping them make their lives better. Our love for others or their love for us may enable us to continue living, even in conditions of extreme hardship. In the Nazi concentration camp where he was imprisoned, Frankl (1963) noted that some of those who kept alive the images of those they loved and retained some measure of hope survived the ordeal, while many who lost any memories of love perished. From his experiences Frankl concluded that "the salvation of man is through love and in love" (p. 59).

Love involves risk, especially the risk of loss or rejection. The act of reaching out to another person entails the possibility of that person's moving away, leaving you more painfully alone than you were before. Loving and living a full life may include pain, but the alternative is choosing not to live or to love fully. Love also involves commitment, which is the foundation of any genuinely loving relationship. Although commitment does not guarantee a successful relationship, it is perhaps one of the most important factors in nurturing and fostering a relationship. Another major characteristic of genuine love is separateness, so that the identity of those in the relationship is maintained and preserved. Love is also an exercise of free choice, for people who love each other are able to live without each other yet choose to live together. When we speak of love relations, we refer to the various kinds of love, such as love between parent and child, love between siblings, friendships, and romantic relationships. Admittedly, these various types of love have some very real differences, but all forms of genuine love embody these basic characteristics in one way or another.

One of the purposes of this chapter is to help you clarify your views and values pertaining to love. As you read, try to apply the discussion to your own experience of love, and consider the degree to which you're now able to appreciate and love yourself. We encourage you to review your own need for love as well as your fears of loving. If you do so, you are likely to recognize whether barriers within you are preventing you from fully experiencing love.

Our Need to Love and to Be Loved

To fully develop as a person and enjoy a rich existence, we need to care about others and have them return this care to us. A loveless life is characterized by joyless isolation and alienation. Our need for love includes the need to know that, in at least one other person's world, our existence makes a difference. If we exclude ourselves from physical and emotional closeness with others, we pay the price in emotional and physical deprivation, which leads to isolation.

A tremendous negative power is involved when people engage in emotional cutoff. In some families relatives have not spoken to one another for years. This act of shunning is generally deliberate and aimed at controlling others. Those who are shunned often feel invisible. Within the Amish culture the practice of shunning is used to sanction members who violate certain norms and religious values. In its most severe form, shunning almost totally cuts off an individual from interaction within the community. Other members will not eat at the same table with those who are shunned, will not do business with them, and will not have anything to do with them socially (Good & Good, 1979). The fear of isolation as a result of being cut off emotionally is so overwhelming that many would not even think of going against their cultural norms. The need for love and acceptance may be far stronger than giving expression to their own individual desires.

People express their need to love and to be loved in many ways, a few of which are revealed in the following statements:

- "I need to have someone in my life I can actively care for. I need to let that person know he [she] makes a difference in my life, and I need to know I make a difference in his [her] life."
- "I want to feel loved and accepted for who I am now, not for what the other person thinks I should be to be worthy of acceptance."
- "Although I enjoy my own company, I also have a need for people in my life. I want to reach out to certain people, and I hope they'll want something from me."
- "I'm finding out that I need others and that I have more of a capacity to give something to others than I thought I had."
- "I'm beginning to realize that I need to learn how to love myself more fully. Until now I've limited myself by discounting my worth. I want to learn how to appreciate myself and accept myself in spite of my imperfections. Then maybe I'll be able to really believe that others can love me."
- "There are times when I want to share my joys, my dreams, my anxieties, and my uncertainties with another person, and at these times I want to feel heard and understood."

Of course, we can harden ourselves so we won't experience a need for love. We can close ourselves off from needing anything from anybody; we can isolate ourselves by never reaching out to another; we can refuse to trust others and to make ourselves vulnerable; we can cling to an early decision that we are basically unlovable. It's important to recognize, however, that *we* make these decisions about love—and *we* pay the price. In whatever way we deaden ourselves to our own need for love, we pay a price. The question you must ask yourself is whether the safety achieved is worth the price you have paid for it.

Barriers to Loving and Being Loved

■ Myths and Misconceptions about Love

Our ability to love fully and to receive love from others may be inhibited by misconceptions we have about the nature of love. We may have unconsciously bought into some myths about love that prevent us from forming realistic views of the nature of love. Our culture, especially the media, influences the way we conceive of love. If we hope to challenge these myths, we must take a critical look at the messages we have received from society about the essence of love. In the following pages we present our views on some common beliefs that need to be challenged.

The Myth of Eternal Love.   Some people assume that if the romance in the relationship fades, this is a sure sign that love never really existed. The notion that love will endure forever without any change is unrealistic. While love can last over

a period of time, love takes on different forms as the relationship matures. Love assumes many complexions and involves both joyful experiences and difficulties. The intensity and degree of your love change as you change. You may experience several stages of love with one person, deepening your love and finding new levels of richness. Conversely, you and your partner may grow in different directions or outgrow the love you once shared.

The Myth that Love Is Fleeting.   On the opposite end of the spectrum is the notion that love is strictly temporary. For example, Joel found himself in love with different women as often as his moods changed. One day he would claim that he loved Sabrina and wanted to be committed to her in an exclusive relationship. But in a short while he would grow tired of Sabrina, find himself in love with Peggy, and maintain that he wanted an intense relationship with her. For him, love was strictly a here-and-now feeling. We don't believe that such changeable feelings constitute real love. In most intense, long-term relationships there are times when the alliance is characterized by deadness, frustration, strife, or conflict. There are inevitable times when we feel "stuck" with a person, and at such times we may consider dissolving the relationship. But if your attitude is "I'll stay while things are rosy, but as soon as things get stormy or dull, I'll split and look elsewhere for something more interesting," then it's worth asking what kind of love it is that crumbles with the first crisis. From our perspective, authentic love means recognizing when we're stuck in an unsatisfying place and being willing to challenge the reasons for this and caring enough about the other person to stay and work on breaking through the impasse. Love involves a commitment, which is a choice you make to work at a relationship even though there are difficulties to be resolved.

The Myth that Love Implies Constant Closeness.   Betina and Luis dated throughout junior high and high school, and they went to college together because they could not tolerate any separation. They are making no friends, either with the same or opposite sex, and they show extreme signs of jealousy when the other indicates even the slightest interest in wanting to be with others. Rather than creating a better balance of time with each other and time with others, the only alternative they see is to terminate their relationship. The mistaken assumption they are operating on is that if they loved each other, they would be fused into one being.

Many of us can tolerate only so much closeness, and at times we are likely to need some distance from others. Gibran's words in *The Prophet* are still timely: "And stand together yet not too near together: For the pillars of the temple stand apart, and the oak tree and the cypress grow not in each other's shadow" (1923, p. 17).

There are times when a separation from our loved one can be very healthy. At these times we can renew our need for the other person and also allow ourselves to become centered again. If we fail to separate when we feel the need to do so, we'll surely strain the relationship. As an example consider the case of Martin, who refused to spend a weekend without his wife and children, even though he said he wanted some time for himself. The myth of constant closeness and constant togetherness in love prevented him from taking private time. It might also have been that the myth covered up certain fears. What if he discovered that his wife and children could manage very well without him? What if he found that he couldn't stand his own company for a few days and that the reason for "togetherness" was to keep him from boring himself?

As a couple, we (Marianne and Jerry) sometimes travel separately. At times Marianne goes to Germany by herself for a visit. In the past, some of the townspeople have let her know that they thought our marriage must be in trouble if we were not always together. Once Marianne and her mother went on a cruise together for a week, and many people wondered why Marianne would go on a vacation without her husband. When Jerry travels alone, whether for personal or professional reasons, he rarely is asked why he is not with his wife. This notion that couples should be inseparable is certainly influenced by what society considers appropriate gender-role behavior. The truth is that we enjoy traveling together and also without each other.

The Myth that We Fall In and Out of Love.   A common notion is that people "fall" in love, that they passively wait for the right person to come along and sweep them off their feet. Part of this misconception is the belief that when love strikes it is so powerful that it renders people helpless and unable to control what they do. According to this view, love is something that happens *to* people. This myth keeps people from assuming personal responsibility for their behavior and decisions. In contrast, we view love as something people themselves create — people *make* love happen.

Peck (1978) believes that falling in love is invariably temporary; eventually people will fall out of love if the relationship continues long enough. Buscaglia (1992) also criticizes the phrase "to fall in love." He contends that it's more accurate to say that we *grow* in love, which implies choice and effort: "We really don't fall out of love any more than we fall into it. When love dies, one or both partners have neglected it, have failed to replenish and renew it. Like any other living, growing thing, love requires effort to keep it healthy" (p. 6). Buscaglia adds: "Love may come to those of us who wait, but it had better be an *active* waiting, not a passive one, or we may wait forever" (p. 26). In *The Art of Loving,* Fromm (1956) also describes love as active: "In the most general way, the active character of love can be described by stating that love is primarily *giving,* not receiving" (p. 22). Although the notion of falling in love is popular, most serious writers on the subject deny that it can be the basis for a lasting and meaningful relationship.

People often say "I love you" and at the same time are hard pressed to describe the active way in which they show this love. Words can easily be overused and become hollow. The loved one may be more convinced by actions than by words. In our professional work with couples, we find that one person may rant and rave about his or her partner's shortcomings. We often ask, "If the situation is as bad as you describe, what keeps you together as a couple?" To this question people often reply that they love the other person. Yet they are slow in identifying ways that they show what their love actually means, and they go on to blame their partner for whatever is awry in their relationship.

In summary, active love is something we can choose to share with others. We don't lose love by sharing it but, rather, increase it. This thought leads to the next myth.

The Myth of the Exclusiveness of Love.   Sometimes you may think of love as something you possess in a limited quantity that you must carefully dole out and conserve. You may believe you are capable of loving only one other person — that there is one right person for you and that your fate is to find this singular soul. One of the signs of genuine love is that it is expansive rather than exclusive. By opening yourself to loving others, you also open yourself to loving one person more deeply.

In some senses, though, we may choose to make our love exclusive or special. For example, two persons may choose not to have sexual relationships with others, because they realize that doing so might interfere with their capacity to freely open up and trust each other. Nevertheless, their sexual exclusivity does not have to mean that they cannot genuinely love others as well.

Jealousy is an issue that can be mentioned here. For example, Joe may feel insecure if he discovers that his wife, Carol, has friendships with other men. Even if Carol and Joe have an agreement not to have sexual relationships with others, Joe might be threatened and angry over the fact that Carol wants to maintain these friendships with other men. He may wrongly reason: "What is the matter with me that Carol has to seek out these friends? Her interest in other men is a sign that something is wrong with me!" The kind of jealousy that is based on ownership of the other is really not flattering. In Joe's case, his jealousy is probably rooted in his feelings of inferiority and the threat posed to him because of the reality that Carol wants to include others in her life. On the other hand, it is wrong to equate an absence of jealousy with an absence of love. For example, Carol might be upset if Joe did not display any jealousy toward her, insisting that this meant that he was indifferent to her or that he had come to take her for granted. The motivations for jealousy need to be understood.

The Myth that True Love Is Selfless.   Lily is a mother who has always given to her children. She never lets them know that she needs anything from them, yet she confides to her friends that she is very hurt that the children do not seem to appreciate her. She complains that if she did not initiate visits with them, they would never see her. She would never say anything about her feelings to her children, nor would she ever tell them that she would like for them to contact her. She harbors the myth that if they really loved her, they would know what she needed without her having to ask for it.

People like Lily are "selfish givers"; that is, they have a high need to take care of others yet appear to have little tolerance for accepting what others want to give to them. Selfish givers create an inequality; the receivers tend to feel guilty because they do not have a chance to reciprocate. Although these receivers may feel guilty and angry, their feelings do not seem appropriate—how could they have angry feelings toward someone who does so much for them? At the same time, selfish givers may feel resentment toward those who are always taking from them, not recognizing how difficult they are making it to receive.

We may have been conditioned to believe that genuine love implies that we forget ourselves. It is a myth that true love means giving selflessly. For one thing, love also means *taking*. If you cannot allow others to give to you and cannot take their expressions of love, you are likely to become drained or resentful. For another thing, in giving to others we do meet many of our own needs. There is not necessarily anything wrong in this, as long as we can admit it. For example, a mother who never says no to any demands made by her children may not be aware of the ways she has conditioned them to depend on her. They may be unaware that she has any needs of her own, for she hides them so well. In fact, she may set them up to take advantage of her out of her need to feel significant. In other words, her "giving" is actually an outgrowth of her need to feel like a good mother rather than an honest expression of love for her children. In *Care of the Soul* (1994), Thomas Moore addresses this notion of selflessness. One of his clients said, "I can't be selfish. My religious upbringing taught me never to be selfish." Moore observes that although she insisted on her selflessness, she was quite preoccupied with herself. Selfless people often depend on others to maintain their feelings of selflessness.

Giving to others or the desire to express our love to others is not necessarily a problem. However, it is important that we recognize our own needs and consider the value of allowing others to take care of us and return the love we show them. One of us (Marianne) is finally learning the importance of letting others return favors. It has always been easy for me to show others kindness and take care of others, yet it has been a struggle for me to be on the receiving end. An old pattern of mine is to do everything by myself and not take the chance of imposing on others by asking for assistance. Lately I have been learning to ask others for help instead of insisting on doing everything by myself. More often than not, when I do ask for help, not only do others not feel any imposition but they express delight that I made the request and are pleased to reciprocate. I continue to learn that it takes a concerted effort to challenge ingrained beliefs about being a selfless giver. One way I am able to give to others is by letting others take care of me at times.

The Myth that Love and Anger Are Incompatible.   Many people are convinced that if they love someone this necessarily implies that they cannot get angry at them. So when they get angry, they tend to deny these feelings or express them in indirect ways. Unfortunately, denied or unexpressed anger can lead to the death of a relationship. Anger needs to be dealt with in a constructive way before it reaches explosive proportions.

Anger and love cannot be compartmentalized: If you deny your anger, you are negating your love. It is difficult to feel loving toward others if we harbor unexpressed grudges. These unresolved issues tend to poison the relationship and can actually prevent deeper intimacy. The harmful effects of unexpressed anger on relationships is explored in some detail by Harriet Goldhor Lerner in *The Dance of Anger* (1985) and *The Dance of Intimacy* (1989).

■ Self-Doubt and Lack of Self-Love

Despite our need for love, we often put barriers in the way of our attempts to give and receive love. One common obstacle consists of the messages we sometimes send to others concerning ourselves. If we enter relationships convinced that nobody could possibly love us, we will give this message to others in many subtle ways. We create a self-fulfilling prophecy; we make the very thing we fear come true by telling both ourselves and others that life can be no other way.

If you are convinced that you're unlovable, your conviction is probably related to decisions you made about yourself during your childhood or adolescent years. At one time, perhaps you decided that you wouldn't be loved *unless* you did certain expected things or lived up to another's design for your life. For example: "Unless I produce, I won't be loved. To be loved, I must produce good grades, become successful, and make the most of my life." Such a decision can make it difficult to convince yourself later in life that you can be loved even if you're not productive.

Jay decided as a child that he would do whatever it took to meet the expectations of others and to gain their acceptance. He gives his all to please people and to get them to like him, yet he has few friends. Through his actions of desperately trying to win people over, he pushes them away even more. Although he thinks he is doing everything right, people don't like the way he behaves around them. He is constantly depressed and complains about how hard life is for him. He seeks sympathy and receives rejection. He needs continual reassurance that he is capable, yet when he does get acceptance and reassurance, he negates it. He seems to work at convincing people that he is really unlovable, and eventually people who know him get frustrated and rebuff him. He may never realize that he has created the cycle of his own rejection. In some important ways he continues to live by the theme that no matter what he does or how hard he tries, people will still not like him, much less love him.

Sometimes people have a difficult time believing that they are lovable for who they are, and they may discount the love others give them. For example, think for a moment of how many times you have completed this sentence in any of the following ways: People love me only because I am . . .

- pretty, bright, and witty.
- good in sports.
- a good student.
- a fine provider.

- attractive.
- accomplished.
- cooperative and considerate.
- a good father [mother].
- a good husband [wife].

If you have limited your ability to receive love from others by telling yourself (and by convincing others) that you are loved primarily for a single trait, it would be healthy to challenge this assumption. For example, if you say "You only love me because of my body," you might try to realize that your body is only *one* of your assets. You can learn to appreciate this asset without assuming that it is all there is to the person you are. If you have trouble seeing any desirable characteristics besides your physical attractiveness, you are likely to give others messages that your primary value is bound up in appearances. Ideally, you will come to accept that being a physically attractive person makes it easier for others to notice you and want to initiate contact with you. However, you don't need to limit yourself by depending exclusively on how you look, for you can work at developing other traits. The danger here consists of relying on physical attractiveness as a basis for building and maintaining a relationship. If you rely exclusively on physical attractiveness as a source of gaining love from others (or from yourself), your ability to be loved is in a tenuous state.

In my own life I, (Jerry) have had to struggle for a long time to recognize and accept my lovability. It would be easy for me to say "People love me only because I'm productive—because I write books, am an energetic teacher, am a good organizer, work hard, and because of my accomplishments." It took me many years to begin to entertain the notion that who and what I am is far greater than all the things I *do* professionally. I continue to learn that my compulsive energy and drive often put distance between those people who love me (and those I love) and myself. One insight that came to me is that the very thing I sometimes believe I *must* do or be to be loved actually gets in the way of others' loving me. I am discovering that my basic worth is not measured by what I accomplish and that there are many lovable dimensions within me if I allow them expression.

We sometimes imagine that other people have expectations we must meet to be loved. This obstructs our ability to love and receive love. In his inspirational book *God's Love Song,* the Reverend Sam Maier (1991) admits that it was a difficult struggle for him to assume responsibility for himself instead of striving for love from others by living up to what they expected of him.

> As a child I was trained to receive satisfaction from meeting other people's expectations of what I should do and be. My parents expected me to behave in certain ways and I tried to please them. My teacher made demands on me and I tried to oblige. When I began my life work, my congregations had expectations of my performance and I tried hard to measure up. (p. 95)

I (Jerry) can relate to Sam Maier's struggle to not buy love and acceptance by meeting the expectations of others. For much of my life, I have been concerned with doing what was expected of me, especially in striving for accomplishments. In my early years I felt that I did not belong, that I was not too useful, and that I did not have much significance. A pattern of my life has been creating my identity through my work, which has led to a sense of being wanted, accepted, and appreciated. I might well have confused the outcomes of my work with being lovable and worthwhile. It's essential for me to remember that the difficulty I sometimes have in feeling worthy apart from my productivity is not a condition I will ever "cure," but it is a pattern I can recognize in myself. And it is possible for me to create a new perspective wherein I feel I am still worthwhile—even if I am not doing something productive at the moment.

■ Our Fear of Love

Despite our need for love, we often fear loving and being loved. Our fear can lead us to seal off our need to experience love, and it can dull our capacity to care about others. Love doesn't come with guarantees. We can't be sure that another person will always love us, and we do lose loved ones. As Hodge (1967) insists, we can't eliminate the possibility that we will be hurt if we choose to love. Our loved ones may die or be injured or become painfully ill, or they may simply be mistrustful of our caring. "These are painful experiences, and we cannot avoid them if we choose to love. It is part of the human dilemma that love always includes the element of hurt" (p. 266).

Most of the common fears of risking in love are related to rejection, loss, the failure of love to be reciprocated, or uneasiness with intensity. Here are some of the ways these fears might be expressed:

- "Since I once got badly hurt in a love relationship, I'm not willing to take the chance of trusting again."
- "I fear allowing myself to love others because of the possibility that they will be seriously injured, contract a terrible illness, or die. I don't want to let them matter that much; that way, if I lose them, it won't hurt as much as if they really mattered."
- "My fear is that love will never be as good as I imagine it to be."
- "I'm afraid of loving others because they might want more from me than I'm willing to give, and I might feel suffocated."
- "I'm afraid that I'm basically unlovable and that when you really get to know me you'll want little to do with me."
- "Emotional closeness is scary for me, because if I care deeply for a person and permit him [her] to care about me, then I'm vulnerable."
- "One great fear is that people will be indifferent to me — that they simply won't give a damn about my existence."
- "In many ways it's easier for me to take rejection than acceptance. It's hard for me to accept compliments or to be close and intimate. If people tell me they want to care for me, I feel I've taken on a burden, and I'm afraid of letting them down."
- "I've never really allowed myself to look at whether I'm lovable. My fear is that I will search deep within myself and find little for another to love. What will I do if I discover that I'm grotesque or hollow and empty or incapable of giving or receiving?"

Sarah has struggled in overcoming early childhood messages in her quest for loving and being loved. At her present age of 26 she is still learning to deal with the fear of love. In her first-person account here she describes the experience of "wearing protective armor" around her heart.

> *Intimacy and trust do not come easy for me. Physical contact and close intimate relationships were not present during my childhood. Yet there is nothing more incredible than sharing your life with someone you love and trust completely. Even after being together almost four years, my boyfriend Al and I are still often engaged in what I sometimes call an emotional tug-of-war. He gives a little, and I feel secure. I give a little, and then feel like I'm the one giving it all. We are always struggling to find a balance.*
>
> *I have become aware that I wear a protective armor around my heart. In my own personal therapy, I have been exploring the ways in which this wall was helpful in my childhood, but may keep people at a distance now. I put my boyfriend through a test every day. If he can take the time to look beneath the tough exterior, he passes the test, and the wall comes down. I sometimes wonder if the game will ever end.*
>
> *I have come to realize the vicious cycle of ebb and flow in my relationship. At times things have gotten so difficult we've actually decided to end it. I sometimes use the analogy of a person on life support for our relationship.*

The loved ones hesitate on pulling the plug, because the person could wake up any day. Sometimes hanging on is what you have to do, so you don't risk ending something that may have come alive the very next day.

No matter what your own fears may be, you can learn, as Sarah has, to choose a different path and to open yourself to the potential for love that awaits you. Can you identify with Sarah's struggle in any way?

➤ *Time Out for Personal Reflection*

1. Who are some of the people who have made the most difference in your life, and in what ways were they important?

   a. _____

   b. _____

   c. _____

   d. _____

   e. _____

2. How do you express your love to others? Check the responses that apply to you, and add any other ways in which you show love, affection, and caring.

   _____ a. by telling the other person that I love him or her
   _____ b. through touching and other nonverbal means
   _____ c. by doing special things for the person
   _____ d. by making myself known to the person
   _____ e. by becoming vulnerable and trusting
   _____ f. by buying the person gifts

   g. _____

   _____

3. How do you express to another person your own need to receive love, affection, and caring?

   _____ a. by telling him or her that I need to be loved
   _____ b. by being open and trusting

   c. _____

   _____

4. List some specific fears you have concerning loving others.

   _____

   _____

_____

_____

5. Mention some barriers within yourself that prevent others from loving you or that prevent you from fully receiving their love. (Examples: being overly suspicious, refusing to accept others' love, feeling a lack of self-worth, needing to return their love.)

_____

_____

_____

_____

6. List some qualities you have that you deem lovable. (Examples: my ability to care for others, my sense of humor.)

_____

_____

_____

_____

7. List some specific ways in which you might become a more lovable person. (Examples: increasing my feelings of self-worth, trusting others more, taking better care of my physical appearance.)

_____

_____

_____

_____

Learning to Love and Appreciate Ourselves

In our counseling sessions clients are at times surprised when we ask them what they actually like and appreciate about themselves. They look uncomfortable and embarrassed, and it is obvious that they are not accustomed to speaking positively about themselves. An indirect way to get people to express some self-appreciation is to ask questions such as: "If your best friends were here, how would they describe you?" "What positive characteristics would they ascribe to you?" "What reasons might they give for choosing you as a friend?" People appear to find it easier to talk about how they see themselves in positive ways when responding to these kinds of questions.

Some people are reluctant to speak of their self-love, because they have been brought up to think of it as purely egocentric. But unless we learn how to love ourselves, we'll encounter difficulties in loving others and in allowing them to express their love for us. We can't very well give to others what we don't possess ourselves. And if we can't appreciate our own worth, how can we believe others when they say that they see value in us? This meditation by Casey and Vanceburg (1985) captures the importance of loving ourselves:

> No one of us is free from the need for love. And most of us search for reassurances of that love from the significant people in our lives. However, the search will be unending until we come to love ourselves. Love of self is assured when we understand our worth, our actual necessity in the larger picture of the events that touch us all. (Meditation of January 17)

Having love for ourselves doesn't imply having an exaggerated picture of our own importance or placing ourselves above others or at the center of the universe. Rather, it implies having respect for ourselves even though we're imperfect. It entails caring about our lives and striving to become the people we are capable of becoming.

Many writers have stressed the necessity of self-love as a condition of love for others. In *The Art of Loving,* Fromm (1956) describes self-love as respect for our own integrity and uniqueness and maintains that it cannot be separated from love and understanding of others. We often ask clients who only give to others and who have a difficult time taking for themselves: "Do *you* deserve what you so freely give to others?" "If your own well runs dry, how will you be able to give to others?" We cannot give what we have not learned and experienced ourselves. Moore (1994) writes that those who try very hard to be loved do not succeed because they do not realize that they have to first love themselves as others before they can receive love from others.

As we grow to treat ourselves with increasing respect and regard, we increase our ability to fully accept the love others might want to give us; at the same time, we have the foundation for genuinely loving others. If we are unable to care for ourselves, we are unable to care for another person. Caring for ourselves and caring for others are mutually dependent.

Inauthentic and Authentic Love

■ "Love" that Stifles

It isn't always easy to distinguish between authentic love, which enhances us and those we love, and the kind of "love" that diminishes us and those to whom we attempt to give it. Some forms of pseudolove parade as real love but cripple us and those we say we love. Certain characteristics are typical of a type of love that stifles. While this list isn't rigid or definitive, it may give you some ideas you can use in thinking about the quality of your love. A person whose love is inauthentic:

- needs to be in charge and make decisions for the other person
- has rigid and unrealistic expectations of how the other person must act to be worthy of love
- attaches strings to loving and loves conditionally
- puts little trust in the love relationship
- perceives personal change as a threat to the continuation of the relationship
- is possessive
- depends on the other person to fill a void in life
- lacks commitment
- is unwilling to share important thoughts and feelings about the relationship
- resorts to manipulation to get the other person to respond in a predetermined manner

Most of us can find some of these manifestations of inauthentic love in our relationships, yet this does not mean that our love is necessarily fraudulent. For instance, at times you may be reluctant to let another person know about your private life, you may have excessive expectations of another person, or you may attempt to impose your own agenda. It is essential to be honest with yourself and to recognize when you are not expressing genuine love, then you can choose to change these patterns.

■ Some Meanings of Authentic Love

So far, we've discussed mostly what we think love is *not*. Now we'd like to share some of the positive meanings love has for us.

Love means that I *know* the person I love. I'm aware of the many facets of the other person — not just the beautiful side but also the limitations, inconsistencies, and flaws. I have an awareness of the other's feelings and thoughts, and I experience something of the core of that person. I can penetrate social masks and roles and see the other person on a deeper level.

Love means that I *care* about the welfare of the person I love. To the extent that it is genuine, my caring is not a smothering of the person or a possessive clinging. On the contrary, my caring liberates both of us. If I care about you, I'm concerned about your growth, and I hope you will become all that you can become. Consequently, I don't put up roadblocks to what you do that enhances you as a person, even though it may result in my discomfort at times.

Love means having *respect* for the *dignity* of the person I love. If I love you, I can see you as a separate person, with your own values and thoughts and feelings, and I do not insist that you surrender your identity and conform to an image of what I expect you to be for me. I can allow and encourage you to stand alone and to be who you are, and I avoid treating you as an object or using you primarily to gratify my own needs.

Love means having a *responsibility* toward the person I love. If I love you, I'm responsive to most of your major needs as a person. This responsibility does not entail my doing for you what you are capable of doing for yourself; nor does it mean that I run your life for you. It does imply acknowledging that what I am and what I do affects you, so that I am directly involved in your happiness and your misery. A lover does have the capacity to hurt or neglect the loved one, and in this sense I see that love entails acceptance of some responsibility for the impact my way of being has on you.

Love means *growth* for both me and the person I love. If I love you, I am growing as a result of my love. You are a stimulant for me to become more fully what I might become, and my loving enhances your being as well. We each grow as a result of caring and being cared for; we each share in an enriching experience that does not detract from our being. Buscaglia (1992) puts this idea well when he writes: "We must not only respect the need for our lover's growth, we must encourage it, even at the risk of losing them. It seems ironic, but it is true, that only in continuing to grow separately is there any hope of individuals growing together" (p. 22).

Love entails *letting go of fear.* Jampolsky (1981) asserts that worrying about past guilts and future fears allows little room to enjoy and savor the present. Not judging others is one way I can let go of fear and experience love. Acceptance means that I am not focused on changing others so that they will conform to my expectations of how they should be.

Love means making a *commitment* to the person I love. This commitment does not entail surrendering our total selves to each other; nor does it imply that the relationship is necessarily permanent. It does entail a willingness to stay with each other in times of pain, uncertainty, struggle, and despair, as well as in times of calm and enjoyment.

Love means that I am *vulnerable.* If I open myself up to you in trust, I may experience hurt, rejection, and loss. Since you aren't perfect, you have the capacity to hurt me; and since there are no guarantees in love, there is no security that your love will endure. Loving involves sharing with and experiencing with the person I love. My love for you implies that I want to spend time with you and share meaningful aspects of your life with you. It also implies that I have a desire to share significant aspects of myself with you.

Love means *trusting* the person I love. If I love you, I trust that you will accept my caring and my love and that you won't deliberately hurt me. I trust that you will find me lovable and that you won't abandon me; I trust the reciprocal nature of our love. If we trust each other, we are willing to be open to each other and can shed masks and pretenses and reveal our true selves.

Love can tolerate *imperfection.* In a love relationship there are times of boredom, times when I may feel like giving up, times of real strain, and times I experience an impasse. Authentic love does not imply perpetual happiness. I can stay during rough times, however, because I can remember what we had together in the past and can envision what we will have together in our future if we care enough to face our problems and work them through.

Love is *freeing.* Love is freely given, not doled out on demand. At the same time, my love for you is not contingent on whether you fulfill my expectations of you. Authentic love does not imply "I'll love you when you become perfect or when you become what I expect you to become." Authentic love is not given with strings attached. There is an unconditional quality about love. Maier believes that the prayer of Saint Francis of Assisi is illustrative of a heart that is filled with unconditional love:

Oh Lord, make me an instrument of Thy peace.
Where there is hatred, let me sow love;
Where there is injury, pardon;
Where there is discord, union;
Where there is despair, hope;
Where there is darkness, light;
Where there is sadness, joy;
O Lord, grant that we seek not to be consoled, but to console;
not to be understood, but to understand;
not to be loved but to love. For it is in giving that we receive, in
forgetting that we find ourselves, in pardoning that we are
 pardoned, and in dying that we are born to eternal life. Amen.
(cited in Maier, 1991, pp. 68–69)

Love is *expansive.* If I love you, I encourage you to reach out and develop other relationships. Although our live for each other and our commitment to each other might preclude certain actions on our parts, we are not totally and exclusively wedded to each other. Only a pseudolove cements one person to another in such a way that he or she is not given room to grow. Casey and Vanceburg (1985) put this notion well:

> The honest evidence of our love is our commitment to encouraging another's full development. We are interdependent personalities who need one another's presence in order to fulfill our destiny. And yet, we are also separate individuals. We must come to terms with our struggles alone." (Meditation of February 21)

Love means having a *want* for the person I love without having a *need* for that person to be complete. If I am nothing without you, then I'm not really free to love you. If I love you and you leave, I'll experience a loss and be sad and lonely, but I'll still be able to survive. If I am overly dependent on you for my meaning and my survival, I am not free to challenge our relationship; nor am I free to challenge and confront you. Because of my fear of losing you, I'll settle for less than I want, and this settling will surely lead to feelings of resentment.

Love means *identifying* with the person I love. If I love you, I can empathize with you and see the world through your eyes. I can identify with you because I'm able to see myself in you and you in me. This closeness does not imply a continual "togetherness," for distance and separation are sometimes essential in a loving relationship. Distance can intensify a loving bond, and it can help us rediscover ourselves, so that we are able to meet each other in a new way.

Love is *selfish.* I can only love you if I genuinely love, value, appreciate, and respect myself. If I am empty, all I can give you is my emptiness. If I feel that I'm complete and worthwhile in myself, I'm able to give to you out of my fullness. One of the best ways for me to give you love is by fully enjoying myself with you.

Love involves *seeing the potential* within the person I love. If I love you, I am able to see you as the person you can become, while still accepting who you are now. Goethe's observation is relevant here: By taking people as they are, we make them worse, but by treating them as if they already were what they ought to be, we help make them better.

Love means *letting go* of the illusion of total *control* of ourselves, others, and our environment. The more I strive for complete control, the more out of control I am. Loving implies a surrender of control and being open to life's events. It implies the capacity to be surprised. Bringing surprise to love, says Buscaglia (1992), is a way to keep a relationship alive: "Love withers with predictability; its very essence is surprise and amazement. To make love a prisoner of the mundane is to take away its passion and lose it forever" (p. 19).

We conclude this discussion of the meanings that authentic love has for us by sharing a thought from *The Art of Loving* (Fromm, 1956); mature love sums up the essential characteristics of authentic love quite well:

> Mature love is union under the condition of preserving one's integrity, one's individuality. In love this paradox occurs that two beings become one and yet remain two. (pp. 20–21)

Is It Worth It to Love?

Often we hear people say something like "Sure, I need to love and to be loved, but is it *really* worth it?" Underlying this question is a series of other questions: "Can I survive without love? Is the risk of rejection and loss worth taking? Are the rewards of opening myself up as great as the risks?"

It would be comforting to have an absolute answer to these questions, but each of us must struggle to decide for ourselves whether it's worth it to love. Our first task is to decide whether we prefer isolation to intimacy. Of course, our choice is not between extreme isolation and constant intimacy; surely there are degrees of both. But we do need to decide whether to experiment with extending our narrow world to include significant others. We can increasingly open ourselves to others and discover for ourselves what that is like for us; alternatively, we can decide that people are basically unreliable and that it's better to be safe and go hungry emotionally.

Perhaps you feel unable to give love, but you'd like to learn how to become more intimate. You might begin by acknowledging this reality to yourself, as well as to those in your life with whom you'd like to become more intimate. In this way you can take a significant beginning step.

In answering the question of whether it's worth it to you to love, you can challenge some of your attitudes and beliefs concerning acceptance and rejection. We've encountered many people who believe that is isn't worth it to love because of the possibility of experiencing rejection. If you feel this way, you can decide whether to stop at this barrier. You can ask yourself: "What's so catastrophic about being rejected? Will I die if someone I love leaves me? Can I survive the emotional hurt that comes with disappointment in love?" Of course, being rejected is not a pleasant experience, yet we hope this possibility will not deter you from allowing yourself to love someone. If a love relationship ends for you, it would surely be worth it to honestly search for your part in contributing to this situation without being severely self-critical. If you identify some ways in which you would like to change, you can then learn from this experience.

Elana, a client we worked with, had to learn to trust again after being deeply hurt in a relationship. She felt that she had a mutual loving bond with Monte, yet most of her friends had a hard time understanding why she continued the relationship. Elana had an idealized picture of Monte and made excuses for his insensitive behavior. She found herself becoming extremely dependent on him and preoccupied with trying to please him at all costs, even if it meant sacrificing her own happiness to keep peace with him. Elana's friends let her know of their concern for her, and they tried to convince her that she deserved better treatment. Elana's response was to cut herself off from her friends so she would not have to deal with their feedback. Eventually, she experienced a betrayal by Monte, which led to a crisis. Even though Elana discontinued her relationship with Monte, she was quite fearful of loving again, and her old wounds were reopened each time she met a new man. She had fears of dragging memories of her past betrayal into other relationships. Indeed, she would approach new relationships with fear and distrust, which made it difficult to open herself to love again. With concerted work on her part, Elana became aware of how clinging to her past hampered her ability to receive love and develop friendships. Elana's immediate impulses were to flee from getting close, yet she challenged her fears with the realization that the risk of rejection did not have to keep her helpless and guarded.

Hodge (1967) writes that, as adults, we're no longer helpless and that we can do something about rejection and hurt. We can choose to leave relationships that aren't satisfying, we can learn to survive pain, and we can realize that being rejected doesn't mean we are fundamentally unlovable. Consider how the last line in Hodge's *Your Fear of Love* may apply to you: "We can discover for ourselves that it is worth the risk to love, even though we tremble and even though we know we will sometimes experience the hurt we fear" (p. 270).

▶ *Time Out for Personal Reflection*

1. The following are some possible reasons for thinking that it is or isn't worth it to love. Check the ones that fit your own thoughts and feelings.
   It's worth it to love, because

   _____ of the joy involved when two people love each other.
   _____ the rewards are greater than the risks.
   _____ a life without love is empty.

   List other reasons:

   _____

   _____

It isn't worth it to love, because

_____   of the pain involved when love is not returned.

_____   the risks are not worth the possible rewards.

_____   it's better to be alone than with someone you might no longer love (or who might no longer love you).

List other reasons:

_____

_____

2. Review our list of the meanings love has for us, and then list some of the meanings love has for you.

_____

_____

_____

_____

3. Think of someone you love. What specifically do you love about that person? (Example: I love his sensitivity.) Then list specific ways that you can show your love to this person. (Example: I spend time with her. I enjoy doing things that make her happy.)

_____

_____

_____

Chapter Summary

Although we have a need to love and to be loved, most of us encounter barriers to meeting these needs. Our doubt that we are worthy of being loved can be a major roadblock to loving others and receiving their love. Although many of us have been brought up believing that self-love is egotistical, in reality we are not able to love others unless we love and appreciate ourselves. How can be give to others something we do not possess ourselves? Our fear of love is another major impediment to loving. Many people would like guarantees that their love for special people will last as long as they live, but the stark reality is that there are no guarantees. It helps to realize that loving and trembling go together and to accept that we must learn to love in spite of our fears.

Myths and misconceptions about love make it difficult to be open to giving and receiving love. A few of these are the myth of eternal love, the myth that love implies constant closeness, the myth of the exclusiveness of love, the myth that true love is selfless, and the myth of falling in love. Although genuine love results in the growth of both persons, some "love" is stifling. Not all that poses as real love is authentic, and one of the major challenges is to decide for ourselves the meanings of authentic love. By recognizing our attitudes about loving, we can increase our ability to choose the ways in which we behave in our love relationships.

Activities and Exercises

1. Think about some early decisions you made regarding your own ability to love or to be loved, such as

   - "I'm not lovable unless I produce."
   - "I'm not lovable unless I meet others' expectations."
   - "I won't love another because of my fears of rejection."
   - "I'm not worthy of being loved."

   Write down some of the messages you've received and perhaps accepted uncritically. How has your ability to feel loved or to give love been restricted by these messages and decisions?

2. For a period of at least a week, pay close attention to the messages conveyed by the media concerning love. What picture of love do you get from television? What do popular songs portray about love? Make a list of some common myths regarding love that you see promoted by the media, such as

   - Love means that two people never argue or disagree.
   - Love implies giving up one's identity.
   - Love implies constant closeness and romance.
   - Love means rarely having negative feelings toward those you love.

3. How much do you agree with the proposition that you can't fully love others unless you first love yourself? How does this apply to you? In your journal you might want to write some notes to yourself concerning the situations in which you don't appreciate yourself. You might also keep a record of the times and events when you do value and respect yourself.

4. How important is love in your life right now? Do you feel that you love others in the ways you'd like to? Do you feel that you're loved by others in the ways you want to be?

5. Are you an active lover or a passive lover? You might try writing down the ways in which you demonstrate your caring for those you love and then ask them to read your list and discuss with you how they see your style of loving.

6. Select one or more of the following books for further reading on the topics explored in this chapter: *Love* (Buscaglia, 1972); *Born for Love: Reflections on Loving* (Buscaglia, 1992); *The Art of Loving* (Fromm, 1956); *Love Is Letting Go of Fear* (Jampolsky, 1981); *God's Love Song* (Maier, 1991); *The Road Less Traveled* (Peck, 1978); *No Hiding Place* (Williams, 1992).

9

Sexuality

It's no easier to achieve
sexual autonomy than it is
to achieve autonomy in other
areas of your life.

✔ *Prechapter Self-Inventory*

Use the following scale to respond: 4 = this statement is true of me *most* of the time; 3 = this statement is true of me *much* of the time; 2 = this statement is true of me *some* of the time; 1 = this statement is true of me *almost none* of the time.

_____ 1. I think that the quality of a sexual relationship usually depends on the general quality of the relationship.

_____ 2. I believe that exercising sexual freedom creates corresponding responsibilities.

_____ 3. I find it easy to talk openly and honestly about sexuality with at least one other person.

_____ 4. For me, sex without love is unsatisfying.

_____ 5. I experience guilt or shame over sexuality.

_____ 6. I have found that gender-role definitions and stereotypes get in the way of mutually satisfying sexual relations.

_____ 7. Sensual experiences do not necessarily have to be sexual.

_____ 8. Performance standards and expectations get in the way of my enjoying sensual and sexual experiences.

_____ 9. I have struggled to find my own values pertaining to sexual behavior.

_____ 10. I believe that I acquired healthy attitudes about sexuality from my parents.

_____ 11. I find safe sex confining.

_____ 12. I wish I knew more about HIV and AIDS.

_____ 13. I don't know what I like or dislike in sexual relationships.

_____ 14. I worry too much about AIDS and other sexually transmitted diseases.

_____ 15. I don't think about safer sex if I really like my partner and think he [she] is HIV negative.

Introduction

People of all ages may experience difficulty talking openly about sexual matters. This lack of communication contributes to the perpetuation of myths and misinformation about sexuality despite the fact that the media are giving increased attention to all aspects of sexual behavior, literally bombarding us with new information and trends. Almost nothing is unmentionable in the popular media. Yet this increased knowledge regarding sexuality does not appear to have resulted in encouraging all people to talk more freely about their own sexual concerns, nor has it always reduced their anxiety about sexuality. For many people sex remains a delicate topic, and they find it difficult to communicate their sexual wants, especially to a person close to them.

One of our goals for this chapter is to help you learn how to recognize and appropriately express your sexual concerns. Too many people suffer from needless guilt, shame, worries, and inhibition merely because they keep their concerns about sexuality secret, largely out of embarrassment. Moreover, keeping your concerns to yourself can hinder your efforts to determine your own values regarding sex. The reality of the AIDS crisis challenges sexually active individuals to rethink their priorities and their sexual behavior. Thus, we address information necessary to prevent HIV infection, and we look at myths and misconceptions surrounding HIV and AIDS. In this chapter we ask you to examine your values and attitudes toward sexuality and to determine what choices *you* want to make in this area of your life.

Myths and Misconceptions about Sexuality

We consider the following statements to be misconceptions about sex. As you read over this list, ask yourself what your attitudes are and where you developed these beliefs. Are they working for you? Could any of these statements apply to you? How might some of these statements affect your ability to make free choices concerning sexuality?

- If I allow myself to become sexual, I'll get into trouble.
- Women should be less active than men in sex.
- Women are not as sexually desirable when they initiate sex.
- By their very nature, men are sexually aggressive.
- Men need to prove themselves through sexual conquests.
- As I get older, I'm bound to lose interest in sex.
- If my partner really loved me, I wouldn't have to tell him or her what I liked or wanted. My partner should know what I need intuitively without my asking.
- My partner would be offended and hurt if I told her or him what I liked and wanted.
- I am not responsible for the level of my sexual satisfaction.
- I can't hope to overcome any negative conditioning I received about sex as I was growing up.
- Acting without any guilt or restrictions is what is meant by being sexually free.
- The more I know about the mechanics of sex, the more satisfied I will be in my sexual relationships.
- The only place I get along well with my partner is in bed.
- Being sexually attracted to a person other than my partner implies that I don't really find my partner sexually exciting.
- Being attracted to someone of the same gender is abnormal.
- There is only one right person for me.
- Multiple sexual relationships enhance a primary relationship.
- Gay men are the majority of those who get AIDS.
- The inability or unwillingness to engage in multiple sexual relationships indicates a lack of trust in myself or at least a basic insecurity.

- The more physically attractive a person is, the more sexually exciting he or she is.
- With the passage of time, any sexual relationship is bound to become less exciting or grow stale.

Learning to Talk Openly about Sexual Issues

As in other areas of your life, you may saddle yourself with beliefs about sex that you have not given much thought to. Open discussions with those you are intimate with, as well as an honest exchange of views in your class, can do a lot to help you challenge the unexamined attitudes you have about this significant area of your life.

Although you might expect that people today would be able to discuss openly and frankly the concerns they have about sex, this is not the case. Students will discuss attitudes about sexual behavior in a general way, but they show considerable resistance to speaking of their own sexual concerns, fears, and conflicts. It is of value to simply provide a climate in which people can feel free to examine their personal concerns. In the groups that we lead, we have found it useful to give women and men an opportunity to discuss sexual issues in separate groups and then come together to share the concerns they've discovered. Typically, both men and women appreciate the chance to explore their sexual fears, expectations, secrets, and wishes, as well as their concerns about the normality of their bodies and feelings. When the male and female groups come together, the participants usually find much common ground, and the experience of making this discovery can be very therapeutic. For instance, men may fear becoming impotent, not performing up to some expected standard, being lousy lovers, or not being "man enough." When the men and women meet as one group, the men may be surprised to discover that women worry about having to achieve orgasm (or several of them) every time they have sex and that they, too, have fears about their sexual desirability. When people talk about these concerns in a direct way, much game playing and putting on of false fronts can be dispensed with.

Although it may be helpful for people to be encouraged to talk more openly about sexual concerns, their privacy should be respected and they should not be pushed to disclose personal sexual thoughts, fantasies, and experiences. What seems more relevant is that they know that their fantasies and feelings are not evil and need not cause them to feel guilty. We do not need to know the specifics of a person's sexual fantasy to help this person overcome feelings of guilt. It is probably helpful to most of us to learn that we are not the only ones to have such fantasies. There is a delicate line between being sexually repressed and being indiscriminately open about our sexual lives.

In the past there was clearly a taboo against openly discussing sexual topics. Today, bookstores are flooded with paperbacks devoted to enhancing sexuality. Although people may come to a counselor with a greater awareness of sexuality, it is clear that many of them have not been able to translate their knowledge into a more satisfying sex life. In fact, an increased awareness of what is normal for

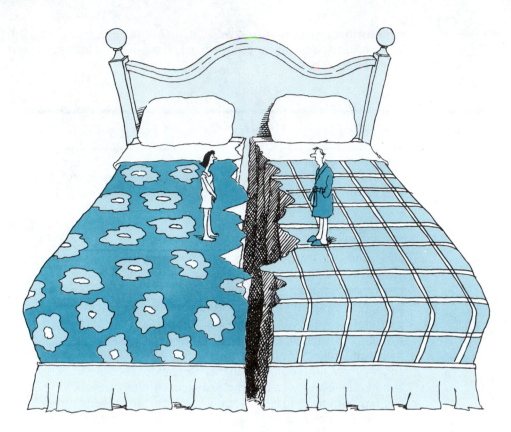

women and men may have compounded their problems. They may burden themselves with expectations of what their sex life *should* be like, according to the latest studies. Counselors discover that couples are often very uncomfortable communicating their sexual likes and dislikes, their personal fears, and the shame and guilt they sometimes have about sex. They still operate on the old myth that if their mate really loves them, he or she should know intuitively what gives them pleasure. To ask for what you want sexually is often seen as diminishing the value of what is received.

Nevertheless, the outlook in this area is not totally negative. Whereas in the past a couple might have kept their sexual problems locked behind their bedroom door, the trend now is toward acknowledging these problems and seeking help. Indeed, many people are able to apply their knowledge about sexuality to enhancing their sex life. Many more are challenging the myths pertaining to sex.

A number of typical concerns are openly aired by both men and women in discussion groups we have participated in. These concerns might be expressed as follows:

- "I often wonder what excites my partner and what she [he] would like, yet I seldom ask. I suppose it's important for me to learn how to initiate by asking and also how to tell the other person what I enjoy."

- "My fear of getting AIDS keeps me from being involved in sexual relationships."
- "Even if my partner has been tested for the AIDS virus, I am still uneasy because of the chance that he or she will have sex with others."
- "So often I doubt my capacity as a lover. I'd like to know what my partner thinks. Perhaps one thing I can learn to do is to share this concern with him [her]."
- "I worry about my body. Am I normal? How do I compare with others? Am I too big? too small? Am I proportioned properly? Do others find me attractive? Do I find myself attractive? What can I do to increase my own appeal to myself and to others?"
- "Am I responsible if my partner is dissatisfied?"
- "I am concerned about sexually transmitted diseases."
- "Sex can be fun, I suppose, but often I'm much too serious. It's really difficult for me to be playful and to let go without feeling foolish — and not just in regard to sex. It isn't easy for me to be spontaneous."
- "Many times I feel that my partner is bored with sex, and that makes me wonder whether I'm sexually attractive to her [him]."
- "There are times when I desire sex and initiate it, and my partner lets me know in subtle or even direct ways that he [she] isn't interested. Then I feel almost like a beggar. This kind of experience makes me not want to initiate anymore."
- "As a woman, I'd really like to know how other women feel after a sexual experience. Do they normally feel fulfilled? What prevents them from enjoying sex? How do they decide who's responsible when they don't have a satisfying experience?"
- "As a man, I frequently worry about performance standards, and that gets in the way of my making love freely and spontaneously. It's a burden to me to worry about doing the right things and being sexually powerful, and I often wonder what other men experience in this area."
- "There seem to two extremes in sex: we can be overly concerned with pleasing our partner and therefore take too much responsibility for their sexual gratification, or we can become so involved with our own pleasure that we don't concern ourselves with our partner's feelings or needs. I ask myself how I can discover a balance — how I can be selfish enough to seek my own pleasure yet sensitive enough to take care of my partner's needs."
- "Sometimes I get scared of women [men], and I struggle with myself over whether I should let the other person know that I feel threatened. Will I be perceived as weak? Is it so terrible to be weak at times? Can I be weak and still be strong?"
- "I frequently feel guilty over my sexual feelings, but there are times when I wonder whether I really want to free myself of guilt feelings. What would happen if I were free of guilt? Would I give up all control?"
- "I worry a lot about being feminine [masculine] and all that it entails. I'm trying to separate out what I've been conditioned to believe about the way a woman [man] is supposed to be, yet I still have a hard time deciding for myself the kind of woman [man] I want to be. I want to find my own standards and not be haunted by external standards of what I should be and feel."
- "Can sex be an attempt to overcome my feelings of isolation and separation? There are times when I think I'm running into a sexual relationship because I feel lonely."

- "I've wondered whether we are by nature monogamous. I know I'd like to experience others sexually, but I don't want my mate to have these same experiences."
- "There are times lately when I don't seem to be enjoying sex much. In the past year I haven't been able to experience orgasms, and the man I'm living with thinks it's his fault. What's happening? Why am I not as sexually responsive as I used to be with him?"
- "I feel very open and trusting in talking about my sexuality in this group, and I'd very much like to experience this with my partner. I want to be able to be direct and avoid getting involved in sexual games. I need to learn how to initiate this kind of open dialogue."
- "There are times when I really don't crave intercourse but would still like to be held and touched and caressed. I wish my partner could understand this about me and not take it as a personal rejection when for some reason I simply don't want intercourse."
- "I really felt humiliated when I became impotent — I was sure she saw me as unmanly. I'm glad to learn that this is a common experience for other men and that I'm not abnormal."

We've included this rather long list here because these are common concerns about sexuality. Knowing that many others have these concerns, we hope you will feel less alone with some of your anxieties about sex. Look over the list again and identify the statements that seem to fit for you. Ask yourself if you are ready to reexamine your feelings about some of these issues.

Sex and Guilt

■ Guilt over Sexual Feelings

Most of us have learned certain taboos about sex. We often feel guilty about our *feelings,* even if we don't act them out. Guilt is commonly experienced in connection with same sex fantasies and impulses, feelings of sexual attraction toward members of your family, sexual feelings toward people other than your partner, enjoyment of sexuality, and too much (or too little) desire for sex. Even though we may intensely fear such feelings, we can and should learn to accept them as legitimate. Moreover, simply having feelings doesn't mean that we're impelled to act on them.

As in the case of shame over our bodies, we need to become aware of our guilt and reexamine it to determine whether we're needlessly burdening ourselves. Not all guilt is unhealthy and irrational, of course, but there is a real value in learning to challenge guilt feelings and to rid ourselves of those that are *unrealistic.*

For many of my earlier years, I (Jerry) experienced a great deal of guilt over my sexual feelings. I believe that my guilt was largely due to the influence of a strict religious education that took a strong stand on sexual morality. Even though I've consciously struggled to overcome some of this influence, I still experience traces of old guilt. As in so many other areas, I find that early lessons in regard to sex are difficult to unlearn. Consequently, it has been important for me to continue to challenge old guilt patterns that interfere with my sexual enjoyment, while at the same time developing a personal ethical code that I can live by with integrity and self-respect.

Contrary to Jerry, I (Marianne) did not have to contend that much with guilt over sexuality. Growing up on a farm in Germany allowed me to realize that sexuality is an important aspect of both animal and human life. Living in close proximity with family members and lacking privacy, I was exposed at an early age to sexual behavior and talk. This helped me to accept sexuality as a natural part of life. Sexual matters were openly discussed and joked about, and sex was not a taboo or heavy subject. Although I don't recall feeling guilty over sexual thoughts or feelings, I had clear boundaries regarding the expression of my sexuality. While there may have been a lack of sexual information, I did not receive negative messages pertaining to sexuality. Many of my clients report that they find it impossible to imagine their parents having sex. I knew that sexuality was a part of my parents' lives and that they enjoyed it. I was not burdened with fears about sex.

Many people express very real fears as they begin to recognize and accept their sexuality. A common fear is that if we recognize or accept our sexual feelings, our impulses will sweep us away, leaving us out of control. It's important to learn that we can accept the full range of our sexual feelings yet decide for ourselves what we will *do* about them. For instance, we remember a man who said that he felt satisfied with his marriage and found his wife exciting but was troubled because he found other women appealing and sometimes desired them. Even though he had made a decision not to have extramarital affairs, he still experienced a high level of anxiety over simply having sexual feelings toward other women. At some level he believed that he might be more likely to *act* on his feelings if he fully accepted that he had them. It was important for him to learn to discriminate between having sexual feelings and deciding to take certain actions and that he learn to trust his own decisions.

In making responsible, inner-directed choices about whether to act on your sexual feelings, consider these questions:

- Will my actions hurt another person or myself?
- Will my actions limit another person's freedom?
- Will my actions exploit another's rights?
- Are my actions consistent with my commitments?

Each of us must decide on our own moral guidelines, but it is unrealistic to expect that we can or should control our feelings in the same way we control our actions. By controlling our actions, we define who we are; by denying or banishing our feelings, we only become alienated from ourselves.

■ Guilt over Sexual Experiences

Although some people are convinced that in these sexually liberated times college students do not suffer guilt feelings over their sexual behaviors, our observations show us that this is not the case. College students, whether single or married, young or middle-aged, report a variety of experiences over which they feel guilty. Guilt may be related to masturbation, extramarital (or "extrapartner") affairs, same sex behavior, sexual practices that are sometimes considered deviant, and the practice of having sex with many partners.

Sex therapists emphasize early sexual learning as a crucial factor in later sexual adjustment because current guilt feelings often stem from both unconscious and conscious decisions made in response to verbal and nonverbal messages about sexuality. Children are often not given the proper words for their body parts and for erotic activities. If parents restrict their vocabulary by referring to the genitals as simply organs of excretion, children tend to assume that sexual pleasure is "dirty" or unnatural. An acquaintance once was shocked and upset when she heard one of our daughters use the word *penis*. When we asked her how she referred to genitals with her children, she replied, "Of course, I call it a weenie!" Such distortions or omissions of information can create an underlying negative attitude through which later information tends to be filtered.

Peers often fill the void left by parents. However, reliance on the same-sex peer group usually results in learning inaccurate sexual information, which can later lead to fears and guilt over sexual feelings and activities. Most sex information from the peer group is imparted during the early teen years. Many distorted notions are incorporated, such as: "If you masturbate, your penis will fall off." "Kissing will get you pregnant." "Babies are born through the navel."

Movies, television, magazines, and newspapers provide information that is often a source of negative learning about sexuality. Material dealing with rape, violent sex, and venereal disease is blatantly presented to children. This slanted information often produces unrealistic and unbalanced attitudes about sexuality and ultimately fosters fears and guilt that can have a powerful impact on the ability to enjoy sex as an adult.

Some ministers of certain churches have contributed to sexual guilt, especially those preachers who shout "hell-and-damnation" sermons. A television evangelist who delivered passionate sermons on the evil and corruption around us shocked many when he was caught going to a prostitute, not once, but on two occasions. To us, this is an example of how repressed sexuality often manifests itself in indirect ways. In Chapter 2 we discussed the use of ego-defense mechanisms to keep anxiety in check. The behavior of this preacher illustrates defense mechanisms such as repression, denial, projection, and reaction formation. This is not an isolated case; stories abound about prominent people who speak out against certain types of sexual behavior only to be caught in such practices themselves.

The main point is that we acquire a sense of guilt over sexual feelings and experiences as a result of a wide diversity of sources of information and *mis*information. Not all guilt is neurotic, nor should it necessarily be eliminated. When we violate our value systems, guilt is a consequence. This guilt can serve a useful purpose, motivating us to change the behavior that is not congruent with our ethical standards. In freeing ourselves of unearned guilt, the first step is to become aware of early verbal and nonverbal messages about sexuality and gender-role behavior. Once we become aware of these messages, we can explore them to determine in what ways we might want to modify them.

➤ *Time Out for Personal Reflection*

1. Complete the following statements pertaining to sexuality:

   a. I first learned about sex through _____

   _____

   b. My earliest memory about sex is _____

   _____

   c. The way this memory affects me now is _____

   _____

   d. One verbal sexual message I received from my parents was _____

   _____

   e. One nonverbal sexual message I received from my parents was _____

   _____

   f. An expectation I have about sex is _____

   _____

   g. When the topic of sexuality comes up I usually _____

   _____

   h. While I was growing up, a sexual taboo I internalized was _____

   _____

2. List a couple of the myths and misconceptions that have most affected you personally.

   _____

   _____

   _____

   _____

3. Are there any steps you'd like to take toward learning to accept your body and your sexuality more than you do now? If so, what are they?

   _____

   _____

   _____

   _____

4. Do you experience guilt over sexual feelings? If so, what specific feelings give rise to guilt?

_____

_____

_____

_____

5. How openly are you able to discuss sexuality in a personal way? Would you like to be more open in discussing your sexuality or sexual issues? If so, what is preventing this openness?

_____

_____

_____

_____

6. What are some personal issues relating to sex that you're willing to discuss in your class group?

_____

_____

_____

Learning to Enjoy Sensuality and Sexuality

Sensual experiences involve all of our senses and can be enjoyed separately from sexual experiences. People often confuse sensuality with sexuality, especially by concluding that sensuality necessarily leads to sexual experiences. Although sexuality involves sensual experiences, sensuality often does not lead to sexual activity.

As we've seen, performance standards and expectations often get in the way of sensual and sexual pleasure, particularly for men. Some men think they must be *supermen,* particularly in the area of sexual attractiveness and performance. They measure themselves by unrealistic standards and may greatly fear losing their sexual power. Instead of enjoying sexual and sensual experiences, they become oriented toward orgasm. For some men, the fact that they or their partner experiences an orgasm signifies that they have performed adequately. They may expect their partner always to have an orgasm during intercourse, primarily out of their need to prove their sexual adequacy. For example, Roland stated in his human sexuality class that he would not continue to date a woman who did not have an orgasm with him. Several of the other male students were in full agreement with

Roland's attitude. With this type of orientation toward sex, it is not surprising that these men harbor intense fears of impotence.

■ Listening to Our Bodies

In a chapter entitled "Thank God for Impotence!" Goldberg (1987) maintains that impotence can simply be a message that a man doesn't want to have sex with this particular woman at this particular time; it doesn't necessarily mean that he has lost his potency in general. Impotence is best viewed as an outgrowth of the interaction between two persons. The man's inability to maintain an erection needs to be understood in the context of a strained relationship.

Although impotence is one of the most anxiety-provoking situations men can experience, it paradoxically creates and promotes the only potential they have for making significant changes, for it can lead to cracking their armor. Goldberg

contends that impotence is potentially a lifesaving and life-giving response. If the context is properly understood and if the man's fragile masculine self-image is able to tolerate the anxiety over not performing adequately, he has the opportunity to become aware of his flawed emotional interaction. His impotence can thus be the only authentic response he has left to measure the defects in the interchange. Although he is telling himself that he *should* be close, his body is telling the real truth, for it knows that he doesn't want to be close. Impotence is a pathway to his deeper feelings because it represents a central threat to his ego, makes him vulnerable, and motivates him to seek help. If men are able to pay attention to their body signals, they can see that the penis serves as a monitoring device in the relationship. Goldberg likens impotence to a psychological heart attack, which can either result in psychological death or be a catalyst for the man to restructure his patterns of living.

It should be added that sexual dysfunction can occur for any one of a number of reasons, including, in some cases, physical ones. Impotence can be a side effect of certain prescription drugs, but in the majority of cases, impotence is due to psychological factors. In addition to the lack of desire to have sex with a certain person at a certain time, for example, impotence may result from feelings of guilt, prolonged depression, hostility or resentment, anxiety about personal adequacy, or a generally low level of self-esteem. Most men for whom impotence becomes a problem might be well advised to ask themselves: "What is my body telling me?"

Some women have difficulty responding sexually, especially experiencing orgasm. Stress is a major factor that can easily interfere with being in a frame of mind that will allow a woman's body to respond. Although her partner may climax and feel some degree of satisfaction, she might be left frustrated. This is particularly true if the couple engages in sex late at night when they are both tired or if they have been under considerable stress. If her body is not responding, it could well be a sign that stress and fatigue are making it difficult for her to relax and give in to a full psychological and physical release. Rather than interpreting her lack of responsiveness as a sign of sexual inadequacy, she would be wise to pay attention to what her body is expressing. Her body is probably saying, "I'm too tired to enjoy this."

■ Asking for What We Want

Paying attention to the messages of our body is only a first step. We still need to learn how to express to our partner *specifically* what we like and don't like sexually. We've found that both women and men tend to keep their sexual preferences and dislikes to themselves instead of sharing them with their partner. They've accepted the misconception that their partner should know intuitively what they like and don't like, and they resist telling their partner what feels good to them out of fear that their lovemaking will become mechanical or that their partner will only be trying to please them.

Often a woman will complain that she doesn't derive as much enjoyment from sex as she might because the man is too concerned with his own pleasure or is orgasm-oriented and sees touching, holding, and caressing only as necessary duties that he must perform to obtain "the real thing." Thus, she may say that he rolls over in bed as soon as he is satisfied, even if she's left frustrated. Although she may require touching and considerable foreplay and afterplay, he may not recognize her needs. Therefore, she needs to express to him what it feels like to be left unsatisfied, but in a way that doesn't feel to him like an attack.

It is not uncommon for a woman to ask a question such as "Does touching always have to lead to sex?" She is probably implying that there is a significant dimension missing for her in lovemaking—namely, the sensual aspect. The case of Tiffani and Ron illustrates this common conflict in lovemaking. Tiffani complains that anytime she wants to be affectionate with Ron, he wants to have sexual intercourse. She harbors considerable resentment over his inability to respond to her need for affection without making a sexual demand. When Tiffani senses that Ron wants to be sexual with her, she tends to start a fight to create distance. In turn, he feels rejected, humiliated, and angry. For this couple, sex becomes a threatening experience instead of a way of expressing closeness.

Being sensual is an important part of a sexual experience. Sensuality pertains to fully experiencing all of our senses, not just sensations in our genitals. Many parts of the body are sensual and can contribute to our enjoyment of sex. Although there is great enjoyment in the orgasmic experience, many people are missing out on other sources of enjoyment by not giving pleasure to themselves and their partners with other stimulation.

It is important to learn how to negotiate for what you want in sex, including safer sex practices. A range of sexual behavior is open to couples if they make their expectations clear and if they talk about sexuality as part of their relationship. You sometimes may engage in sexual intercourse when what you actually want is to be touched and embraced and to feel sensual in all parts of your body. When this need for a sensual experience quickly culminates with an orgasm, you may feel deeply frustrated. If this becomes a pattern, you may find that there is a feeling of emptiness attached to your sex life. Sex then becomes either a duty or a routine event, and one or both of the partners are likely to feel used or cheated and eventually may find reasons to avoid sex.

Sex and Intimacy

Intimacy can be conceived of as a close emotional relationship characterized by a deep level of caring for another person. It is a basic component of all loving relationships. Although intimacy is part of all loving relationships, it is a mistake to assume that sexuality is part of all loving and intimate relationships. In Chapter 10 we explore many forms of intimate relationships that do not involve sex.

Increasing our sexual awareness can include becoming more sensitive to the ways in which we sometimes engage in sex as a means to some end. For instance, sexual activity can be used as a way to actually prevent the development of intimacy. It can also be a way to avoid experiencing our aloneness, our isolation, and our feelings of distance from others. Sex can be an escape into activity, a way of avoiding inner emptiness. When used in any of these ways, sex takes on a driving or compulsive quality that detracts from its spontaneity and leaves us unfulfilled. Used as a way of filling inner emptiness, sex becomes a mechanical act, divorced from any passion, feeling, or caring. Then it only deepens our feelings of isolation and detachment.

In her personal therapy, Evelyn, who's 23 and single, reveals her extreme feelings of isolation and despair. Although she is seen by her friends as outgoing, attractive, and vivacious, she feels an inner emptiness. She has had many sexual partners and sexual conquests, which have only left her feeling even more empty. In all of her sexual experiences she has ended up feeling more removed from her partner. She longs for a relationship in which she can feel both emotional and sexual satisfaction.

Another case illustrates how sexual activity can be used to avoid boredom. Earl, who is middle-aged and married, sought out an affair to bring more vitality to what he felt was a dead life. Although he found excitement in his affair initially, he soon discovered that he could not run from his meaningless existence. Sex proved to be no "cure" for his restlessness in his marriage, his stagnation in his work, and his inability to enjoy leisure activities.

In our professional work with clients and college students we have observed a trend away from casual sexual encounters without any emotional attachment.

Those who have left sexually exclusive relationships may look forward to sex with a variety of partners. For a time, some of them may be drawn to "sport sex" as they experience their newfound "freedom." Many report, however, that they eventually tire of such relationships and find themselves searching for intimacy as a vital part of their sexual involvements. Of course, the impact of AIDS on sexual behavior probably accounts for some of the caution in getting involved with multiple partners. The fear of becoming infected certainly makes casual sex much less attractive than it might otherwise be. As one student put it, "When you are sexually intimate with someone, it could be a life-or-death matter. You are really trusting them with your life." In our discussions with college students, we are finding that they are seeking to be loved by a special person, and they want to trust giving their love in return.

Take a moment to reflect on how sex can be used to either enhance or diminish you and your partner as persons. Ask yourself: "Are my intimate relationships based on a need to conquer or exert power over someone else? Or are they based on a genuine desire to become intimate, to share, to experience joy and pleasure, to both give and receive?" Asking yourself what you want in your relationships and what uses sex serves for you may also help you avoid the overemphasis on technique and performance that frequently detracts from sexual experiences. Although technique and knowledge are important, they are not ends in themselves, and overemphasizing them can cause us to become oblivious to the *persons* we have sex with. An abundance of anxiety over performance and technique can only impede sexual enjoyment and rob us of the experience of genuine intimacy and caring.

► *Time Out for Personal Reflection*

1. Complete the following sentences:

   a. To me, being sensual means _____

   _____

   b. To me, being sexual means _____

   _____

   c. Sex without intimacy is _____

   _____

   d. Sex can be an empty experience when _____

   _____

   e. Sex can be most fulfilling when _____

   _____

2. Look over the following list, quickly checking the words that you associate with sex:

____ fun	____ dirty	____ routine
____ ecstasy	____ shameful	____ closeness
____ procreation	____ joy	____ release
____ beautifull	____ pressure	____ sinful
____ duty	____ performance	____ guilty
____ trust	____ experimentation	____ vulnerability

Now look over the words you've checked and see whether there are any significant patterns in your responses. What can you say by way of summary about your attitudes toward sex?

_____

_____

_____

_____

AIDS: A Crisis of Our Time*

If you have not already done so, you will inevitably come in contact with people who have tested positive for HIV, people who have AIDS, people who have had sexual contact with someone who has tested HIV-positive, and people who are close to individuals with HIV or AIDS.

AIDS already affects a wide population and will continue to be a major health problem. You simply cannot afford to be unaware of the personal and societal implications of this epidemic. Unless you are educated about the problem, you are likely to engage in risky behaviors or live needlessly in fear. Accurate information is vital if you are to deal with the personal and societal implications of the AIDS epidemic.

You need to be able to differentiate between fact and fiction about the virus and about this disease. Because this is a relatively new disease, we continue to discover new information. Thus, the facts we provide here might be outdated by the time this book is published. You can contact the national HIV and AIDS hotline (1-800-342-AIDS) for free written material, as well as answers to your questions.

There is much ignorance and fear of AIDS, fueled by conflicting reports. Misinformation about the ways in which the disease is spread results in apprehension among many people. There is no reason to remain ignorant; the basic information you need about this disease is available through the sources listed at the end of this section. Reading is a minimum step. You can also attend an AIDS workshop or

*We want to acknowledge the helpful suggestions of Jerome Wright, Lynn Mountain, and Mark Bidell in providing an updated perspective on the AIDS issue.

I HAVE AIDS
Please hug me

I can't make you sick

AIDS HOT LINE FOR KIDS
CENTER FOR ATTITUDINAL HEALING
33 BUCHANAN DRIVE, SAUSALITO, CA 94965 (415) 331-6161

contact your local public health department or one of the HIV clinics that are being started all over the country.

As well as finding out about HIV and AIDS, we urge you to explore your own sexual practices, drug behaviors, and your attitudes, values, and fears pertaining to AIDS. Better understanding on all fronts will better equip you to make informed, wise choices.

■ Basic Facts about AIDS

What Is AIDS?   *Acquired immunodeficiency syndrome* (AIDS) is the last stage of a disease caused by the *human immunodeficiency virus* (HIV), which attacks and weakens the body's natural immune system. Without a working immune system, the body gets infections and cancers that it would normally be able to fight off. HIV was first isolated by French and American scientists in late 1983 and early 1984. People who have AIDS are vulnerable to serious illnesses that would not be a threat to anyone whose immune system was functioning normally. These illnesses are referred to as "opportunistic" infections or diseases. AIDS weakens the body against invasive agents so that other diseases can prey on the body.

What Causes AIDS?   At this time, much is known about HIV, such as how it is transmitted, and also how it can be avoided. What is not known is how to destroy the virus. Although there is not yet a vaccine, treatment is improving with early detection and intervention. Infection with HIV does not always lead to AIDS. Research suggests that more than 50 percent of HIV-infected persons may develop AIDS; and almost everyone with the virus will ultimately become ill to some degree within five to ten years after infection. However, the complete natural history of the disease is still not known.

How Is HIV Transmitted?   HIV can be transmitted by unprotected sexual intercourse (vaginal and anal) with a person infected with the virus or by sharing needles with an infected person during intravenous drug use. A woman infected with HIV who becomes pregnant or breastfeeds can pass the virus to the baby. Although some cases have developed through blood transfusions, this risk has been virtually eliminated by testing donated blood for HIV antibodies (San Francisco AIDS Foundation, 1990). "High concentration" agents of transmission of HIV include blood, semen, vaginal secretions, and breast milk. The virus can be spread by women or men through heterosexual or homosexual contact. It may also be possible to become infected with HIV through oral intercourse because the act often involves semen and vaginal secretions that may contain HIV. The virus can enter the body through the vagina, penis, rectum, or mouth or through breaks in the skin. The risk of infection with the virus is increased by having multiple sexual partners and by sharing needles among those using drugs. People are most able to infect someone in the first few months of being infected themselves. This is a major problem, since individuals can test HIV-negative during this time.

The virus has been found in "low concentration" in a number of body fluids and secretions, such as saliva, urine, and tears. However, you *do not* "catch" AIDS in the same way you catch a cold or the flu. It cannot be passed through a glass or eating utensils. The AIDS virus is not transmitted through everyday contact with people around you in the workplace, at school, and at social functions. You cannot get AIDS by being near someone who carries the virus. The virus is hard to get and easily avoided. It is a misconception that it is spread through casual contact or from a mosquito bite, a casual kiss, or a toilet seat.

Who Gets AIDS?   Most of the AIDS public health effort has been focused on persons with high-risk behavior such as bisexual and gay men, intravenous drug users, and blood transfusion recipients. Some people have been lulled into feeling safe if they are not associated with a high-risk group, yet the epidemic is shifting and is spreading to women, youth, and minorities. AIDS has been called an "equal opportunity disease" because it is found among people of all ages, genders, races, and sexual orientations. Unlike people, AIDS does not discriminate, but it is *behavior* that puts people at risk, not the group to which they belong. Perhaps the largest growth in HIV infection is occurring among women. The World Health Organization estimates that 8 to 10 million women worldwide are infected with HIV. By the year 2000 the number of worldwide cases of HIV is expected to be 40 million. It is predicted that, at the same time, AIDS will have become the third most common cause of death in the United States. Presently, in this country the leading cause of death for individuals in the 25 to 44 age group is AIDS.

What Symptoms Are Associated with HIV Infection?   HIV may live in the human body for years before symptoms appear. These people are asymptomatic. Although many individuals infected with the virus have no symptoms, some victims develop severe and prolonged fatigue, night sweats, fever, loss of appetite and weight, diarrhea, and swollen lymph glands in the neck. Anyone having one or more of these symptoms for more than two weeks should see a health care provider. Of course, other diseases besides AIDS can cause similar symptoms.

What Kind of Test Is There for AIDS?   An HIV antibody test looks for antibodies, not the virus. Couples can test negative but be positive during a six-month window period. This is why it is important to get a second test about six months after a person thinks he or she might have been exposed to the virus. A positive test result does not mean that the person will get AIDS, because many people who test positive either remain symptom-free or develop less serious illnesses. The antibody test cannot tell whether the individual will eventually develop signs of illness related to the viral infection or, if so, how serious the illness might be. Early intervention is the key. What a positive test result does indicate is that the person has been infected by the virus and can transmit it to others. It does not mean that you have AIDS. It means that you have been infected with the virus and your body has developed a reaction to it. If you suspect that you have been exposed to the virus, it is crucial that you get tested. With early medical attention, it is possible to delay the diseases that stem from AIDS. Testing is completely anonymous and confidential, but you should inquire if the test site provides these safeguards. It is generally free if you go to the health department in your county.

What Are Common Reactions to Testing HIV-Positive?   People who believe or have discovered that they are carriers of HIV are typically highly anxious. Both those who have tested positive and those who have contracted AIDS need immediate help. Upon learning that they are HIV-positive, it is not uncommon to experience a gamut of emotional reactions from shock, to anger, to fear and anxiety, to grieving for the loss of sexual freedom, to alarm over the uncertain future. Some feel that they have been given a death sentence. They will need to find a support system to help them cope with the troubled times that lie ahead. In *AIDS: The Ultimate Challenge* (1993), Elizabeth Kübler-Ross applied the five stages of dying—denial, anger, bargaining, depression, and acceptance—to AIDS patients. As is the case with any loss, individuals tend to experience emotional reactions to the news that they have tested HIV-positive. (See Chapter 12 for a detailed discussion of Kübler-Ross's stages as applied to both loss and dying.)

It needs to be emphasized that HIV-positive individuals can live long and relatively symptom free lives for many years. Many new medications are now available to treat the opportunistic infections that often kill people with AIDS. Today, much more is known about the disease than was the case when AIDS was first discovered.

Why Is a Stigma Attached to AIDS?   Both those who have AIDS and those who discover that they have the virus within them struggle with the stigma attached to this disease. People who are HIV-positive live with the anxiety of wondering whether they will come down with this incurable disease. Most of them also struggle with the stigma attached to AIDS. They live in fear not only of developing a life-threatening disease but also of being discovered and thus being rejected by society in general and by significant persons in their life. Of course, those who develop AIDS must also deal with this stigma. The stigma stems from the fact that during the early years when this disease was discovered, those who contracted AIDS belonged primarily to the sexually active gay male or bisexual male population or were present or past abusers of intravenous drugs. Among the mainstream population there is still a general negative reaction toward gay men, lesbians, and bisexuals. However, increasing numbers of the general population are being infected, in addition to these "risk groups."

For some, the stigma may be worse than the diagnosis itself. Very often people afflicted with AIDS stigmatize themselves and perpetuate beliefs such as "I feel guilty and ashamed." "I'm a horrible person, and therefore I deserve to suffer." "I'm to blame for getting this disease."

Many of the social fears felt by people with HIV or AIDS are realistic. Some family members actually disown the person with AIDS out of fear. This type of treatment naturally inspires anger, depression, and feelings of hopelessness in the person who has been rejected. He or she may express this anger by asking, over and over: "What did I do to deserve this? Why me?" This anger is sometimes directed at God for letting this happen, and then the person may feel guilty for having reacted this way. Anger is also directed toward others, especially those who are likely to have transmitted the virus.

How Is AIDS Treated?   At this point, those who carry the virus are likely to have it for the rest of their lives. No drugs have been shown to cure AIDS, but an antiviral agent called azidothymidine (AZT), dideoxyinosine, and others, appear to retard the progress of the disease in some patients. Several experimental drugs have also shown potential efficacy in delaying the onset of AIDS. Although no treatment has yet been successful in restoring the immune system, doctors have been able to treat the various acute illnesses affecting those with AIDS.

How Can the Spread of HIV Be Prevented?   There are conflicting reports and evidence about the disease. The changing nature of information about AIDS and misinformation about the ways in which the disease is spread can block programs aimed at prevention.

Because the AIDS crisis shows no signs of decreasing, education to stop the spread of the disease is the key to prevention. Individuals can do a lot to avoid contracting the disease. The following specific steps aimed at prevention have been taken from a number of sources:

- All sexually active individuals need to know the basic facts about this disease and how to avoid the risk of infection.
- Talk to your partners about past and present sexual practices and drug use.
- Engage in sexual activities that do not involve vaginal, anal, or oral intercourse.
- Avoid having sex with multiple partners. The more partners you have, the more you increase your risk. Have intercourse only with one uninfected partner.
- Avoid sex with persons with AIDS, with those at risk for AIDS, or with those who have had a positive result on the HIV antibody test.
- Effective and consistent use of condoms and spermicidal barriers will reduce the possibility of transmitting the virus, but they are not 100 percent effective in preventing HIV or other STDs. Use latex condoms correctly from start to finish with each act of intercourse.
- It is essential to talk with your partner about his or her sexual history, STD history, and safer sex history. It is important to negotiate safer sex with your partner.
- Making responsible choices is of the utmost importance in avoiding sexually transmitted diseases, including HIV infection. Sexual abstinence is certainly a safe course to follow. If you choose to practice abstinence as a way to prevent infection, this strategy will be effective only if you always abstain.
- If you intend to have unprotected sexual intercourse, you are *not* safe, and you need to recognize the risks of infection. Rather than thinking in terms of "safe sex," it is helpful to consider practices that are "unsafe," "relatively safe," and "safer." In his book, *What You Can Do to Avoid AIDS* (1992), Earvin "Magic" Johnson emphasizes that "the most responsible thing you can do is to act as though you yourself and anybody you want to have sex with could have HIV and to practice safer sex every time" (p. 67).
- "Safer" behavior includes choosing not to be sexually active; restricting sex to one mutually faithful, uninfected partner; and not injecting drugs. Safer sex practices are especially critical if you sense that your partner may not be totally honest about his or her past or present sexual practices.
- If you use intravenous drugs, don't share needles.
- Avoid using drugs and alcohol, which cloud your judgment. Many college students attend parties in which there is a great deal of peer pressure to "drink and have fun." Intoxication lessens inhibitions, which often leads to unprotected sex. It takes a good bit of courage to take a stand and not engage in irresponsible use of drugs and alcohol, especially when many of your friends may be drinking excessively.
- People who carry the AIDS virus are often not sick and often are unaware that they are infected. They can be HIV-positive and still look fine and feel well.
- Although AIDS has created a tremendous amount of fear for most people, it can be reassuring to know that it's *unprotected* sex that can lead to HIV infection, not any and all sexual experiences.

■ Educate Yourself

Educate yourself on the major issues surrounding AIDS and explore your own attitudes and choices pertaining to sexual behavior. Because information is changing rapidly, it is difficult for people who are at risk to trust what they hear from the medical profession. Some individuals become defensive about education because they don't believe what is presented to them. They also may remain in a state of denial because they do not want to change their sexual lifestyle.

Kübler-Ross (1993) views it as a matter of choice as to whether we will learn from the AIDS epidemic or will live in ignorance about this reality: "Since we can no longer deny that AIDS is a life-threatening illness that will eventually involve millions of people and decimate large portions of our human population, it is our choice to grow and learn from it, to either help the people with this dread disease or abandon them. It is our choice to live up to this ultimate challenge or to perish" (p. 13).

And in the epilogue of her book, Kübler-Ross concludes that AIDS poses a threat to mankind: "Are we going to choose hate and discrimination, or will we have the courage to choose love and service? Yes, I truly believe that AIDS is the ultimate challenge for all of us. Choose wisely, take the highest road you can, so that you will have no regrets at the end" (1993, pp. 320–321).

Simply having information will not prevent you from getting AIDS, but it will help you make sound behavioral choices. In the early days of the epidemic, the emphasis was on providing information and education only. We now know that information alone is never enough to create the environment for individuals to change. For example, although many smokers are well aware of the dangers their habit poses, they often say that they cannot quit or aren't motivated enough to quit. Likewise, many people have the information about the effects of alcohol on impairing judgment, yet may go ahead and become intoxicated, which often leads to unprotected sex. These examples illustrate how difficult it is to act on information. Indeed, behavior change is tough, especially when dealing with very personal behaviors, including sexuality. What it boils down to is this: If you choose to be sexually active, in addition to getting information and educating yourself about a safer sex plan, it is essential that you develop the skills to negotiate your safer sex plan with your partner.

Magic Johnson (1992) has some outstanding advice for those who are considering becoming sexually active. He suggests asking:

- Am I prepared to practice safer sex each time I have sex?
- Am I prepared to use contraception each time I have woman-man sex?
- Am I prepared to deal with the consequences if I or my partners become infected with HIV or another STD or become pregnant?
- Am I prepared to say "no" when I think it's not right for me?

One practical way of educating yourself about HIV/AIDS is to read on the subject. Magic Johnson has a readable and down-to-earth book, *What You Can Do to Avoid AIDS* (1992). In addition to writing about HIV and AIDS, Magic deals in a frank way with sexual responsibility, safer sex, and protecting yourself from STDs. Lorraine Jones wrote an informative and practical book, *HIV/AIDS: What to Do about It* (1996). Our discussion of HIV/AIDS in this section is brief and is merely an overview. Jones's brief book provides facts about HIV/AIDS, identifies ways to protect yourself, focuses on rights and responsibilities, and talks about where to find help. She emphasizes the importance of keeping up to date with the facts about HIV infection, especially in light of the fact that new information becomes available almost daily.

■ Resources for Further Information

More information about AIDS and AIDS-related illnesses can be obtained from your doctor, your state or local health department, your local chapter of the American Red Cross, and the Public Health Service's toll-free HIV and AIDS hotline (1-800-342-AIDS). This national hotline is for anyone with questions about HIV and AIDS. It functions 24 hours a day in every state. The information specialists are well trained and they respect privacy. In addition to providing information, they provide referrals to appropriate sources among the more than 8,000 entries in the hotline database. The hotline is the place to call for free pamphlets and booklets with updated information about HIV and AIDS. Information and many of these pamphlets are available from the National AIDS Clearinghouse by calling 1-800-458-5231:

- *Facts about Condoms and Their Use in Preventing HIV Infection and Other STDs.* (Centers for Disease Control and Prevention, 1993a).
- *National AIDS Clearinghouse.* (Centers for Disease Control and Prevention, 1993b).
- *AIDS and Families.* (American Association for World Health, 1994).
- *Facts about AIDS.* (U.S. Department of Health and Human Services, 1987).
- *Understanding AIDS.* (U.S. Department of Health and Human Services, 1988a).
- *Women, Sex, and AIDS.* (U.S. Department of Health and Human Services, 1988b).
- *Many Teens Are Saying No.* (U.S. Department of Health and Human Services, 1989).
- *AIDS and You.* (U. S. Department of Health and Human Services, 1991a.).
- *Caring for Someone with AIDS.* (U.S. Department of Health and Human Services, 1991b).
- *HIV Infection and AIDS: Are You at Risk?* (U.S. Department of Health and Human Services, 1991c).
- *How You Won't Get AIDS.* (U.S. Department of Health and Human Services, 1991d).
- *Voluntary HIV Counseling and Testing: Facts, Issues, and Answers.* (U.S. Department of Health and Human Services, 1991e).

■ Concluding Comments

As we have stressed, it is essential that you educate yourself on the major issues surrounding AIDS and that you explore your own attitudes and choices pertaining to sexual behavior. Because information is changing rapidly, it is difficult for people who are at risk to trust what they hear from the medical profession. Some individuals become defensive about education because they don't believe what is presented to them. An observation of one of the reviewers of this book is that his students are less concerned about contracting HIV. Youth often feel that they are immune to any harm, and thus they tend to disregard good advice. Some may remain in a state of denial because they do not want to change their sexual lifestyle.

Simply having information will not prevent you from getting AIDS, but it can help you make sound behavioral choices. You do have a choice in how aware and safe you can be. We hope you will take the warnings seriously and use knowledge to help you make better choices. Even though some young people are behaving recklessly, many others are changing their sexual behaviors because of the possibility of contracting the disease.

Magic Johnson sums up beautifully the message we have attempted to convey in this section on HIV and AIDS. His message deserves reflection.

> Take responsibility. It's your life. Remember: The safest sex is no sex, but if you choose to have sex, have safer sex each and every time. HIV happened to me, so I know it could happen to you. I want you to stay safe. Your life is worth it. (1992, p. 156)

Developing Your Own Sexual Values

The AIDS epidemic has challenged our sexual attitudes and behaviors. People are seriously considering changing some of their behaviors because of the possibility of contracting a sexually transmitted disease or because of the risk of an unwanted pregnancy. During the last 25 years, people have openly questioned society's sexual standards and practices, and a belief has grown that individuals can and should decide for themselves what sexual practices are acceptable. It is desirable to bring sexual issues into the open and talk freely without guilt and shame, but it is also important that your sexual behavior be consistent with your value system.

Take a few minutes to reflect on your attitudes about sexual behavior and consider these questions that Corey, Corey, and Corey (1997) raise in exploring the pros and cons of being sexually active:

- How do I feel about my decision?
- Does my choice to be sexually active interfere with my religious beliefs or cultural values?
- Do I attach feelings of shame or guilt to not having sex?
- Do I feel pressured into having sex?
- Am I afraid that I will be abandoned by someone if I don't have sex?
- Am I choosing to have sex so that I can "fit in"?
- Do I feel pressure to engage in sex because of gender expectations?
- What are my reasons for choosing to have sex at this time?

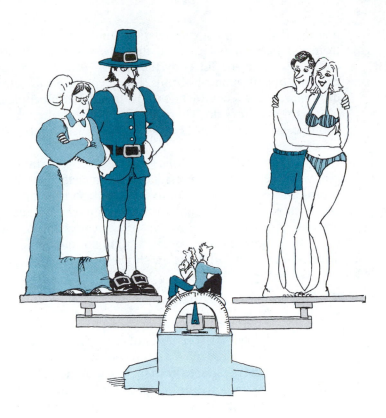

- Whose expectations am I trying to meet?
- What are my expectations about sex?
- Am I willing to talk openly with my partner about sex beforehand?
- Am I prepared for the emotional complications of a sexual relationship?
- If birth control is an issue, have I considered my options and chosen a safe and effective method?
- Have my partner and I discussed our sexual histories?
- Am I prepared to discuss and effectively use protection against sexually transmitted diseases?

■ Fear of Being a Virgin

Many people accept external standards, such as those of their church or their parents, and eventually internalize a set of sexual values that they can best live with. At an earlier time people were afraid to reveal that they had had sexual experiences before marriage; now some people are anxious about revealing that they have refrained from sexual intercourse. We are reminded of Elvira, a 23-year-old client, who with some embarrassment revealed that she was a virgin. She and her boyfriend had decided to delay sexual relations until after marriage. But she felt pressure from her peers and was afraid that she was behaving strangely because of the choice she had made. Recently, the evening news featured a discussion of an international organization of virgins. Many young people are deciding that celibacy until marriage is a worthwhile value. It could help people like Elvira to know that others think as they do. There are many others who, like Elvira, make a decision about their sexual behavior based on their values rather than on a fear of pregnancy or venereal disease.

Deciding what sexual choices are right for you can be a difficult task, yet it can give you a sense of empowerment and independence. There are many things to consider when choosing to have sex or not. Some people, however, just let it happen without much thought to the possibility of sexually transmitted diseases, pregnancy, religious or moral values, or consideration of feelings for the other party. While we neither encourage you to nor discourage you from having sex, we do feel that you should make the choice a conscious one.

■ Celibacy as an Option

If you decide that abstaining from sexual intercourse until marriage is congruent with your value system, you need not apologize for your choice. A recent news special reported that between 50 and 75 percent of adolescents engage in sexual intercourse before they graduate from high school. However, the television special dealt with a growing movement of young people committed to sexual abstinence until marriage. The program described purity seminars, which partly includes providing support to the choice for celibacy. Choosing celibacy or abstinence is a viable option. Some choose it out of moral or cultural convictions, others out of various fears about sex. Fear is not necessarily a bad reason. For example, the fear of driving under the influence of drugs and alcohol makes good sense. So does the fear of an unwanted pregnancy. Whatever your reasons for choosing to abstain from sex, you should know that you are not alone.

If you are choosing celibacy, Corey, Corey, and Corey (1997) offer the following questions to consider:

- What meaning do I attach to celibacy?
- How do I feel about my decision?
- Is this choice based on my own values or on what someone else told me I should value?
- How will I feel about myself if I go against my decision to be celibate?
- Do I feel compelled to abstain from sex because of gender-role expectations? (For example, "Good girls don't!")
- Is my choice to be celibate based on a full acceptance of my body?
- Do I believe that I am a sexually desirable person?
- Do I fear that being celibate stands in the way of the level of intimacy I desire?
- In choosing celibacy, am I denying myself the possibility of intense emotional feelings?
- Am I choosing celibacy mainly out of a fear of getting involved with someone who might then abandon me?

- Do I attach feelings of shame or guilt to having sex?
- Do I have confidence in my sexual ability?

Even in marriage or other committed relationships, celibacy is sometimes necessary due to illness or other physical conditions. It is important to cultivate emotional intimacy without physical intimacy.

■ Formulating Your Sexual Ethics

Designing a personal and meaningful set of sexual ethics is not an easy task. It can be accomplished only through a process of honest questioning. Your questioning can start with the values you now have. What is their source? Do they fit in with your views of yourself in other areas of your life? Which of them are important in allowing you to live responsibly and with enjoyment? Which should you reject? Achieving freedom doesn't have to mean shedding all your past beliefs or values. Whether you keep or reject them in whole or in part, you can refuse to allow someone besides yourself to make decisions for you. It can be tempting to allow others (whether past authorities or present acquaintances) to tell you what is right and wrong and design your life for you; then you don't have to wrestle with tough decisions yourself. If you fail to create your own values and choose for yourself, however, you surrender your autonomy and run the risk of becoming alienated from yourself.

Also, there is the matter of realistic and appropriate guilt when we engage in sexual practices that are not in accordance with our value system. For instance, some people struggle with wanting to act out sexually with many partners, even though this behavior goes against their personal value system. Their struggle is between giving behavioral expression to their sexual desires and feeling guilty because they are not living by their values.

Developing your own values means assuming responsibility for yourself, which includes taking into consideration how others may be affected by your choices while allowing them to take responsibility for themselves. In an adult relationship, the parties involved are capable of taking personal responsibility for their own actions. For example, in the case of premarital or extramarital sex, each person must weigh such questions as: "Do I really want to pursue a sexual relationship with this person at this time? Is the price worth it? What are my commitments? Who else is involved, and who could be hurt? Might this be a positive or a negative experience? How does my decision fit in with my values generally?"

It is no easier to achieve sexual autonomy than it is to achieve autonomy in other areas of your life. While challenging your values, you need to take a careful look at how you could easily engage in self-deception by adjusting your behavior to whatever you might desire at the moment. You also need to pay attention to how you feel about yourself in regard to your past sexual experience. Perhaps, in doing so, you can use your level of self-respect as one important guide to your future behavior. You might ask: "Do I feel enhanced or diminished by my past experience?"

Sex can be a positive or a negative force, depending on how it is used. At its best, sex can be a deep source of enjoyment, bringing pleasure, enhancing overall well-being, and demonstrating love, caring, and affection. At its worst, sex can be used to hurt others. Sex is abused when it is manipulative, a punishing force, used to get favors, the tool of aggression and control, aimed at dominating another, and when it evokes guilt. In the next section, we consider some of the ways sex is frequently abused and used as a ploy to assume power and control over others.

➤ *Time Out for Personal Reflection*

1. What influences have shaped your attitudes and values concerning sexuality? In the following list, indicate the importance of each factor by placing a 1 in the blank if it was *very important,* a 2 if it was *somewhat important,* and a 3 if it was *unimportant.* For each item you mark with a 1 or a 2, indicate briefly the nature of that influence.

_____   parents _____

_____   church _____

_____   friends _____

_____   siblings _____

_____   movies _____

_____   school _____

_____   books _____

_____   television _____

_____   spouse _____

_____   grandparents _____

_____   your own experiences _____

_____   other influential factors _____

_____

2. Try making a list of specific values that you hold regarding sexual issues. As a beginning, respond to the following questions:

   a. How do you feel about sex with multiple partners?

   _____

   _____

   _____

   _____

   b. What is your view of sex outside of marriage?

   _____

   _____

_____

_____

c. Do you think it's legitimate to separate love and sex?

_____

_____

_____

d. How do you feel about having sex with a person you don't like or respect?

_____

_____

_____

_____

Sexual Abuse and Harassment

In this section, we discuss three topics that involve some form of abuse of sexuality: incest, rape, and sexual harassment. In each of these cases, power is misused or a trusting relationship is betrayed for the purpose of gaining control over the individual. Individuals are robbed of choice—except for the choice of how to react to being violated. Incest, date and acquaintance rape, and sexual harassment all entail abusive power, control, destructiveness, and violence. As such, these practices are never justifiable. In all of these forms of sexual abuse, a common denominator is the reluctance of victims to disclose that they have been wronged. In fact, many victims suffer from undue guilt and believe that they were responsible for what occurred. This guilt is exacerbated by segments of society that contribute to the "blaming the victim" syndrome. The victims should not be given further insult by being blamed for cooperating or contributing to the violence that was forced upon them. Victims often carry psychological scars from these experiences that stifle their ability to accept and express the full range of their sexuality.

■ Incest: A Betrayal of Trust

In our therapeutic groups we continue to meet women who suffer tremendous guilt related to early incestuous experiences. To a lesser extent, we come across men who have been subjected to incest or some form of molestation. Because incest is a betrayal of trust and a misuse of power and control, it can never be rationalized away. The responsibility of the perpetrator can never be diminished. This subject is being given much-deserved attention by both helping professionals and the general public. It appears that incest is far more widespread than ever before thought. It occurs on all social, economic, educational, and professional levels. At least one out of ten children is molested by a trusted family member (Forward & Buck, 1988). This number of victims is conservative, since many incidents are never reported. Many women do not remember their incestuous experiences until something triggers a certain memory in their adult years (Maltz & Holman, 1987).

In our personal-growth groups for relatively well-functioning people, we find a startling number of women who report incidents of incest and sexual experimentation with fathers, uncles, stepfathers, grandfathers, and brothers. Black (1987) defines incest as "inappropriate sexual behavior, usually perpetrated by an adult family member with a minor child, brought about by coercion, deception, or psychological manipulation. It includes inappropriate touching, fondling, oral sex, and/or intercourse" (p. 154). The definition used by Vanderbilt (1992) is "any sexual abuse of a child by a relative or other person in a position of trust and authority over the child. It is the violation of the child where he or she lives — literally and metaphorically" (p. 51). Vanderbilt indicates that incest is a felony offense in all 50 states, although its definition varies from state to state, as does the punishment. Although father/daughter incest is the most common type of adult/child incest, sexual relations also occur between mother and daughter, mother and son, and father and son (Forward & Buck, 1988). Although females are more often incest victims, males also suffer the effects of incestual experiences.

In our groups, many women will bring up the matter because they feel burdened with guilt, rage, hurt, and confusion over having been taken advantage of sexually and emotionally. Some feel both confused and guilty, because even though they feel like a victim, at the same time they see themselves as a conspirator. They may believe that they were to blame, a belief that is often reinforced by others. They may have liked the affection and love they received even though they were probably repulsed by the sexual component. Because children realize that adults have power over them, they tend to be compliant, even in situations that seem strange. Typically, these experiences happen in childhood or early adolescence; the women remember feeling helpless at the time, not knowing how to stop the man, and also being afraid to tell anyone. Some of the reasons children give for not telling others about the abuse include not knowing that it was wrong, feeling ashamed, being frightened of the consequences of telling, fearing that others might not believe that such abuse occurred, and hoping to protect other siblings from incest. However, once they bring out these past experiences, intense, pent-up emotions surface, such as hatred and rage for having been treated in such a way and feelings of having been raped and used.

In *Betrayal of Innocence,* Forward and Buck (1988) describe recurring themes that emerge from the incest experiences of almost every victim. From the victim's perspective, these themes include a desire to be loved by the perpetrator; a tendency to put up little resistance; an atmosphere of secrecy surrounding the incest; feelings of repulsion, fear, and guilt; the experience of pain and confusion; fears of being punished or removed from the home; and feelings of tremendous isolation and of having no one to turn to in a time of need. Most often the victim feels responsible for what occurred.

Children who have been sexually abused by someone in their family feel betrayed and typically develop a mistrust of others who are in a position to take advantage of them. Oftentimes the sexual abuse is only one facet of a dysfunctional family. There may also be physical abuse, neglect, alcoholism, and other problems. These children are often unaware of how psychologically abusive their family atmosphere really is for all members of the family.

The effects of these early childhood experiences can carry over into adulthood. The woman's ability to form sexually satisfying relationships may be impaired by events she has kept inside for many years. She may resent all men, associating them with the father or other man who initially took advantage of her. If she couldn't trust her own father, then what man can she trust? She may have a hard time trusting men who express affection for her, thinking that they, too, will take advantage of her. She may keep control of relationships by not letting herself be open or sexually playful and free with men. She may rarely or never allow herself to fully give in to sexual pleasure during intercourse. Her fear is that if she gives up her control, she will be hurt again. Her guilt over sexual feelings and her negative conditioning prevent her from being open to enjoying a satisfying sexual relationship. She may blame all men for her feelings of guilt and her betrayal and victimization. She may develop severe problems with establishing and maintaining intimate relationships, not only with her partner but also with her own children. In adulthood she may marry a man who will later victimize their own children, which perpetuates the pattern of her experiences in growing up. In this way the dynamics from childhood are repeated in adulthood.

Veronika Tracy (1993) conducted a research study to determine the impact of childhood sexual abuse on women's sexuality. Her study compared a group of women who were sexually abused with a group of women who had not experienced sexual abuse. She found that the women with a reported history of sexual abuse in childhood tended to have lower self-esteem, a greater number of sexual problems, less sexual satisfaction with a partner, less interest in engaging in sex, a higher propensity for sexual fantasies that involved force, and more guilt feelings about their sexual fantasies. Many of the women who were sexually abused reported that they were not able to achieve orgasm with a partner, but only by themselves. Her research revealed that women who were sexual abuse survivors often blocked out their negative experiences, only to remember the sexual abuse as they became sexually active. Paradoxically, as the women began to feel safer with a partner, their sexual activity often triggered memories of the abuse, which tended to interfere with their ability to maintain satisfying intimate relationships.

In our work with people in groups, we've found that it is therapeutic for most women who have a history of sexual abuse to simply share the burden associated with their abuse that they've been carrying alone for so many years. In a climate of support, trust, care, and respect, these women can *begin* a healing process that will eventually allow them to shed needless guilt. Before this healing can occur, they generally need to fully express bottled-up feelings, usually of anger and hatred. A major part of their therapy consists of accepting the reality that they were indeed victims and learning to direct their anger outward, rather than blaming themselves. We stress that it is important for this catharsis to occur in the group in

symbolic ways. With the assistance of their therapist, they may be able to confront the perpetrator and those who did not protect them. Sometimes the man in question will no longer be alive, or the woman may decide that she does not want to confront the aggressor.

As we mentioned, it is not uncommon for a woman to assume the guilt and responsibility for these inappropriate sexual activities. Even though she may have been only 7 years old, she firmly believes that she should have prevented the abuse from happening. She fails to realize that the adults in her life were violating her and failing to provide the safe environment in which she could have developed and matured as a sexual being. A very moving account that describes a long period of incest between a lonely and disturbed man and his daughter is the subject of *If I Should Die Before I Wake* by Michelle Morris (1984). This book depicts the terror experienced by the victim and shows the psychological scars she carried beyond childhood.

The process of recovery from the psychological wounds of incest varies from individual to individual, depending on a number of complex factors. Many incest victims cut off their feelings as a survival tactic. Part of the recovery process involves regaining the ability to feel, getting in touch with buried memories, and speaking truths. They will likely have to deal with questions such as: "What is wrong with me? Why did this happen in my life? Why didn't I stop it? What will my future be like?" Victims may vacillate between denying the incestuous experiences and accepting what occurred. As they work through their memories surrounding the events, they eventually accept the fact that they were involved in incest. They typically feel sadness and grief, and then rage. If recovery is successful, they are finally able to forgive themselves and find a resolution to being stuck (Vanderbilt, 1992).

According to Forward and Buck (1988), one of the greatest gifts that therapy can bestow is a full and realistic reversal of blame and responsibility from the victim to the victimizers. In her therapeutic practice with victims of incest, Susan Forward attempts to achieve three major goals:

- Assist the client in externalizing the guilt, rage, shame, hurt, fear, and confusion that are stored up within her.
- Help the victim place the responsibility for the events primarily with the aggressor and secondarily with the silent partner.
- Help the client realize that although incest has damaged her dignity and self-esteem, she does not have to remain psychologically victimized for the rest of her life.

Through role playing, release of feelings, and sharing her conflicts with others in the group, the victim often finds that she is not alone in her plight, and she begins to put these experiences into a new perspective. Although she will never forget these experiences, she can begin the process of letting go of feelings of self-blame and eventually arrive at a place where she is not controlled by these past experiences. In doing so, she is also freeing herself of the control that these sexual experiences (and the feelings associated with them) have had over her ability to form an intimate relationship with her partner.

We have worked with some adult men who were incest victims during childhood and adolescence. Regardless of gender or cultural background, the dynamics

of incest are similar, and thus the therapeutic work is much the same for both women and men. However, the incestual traumas experienced by men have a different focus because of the roles men have traditionally held. Men are socialized to be in control and to demonstrate "masculinity." To be stripped of control and power is devastating to anyone, but that devastation takes a different toll on men who have been socialized to reflect the supposedly masculine qualities of being strong and in charge at all times.

If you have been sexually abused in any way, regardless of whether you are a woman or a man, we encourage you to seek counseling. It is not uncommon for people to block out experiences such as sexual abuse, only to have memories and feelings surfaced in a course that deals with the subject. Counseling can provide you with an opportunity to deal with unresolved feelings and problems that may linger because of earlier experiences. Support groups for incest survivors also can be most beneficial.

In addition to counseling or support groups, many fine books deal with sexual abuse, which can be of value. If you are interested in doing further reading on the psychological aspects of incest, including its causes, effects, and treatment approaches, a number of recommended readings are given in the "Activities and Exercises" section at the end of this chapter.

■ Date and Acquaintance Rape

In our contacts with college students it has become clear to us that date rape is prevalent on the campus. *Acquaintance rape* takes place when a woman is forced to have unwanted sex with someone she knows. This might involve friends, co-workers, neighbors, or relatives. *Date rape* occurs in those situations where a woman is forced to have unwanted intercourse with a person in the context of dating.

Some writers consider acquaintance rape and date rape as examples of communication gone awry (Weiten & Lloyd, 1994). Earlier in this chapter we identified some myths and misconceptions about sexuality. One of these myths is that men are by nature sexually aggressive. Thus, men may feel that they are expected to be this way. As a consequence, they may misinterpret a woman's "no" as a "maybe" or a sign of initial resistance that can be broken down. Dating partners may not say what they really mean, or they may not mean what they say. This phenomenon is reinforced by the linkage of sex with domination and submission. In our society, masculinity is equated with power, dominance, and sexual aggressiveness, while femininity is associated with pleasing men, sexual passivity, and lack of assertiveness (Basow, 1992).

Weiten and Lloyd (1994) indicate that inadequate communication between dating partners is often a key factor contributing to date rape, and they offer these suggestions to people in dating relationships:

- Recognize that date rape is an act of sexual aggression.
- Beware of using excessive alcohol or drugs, which can lower your resistance and distort your judgment.
- Clarify your values and attitudes about sex before you are in situations where you have to make a decision about sexual behavior.

- Communicate your feelings, thoughts, and expectations about sex in a clear and open manner.
- Listen carefully to each other and respect each other's values, decisions, and boundaries.
- Exercise control over your environment.
- Know the warning signs associated with pre-rape behavior.
- Be prepared to act aggressively if assertive refusals don't stop the unwanted sexual advances.

Both date rape and acquaintance rape can be considered as a betrayal of trust. Much like in incest, when a woman is forced to have sex against her will, her dignity as a person is violated. Not believing that she is in danger, she may make herself vulnerable to a man, and then experience hurt. She might have explicit trust in a man she knows, only to discover that he is intent on getting what he wants, regardless of the cost to her. The emotional scars that are a part of date rape are similar to the wounds inflicted by incest. As is the case with incest victims, women who are raped by people they know often take responsibility and blame themselves for what occurred, and they are often embarrassed about or afraid of reporting the incident.

Currently, many college campuses offer education directed at the prevention of date rape. The focus of this education is on the importance of being consistent and clear about what you want or don't want with your dating partner, as well as providing information about factors contributing to date rape. Many prevention programs are designed for women to increase their awareness of high-risk situations and behaviors and to teach them how to protect themselves. Basow (1992) emphasizes the reality that because men rape, only they can stop rape. It is the man's responsibility to avoid forcing a woman to have sex with him, and he must learn that her "no" really does mean "no." Basow reports that innovative campus programs aimed at men are just beginning, especially programs for men in fraternity groups.

It is clear that campus preventive programs need to be designed for both women and men. Both could benefit from discussion groups or workshops on this topic so that they can explore myths and misconceptions that drive certain behavior. Basow believes that all of us are part of the problem and that all of us need to be part of the solution. She points out that rape can be viewed as an outgrowth of a culture that glorifies sex and violence; prevention programs need to address ways of changing those attitudes and behaviors that lead to the exploitation of women.

■ Sexual Harassment

Sexual harassment is repeated and unwanted sexually oriented behavior in the form of comments, gestures, or physical contacts. This phenomenon is of concern on the college campus, in the workplace, and in the military. Women experience sexual harassment more frequently than do men. Sexual harassment is abuse of the power differential between two people. Those who have more power tend to engage in sexual harassment more frequently than those with less power (Basow, 1992). Some of the many forms of sexual harassment include:

- comments about one's body or clothes
- physical or verbal conduct of a sexual nature
- jokes about sex or gender-specific traits
- repeated and unwanted staring, comments, or propositions of a sexual nature
- demeaning references to one's gender
- unwanted touching or attention of a sexual nature
- conversations tinted with sexually suggestive innuendoes or double meanings
- questions about one's sexual behavior

Men sometimes make the assumption that women like sexual attention, when in fact they resent being related to in strictly sexual terms. Sexual harassment dimin-ishes choice, and surely it is not flattering. Harassment reduces people to objects to be demeaned. The person doing the harassing may not see this behavior as being problematic and may even joke about it. Yet it is never a laughing matter. Those on the receiving end of harassment often report feeling responsible. However, as in the case of incest and date rape, the victim should never be blamed.

As is true in cases of incest and date or acquaintance rape, many incidences of sexual harassment go unreported because the individuals involved fear the consequences, such as getting fired, being denied a promotion, risking a low grade in a course, and encountering barriers to pursuing their careers. Fear of reprisals is a foremost barrier to reporting. Riger (1991) suggests that gender bias in policies and procedures discourages women from making complaints.

If you are on the receiving end of unwanted behavior, you are not powerless. Because sexual harassment is never appropriate, you have every right to break the pattern. Make it clear to the person doing the harassing that his or her behavior is unacceptable to you and that you want it stopped. If this does not work, or if you feel it would be too much of a risk to confront this individual, you can talk to someone else. If the offensive behavior does not stop, keep a detailed record of what is taking place. This will be useful in showing a pattern of unwanted behavior when you issue a complaint.

Most work settings and colleges have policies and procedures for dealing with sexual harassment complaints. You do not have to deal with this matter alone if your rights are violated. Realize that the college community does not take abusing power lightly and that procedures are designed to correct abuses. When you report a problematic situation, know that your college most likely has staff members who will assist you in bringing resolution to this situation. As is true for preserving the secret of incest, it will not help if you keep the harassment a secret. By telling someone else, you are breaking the pattern of silence that burdens sexual harassment victims.

Chapter Summary

Sexuality is part of our personhood and should not be thought of as an activity divorced from our feelings, values, and relationships. Although childhood and adolescent experiences do have an impact on shaping our present attitudes toward sex and our sexual behavior, we are in a position to modify our attitudes and behavior if we are not satisfied with ourselves as sexual beings.

One significant step toward evaluating your sexual attitudes is to become aware of the myths and misconceptions you may harbor. It helps to review where and how you acquired your views about sexuality. Have the sources of your sexual knowledge and values been healthy models? Have you questioned how your attitudes affect the way you feel about yourself sexually? Is your sexuality an expression of yourself as a complete person?

Another step toward developing your own sexual views is to learn to be open in talking about sexual concerns, including your fears and desires, with at least one other person you trust. Guilt feelings may be based on irrational premises, and you may be burdening yourself needlessly by feeling guilty about normal feelings and behavior. You may feel very alone when it comes to your sexual feelings, fantasies, fears, and actions. By sharing some of these concerns with others, you are likely to find out that you are not the only one with such concerns.

If we are successful in dealing with barriers that prevent us from acknowledging, experiencing, and expressing our sexuality, we increase our chances of learning how to enjoy both sensuality and sexuality. Sensuality can be a significant path toward creating satisfying sexual relationships, and we can learn to become sensual beings even if we decide not to have sexual relationships with others. Sensuality implies a full awareness of and a sensitivity to the pleasures of sight, sound, smell, taste, and touch. We can enjoy sensuality without being sexual, and it is a mistake to conclude that sensuality necessarily leads to sexual behavior. Nevertheless, sensuality is very important in enhancing sexual relationships. Intimacy, or the emotional sharing with a person we care for, is another ingredient of joyful sex. As a habitual style, sex without intimacy tends to lead to a basic sense of frustration, emptiness, and emotional deadness.

The AIDS crisis has had a significant impact on sexual behavior. Although ignorance and fear of AIDS are rampant, education can be the key to dispelling them. There are many myths and misconceptions pertaining to who gets AIDS, how it is transmitted, and the stigma attached to it. Along with a better understanding of this disease, education can put you in a good position to make informed choices in expressing your sexuality.

The place that sex occupies in your life and the attitudes you have toward it are very much a matter of free choice. It is no easier to achieve sexual autonomy than it is to achieve autonomy in other areas of your life.

Incest, date or acquaintance rape, and sexual harassment are all forms of sexual abuse that have the capacity to render the victims powerless and helpless. They are all embedded in gender and power dynamics. Incest and date rape are examples of betrayals of trust, sexual aggression, and violence. Those involved do not have much choice in a situation that is foisted upon them. The consequences are potentially dire both physically and psychologically, for the victims often have difficulty forming trusting relationships and enjoying sexuality.

The themes explored in the previous chapter on love and in the following chapter on relationships and lifestyles are really impossible to separate from the themes of this chapter. Think about love, sex, and relationships as an integrated dimension of a rich and full life.

Activities and Exercises

1. Write down some of your major questions or concerns regarding sexuality. You might consider discussing these issues with a friend, your partner (if you're involved in an intimate relationship), or your class group.

2. In your journal trace the evolution of your sexual history. What were some important experiences for you, and what did you learn from these experiences?

3. List as many common slang words as you are able to think of pertaining to (a) the male genitals, (b) the female genitals, and (c) sexual intercourse. Review this list and ask yourself what sexual attitudes seem to be expressed. What do you think this list implies about your culture's attitude toward sexuality? Explore the hypothesis that the more rigid, uncomfortable, and embarrassed a particular culture is about sex, the more negative are the words used to describe sexual functioning.

4. Incest is a universal taboo. Explore some of the reasons for this taboo. You might investigate cross-cultural attitudes pertaining to incest. Do you view sexual experimentation between siblings during childhood as incest? Discuss.

5. The media are giving increasing attention to the topics of incest and sexual abuse of children. What do you think this current interest in these subjects implies?

6. What sexual modeling did you see in your parents? What attitudes and values about sex did they convey to you, both implicitly and explicitly? What would you most want to communicate to your children about sex?

7. Select one or more of the following books for further reading on the topics explored in this chapter. If you are interested in doing further reading on the psychological aspects of incest, including its causes, effects, and treatment approaches, the following resources are recommended: *The Courage to Heal: A Guide for Women Survivors of Child Sexual Abuse* (Bass & Davis, 1994); *It Will Never Happen to Me* (Black, 1987); *Child Sexual Abuse* (Finkelhor, 1984); *Betrayal of Innocence* (Forward & Buck, 1988); *Father-Daughter Incest* (Herman, 1981); *The Broken Taboo* (Justice & Justice, 1979); *The Sexual Healing Journey* (Maltz, 1991); *Incest and Sexuality* (Maltz & Holman, 1987); *Incest* (Meiselman, 1978); *Resolving the Trauma of Incest* (Meiselman, 1990); *If I Should Die Before I Wake* (Morris, 1984); and *The Best Kept Secret* (Rush, 1980).

   Vanderbilt (1992) lists some self-help resources that can be useful for victims of child sexual abuse, including these four resources:

- Self-Help Clearinghouse, St. Clare's-Riverside Medical Center, Denville, NJ 07834 (201-625-9565). Publishes *The Self-Help Directory*, a guide to mutual-aid self-help groups and how to form them.

- Incest Survivors Anonymous, P.O. Box 5613, Long Beach, CA 90805-0613 (213-428-5599). Assists in forming 12-step groups.

- SARA (Sexual Assault Recovery Anonymous) Society, P.O. Box 16, Surrey, British Columbia V3T 4W4 Canada (604-584-2626). Provides self-help information for adults and teens who were sexually abused as children.

- National Council on Child Abuse and Family Violence, 1155 Connecticut Avenue NW, Suite 400, Washington, DC 20036 (202-429-6695).

10 *Relationships*

It takes both imagination
and effort to think of ways
to revise our relationships so
that they will remain alive.

✔ *Prechapter Self-Inventory*

Use the following scale to respond: 4 = this statement is true of me *most* of the time; 3 = this statement is true of me *much* of the time; 2 = this statement is true of me *some* of the time; 1 = this statement is true of me *almost none* of the time.

_____ 1. I consider the absence of conflict and crisis to be a sign of a good relationship.

_____ 2. It's difficult for me to have many close relationships at one time.

_____ 3. If I'm involved in a satisfactory relationship, I won't feel attracted to others besides my partner.

_____ 4. I believe that the mark of a successful relationship is that I enjoy being both with and without the other person.

_____ 5. I would like to find intimacy with one other person.

_____ 6. At times, wanting too much from another person causes me difficulties in the relationship.

_____ 7. I think that an exclusive relationship is bound to become dull, predictable, and unexciting.

_____ 8. I know what I'm looking for in a relationship.

_____ 9. I have what I want in terms of intimacy with others.

_____ 10. I can be emotionally intimate with another person without being physically intimate with that person.

Introduction

Relationships play a significant role in our lives. In this chapter we deal with friendships, marital relationships, intimacy between people who are not married, dating relationships, relationships between parents and children, same-gender relationships as well as opposite-gender relationships, and other meaningful personal relationships.

Marriage — when construed broadly to encompass all committed, intimate partnerships, whether legally sanctioned or less formally ordered — is the dominate relationship in our society. Whether you choose to marry or not, whether your primary relationship is with someone of the same gender or the opposite gender, you will face many of the same relationship challenges. What is true for marriage is largely true for these other intimate relationships as well. Allowing for the differences in relationships, the signs of growth and meaningfulness are much the same, and so are the problems. You can use the ideas in this chapter as a basis for thinking about the role relationships play in your life. In this chapter we hope to encourage you to reflect on what you want from your relationships, and we will assist you in examining the quality of these relationships.

Types of Intimacy

The challenge of forming intimate relationships is the major task of early adulthood (Erikson, 1963). Intimacy implies that we are able to share significant aspects of ourselves with others. The issues we raise here concerning barriers to intimacy and ways of enhancing intimacy can help you better understand the many different types of relationships in your life. The ideas in this chapter are useful tools in rethinking what kind of relationships you want, as well as in clarifying some new choices you may want to make. Take a fresh look at your relationships, including both their frustrations and their delights, and decide whether you might want to initiate some changes.

Consider the case of Donald, who told us about how little closeness he had experienced with his father. He saw his father as uncaring, aloof, and preoccupied with his own concerns. Donald deeply wished that he could be physically and emotionally closer to his father, but he had no idea how to bring this about. He made the difficult decision to talk to his father and tell him how he felt and what he wanted. His father appeared to listen, and his eyes moistened, but then without saying much he quickly left the room. Donald reported how hurt and disappointed he was that his father had not been as responsive as he had hoped he would be. Donald was missing the subtle yet significant signs that his father had been touched and was not as uncaring as he had imagined. That his father listened to him, that he responded with even a few clumsy words, that he touched Donald on the shoulder, and that he became emotional were all manifestations that Donald's overtures had been received. Donald needs to understand that his father is probably very uncomfortable in talking personally. His father may well be every bit as afraid of his son's rejection as Donald is of his father's rebuffs. Donald will need to show patience and continue "hanging in there" with his father if he is really interested in changing the way they relate to each other.

The experience Donald had with his father could have occurred in any intimate relationship. We can experience feelings of awkwardness, unexpressed desires, and fears of rejection with our friends, lovers, spouses, parents, or children. A key point is that we have the power to bring about change if we ourselves change and do not insist that the other person make quick and total changes. It is up to us to teach others specific ways of becoming more personal. It does little good to invest our energy in lamenting all the ways in which the other person is not fulfilling our expectations, nor is it helpful to focus on remaking others. Time and again, in this chapter we will encourage you to focus on your own wants, to look at what you are doing, and to make some decisions about how you can assume increased control of your relationships. When you take a passive stance and simply hope the other person will change in the ways that you would like, you are giving away your own power.

The intimacy we share with another person can be emotional, intellectual, physical, spiritual, or any combination of these. It can be exclusive or nonexclusive,

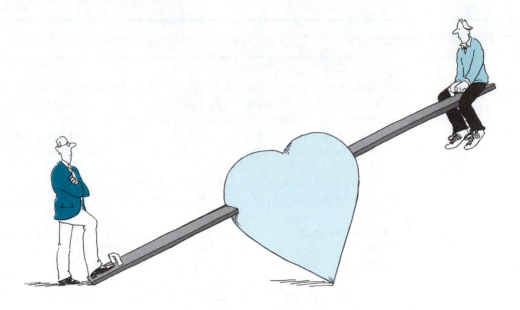

long-term or brief. For example, many of the participants in the personal-growth groups we conduct become emotionally involved with one another. During the space of a week in which they share their struggles, they develop a meaningful closeness, even though they may not keep in touch once the week is over. This closeness does not come about magically or automatically. They earn it by daring to be different in how they relate. Instead of keeping their thoughts, feelings, and reactions to themselves, they let others know them in ways that they typically do not allow outside of the group setting. The cohesion comes about when people discover that they have very similar feelings and when they are willing to share their pain, anger, frustration—and their joys. We've observed how reluctant many people are to open themselves up emotionally in such short-term situations, because they want to avoid the sadness of parting. Bonds of intimacy and friendship can be formed in a short period, however, and subsequent distance in space and time need not diminish the quality of the friendships we form. We caution that developing intimacy with people in the group should not be the final goal. What is important is that the members translate this learning to their outside lives.

When we avoid intimacy, we only rob ourselves. We may pass up the chance to really get to know neighbors and new acquaintances, because we fear that either we or our new friends will move and that the friendship will come to an end. Similarly, we may not want to open ourselves to intimacy with sick or dying persons, because we fear the pain of losing them. Although such fears may be natural ones, too often we allow them to cheat us of the uniquely rich experience of being truly close to another person. We can enhance our lives greatly by daring to care about others and fully savoring the time we can share with them now.

The idea that we most want to stress is that you can choose the kinds of relationships you want to experience. Often, we fail to make our own choices and instead fall into a certain type of relationship because we think "this is the way it's *supposed* to be." For example, some people marry who in reality might prefer to remain single—this is particularly true for women who feel the pressure to have a family because it's "natural" for them to do so. Sometimes people choose an opposite-sex relationship because they think that it is what is expected of them, when they would really prefer a same-sex relationship. Instead of blindly accepting what others think you "ought" to do, you have the choice of giving real thought to the question of what types of intimacy have meaning for you.

As you read the remainder of this chapter, spend some time thinking about the quality of all the various kinds of intimacy you are experiencing in your life. Are you involved in the kinds of relationships that you want? How can you enhance your relationships? What are *you* willing to do to improve them? What is your view of a growing relationship?

➤ *Time Out for Personal Reflection*

1. What do you look for in a person you'd like to form an intimate relationship with? For each item, put a 1 in the space if the quality is *very important* to you, a 2 if it is *somewhat important,* and a 3 if it is *not very important.*

_____	intelligence
_____	character (a strong sense of values)
_____	physical appearance and attractiveness
_____	money and possessions
_____	charm
_____	prestige and status
_____	a strong sense of identity
_____	expressiveness and a tendency to be outgoing
_____	a sense of humor
_____	caring and sensitivity
_____	power
_____	independence
_____	a quiet person
_____	someone who will make decisions for me
_____	someone I can lean on
_____	someone who will lean on me
_____	someone I can't live without
_____	someone who works hard and is disciplined
_____	someone who likes to play and have fun
_____	someone who has values similar to mine
_____	someone I'd like to grow old with

Now list the three qualities that you value most in a person when you are considering an intimate relationship.

_____

_____

_____

2. Why do you think a person might want an intimate relationship with you? Look over the qualities listed above, and then list the qualities you see yourself as having.

_____

_____

_____

3. Identify the kinds of intimate relationships you have chosen so far in your life. If you aren't presently involved in any significant intimate relationships, would you like to be?

_____

_____

_____

4. What do you get from being involved in a significant relationship? Check the responses that apply to you, and add your own on the lines provided.

_____   a feeling of being cared for
_____   a sense of importance
_____   joy in being able to care for another person
_____   excitement
_____   the feeling of not being alone in the world
_____   sharing and companionship

Other:

_____

_____

_____

Meaningful Relationships: A Personal View

In this section we share some of our ideas about the characteristics of a meaningful relationship. Although these guidelines pertain to couples, they are also relevant to other personal relationships, such as those between parent and child and between friends of the same or opposite gender. Take, for example, the guideline

"The persons involved are willing to work at keeping their relationship alive." Parents and children often take each other for granted, rarely spending time talking about how they are getting along. Either parent or child may expect the other to assume the major responsibility for their relationship. The same principle applies to friends or to partners in a primary relationship. As you look over our list, adapt it to your own relationships, keeping in mind your particular cultural values. Your cultural background plays an influential role in your relationships, and you may need to adapt our ideas to better fit your core values. As you review our list, ask yourself what qualities *you* think are most important in your relationships.

We see relationships as most meaningful when they are dynamic and evolving rather than fixed or final. Thus, any relationship may have periods of joy and excitement followed by times of struggle, pain, and distance. As long as the individuals in a relationship are growing and changing, their relationship is bound to change as well. The following qualities of a relationship seem most important to us.

■ *Each person in the relationship has a separate identity.* Kahlil Gibran (1923) expresses this thought well in *The Prophet:* "But let there be spaces in your togetherness, and let the winds of the heavens dance between you" (p. 16). In *The Dance of Anger,* Harriet Goldhor Lerner (1985) says that making long-term relationships work is difficult because it is necessary to create and maintain a balance between separateness and togetherness. If there is not enough togetherness in a relationship, people typically feel isolated and do not share feelings and experiences. If there is not enough separateness, they give up a sense of their own identity and control, devoting much effort to becoming what the other person expects.

■ *Although each person desires the other, each can survive without the other.* This characteristic is an extension of the prior one, and it implies that people are in a relationship by choice. They are not so tightly bound together that if they are separated one or the other becomes lost and empty. Thus, if a young man says "I simply can't live without my girlfriend," he is indeed in trouble. His dependency should not be interpreted as love but as seeking for an object to make him feel complete.

■ *Each is able to talk openly with the other about matters of significance to the relationship.* Both people can openly express grievances and let each other know the changes they desire. They ask for what they want, rather than expecting the other to intuitively know what they want and give it to them. For example, assume that you are not satisfied with how you and your mother spend time together. You can take the first step by letting her know, in a nonjudgmental way, that you would like to talk more personally. Rather than telling her how she is, you can focus more on telling her how you feel in your relationship with her.

■ *Each person assumes responsibility for his or her own level of happiness and refrains from blaming the other if he or she is unhappy.* Of course, in a close relationship or friendship the unhappiness of the other person is bound to affect you, but you should not expect another person to *make* you happy, fulfilled, or excited. Although the way others feel will influence your life, they do not create or cause your feelings. Ultimately, you are responsible for defining your goals and your life, and you can take actions to change what *you* are doing if you are unhappy with a situation.

■ *Both people are willing to work at keeping their relationship alive.* If we hope to keep a relationship vital, we must reevaluate and revise our way of being with each other from time to time. Consider how this guideline fits for your friendships. If you take a good friend for granted and show little interest in doing what is necessary to maintain your friendship, that person may soon grow disenchanted and wonder what kind of friend you are. Buscaglia (1992) puts this notion as follows: "If we want love in our relationships, then we are directly responsible for creating and maintaining it" (p. 190).

■ *They are able to have fun and to play together; they enjoy doing things with each other.* It is easy to become so serious that we forget to take time to enjoy those we love. One way of changing drab relationships to become aware of the infrequency of playful moments and then determine what things are getting in the way of enjoying life. Again, think of this guideline as it applies to your close friends.

■ *Each person is growing, changing, and opening up to new experiences.* When you rely on others for your personal fulfillment and confirmation as a person, you are in trouble. The best way to build solid relationships with others is to work on developing your own personality. But do not be surprised if you encounter resistance to your growth and change. This resistance can come from within yourself as well as from others.

■ *If the relationship contains a sexual component, each person makes some attempt to keep the romance alive.* Although sexual partners may not always experience the intensity and novelty of the early period of their relationship, they can devise ways of creating a climate of romance and closeness. They may go to places they haven't been before or otherwise vary their routine in some ways. They recognize when life is getting dull and look for ways to eliminate its boring aspects. In their lovemaking they are sensitive to each other's needs and desires; at the same time, they are able to ask each other for what they want and need.

■ *The two people are equal in the relationship.* People who feel that they are typically the "givers" and that their partners are usually unavailable when they need them might question the balance in their relationships. In some relationships one person may feel compelled to assume a superior position relative to the other — for example, to be very willing to listen and give advice yet unwilling to go to the other person and show any vulnerability or need. Both parties need to be willing to look at aspects of inequality and demonstrate a willingness to negotiate changes.

■ *Each person actively demonstrates concern for the other.* In a vital relationship the participants do more than just talk about how much they value each other. Their actions show their care and concern more eloquently than any words. Each person has a desire to give to the other. They have an interest in each other's welfare and a desire to see that the other person is fulfilled.

■ *Each person finds meaning and sources of nourishment outside the relationship.* Sometimes people become very possessive in their friendships. A sign of a healthy relationship is that each avoids assuming an attitude of ownership toward the other. Although they may experience jealousy at times, they do not demand that the other person deaden his or her feelings for others. Their lives did not begin when they met each other, nor would their lives end if they should part.

■ *Each avoids manipulating, exploiting, and using the other.* Each respects and cares for the other and is willing to see the world through the other's eyes. At times parent/child relationships are strained because either or both parties attempt to manipulate the other. Consider the father who brags about his son, Roger, to others and whose affection is based on Roger's being an outstanding athlete. Roger may feel used if his father is able to talk only of sports. What if he were to decide to quit playing sports? Would he still be earning his father's approval?

■ *Each person is moving in a direction in life that is personally meaningful.* They are both excited about the quality of their lives and their projects. Applied to couples, this guideline implies that both individuals feel that their needs are being met within the relationship, but they also feel a sense of engagement in their work, play, and relationships with other friends and family members.

■ *If they are in a committed relationship, they maintain this relationship by choice, not simply for the sake of any children involved, out of duty, or because of convenience.* They choose to keep their ties with each other even if things get rough or if they sometimes experience emptiness in the relationship. They share some common purposes and values, and therefore, they are willing to look at what is lacking in their relationship and to work on changing undesirable situations.

■ *They are able to cope with anger in their relationship.* Couples often seek relationship counseling with the expectation that they will learn to stop fighting and that conflict will end. This is not a realistic goal. More important than the absence of fighting is learning how to fight cleanly and constructively, which entails an ongoing process of expressing anger and frustrations. In writing about love and anger, Buscaglia (1992) claims that many people try to disguise anger, sublimate it, suppress it, or project it where it doesn't belong. He adds that expressing anger often takes care of the situation, while repressed anger festers until it explodes. It is the buildup of these emotions that creates trouble. If anger is not expressed and dealt with constructively, it will sour a relationship. Stored-up anger usually results in the target person getting more than his or her share of deserved anger. At other times bottled-up anger is let out in indirect ways such as sarcasm and hostility. If the parties in a relationship are angry, they should try to express it in a direct and honest way.

■ *Each person recognizes the need for solitude and is willing to create the time in which to be alone.* Each allows the other a sense of privacy. Because they recognize each other's individual integrity, they avoid prying into every thought or manipulating the other to disclose what he or she wants to keep private. Sometimes parents are guilty of not respecting the privacy of their children. A father may be hurt if his daughter does not want to talk with him at any time that *he* feels like talking. He needs to realize that she is a separate person with her own needs and that she may be needing time alone when he wants to talk.

■ *They do not expect the other to do for them what they are capable of doing for themselves.* They don't expect the other person to make them feel alive, take away their boredom, assume their risks, or make them feel valued and important. Each is working toward creating his or her own autonomous identity. Consequently, neither person depends on the other for confirmation of his or her personal worth; nor does one walk in the shadow of the other.

■ *They encourage each other to become all that they are capable of becoming.* Unfortunately, people often have an investment in keeping those with whom they are intimately involved from changing. Their expectations and needs may lead them to resist changes in their partner and thus make it difficult for their partner to grow. If they recognize their fears, however, they can challenge their need to block their partner's progress.

■ *Each has a commitment to the other.* Commitment is a vital part of an intimate relationship. It means that the people involved have an investment in their future together and that they are willing to stay with each other in times of crisis and conflict. Although many people express an aversion to any long-term commitment in a relationship, how deeply will they allow themselves to be loved if they believe that the relationship can be dissolved on a whim when things look bleak? Perhaps, for some people, a fear of intimacy gets in the way of developing a sense of commitment. Loving and being loved is both exciting and frightening, and we may have to struggle with the issue of how much anxiety we want to tolerate. Commitment to another person involves risks and carries a price, but it is an essential part of an intimate relationship.

Creating and maintaining friendships, especially intimate relationships, is a primary interest among many college students. There is no single or easy prescription for success; developing meaningful relationships entails the willingness to struggle. You may have encountered difficulties keeping your relationships alive. Many students say that they don't have enough time to maintain their friendships and other relationships. If this fits for you, realize that your relationships and friendships are likely to dissolve if you neglect them. Time must be devoted to nourishing and revitalizing your relationships if you expect them to last.

You can make choices that will increase your chances of developing lasting friendships:

- be tolerant of differences between your friends and yourself
- learn to become aware of conflicts and deal with them constructively
- be willing to let the other person know how you are affected in the relationship
- stay in the relationship even though you may experience a fear of rejection
- check out your assumptions with others instead of deciding for them what they are thinking and feeling
- be willing to make yourself vulnerable and to take risks

▪ avoid the temptation to live up to others' expectations instead of being true to yourself

Creating and maintaining friendships and intimate relationships requires time, work, and the willingness to ride out hard times. Further, to be a good friend to another, you must first be a good friend to yourself, which implies knowing yourself and caring about yourself. The following "Time Out" asks you to focus on some of the ways in which you see yourself as an alive and growing person, which is the foundation of building meaningful relationships.

➤ *Time Out for Personal Reflection*

1. What are some ways in which you see yourself as growing? In what ways do you see yourself as resisting personal growth by sticking with old and comfortable patterns, even if they don't work? To facilitate your reflection, look over the following statements and mark each one with a "T" or an "F," depending on whether you think it generally applies to you.

_____ If I'm involved in an intimate relationship, I tell the other person what I want.
_____ I'm willing to try new things.
_____ Rather than settling for comfort in a relationship or in life, I ask for more.
_____ If I'm involved in an intimate relationship, I tell the other person what I'm feeling.
_____ I'm engaged in projects that are meaningful to me.

2. List other ways in which you're growing:

_____

_____

3. List some ways in which you resist personal growth:

_____

_____

4. In what ways do you see the person with whom you're most intimate growing or resisting growth?

_____

_____

5. If you're involved in a couple relationship, in what ways do you think you and your partner are growing closer? In what ways are you going in different directions?

_____

_____

_____

_____

6. Are you satisfied with the relationship you've just described? If not, what would you most like to change? How might you go about it?

_____

_____

_____

_____

A suggestion: If you're involved in a couple relationship, have your partner respond to the questions on a separate sheet of paper. Then compare your answers and discuss areas of agreement and disagreement.

Dealing with Communication Blocks

A number of barriers to effective communication can inhibit developing and maintaining intimate relationships. Some of these barriers are: failing to really listen to another person; selective listening—that is, hearing only what you want to hear; being overly concerned with getting your point across without considering

the other's views; silently rehearsing what you will say next as you are "listening"; becoming defensive, with self-protection your primary concern; attempting to change others rather than first attempting to understand them; telling others how they are, rather than telling them how they affect you; reacting to people on the basis of stereotypes; being blinded by prejudice; bringing old patterns into the present and not allowing the other person to change; overreacting to a person; failing to state what your needs are and expecting others to know intuitively; making assumptions about another person without checking them out; using sarcasm and hostility instead of being direct; and speaking in vague terms such as "You manipulate me!"

In most of these cases you tend to be so concerned with getting your point across, defending your view of yourself, or changing another person that you cannot appreciate what the other person is thinking and feeling. These blocks make it very difficult to have I/Thou encounters, in which both people are open with themselves and each other, expressing what they think and feel and making genuine contact. Barriers between people who are attempting to communicate typically leave the participants feeling distant from each other.

Deborah Tannen has written two best-selling books on the subject of communication between women and men. In *That's Not What I Meant* (1987), Tannen focuses on how conversational styles can make or break a relationship. She maintains that male-female communication can be considered cross-cultural. The language we use as we are growing up is influenced by our gender, ethnicity, class and cultural background, and location. Boys and girls grow up in different worlds, even if they are part of the same family. Furthermore, they carry many of the patterns they established in childhood into their transactions as adults. For Tannen, these cultural differences include different expectations about the role of communication in relationships. These factors make up our conversational style, and the subtle differences in this style can lead to overwhelming misunderstandings and disappointments. In her other book, *You Just Don't Understand* (1991), Tannen develops the idea that conversational style differences do not explain all the conflicts in relationships between women and men, but many problems result because partners are expressing their thoughts and feelings in different ways. She believes that if we can sort out these differences based on conversational style we will be better able to confront real conflicts and find a form of communication that will allow for negotiation of these differences.

Rogers (1961) has written extensively on ways to improve personal relationships. For him, the main block to effective communication is our tendency to evaluate and judge the statements of others. He believes that what gets in the way of understanding another is the tendency to approve or disapprove, the unwillingness to put ourselves in the other's frame of reference, and the fear of being changed ourselves if we really listen to and understand a person with a viewpoint different from our own. Rogers suggests that the next time you get into an argument with your partner, your friend, or a small group of friends, just stop the discussion for a moment and, for an experiment, institute this rule: "Each person can speak up for himself *only* after he has restated the ideas and feelings of the previous speaker accurately, and to that speaker's satisfaction" (1961, p. 332).

Carrying out this experiment requires that you strive to genuinely understand another person and achieve his or her perspective. Although this may sound simple, it can be extremely difficult to put into practice. It involves challenging yourself to go beyond what you find convenient to hear, examining your assumptions and prejudices, not attributing to statements meanings that were not intended, and not coming to quick conclusions based on superficial listening. If you are successful in challenging yourself in these ways, you can enter the subjective world of the significant person in your life; that is, you can acquire empathy, which is the necessary foundation for all intimate relationships. Rogers (1980) contends that the sensitive companionship offered by an empathic person is healing and that such a deep understanding is a precious gift to another.

■ Stereotypes as Barriers to Interpersonal Communication

A stereotype is a judgmental generalization applied to an individual without regard to his or her own uniqueness. A few examples of stereotypes are: "Men are unemotional and uncaring." "Lesbians hate men." "Asians are talented in mathematics." "Italians are emotional." "Women are passive." Stereotypes get in the way of communicating with others because they put people in categories, which does not allow for authentic relating. These stereotypes create boundaries that prevent us from seeing our interconnectedness as members of the human family. Our social isolation limits our capacity to experience the richness that can be part of diverse human relationships. Unless challenged, our stereotypes can keep us separate and prevent us from getting to know people who could enhance our lives.

Prevailing assumptions are generally held onto tenaciously. People have a tendency to see evidence that supports their assumptions more clearly than evidence that challenges those assumptions. Rather than challenge their beliefs, people often look for evidence to support their preconceived notions. Stereotypes are very common in our society, but belief in them ranges along a continuum. Most people do not believe that every member of a specific group has common characteristics, values, and behaviors. And once we get to know someone from a group, our belief in the stereotype for that group is often lessened — and certainly doesn't apply to the person we know.

Ask yourself how stereotypes get in your way of understanding people on an individual basis. Consider stereotypes you may hold and reflect on ways that they serve as barriers to getting to know another person:

- How are you affected by having certain characteristics assigned to you based on your gender, sexual orientation, ethnicity, culture, religion, age, or ability?
- How does the act of placing a label on you or on others affect your relationships?

Once you become aware of some stereotypes you may have bought into, explore where you acquired those beliefs. Did you get messages from your parents? from people in your community? from your friends? from your teachers? While you may have acquired stereotypes on a less than conscious level, once you become aware of their existence you are in a position to question their validity.

■ Effective Personal Communication

Your culture influences both the content and the process of your communication. Some cultures prize direct communication, while other cultures see this behavior as rude and insensitive. In certain cultures direct eye contact is as insulting as the avoidance of eye contact is in other cultures. Harmony within the family is a cardinal value in certain cultures, and it may be inappropriate for adult children to confront their parents. As you read the following discussion, recognize that variations do exist among cultures. Our discussion has a Euro-American slant, which makes it essential that you adapt the principles we present to your own cultural framework. Examine the ways your communication style has been influenced by your culture, and decide if you want to modify certain patterns that you have learned. For example, your culture might have taught you to control your feelings. You might decide to become more emotionally expressive if you discover that this pattern is restricting you in areas of your life where you would like to be freer.

From our perspective, when two people are communicating meaningfully, they are involved in many of the following processes:

- They are facing each other and making eye contact, and one is listening while the other speaks.
- They do not rehearse their response while the other is speaking. The listener is able to summarize accurately what the speaker has said. ("So you're hurt when I don't call to tell you that I'll be late.")

- The language is specific and concrete. (A vague statement is "I feel manipulated." A concrete statement is "I don't like it when you bring me flowers and then expect me to do something for you that I already told you I didn't want to do.")
- The speaker makes personal statements instead of bombarding the other with impersonal questions. (A questioning statement is "Where were you last night, and why did you come home so late?" A personal statement is "I was worried and scared because I didn't know where you were last night.")
- The listener takes a moment before responding to reflect on what was said and on how he or she is affected. There is a sincere effort to walk in the shoes of the other person. ("It must have been very hard for you when you didn't know where I was last night and thought I might have been in an accident.")
- Although each has reactions to what the other is saying, there is an absence of critical judgment. (A critical judgment is "You never think about anybody but yourself, and you're totally irresponsible." A more appropriate reaction would be "I appreciate it when you think to call me, knowing that I may be worried.")
- Each of the parties can be honest and direct without insensitively damaging the other's dignity. Each makes "I" statements, rather than second-guessing and speaking for the other. ("Sometimes I worry that you don't care about me, and I want to check that out with you, rather than assuming that it's true.")
- There is a respect for each other's differences and an avoidance of pressuring each other to accept a point of view. ("I look at this matter very differently than you do, but I understand that you have your own opinion.")

- There is a congruency (or matching) between the verbal and nonverbal messages. (If she is expressing anger, she is not smiling.)
- Each person is open about how he or she is affected by the other. (An ineffective response is "You have no right to criticize me." An effective response is "I'm very disappointed that you don't like the work I've done.")
- Neither person is being mysterious, expecting the other to decode his or her messages.

These processes are essential for fostering any meaningful relationship. You might try observing yourself while you are communicating and take note of the degree to which you practice these principles. Decide if the quality of your relationships is satisfying to you. If you determine that you want to improve certain relationships, it will be helpful to begin by working on one of these skills at a time.

Although communication skills are basic to solid relationships, they alone are not sufficient to enable two people to understand and work through their difficulties. Goldberg (1987) believes that men and women have trouble communicating mainly because of their polarized and unconscious defenses. Gender-defensive polarization develops because of gender-role conditioning (discussed in Chapter 4). Both genders have difficulties grasping the world of the other. According to Goldberg, if women and men are engaged in defending themselves, they will be using different languages and living in different psychological worlds. He emphasizes that the starting point for effective communication is an absence of gender-defensive polarization.

■ Communicating with Your Parents

Parents are powerful people in our lives. We often expect them to change in the way we want and to do so quickly. We often insist that they undo years of unfair treatment or pain that they have caused us. If we persist in this behavior, our parents will eventually withdraw from us. It would be a good idea to decide what you want with your parents now. If you decide you want a different kind of life with them in the present, you will probably have to let go of some past grudges. It is important to learn how to forgive and how to make peace.

In our personal-growth groups we find that people don't give their parents much room to be imperfect. Time and again they blame their parents for having done or having failed to do something. In the group they express this blame in a symbolic way, such as in role-playing exercises. But before they got involved in a group, they might have been engaging in blaming behavior for years.

If you desire intimacy with your parents, it is a good idea to put aside your need to remake them and to accept any small changes that they may make. This recommendation was illustrated earlier in the chapter by the example of Donald's attempt to confront his father. Furthermore, rather than expecting your parents to make the first move, it would be more realistic to take the first step by initiating the changes in yourself that you are hoping they will make. For example, if you hope for more physical signs of affection between you and your parents, you might initiate touching. If you want more time with your mother and are angry that she doesn't ask for this time, ask yourself what is stopping you from taking this time with her. Persistence in asking for what you want sometimes does pay off. Too many people withdraw quickly when their expectations of others are not fully and immediately met.

Our experience with personal-growth groups has taught us how central our relationship with our parents is and how it affects all of our other interpersonal relationships. We learn from our parents how to deal with the rest of the world. We are often unaware of the impact our parents had, and continue to have, on us. Our groups are made up of people of various ages, sociocultural backgrounds, life experiences, and vocations; yet many of the members have ongoing struggles with their parents. It is not uncommon to have a 60-year-old man and a 20-year-old woman both expressing their frustration over not being accepted and affirmed by their parents. They are both intent on obtaining parental approval that they are convinced they need.

It is important to recognize the present effect that your parents are having on you and to decide the degree to which you like this effect. On one hand, you may have problems letting them be other than they were when you were a child. Although they may continue to treat you as a child, it could be that you behave around them as you did as a child and provoke this response. On the other hand, parents at times are reluctant to give up old parental roles; this does not mean that you cannot be different with them. You might become angry at your parents for the very things you are not willing to do, such as initiating closer contact or making time for the relationship. If you really want to be able to talk with your parents more intimately, you can take the first step. You can apply the principles of effective communication to enrich the time you spend with your parents.

Gay and Lesbian Relationships

Same-sex primary relationships are preferred by many people. But gay and lesbian relationships are not accepted as normal in our society. Our intention in including a discussion of gay and lesbian relationships is to dispel the myth that these relationships are basically different from heterosexual relationships. Common factors underlie all forms of intimate relationships; the guidelines for meaningful relationships presented earlier can be applied to friendships, parent/child relationships, and relationships between couples who are married or unmarried, gay or straight.

This section is not designed to be a comprehensive discussion of such a complex issue; rather, it is aimed at dispelling some of the myths and challenging some of the prejudices that lead to homophobia. You may be struggling over making a decision to declare your gay inclinations to others (or to acknowledge and accept them in yourself). You may be affected by the prejudices of others, and you may be trying to clarify your values and decide how you want to behave. We hope that this discussion will assist you in thinking about your views, assumptions, values, and possible prejudices.

■ Psychological Views of Homosexuality

How sexual orientation is established is still not understood. Some experts argue that sexual preference is at least partly a function of genetic or physiological factors, and others contend that homosexuality is entirely a learned behavior. Some maintain that both an internal predisposition and an environmental dimension come together to shape one's sexual orientation. And there are those who assert that sexual identity is strictly a matter of personal choice. Many gay men, lesbians, and bisexuals report that they did not actively choose their sexual orientation anymore than they did their sex. Where they see choice entering the picture is in deciding how they will act on their inclinations. Some will see that they have a choice of keeping their sexual orientation a secret or "coming out" and claiming their affectional preference.

The American Psychiatric Association in 1973 and the American Psychological Association in 1975 stopped calling homosexuality a form of mental illness, ending a long and bitter dispute. Along with these changes came the challenge to mental health professions to modify their thinking and practice to reflect a view of homosexuality as normal and healthy. Same-sex sexual orientation can be regarded as another style of expressing sexuality. And as with any form of sexual expression, this style can be healthy or unhealthy, depending on the person and the social and psychological dynamics.

In the helping professions, there has been a trend toward treating the *problems* encountered by lesbians and gay men rather than treating the condition of their sexual orientation (Fassinger, 1991). Still, in the training workshops we offer for counselors and other mental health professionals, we are surprised at the number of heterosexual counselors who see their proper role as actively trying to convert gay couples or gay individuals to a heterosexual preference, even if these clients do not have a problem with their sexual orientation.

Many gay people are not interested in changing their sexual orientation but seek counseling for many of the same reasons as do nongay people. In our consulting with counselors, we make our views quite clear. We see the counselor's job as helping clients clarify their own values and decide for themselves the course of action to take. We strongly oppose the notion that it is the role of counselors to impose their values on their clients, to tell others how to live, or to make their decisions for them. We believe that it is unethical for counselors who are opposed to homosexuality on moral grounds to work with gay clients if they are unable to retain the objectivity necessary to effectively help them. The ethical course would be to acknowledge their bias and provide referrals to other professionals who are in a position to work with these clients objectively. It is not the counselor's job to persuade these individuals to change.

■ Prejudice and Discrimination against Lesbians and Gay Men

In the past many people felt ashamed and abnormal because they had homosexual preferences. Heterosexuals frequently categorized them as deviants and as sick or immoral. For these and other reasons many gay and lesbian individuals were forced to conceal their preferences, perhaps even to themselves. Today, the gay liberation movement is actively challenging the stigma attached to sexual preference, and those who choose same-sex partners are increasingly asserting their right to live as they choose, without discrimination. However, just as gay men, lesbians, and bisexuals had won some rights and were more willing to disclose their sexual orientation, the AIDS crisis arose, once again creating animosity, fear, and antipathy toward the gay population. Much of the public continues to cling to stereotypes, prejudices, and misconceptions regarding behavior between same-sex couples.

Like any minority group, lesbians, gay men, and bisexual individuals are subjected to discrimination. This discrimination manifests itself when gay people seek employment or a place of residence. For instance, the Department of Defense does not allow openly homosexual individuals in the military. The "Don't ask, don't tell" policy formulated under President Clinton still does not allow military personnel to be open about their sexual orientation. A special issue that lesbians, gay men, and bisexuals often bring to counseling is the struggle of concealing their identity versus "coming out." Dealing with other family members is of special importance to gay couples. They may want to be honest with their parents, yet they may fear hurting their parents or receiving negative reactions from them.

In a study designed to examine common psychosocial assumptions pertaining to lesbian mothers, Falk (1989) found that discrimination has persisted in court decisions denying lesbian mothers' petitions for custody of their children. The courts often assume that lesbians are emotionally unstable or unable to perform a maternal role. They also assume that children with lesbian mothers are more likely to be emotionally harmed, that they will be subject to molestation, that their role development will be negatively affected, or that they will themselves become homosexual. Falk came to the conclusion that research has yet to identify significant differences between lesbian mothers and their heterosexual counterparts or the children raised by these groups. Researchers have not been able to establish scientifically that children suffer detrimental results from being raised by lesbian mothers.

■ Helping Gay People

At the 1995 American Counseling Association convention, a large number of programs dealt with issues pertaining to gay men and lesbians. The thousands of counselors who attended this conference seemed quite supportive of gays and lesbians in their quest for equality in this society. One of the keynote speakers, Mel White, dean of the nation's largest gay-lesbian congregation, expressed his appreciation to counselors who have an accepting attitude toward a group of people who face a hostile and prejudicial world. As a minister and gay-activist, White called on counselors to help individuals accept who they are. He said that counselors need to say: "I love you and accept you as you are. God loves you and accepts who you are. If the world doesn't—it's their loss" (cited in Morrissey, 1995, pp. 46–47). White disclosed that as an adolescent he felt alone, confused, and terrified. When he was 12 he saw his first counselor who told him that it is a sin to be gay and that he needed to fast and pray to "throw out the demon of homosexuality."

At the American Psychological Association meetings, we attended several presentations related to the social and political dimensions of gay and lesbian life. At an invited symposium entitled "Beyond Stigma: Lesbian and Gay Policy Issues in the 1990s," a panel of five participants addressed concerns relating to family life, school life, the struggles for civil rights, job discrimination, and the future of AIDS politics. This dynamic panel dealt with fundamental concerns related to gaining a voice in society. As the symposium presenters addressed some of the political challenges facing gay and lesbian people in the 1990s, it was clear that there is still a critical need for the general public to become educated about what it means to be gay and lesbian.

In his very informative book *The New Loving Someone Gay,* psychologist Don Clark (1987) makes these generalizations about the problems facing people involved in same-sex relationships:

- Gay people have learned to feel different. Even though they may be outwardly successful, they often feel devalued.
- Gay people have learned to distrust their own feelings, for many of them have accepted the myth that they have "perverted" feelings.
- Often being "invisible" to others, gay people are subject to daily attacks on their character and ability; they experience antigay jokes and statements as well as discrimination.
- They feel alone and wrong and fear further lack of support and affection if they reveal what they really think and feel; therefore, they often struggle over keeping their true identity a secret.
- They are likely to experience depression.
- Gay people are often tempted to numb the pain they experience by using drugs and alcohol to end their pain through suicide.

Clark suggests the following guidelines for those who are interested in being helpful to gay people:

- Help cannot be forced but only offered. Gay people tend to be suspicious of an overture of help until they can sense its personal validity. They will not accept help until trust is established.
- The primary goal in helping gay people should be to encourage them to become more truly themselves through developing self-appreciation and integrity.
- Those who want to help gay people had better discover any homophobic or anti-gay feelings of their own and seek whatever help may be necessary to rid themselves of these feelings. Growing up in this culture entails some degree of homophobic feelings.
- It is important for you to admit to yourself and others any homosexual feelings of your own as well as your general feelings of attraction to people of the same sex.
- It is essential that you not inform on gay people by telling others what you know, especially their family. To divulge information is a breach of trust.

Clark contends that neglecting these ground rules retards, disrupts, or terminates the helping process with gay people. He also urges us to avoid prejudging gay and lesbian people and instead to accept them as individuals.

■ Ann and Berit: The Struggle to Be True to Oneself

Ann and Berit, friends of ours from Norway, wrote this personal account of the development of their relationship.

> *We met when we were in our early twenties while attending a teacher credentialing program in Norway. Over the years we became close friends and spent more and more time together. Even though neither of us ever married, both of us had various relationships with men, which for the most part, were not very satisfying. As our friendship deepened, our interest in male companionship diminished and, when it was there, it seemed to be more in response to a societal "should" than an inner need.*
>
> *Our families and friends often expressed concern and disapproval about the closeness of our relationship, which didn't appear "natural" or "normal" to them and which, they thought, might interfere with our "settling down with a good man" and starting a family. So we tried to keep our feelings for each other a secret for fear of rejection.*
>
> *At one point, our relationship became a sexual one, a fact that brought out many of our self-doubts and vulnerabilities and the concern that, should we become separated, being sexually involved would make the parting even more difficult. Even though the sexual aspect didn't last long because of our concerns and doubts, our relationship continued. But the burden of pretending to be other than we were became increasingly heavy for us. We felt insincere and dishonest both toward each other and toward our families and friends, and we found the need to invent pat answers when others asked us why we were still single. We both felt that, if we had been honest, we would have said instead, "I'm not interested at all in a traditional marriage. I have a significant other, and I wish I didn't have to hide this very important part of my life."*

Ann and Berit's situation was complicated by the fact that Ann lived in a small rural community near her extended family, which made it almost impossible to maintain a sense of privacy. Although Berit did not live near her family, she too felt she couldn't openly acknowledge her relationship with Ann for fear of being rejected by family, friends, and co-workers. In her early thirties, Berit developed severe panic attacks that manifested themselves in acute anxiety over driving, being in a store, or even just going out of her house.

> *I believed that I was being watched, and I couldn't bear the thought of my parents finding out about my relationship with Ann, because I was sure they would interpret it as their failure to raise me properly. Because of my anxiety attacks, I went into therapy, and soon afterward my symptoms decreased greatly. I never felt a need to explore my preference for women, but I did spend a good deal of time on the conflict between my need to do what I thought was right for me and my need to give in to external pressure to be "normal."*
>
> *Neither of us knew that we were lesbians. We were aware, however, of being somewhat "different" from other girls our age when we were going to school; we didn't have the same interest in boys as did most of our friends, and as we matured we still felt more comfortable with women.*

At the age of 40, we made the decision that we could no longer live with the duplicity and that something had to be done. Either we would go separate ways, or we would share a life and acknowledge our situation openly. We decided to do the latter. After years of struggling, we were finally able to face ourselves, each other, and then the other significant people in our lives. Much to our surprise, when we did disclose the truth about our relationship, most of our relatives and friends were supportive and understanding, and some even told us that they knew of our "special" relationship. We felt a great burden had been lifted from us and began to experience a new sense of peace and happiness.

We have many things in common and feel our relationship is quite unique compared to those of many of our heterosexual friends. We do not have "power fights" and feel a sense of equality in our relationship. We care about each other deeply and are sensitive to each other's needs. We are both hard working and engage in practical work that many women we know would never even think of involving themselves in. We enjoy boating, fishing, hiking, and being with close friends. We both play several musical instruments and like to gather with other musical friends to play.

Just last year we got married. Ann's mother's first reaction to this was somewhat negative, probably because of her concern over what the neighbors and other relatives would think. However, when Ann's mother experienced nothing but positive reactions from her friends and family, her attitude changed and she accepted our marriage. Berit's parents acted as if the marriage never took place. No remarks were ever made about the event, but they continued to treat both of us with respect, friendliness, and hospitality. The fact that they ignored the marriage hurt Berit's feelings, a fact that she dealt with in therapy.

We got married first and foremost to protect each other financially. Neither of us thought marriage would make any difference in our relationship. However, we now see that the marriage itself has been an important aspect in our lives. It has made us feel more confident being the "number one" in each other's lives. It also makes a difference as to how others view us as a couple. After the marriage we even put an ad in the newspaper announcing our marriage. To us, it expressed that we were not embarrassed to tell everyone about our choice. We were quite happy with the responses we received by way of flowers and gifts. We are both happy to live in Norway, a country that allows people of the same sex to marry.

■ Concluding Comments

Ann and Berit's case illustrates the struggle that many couples go through as they make the choice of how they will live. Many of the issues that concern Ann and Berit are the same interpersonal conflicts that any couple will eventually face and need to resolve. However, they must also deal with the pressure of being part of a segment of society that many consider unacceptable. Thus, being involved in a gay or lesbian relationship is not simply a matter of sexual preference, because it involves a whole spectrum of interpersonal and practical issues. All the concerns about friendships, heterosexual relationships, and traditional marriage that we explore in this chapter apply to gay and lesbian relationships as well. Indeed, barriers to effective communication are found in every kind of intimate relationship. The challenge is to find ways of removing the blocks that obstruct communication and intimacy.

In categorizing relationships as heterosexual or homosexual, we sometimes forget that sex is not the only aspect of a relationship. Whatever choice we make, we need to examine whether it is the best choice for us and whether it is compatible with our own values. Some people choose or reject specific gender roles because of others' expectations, and in the same fashion people may reject being gay merely because others condemn it or adopt it merely because they are unquestioningly following a liberation movement. What we think is important is that you define yourself, that you assume responsibility and accept the consequences for your own choices, and that you live out your choices with peace and inner integrity.

➤ Time Out for Personal Reflection

1. How do you generally cope with conflicts in your relationship? Check the items that most apply to you.

_____   open dialogue
_____   avoidance
_____   fighting and arguing
_____   compromising
_____   getting involved with other people or in projects

List other ways in which you deal with conflicts in your relationship:

_____

_____

_____

2. List some ways in which you've changed during the period of your relationship. How have your changes affected the relationship?

_____

_____

_____

3. To what extent do you have an identity apart from the relationship? How much do you need (and depend on) the other person? Imagine that he or she is no longer in your life, and write down how your life might be different.

_____

_____

_____

4. What are your reactions to people who have a same-sex sexual orientation?

_____

_____

_____

5. How do you feel about homosexual experiences for yourself?

_____

_____

_____

6. What are your views concerning the gay liberation movement? Do you believe that the rights of gay men and lesbians have been denied? Do you think that people who openly admit they are gay should have rights equal to those of heterosexuals and should not be denied a specific job because of their sexual orientation alone?

_____

_____

_____

Separation and Divorce

The principles we discuss here can be applied to separations between people who are friends, to unmarried people involved in an intimate relationship, or to married couples who are contemplating a divorce. The fear of being alone forever often keeps people from dissolving a relationship, even when they agree that there is little left in that relationship. People may say something like this: "I know what I have, and at least I have somebody. So maybe it's better to have that than nothing at all." Because of their fears, many people remain stuck in stagnant relationships.

■ Freeing Ourselves from Deadening Ways of Being Together

An alternative to separating or stagnating is to remain in the relationship but challenge both yourself and your partner to create a different way of relating to each other. Sidney Jourard (1975) developed the idea of having several different "marriages" with the same person. His key point was that people should develop

new dimensions to intimate relationships, and he described marriage as a dialogue that ends as soon as habitual ways of acting set in. Jourard maintained that people are frequently not very creative when it comes to finding new ways of living with each other and that they tend to fall into the same ruts day after day, year after year.

At its best, marriage is a relationship that generates change through dialogue. Instead of being threatened by change, we can welcome it as necessary for keeping the relationship alive. In this way an impasse can become a turning point that enables two people to create a new way of life together. If both partners care enough about their investment in each other, and if they are committed to doing the work necessary to change old patterns and establish more productive ones, a crisis can actually save their relationship. People often terminate their relationships without really giving themselves or others a chance to face a particular crisis and work it through. For example, a man begins to see how deadening his marriage is for him and to realize how he has contributed to his own unhappiness in it. As a result of changes in his perceptions and attitudes, he decides that he no longer wants to live with a woman in this deadening fashion. However, rather than deciding to simply end the marriage, he might allow his partner to really see and experience him as the different person he is becoming. Moreover, he might encourage her to change as well, instead of giving up on her too quickly. His progress toward becoming a more integrated person might well inspire her to work actively toward her own internal changes. This kind of work on the part of both people takes understanding and patience, but they may find that they can meet each other as new and changing persons and form a very different kind of relationship.

Sometimes, of course, ending a relationship is the wisest course, and ending a relationship can be an act of courage that makes a new beginning possible. Our concern is that too many people may not be committed enough to each other to stay together in times of crisis and struggle. As a result, they may separate at the very time when they could be making a new start.

■ When to Separate or Terminate a Relationship

How do two people know when a separation is the best solution? No categorical answer can be given to this question. However, before two people decide to terminate their relationship, they might consider these questions:

■ *Has each of you sought personal therapy or counseling?* Perhaps their exploration of themselves would lead to changes that would allow them to renew or strengthen their relationship.

■ *Have you considered seeking relationship counseling?* If they do get involved in relationship counseling of any type, is each doing so willingly, or is one of them merely going along to placate the other?

■ *Are you both really interested in maintaining your relationship?* Perhaps one or both are not interested in keeping the *old* relationship, but it is vital that they both at least want time together. We routinely ask both partners in a significant relationship who are experiencing difficulties to decide whether they even want to preserve their relationship. Some of the responses people give include: "I don't really know. I've lost hope for any real change, and at this point I find it difficult to care whether we stay together or not." "I'm sure that I don't want to live with this person anymore; I just don't care enough to work on improving things between us. I'm here so that we can separate cleanly and finish the business between us." "Even though we're going through some turmoil right now, I would very much like to care enough to make things better. Frankly, I'm not too hopeful, but I'm willing to give it a try." Whatever their responses, it's imperative that they each know how they feel about the possibility of renewing their relationship.

■ *Have you each taken the time to be alone, to get in focus, and to decide what kind of life you want for yourself and with others?*

■ *If you are a couple, have you taken time to be with each other for even a weekend?* Few couples in troubled relationships arrange for time alone with each other. It's almost as if couples fear discovering that they really have little to say to each other. This discovery in itself might be very useful, for at least they might be able to do something about the situation if they confronted it; but many couples seem to arrange their lives in such a way that they block any possibilities for intimacy. They eat dinner together with the television set blasting, or they spend all their time together taking care of their children, or they simply refuse to make time to be together.

▪ *If you are married, what do you each expect from the divorce?* Frequently, problems in a marriage are reflections of internal conflicts within the individuals in that marriage. In general, unless there are some changes within the individuals, the problems they experienced may not end with the divorce. In fact, many who do divorce with the expectation of finding increased joy and freedom discover instead that they are still miserable, lonely, depressed, and anxious. Lacking insight into themselves, they may soon find a new partner very much like the one they divorced and repeat the same dynamics. Thus, a woman who finally decides to leave a man she thinks of as weak and passive may find a similar man to live with again, unless she comes to understand why she needs or wants to align herself with this type of person. Or a man who contends that he has "put up with" his wife for over 20 years may find a similar person unless he understands what motivated him to stay with his first wife for so long. It is essential, therefore, that each come to know as clearly as possible why they are divorcing and that they look at the changes they may need to make in themselves as well as in their circumstances.

Sometimes one or both members of a couple identify strong reasons for separating but say that, for one reason or another, they are not free to do so. This kind of reasoning is always worth examining; an attitude of "I couldn't possibly leave" will not help either partner make a free and sound choice. Some of the reasons people give for refusing to call an end to their relationship include:

▪ "I have an investment of 15 years with this person, and to end our relationship now would mean that these 15 years have been wasted." A person who feels this way might ask: "If I really don't see much potential for change, and if my partner has consistently and over a long period of time rebuffed any moves that might lead to improving our relationship, should I stay another 15 years and have 30 years to regret?"

▪ "I can't leave because of the kids, but I do plan to leave as soon as they get into high school." This kind of thinking often burdens children with unnecessary guilt. In a sense, it makes them responsible for the unhappiness of their parents. We would ask: Why place the burden on them if *you* stay in a place where you say you don't want to be? And will you find another reason to cement yourself to your partner once your children grow up?

"Since the children need both a mother and a father, I cannot consider breaking up our marriage." True, children do need both a father and a mother. But it's worth asking whether they will get much of value from either parent if they see them despising each other. How useful is the model that parents present when they stay together and the children see how little joy they experience? Might they not get more from two parents separately? Wouldn't the parents set a better and more honest example if they openly admitted that they no longer really choose to remain together?

▪ One man in a gay relationship may say, "I'm afraid to break off the relationship because I might be even more lonely than I am now." Certainly, loneliness is a real possibility. There are no guarantees that a new relationship will be established after one relationship is terminated. He might be reluctant to leave the relationship because his parents warned him of the problems he was getting into when he decided on an arrangement of living together. However, he might be more lonely living with someone he doesn't like, much less love, than he would be if he were living alone. Living alone might bring far more serenity and inner strength than remaining in a relationship that is no longer right for him. If he refuses to get out of a relationship because of what his parents might say about his original choice, he is almost certain to experience more alienation than he already does.

■ "One thing that holds me back from separating is that I might discover that I left too soon and that I didn't give us a fair chance." To avoid this regret, partners should explore all the possibilities for creating a new relationship *before* making the decision to dissolve their relationship. There does come a point, however, at which a person must finally take a stand and decide. Once the decision to separate is made, it is fruitless to brood continually over whether he or she did the right thing.

At times, people find themselves in relationships that are emotionally or physically abusive, yet they are hesitant to leave these relationships. Abusive relationships have been getting a great deal of media attention, and people who have left abusive relationships often report that they did not recognize the full extent to which the relationship was toxic. Although they may have had opportunities to terminate the relationship, they rationalized that their situation was not really so bad. They often excuse the partner's behavior and find fault with themselves for bringing about the abuse. The individual doing the abuse might well demonstrate regret for hurting the partner and gives promises to reform. However, soon afterward the same cycle repeats itself, and one person in the relationship feels trapped. Many times people stay in a relationship that is less than desirable because they do not know where else to go, nor do they know who can help them. Here are some signs that could indicate an abusive relationship:

■ verbal put downs
■ withholding love and affection
■ striking, hitting, pushing, shoving
■ using physical or psychological threats
■ making promises, yet never keeping them
■ unpredictable behavior
■ extreme jealousy and possessiveness
■ chronic hostility and sarcasm

Not all abusive relationships involve physical violence. Subtle emotional abuse over a period of time can also erode a relationship. Remaining in such a relationship generally makes it difficult for an individual to want to reach out and form new friendships. He or she often becomes numb and is cautious about trusting again for some time.

People sometimes remain in unhealthy relationships in the hopes that their situation will improve. Perhaps one of the partners believes that he or she can change the other person. Frequently, this attempt ends in frustration. If you think you are involved in an abusive relationship, you need not remain a victim. Recognize what you are not getting with your partner, and do not discount reality.

In summary, we limit our options unnecessarily whenever we tell ourselves that we *can't possibly* take a certain course of action. Before deciding to terminate a relationship, ask whether you have really given the other person (and yourself) a chance to establish something new. By the same token, if you decide that you want to end the relationship but can't, it's worth asking whether you are not simply evading the responsibility for creating your own happiness. Neither keeping a relationship alive and growing nor ending one that is no longer right for you is easy, and it's tempting to find ways to put the responsibility for your decisions on your children, your mate, or circumstances. You take a real step toward genuine freedom when you fully accept that the choice is yours to make.

■ Coping with Ending a Long-Term Relationship

When a long-term relationship comes to an end, a mixture of feelings, ranging from a sense of loss and regret to relief, may be present. Betty, an unmarried college student in her mid-twenties, is going through some typical reactions to the breakup of a three-year relationship with her boyfriend Isaac. At first, she felt abandoned and was afraid of never finding a suitable replacement. She found herself ruminating over who was at fault. She switched back and forth between blaming herself and blaming him. She felt severe depression, which affected her eating and her sleeping patterns. Then she began to withdraw from other relationships. She told herself that she was not enough as a person, which led to feelings of worthlessness and inadequacy. She went from the extreme of shying away from other relationships so she would not get hurt again to wanting too many new relationships to take away the hurt. Her feelings and behavior were largely the product of her irrational beliefs. She continued to tell herself: "This relationship didn't work out, and it proves that I'm a failure and unlovable and that I won't be able to establish and keep any further relationships." "Because things didn't work out between Isaac and me, this is a sure sign that I'll never get along with any man." "If Isaac found me undesirable, it must prove that I'm the kind of person he said I was." "I don't think I can stand the pain of this rejection." Internal dialogue such as this kept Betty miserable and kept her from taking any action that could change her situation. It was not the breakup itself that was causing Betty's reactions; rather, her beliefs about and her interpretations of the breakup were giving her trouble.

There are no easy ways to ending a long-standing relationship. After a breakup or loss of a friend or significant other, you will have feelings of pain, anger, and grief. However, if you find yourself in such a situation, we hope you'll realize that there are some attitudes you can assume and some behaviors you can choose that are likely to help you work through your feelings associated with the breakup. Corey, Corey, and Corey (1997) give the following suggestions for living with and learning from the termination of a meaningful relationship:

- *Allow yourself to grieve.* Although grieving can be both overwhelming and painful, the alternative of cutting off your feelings will keep you stuck and make it difficult to move on.
- *Give yourself time.* As the saying goes, "Time heals all wounds." However long or short it takes, it is important to permit yourself to grieve based on your own time clock and not because others feel you should be over it by now.
- *Express your anger.* Sometimes breakups leave us feeling angry and bitter. Remember that anger is a normal reaction, yet if unexpressed or overindulged in, it can poison you.

- *De-personalize your partner's actions.* Often when one person ends a relationship the other is left feeling rejected and as if they were a failure for not making the relationship work. A person's decision to end a relationship may be more a reflection of them than it is of you.
- *Take responsibility for your own part in the relationship.* It may be easier to find fault in the other person, but exploring your own behaviors can be helpful in your healing process. The point is not to find blame but to gain insight into how you relate to people in both negative and positive ways.
- *Find a support network.* Whether you are shy or social, having people there to support you can provide you with some level of stability in a time of loss and change. Seek counseling or professional help if you feel that you can't cope with the loss on your own. Most universities offer free student counseling.
- *Keep busy.* Setting aside time to grieve is important, yet obsessing over your situation does not change it. Pushing yourself to engage in some form of activity can help you stay connected to the aspects of your life that continue outside the relationship.
- *Write in your journal.* Writing can help you release emotions even if you are not able to talk to others about how you are feeling. Later, it can be useful to re-read what you wrote and see how you may have grown since then.
- *Make amends.* Making amends and forgiving both yourself and your partner can free you from carrying the pain and anger into future relationships.
- *Get closure.* Coming to some type of closure is essential to moving forward. To one person it may mean forgiveness and for another it may include some type of a ritual or final letter.
- *Love and learn.* At some point you will find that it can be freeing to reflect on what you have learned from the experience. Even the most abusive or unhealthy relationship can teach us something about ourselves and the types of relationships we want to have.

▶ *Time Out for Personal Reflection*

Complete the following sentences by writing down the first responses that come to mind. Suggestion: Ask your partner or a close friend to do the exercise on a separate sheet of paper; then compare and discuss your responses.

1. To me, intimacy means _____

   _____

2. The most important thing in making an intimate relationship successful is _____

   _____

3. The thing I most fear about an intimate relationship is _____

   _____

4. When an intimate relationship becomes stale, I usually _____

_____

5. One of the reasons I need another person is _____

_____

6. One conflict that I have concerning intimate relationships is _____

_____

7. In an intimate relationship, it's unrealistic to expect that _____

_____

8. To me, commitment means _____

_____

9. I have encouraged my partner to grow by _____

_____

10. My partner has encouraged me to grow by _____

_____

On Choosing the Single Life

You may choose to remain single (for a time or throughout your life) due to a desire for personal autonomy, the failure to find a suitable mate, a distrust of marriage perhaps based on the failure of your parents' marriage, or incompatibility between marriage and a career. Being single is now a more accepted status than it was in the past, and there is a greater recognition of the idea that some people choose to remain unmarried. Being single does not mean that you are deficient in social skills. Attitudes toward never-married people are becoming more positive, and such people are no longer necessarily seen as losers.

Americans are staying single longer and getting married later than ever before (Carr, 1988). The percentage of single women and men in this country has risen sharply and continues to rise. Some women do not see marriage as a requirement for parenthood or for emotional, social, and economic support. It is clear that more women today are resisting societal pressure to get married and have a family, and more women are waiting until later in life to become involved in a committed relationship. It is not uncommon for women to have children in their forties. There are intrinsic values and limitations in both a marriage and a single life. What is critical is that you weigh the pros and cons of each and freely make the choice of how you want to live, rather than merely giving in to the pressure to do what you think you "should" do.

■ The Struggles of a Single Person

The following case typifies the problems and challenges many young women face
if they choose to remain single. June likes the advantages of being single, yet she
struggles with nagging doubts over whether she is missing more by not becoming
involved in a committed relationship, particularly as she is fond of someone.

June has a successful teaching career at age 27. She earns a good salary, is living
in her own house, is free to pursue additional education, and enjoys the freedom of
traveling in many countries of the world. She has nobody to answer to in terms of
considering changing her career. She says that her many male and female friends
provide nourishment to her. She also enjoys many sports and other leisure activities. She feels a sense of accomplishment and independence, something that perhaps not many people her age do.

At times June struggles with the internal pressure of fearing that she will never be in a committed relationship. She also feels external pressure from the man she is now having a close relationship with. But she is also very afraid to give in to his urgings to get married. While she enjoys intimacy with him, she does not feel ready to commit herself. She tells herself that she really *should* be ready at her age to take this step, but she realizes that the price of making this commitment would be giving up much of what she values.

June judges herself as being too selfish to make compromises and consider her friend's needs and demands. She tells herself at times that perhaps she should be willing to give up more of what she wants so she could share a life with him. She wonders about her chances for ever having a significant other in her life if she fails to take this opportunity. At this time June is still searching within herself for her answer. Does she really want to be in a long-term relationship? Does she equate being single with a lonely life?

Many people choose to be single and are happy about their choice. Being single does not necessarily entail remaining isolated or being without friends. Lewis and Borders (1995) conducted a study to determine the degree to which single middle-aged professional women were satisfied with their lives. The researchers found the following five factors to be the most highly related to life satisfaction of single professional women:

- Job satisfaction was the best single predictor of life satisfaction.
- Sexual satisfaction was the second best predictor of life satisfaction.
- The absence of regrets was a significant predictor of life satisfaction. The women in this study did not seem to be filled with doubts about "what life could have been."
- An internal locus of control was related to life satisfaction; that is, many of these women believed that the quality of their lives was the result of their own attitudes and efforts.
- The last predictor of life satisfaction was leisure-time activities. The women in this study reported they valued their leisure.

Taken together, these five predictors of satisfaction indicate the importance of a balanced life of work and leisure for these single professional women. In general, the women in this study found satisfaction in life through their careers, friends, and leisure activities.

Chapter Summary

In this chapter we've encouraged you to think about what characterizes a growing, meaningful relationship and to ask yourself such questions as: Do I have what I want in my various relationships? Do I desire more (or less) intimacy? What changes would I most like to make in my intimate relationships? In each of my relationships, can both the other person and I maintain our separate identities and at the same time develop a strong bond that enhances us as individuals?

The themes explored in this chapter can be applied to all intimate relationships, regardless of one's sexual orientation. Although same-sex relationships are not well accepted in our society, it is important to realize that all couples share some common challenges. Rather than judging lesbians and gay men because of their sexual orientation, focus on understanding concerns and struggles that we all share.

A major barrier to developing and maintaining relationships is our tendency to evaluate and judge others. By attempting to change others we typically increase their defensiveness. A key characteristic of a meaningful relationship is the ability of the people involved to listen and to respond to each other. They are able to communicate effectively, and they are committed to staying in the relationship even when communication appears to have broken down. It is important to pay attention to both cultural and gender differences that make up our conversational style. Many misunderstandings are due to the different ways women and men express their thoughts and feelings.

Maintaining a relationship entails dedication and hard work. Although there are many sources of conflict in intimate relationships, a major problem is a sense of predictability that comes with knowing another person well. It takes both imagination and effort to think of ways to revise our relationships so that they remain alive. At times people decide that a relationship is "dead," and they give serious consideration to separating. Although this may be a solution for some situations, a relationship that has lost life can also be reinvented. Again, commitment is essential, because time will be required to resolve certain issues that are divisive and that cause conflict.

People can still experience intimacy with others even though they choose to remain single. Today remaining single is more acceptable, and this way of living is no longer thought of as "second best." Although there are difficulties in being single, there are also some distinct advantages and rewards.

The ideal picture we've drawn of a growing relationship is not a dogmatic or necessarily complete one; nor will your relationships, however good they are, always approximate it. Our hope is that these reflections will stimulate your own independent thinking. You can begin by honestly assessing the present state of your intimate relationships and recognizing how they really are (as opposed to how you wish they were). Then you can consider the choices that can lead to positive change in those areas over which you are dissatisfied.

Throughout this chapter we've emphasized that we must actively work to recognize problems in ourselves and in our relationships if we are to make intimacy as rewarding as it can be. You can choose the quality of the relationships you want in your life.

Activities and Exercises

Some of the following activities are appropriate for you to do on your own; others are designed for two persons in an intimate relationship to do together. Select the ones that have the most meaning for you, and consider sharing the results with the other members of your class.

1. In your journal write down some reflections on your parents' relationship. Consider such questions as the following:

   ▪ Would you like the same kind of relationship your parents have had? What are some of the things you like best about their relationship? What are some features of their relationship that you would not want in your own relationships?
   ▪ How have your own views, attitudes, and practices regarding intimacy been affected by your parents' relationship?

2. How much self-disclosure, honesty, and openness do you want in your intimate relationships? Reflect in your journal on how much you would share your feelings concerning each of the following with your partner. Then discuss how you would like your partner to respond to this same question.

   ▪ your sexual fantasies about another person
   ▪ your secrets
   ▪ your need for support from your partner
   ▪ your angry feelings
   ▪ your dreams
   ▪ your friendships with other persons
   ▪ your ideas on religion and your philosophy of life
   ▪ the times when you feel inadequate as a person
   ▪ the times when you feel extremely close and loving toward your partner
   ▪ the times in your relationship when you feel boredom, staleness, hostility, or detachment

   After you've answered this question for yourself, think about how open you want *your partner* to be with *you*. If your partner were doing this exercise, what answers do you wish he or she would give for each of these items?

3. Over a period of about a week, do some writing about the evolution of your relationship and ask your partner to do the same. Consider issues such as: Why were we initially attracted to each other? How have we changed since we first met? Do I like these changes? What would I most like to change about our life together? What are the best things we have going for us? What are some problem areas we need to explore? If I could do it over again, would I select the same person? What's the future of our life together? What would I like to see us doing differently? After you've each written about these and any other questions that are significant for you, read each other's work and discuss where you want to go from here. This activity can stimulate you to talk more openly with each other and can also give each of you the chance to see how the other perceives the quality of your relationship.

4. As you look at various television shows, keep a record of the messages you get regarding marriage, family life, and intimacy. What are some common stereotypes? What sex roles are portrayed? What myths do you think are being presented? After you've kept a record for a couple of weeks or so, write down some

of the attitudes that you think you have incorporated from television and other media about marriage, family life, and intimacy.

5. Select one or more of the following books for further reading on the topics explored in this chapter: *Counseling Gay Men and Lesbians: Journey to the End of the Rainbow* (Dworkin & Gutierrez, 1992); *Close Relationships: What Couple Therapists Can Learn* (Hendrick, 1995); *The Dance of Anger* (Lerner, 1985); *The Dance of Intimacy* (Lerner, 1990); *The Fragile Bond: In Search of an Equal, Intimate and Enduring Marriage* (Napier, 1990). Within the chapter we have given a number of other specific recommendations for a reading program.

11

Loneliness and Solitude

In solitude we make the time to be with ourselves, to discover who we are, and to renew ourselves.

✔ *Prechapter Self-Inventory*

Use the following scale to respond: 4 = this statement is true of me *most* of the time; 3 = this statement is true of me *much* of the time; 2 = this statement is true of me *some* of the time; 1 = this statement is true of me *almost none* of the time.

_____ 1. I stay in unsatisfactory relationships just to avoid being lonely.
_____ 2. Knowing that I am ultimately on my own in the world scares me.
_____ 3. I don't know what to do with my time when I'm alone.
_____ 4. Sometimes when I'm with people I feel lonely and shut out.
_____ 5. I can't escape loneliness completely.
_____ 6. I know the difference between being lonely and being alone.
_____ 7. My childhood was a lonely period of my life.
_____ 8. My adolescent years were lonely ones for me.
_____ 9. Loneliness is a problem for me in my life now.
_____ 10. I generally arrange for time alone so that I can reflect on the way my life is going.

Introduction

We are ultimately alone. Although the presence of others can surely enhance our lives, no one else can completely become us or share our unique world of feelings, thoughts, hopes, and memories. In addition, none of us knows when our loved ones may leave us or die, when we will no longer be able to involve ourselves in a cherished activity, or when the forest we love will be burned or cut down. We come into the world alone, and we will be alone again when the time comes to leave it.

In the last chapter our focus was on intimacy and interpersonal relationships. We now turn to the experience of loneliness and the creative use of solitude. Being with others and being with ourselves are best understood as two sides of the same coin. If we do not like our own company, why should others want to be with us? If we have a good relationship with ourselves and enjoy our solitude, we have a far greater chance of creating solid, give-and-take relationships with others.

We invite you to think of being alone as a natural and potentially valuable part of human experience. It is important to distinguish between being alone and being lonely. Casey and Vanceburg (1985) write about being alone but not lonely as we search for understanding, serenity, and certainly about the path of life we are traveling. All of us are ultimately alone in the world, but appreciating that aloneness can actually enrich our experience of life. Moreover, we can use times of solitude to look within ourselves, to renew our sense of ourselves as the center of choice and direction in our lives, and to learn to trust our inner resources instead of allowing circumstances or the expectations of others to determine the path we travel. If we fundamentally accept our aloneness and recognize that no one can take away *all* our loneliness, we can deal more effectively with our experiences of

loneliness and give ourselves to our projects and our relationships out of our freedom instead of running to them out of our fear.

The Value of Loneliness and Solitude

Loneliness and solitude are different experiences, and each has its own potential value. Loneliness generally results from certain events in life — the death of someone we love, the decision of another person to leave us for someone else, a move to a new city, a long stay in a hospital. Loneliness can occur when we feel set apart in some way from everyone around us. And sometimes feelings of loneliness are simply an indication of the extent to which we've failed to listen to ourselves and to our own feelings. However it occurs, loneliness is generally something that happens to us rather than something we choose to experience; but we *can* choose the attitude we take toward it. If we allow ourselves to experience our loneliness, even if it is painful, we may be surprised to find sources of strength and creativity within ourselves.

Unlike loneliness, solitude is something that we often choose for ourselves. In solitude, we make the time to be with ourselves, to discover who we are, and to renew ourselves. Casey and Vanceburg (1985) say that solitude is a pathway to self-knowledge:

> It's in our solitude that we come to know ourselves, to appreciate the many nuances that distinguish us from others. It's in the stillness that we detect our soul's

inclinations. The privacy of silence offers us the answers we need. The distractions that stood in our way no longer fetter us when we've invited solitude to be our guest. (Meditation of January 10)

In her beautiful and poetic book *Gift from the Sea*, Anne Morrow Lindbergh (1955/1975) describes her own need to get away by herself to find her center, to simplify her life, and to nourish herself so that she could give to others again. She relates how her busy life, with its many and conflicting demands, fragmented her, so that she felt "the spring is dry, and the well is empty" (p. 47).* Through solitude, she found replenishment and became reacquainted with herself:

> When one is a stranger to oneself, then one is estranged from others too. If one is out of touch with oneself, then one cannot touch others . . . Only when one is connected to one's own core is one connected to others . . . For me, the core, the inner spring, can best be refound through solitude. (pp. 43–44)

If we don't take time for ourselves but instead fill our lives with activities and projects, we run the risk of losing a sense of centeredness. As Lindbergh puts it, "Instead of stilling the center, the axis of the wheel, we add more centrifugal activ-

*This and all other quotations from this source from *Gift from the Sea*, by A. M. Lindbergh. Copyright 1955 by Pantheon Books, a division of Random House, Inc.

ities to our lives—which tend to throw us off balance" (p. 51). Her own solitude taught her that she must remind herself to be alone each day, even for a few minutes, to keep a sense of herself that would then enable her to give of herself to others. She expressed this thought in words addressed to a seashell she took with her from an island where she had spent some time alone:

> You will remind me that I must try to be alone for part of each year, even a week or a few days; and for part of each day, even for an hour or for a few minutes, in order to keep my core, my center, my island-quality. You will remind me that unless I keep the island-quality intact somewhere within me, I will have little to give my husband, my children, my friends or the world at large. (p. 57)

In much the same way as Lindbergh describes solitude as a way of discovering her core and putting her life in perspective, Clark Moustakas (1977) relates that a critical turning point in his life occurred when he discovered that loneliness could be the basis for a creative experience. He came to see that his personal growth and changed relationship with others were related to his feelings of loneliness. Accepting himself as a lonely person gave him the courage to face aspects of himself that he had never dared to face before and taught him the value of listening to his inner self. For him, solitude became an antidote to loneliness. He writes: "In times of loneliness, my way back to life with others required that I stop listening to others, that I cut myself off from others and deliberately go off alone, to a place of isolation" (p. 109). In doing so, Moustakas became aware of how he had forsaken himself and of the importance of returning to himself. This process of finding himself led him to find new ways of relating to others: "In solitude, silent awareness and self-dialogues often quickly restored me to myself, and I was filled with new energy and the desire to renew my life with others in real ways" (p. 109).

Solitude can provide us with the opportunity to sort out our lives and gain a sense of perspective. It can give us time to ask significant questions, such as: "How much have I become a stranger to myself? Have I been listening to myself, or have I been distracted and overstimulated by a busy life? Am I aware of my sense experiences, or have I been too involved in doing things to be aware of them?"

Most of us need to remind ourselves that we can tolerate only so much intensity with others and that ignoring our need for distance can breed resentment. For instance, a mother and father who are constantly with each other and with their children may not be doing a service either to their children or to themselves. Eventually they are likely to resent their "obligations." Unless they take time out, they may be there bodily and yet not be fully present to each other or to their children.

Many of us fail to experience solitude because we allow our lives to become more and more frantic and complicated. Unless we make a conscious effort to be alone, we may find that days and weeks go by without our having the chance to be with ourselves. Moreover, we may fear that we will alienate others if we ask for private time, so we alienate ourselves instead. Perhaps we fear that others will think us odd if we express a need to be alone. Indeed, others may sometimes fail to understand our need for solitude and try to bring us into the crowd or "cheer us up." People who are close to us may feel vaguely threatened, as if our need for time alone somehow reflected on our affection for them. Their own fears of being left alone may lead them to try to keep us from taking time away from them. It is not uncommon to feel uneasy about wanting and taking time alone for ourselves. We may feel a need to make up excuses if we want to decline an invitation to be with others so that we can have some time alone. Claiming what we need and want for ourselves can involve a certain risk; if we fail to take that risk, however, we give up the very thing solitude could provide — a sense of self-direction and being centered.

Learning to Confront the Fear of Loneliness

Many people fear being lonely. If we associate the lonely periods in our lives with pain and struggle, we may think of loneliness only as a condition to be avoided as much as possible. Furthermore, we may identify being alone with being lonely and either actively avoid having time by ourselves or fill such time with distractions and diversions. We may associate being alone with rejection of self and being cut off from others. Paradoxically, out of fear of rejection and loneliness, we may even make ourselves needlessly lonely by refusing to reach out to others or by holding back parts of ourselves in our intimate relationships. On the other hand, because of our fear of loneliness, we sometimes deceive ourselves by convincing ourselves that we can overcome loneliness by anchoring our life to another's life. The search for relationships, especially ones in which we think we will be taken care of, is often motivated by the fear of being isolated.

Here are some ways we attempt to escape from facing and coping with loneliness:

- We busy ourselves in work and activities, so we have little time to think or to reflect by ourselves.
- We schedule every moment and overstructure our lives, so we have no opportunity to think about ourselves and what we are doing with our lives.
- We strive for perfect control of our environment, so we won't have to cope with the unexpected.
- We surround ourselves with people and become absorbed in social functions in the hope that we won't have to feel alone.
- We try to numb ourselves with television, alcohol, or drugs.
- We immerse ourselves in our "responsibilities."
- We eat compulsively, hoping that doing so will fill our inner emptiness and protect us from the pain of being lonely.
- We make ourselves slaves to routine, become stuck in a narrow and predictable rut, becoming machines that don't feel much of anything.
- We go to night clubs and other centers of activity, trying to lose ourselves in a crowd. By escaping into crowds we hope to avoid coming to terms with deeper layers of our inner world.

Most of us lead a hectic life in a crowded, noisy environment. We are surrounded by entertainment and escapes, which makes it impossible to hear the voice within us. Paradoxically, in the midst of our congested cities and with all the activities available to us, we are often lonely because we are alienated from ourselves.

Stella's Fear of Separateness.   Stella is a young woman who often fears separateness from others, even though she immerses herself in many relationships and activities. Outsiders tend to envy her "fun-filled" life and wish they were in her place. In a moment of candor, however, she will admit that she feels her life to be empty and that she is in a desperate search for substance.

> *I am petrified when I have to spend any time alone in my apartment. I schedule my life so that I spend as little time by myself as possible. I have a long list of phone numbers to call, just in case my panic overwhelms me. My stereo or television is typically blaring so that I am unable to pay attention to what is going on with me. I want so much to fill my inner emptiness. I have a hard time liking myself or thinking I have much value. I look to others for my security, yet I never really find it. In my therapy I am learning to stay with being uncomfortable with myself long enough to face some of my fears.*

In some ways Stella illustrates the quiet desperation that is captured in Edward Arlington Robinson's poem "Richard Cory" (1897):

Whenever Richard Cory went down town,
We people on the pavement looked at him:
He was a gentleman from sole to crown,
Clean favored, and imperially slim.
And he was always human when he talked;
But still he fluttered pulses when he said,
"Good morning," and he glittered when he walked.
And he was rich — yes, richer than a king —
And admirably schooled in every grace:
In fine, we thought that he was everything
To make us wish that we were in his place.
So on we worked and waited for the light,
And went without the meat, and cursed the bread;
And Richard Cory, one calm summer night,
Went home and put a bullet through his head.

There is a loneliness in living in ways that belie the way we present ourselves to the world, as the cases of Stella and Richard Cory demonstrate. Pretending to others to be what we are not, as well as anchoring our lives to others as a way of avoiding facing ourselves, results in our losing a sense of selfhood and feeling alienated.

In our work with clients in therapy groups, we meet people who hide dimensions of themselves from others. Out of their fear of being rejected, they deprive others of getting to know them fully. During the group sessions they reveal themselves in ways that are totally unknown to even the most intimate people in their lives. As they reveal themselves in the context of the group, and generally receive support and reinforcement, they are more willing to show their hidden self to the significant people in their lives. Through this self-disclosure, individuals learn to appreciate facets of themselves that were strangers to them.

If we want to get back into contact with ourselves, we can begin by looking at the ways we have learned to escape being lonely. We can examine the values of our society and question whether they are contributing to our estrangement from ourselves and to our sense of isolation. We can ask whether the activities that fill our time actually satisfy us or whether they leave us hungry and discontented. To truly confront loneliness, ironically, we may have to spend more time alone, strengthening our awareness of ourselves as the true center of meaning and direction in our lives.

Creating Our Own Loneliness through Shyness

Shyness can lead to loneliness. Shy people tend to be easily frightened, timid, inhibited, uncomfortable in social situations, and relatively unassertive. Some specific characteristics that identify shy individuals are timidity in expressing themselves; being overly sensitive to how others are perceiving and reacting to them; getting embarrassed easily; and experiencing bodily symptoms such as blushing, upset stomach, anxiety, and racing pulse (Weiten & Lloyd 1994).

According to Phil Zimbardo (1987), founder of the shyness clinic at Stanford University, shyness is an almost universal experience. In one study 80 percent of those questioned reported that they had been shy at some point in their lives. Of those, more than 40 percent considered themselves shy at that time. This means that four out of every ten people you meet, or 84 million Americans, are shy. Shyness exists on a continuum. That is, some people see themselves as *chronically* shy, whereas others are shy with certain people or in certain situations.

Shyness can lead directly to feelings of loneliness. Zimbardo (1987) believes that shyness can be a social and a psychological handicap as crippling as many physical handicaps, and he lists these consequences of shyness:

- Shyness prevents people from expressing their views and speaking up for their rights.
- Shyness may make it difficult to think clearly and to communicate effectively.
- Shyness holds people back from meeting new people, making friends, and getting involved in many social activities.
- Shyness often results in feelings such as depression, anxiety, and loneliness.

You may be aware that shyness is a problem for you and that you are creating your own loneliness, at least in part. You may well be asking "What can I do about it?" For one thing, being shy is not necessarily only negative. We are not suggesting that you try to make yourself into an extroverted personality if this is not the person you are, but you can challenge those personal fears that keep you from expressing yourself the way you'd like to. It is likely that one reason for your shyness is not having the interpersonal skills that make it possible to express your feelings and thoughts. You can put yourself in situations where you will be forced to make contact with people and to engage in social activities, even if you are intimidated.

It helps to understand the context of your shyness, especially to identify those social situations that bring out your shy behavior. Also, it is useful to pinpoint

the reasons or combination of factors underlying your shyness. According to Zimbardo (1987), a constellation of factors explain shyness: being overly sensitive to negative feedback from others, fearing rejection, lacking self-confidence and specific social skills, being frightened of intimacy, and personal handicaps. A good way to identify those factors that contribute to your shyness is to keep track in your journal of those situations that elicit your shy behavior. It is also helpful to write down the symptoms you experience and what you actually do in such situations. Pay attention to what you tell yourself when you are in difficult situations. For example, your "self-talk" may be negative, actually setting you up to fail. You may say silently to yourself: "I'm ugly, so who would want anything to do with me?" "I'd better not try something new, because I might look like a fool." "I'm afraid of being rejected, so I won't even approach a person I'd like to get to know." "If people really knew what I was like, they wouldn't like what they saw." "Others are constantly evaluating and judging me, and I'm sure I won't measure up to what they expect."

These are the very statements that are likely to keep you a prisoner of your shyness and prevent you from making contact with others. You can do a lot yourself to control how your shyness affects you by learning to challenge your self-defeating beliefs and by substituting constructive statements. Learning new ways of thinking about yourself involves self-discipline in pushing yourself to test out your new beliefs by acting in new ways.

Don't Let Shyness Hold You Back.   Tracy's experience in coping with shyness illustrates how you can overcome inhibitions and can come out of your shell.

> *When I first began my college education, I was really shy. I would not raise my hand to ask questions in class, I studied by myself, and did not pursue friendships with my peers. My shyness developed out of a belief that I would look stupid if I asked questions and that my peers would think I was not really smart if they studied with me. If I pursued friendships, I was convinced that people would eventually realize I was not fun or outgoing. I believe my shyness in these early years contributed to my failure at my first college.*
>
> *When I decided to leave my first college, I made a commitment to myself that I would do what it took to succeed in earning my education at my new school. Part of this commitment was to speak up in class, ask questions, form study groups, and make friends. This was really scary for me, but I knew that not reaching out kept me lonely. I did not want to live that way anymore. I made contact with my teachers and actually became involved in my learning process. As I became involved with my studies and my peers, my self-confidence increased. Along with this came higher grades. I began to believe that I was smart, that I did ask good questions, that others were not judging me, and that others liked who I was, and most important, I liked who I was.*

If shyness is a problem for you and if it is something you'd like to change about yourself, we encourage you to monitor your thoughts, feelings, and actions to become more aware of the effects of shyness in your life. Like Tracy, you can take steps to make contact with others and challenge negative self-talk that is keeping you in your shell. One way to understand your own shyness and learn some ways of dealing with it would be to read Zimbardo's excellent book *Shyness* (1987).

▶ *Time Out for Personal Reflection*

---

1. Do you try to escape from your loneliness? In what ways? Check any of the following statements that you think apply to you.

_____   I bury myself in work.
_____   I constantly seek to be with others.
_____   I drink excessively or take drugs.
_____   I schedule every moment so that I'll have very little time to think about myself.

_____   I attempt to avoid my troubles by watching television or listening to music.
_____   I eat compulsively.
_____   I sleep excessively to avoid the stress in my life.
_____   I become overly concerned with helping others.
_____   I rarely think about anything if I can help it; I concentrate on playing and having fun.

List other specific ways in which you sometimes try to avoid loneliness:

_____

_____

_____

2. Would you like to change any of the patterns you've just identified? If so, what are they? What might you do to change them?

_____

_____

_____

3. Is shyness a problem for you? In what ways might you be creating your own loneliness through your shyness?

_____

_____

_____

4. Do you see time spent alone as being valuable to you? If so, in what ways?

_____

_____

_____

_____

5. List a few of the major decisions you've made in your life. Did you make these decisions when you were alone or when you were with others?

_____

_____

_____

_____

A journal suggestion: If you find it difficult to be alone, without distractions, for more than a few minutes at a time, try being alone for a little longer than you're generally comfortable with. During this time you might simply let your thoughts wander freely, without hanging on to one line of thinking. In your journal describe what this experience is like for you.

Loneliness and Our Life Stages

How we deal with feelings of loneliness can depend to a great extent on our experiences of loneliness in childhood and adolescence. Later in life we may feel that loneliness has no place or that we can and should be able to avoid it. It's important to reflect on our past experiences, because they are often the basis of our present feelings about loneliness. In addition, we may fear loneliness less if we recognize that it is a natural part of living in every stage of life. Once we have accepted our ultimate aloneness and the likelihood that we will feel lonely at many points in our lives, we may be better able to take responsibility for our own loneliness and recognize how we may be contributing to it.

■ Loneliness and Childhood

Reliving childhood experiences of loneliness can help you come to grips with present fears about being alone or lonely. Some typical memories of lonely periods that people we've worked with in therapy have relived are:

- A woman recalls the time her parents were fighting in the bedroom and she heard them screaming and yelling. She was sure that they would divorce, and in many ways she felt responsible. She remembers living in continual fear that she would be deserted.
- A man recalls attempting to give a speech in the 6th grade. He stuttered over certain words, and children in the class began to laugh at him. Afterwards he developed extreme self-consciousness in regard to his speech, and he long remembered the hurt he had experienced.
- An African-American man recalls how excluded he felt in his all-white elementary school and how the other children would talk to him in derogatory ways. As an adult he can still cry over these memories.
- A woman recalls the fright she felt as a small child when her uncle made sexual advances toward her. Although she didn't really understand what was happening, she remembers the terrible loneliness of feeling that she couldn't tell her parents for fear of what they would do.
- A man recalls the boyhood loneliness of feeling that he was continually failing at everything he tried. To this day, he resists undertaking a task unless he is sure he can handle it, for fear of rekindling those old feelings of loneliness.
- A woman vividly remembers being in the hospital as a small child for an operation. She remembers the loneliness of not knowing what was going on or whether she would be able to leave the hospital. Since no one talked with her, she was all alone with her fears.

As we try to relive these experiences, remember that children do not live in a logical, well-ordered world. Our childhood fears may have been greatly exaggerated, and the feeling of fright may remain with us even though we may now think of it as irrational. Unfortunately, being told by adults that we were foolish for having such fears may only have increased our loneliness while doing nothing to lessen the fears themselves.

At this point you may wonder: "Why go back and recall childhood pain and loneliness? Why not just let it be a thing of the past?" It is important that we re-experience some of the pain we felt as children to understand how we may still be affected by this pain now. We can also look at some of the decisions we made during these times of extreme loneliness and ask whether these decisions are still appropriate. Frequently, strategies we adopted as children remain with us into adulthood, when they are no longer appropriate. For instance, suppose that your family moved to a strange city when you were 7 years old and that you had to go to a new school. Kids at the new school laughed at you, and you lived through several months of anguish. You felt desperately alone in the world. During this time you decided to keep your feelings to yourself and build a wall around yourself so others couldn't hurt you. Although this experience is now long past, you still defend yourself in the same way, because you haven't *really* made a new decision to open up and trust some people. In this way old fears of loneliness might contribute to a real loneliness in the present. If you allow yourself to experience your grief and work it through, emotionally as well as intellectually, you can overcome past pain and create new choices for yourself.

➤ Time Out for Personal Reflection

Take some time to decide whether you're willing to recall and relive a childhood experience of loneliness. If so, try to recapture the experience in as much detail as you can, reliving it in fantasy. Then reflect on the experience, using the following questions as a starting point.

1. Describe in a few words the most intense experience of loneliness you recall having as a child.

_____

_____

_____

_____

2. How do you think the experience affected you then?

_____

_____

_____

_____

3. How do you think the experience may still be affecting you now?

_____

_____

_____

_____

Journal suggestions: Consider elaborating on this exercise in your journal. Here are a few questions you might reflect on: How did you cope with loneliness as a child? How has this influenced the way you deal with loneliness in your life now? If you could go back and put a new ending on your most intense childhood experience of loneliness, what would it be? You might also think about times in your childhood when you enjoyed being alone. Write some notes to yourself about what these experiences were like for you. Where did you like to spend time alone? What did you enjoy doing by yourself? What positive aspects of these times do you recall?

■ Loneliness and Adolescence

For many people loneliness and adolescence are practically synonymous. Adolescents often feel that they are all alone in their world, that they are the first ones to have had the feelings they do, and that they are separated from others by some abnormality. Bodily changes and impulses alone are sufficient to bring about a sense of perplexity and loneliness, but there are other stresses to be undergone as well. Adolescents are developing a sense of identity. They strive to be successful yet fear failure. They want to be accepted and liked, but they fear rejection, ridicule, or exclusion by their peers. Most adolescents know the feeling of being lonely in a crowd or among friends. They often have fears of being ostracized. Conformity can bring acceptance, and the price of nonconformity can be steep.

As you recall your adolescent years — and, in particular, the areas of your life that were marked by loneliness — reflect on the following questions:

- Did I feel included in a social group? Or did I sit on the sidelines, afraid of being included and wishing for it at the same time?
- Was there at least one person I felt I could talk to — one who really heard me, so that I didn't feel desperately alone?
- What experience stands out as one of the loneliest times during these years? How did I cope with my loneliness?
- Did I experience a sense of confusion concerning who I was and what I wanted to be as a person? How did I deal with my confusion? Who or what helped me during this time?
- How did I feel about my own worth and value? Did I believe that I had anything of value to offer anyone or that anyone would find me worth being with?

- How did my culture affect the way I viewed loneliness? Did I learn that loneliness is a natural condition? Or did I pick up the message that loneliness is a disease to cure?

A Stranger in My Own Land.   Ethnic minority adolescents often face unique challenges in terms of feeling connected to others, knowing who they are, and believing in their abilities. They may buy into stereotypes that contribute to feeling alone and different. Natalie's story shows how a person can find an identity and begin to trust herself.

> *In high school I was told that I was not college material and that "Mexicans are good with their hands." A block that I've had to deal with is the stereotype of Mexican women as being submissive and unable to stand up for themselves—which I've heard all my life from many teachers.*
>
> *During my senior year in high school, I met Sal, who invited me to a Chicano Youth Leadership Conference. This conference made my outlook about myself change. Up to that point I was a stranger in my own land. I had no cultural identity, and no strength to speak up. People there believed in me and told me that I could go to college and be successful. It was the first time that others had more faith in my abilities than I did. Sal became my mentor and challenged me to never underestimate the power I have. He made me feel so proud as a young Chicana and proud of my people. This was my spark to stand up and help the Chicano community.*

Can you identify in any way with Natalie's story? Have you ever had difficulty believing in yourself? If so, did this affect your ability to feel connected to others? As you reflect on your adolescence, try to discover some of the ways in which the person you now are is a result of your experiences of loneliness as an adolescent. Do you shrink from competition for fear of failure? In social situations are you afraid of being left out? Do you feel some of the isolation you did then? If so, how do you deal with it? How might you have changed the way you deal with loneliness?

➤ *Time Out for Personal Reflection*

1. Describe the most intense experience of loneliness of your adolescent years.

   _____

   _____

   _____

   _____

2. How did you cope with the loneliness you've just described?

   _____

   _____

_____

_____

3. What effect do you think the experience you've described has on you today?

_____

_____

_____

_____

■ Loneliness and Young Adulthood

In our young-adult years we experiment with ways of being, and we establish lifestyles that may remain with us for many years. You may be struggling with the question of what to do with your life, what intimate relationships you want to establish, and how you will chart your future. Dealing with all the choices that face us at this time of life can be a lonely process.

How you come to terms with your own aloneness can have significant effects on the choices you make — choices that, in turn, may determine the course of your life for years to come. For instance, if you haven't learned to listen to yourself and to depend on your own inner resources, you might succumb to the pressure to choose a relationship or a career before you are really prepared to do so, or you might look to your projects or partners for the sense of identity that you ultimately can find only in yourself. Alternatively, you may feel lonely and establish patterns that only increase your loneliness. This last possibility is well illustrated by the case of Saul.

Saul was in his early twenties when he attended college. He claimed that his chief problem was his isolation, yet he rarely reached out to others. His general manner seemed to say "Keep away." Although he was enrolled in a small, informal class in self-awareness and personal growth, he quickly left after each session, depriving himself of the chance to make contact with anyone.

One day, as I (Jerry) was walking across the campus, I saw Saul sitting alone in a secluded spot, while many students were congregated on the lawn, enjoying the beautiful spring weather. Here was a chance for him to do something about his separation from others; instead, he chose to seclude himself. He continually told himself that others didn't like him and, sadly, made his prophecy self-fulfilling by his own behavior. He made himself unapproachable and, in many ways, the kind of person people would avoid.

In this time of life we have the chance to decide on ways of being toward ourselves and others as well as on our vocation and future plans. If you feel lonely on the campus, we'd like to challenge you to ask yourself what *you* are doing and can do about your own loneliness. Do you decide in advance that the other students and instructors want to keep to themselves? Do you assume that there already are well-established cliques to which you cannot belong? Do you expect others to reach out to you, even though you don't initiate contacts yourself? What fears

might be holding you back? Where do they seem to come from? Are past experiences of loneliness or rejection determining the choices you make now?

Often we create unnecessary loneliness for ourselves by our own behavior. If we sit back and wait for others to come to us, we give them the power to make us lonely. As we learn to take responsibility for ourselves in young adulthood, one area we can work on is taking responsibility for our own loneliness and creating new choices for ourselves.

■ Loneliness and Middle Age

Many changes occur during middle age that can result in new feelings of loneliness. Although we may not be free to choose some of the things that occur at this time in our lives, we *are* free to choose how we relate to these events. Some possible changes and crises of middle age are:

■ Our significant other may grow tired of living with us and decide to leave. If this happens, we must decide how to respond. Will we blame ourselves and become absorbed in self-hate? Will we refuse to see any of our own responsibility for the breakup and simply blame the other person? Will we decide never to trust anyone again? Will we mourn our loss and, after a period of grieving, actively look for another person to live with?

■ Our life may not turn out the way we had planned. We may not enjoy the success we had hoped for, we may feel disenchanted with our work, or we may feel that we passed up many fine opportunities earlier. But the key point is what we can do about our life now. What choices will we make in light of this reality? Will we slip into hopelessness and berate ourselves endlessly about what we could have done and should have done? Will we allow ourselves to stay trapped in meaningless work and empty relationships, or will we look for positive options for change?

- Our children may leave home, and with this change we may experience emptiness and a sense of loss. If so, what will we do about this transition? Will we attempt to hang on? Can we let go and create a new life with new meaning? When our children leave, will we lose our desire to live? Will we look back with regret at all that we could have done differently, or will we choose to look ahead to the kind of life we want to create for ourselves now that we don't have the responsibilities of parenthood?

- Up to this time in our lives, we may have been absorbed in work and family responsibilities. We may have an overwhelming sense of regret over all the time we missed with friends and the time we did not have for recreation, and we may feel a strong desire to change our lives in the direction of integrating leisure time with work.

These are just a few of the changes that many of us confront during midlife. Although we may feel that events are not in our control, we can still choose how we respond to these life situations. To illustrate, we'd like to present a brief example that reflects the loneliness many people experience after a divorce and show how the two people involved made different decisions about how to deal with their loneliness.

Amy and Gary had been married for more than 20 years before their recent divorce, and they have three children in their teens. Amy is 43; Gary is 41. Although they have both experienced a good deal of loneliness since their divorce, they have chosen different attitudes toward their loneliness. Here is Gary's story.

> *I felt resentful at first and believed that somehow we could have stayed together if only Amy had changed her attitude. I live alone in a small apartment and get to see my kids only on weekends. I see my divorce as a personal failure, and I still feel a mixture of guilt and resentment. I hate to come home to an empty apartment with no one to talk to and no one to share my life with. In some ways I've decided not to cultivate other relationships, because I'm still raw over my first failure. I wonder whether women would find me interesting once they got to know me, and I fear that it's too late to begin a new life with someone else.*
>
> *I say no to most of my friends' invitations, because I worry about them asking me out of pity. At times I feel like climbing the walls. I've tried to numb my loneliness by burying myself in work, but that doesn't do the trick. I'm pretty much convinced that it isn't really possible for me to develop a new relationship.*

For her part, Amy had many ambivalent feelings about divorcing. Here is Amy's story.

> *After the divorce I experienced panic and aloneness as I faced the prospect of rearing my children and managing the home on my own. I wonder*

whether I can meet my responsibilities and still have time for any social life. I am concerned that men may not be interested in me, especially with my three teenagers. I sometimes anguish over my future and ask myself: "Will I be able to have another life with someone else? Do I want to live alone? Can I take care of my emotional needs and still provide for the family?"

Even though I'm unsure of myself, I have dated some. At first I felt pressured by my parents to get married again. Yet I'm doing my best to resist this pressure. I'm choosing to remain single for the time being. Although I feel lonely at times, I don't feel trapped.

Experiences like those of Gary and Amy are very common among middle-aged people who find themselves having to cope with feelings of isolation and abandonment after a divorce. Some, like Gary, may feel panic and either retreat from people or quickly run into a new relationship to avoid the pain of separation. If they don't confront their fears and their pain, they may be controlled by their fear of being left alone for the rest of their lives. Others, like Amy, may go through a similar period of loneliness after a divorce yet refuse to be controlled by a fear of living alone. Although they might want a long-term relationship again some day, they avoid rushing impulsively into a new relationship to avoid feelings of pain or loneliness.

■ Loneliness and the Later Years

Our society emphasizes productivity, youth, beauty, power, and vitality. As we age, we may lose some of our vitality and sense of power or attractiveness. Many people face a real crisis when they reach retirement, for they feel that they're being put out to pasture — that they aren't needed anymore and that their lives are really over. Loneliness and hopelessness are experienced by anyone who feels that there is little to look forward to or that he or she has no vital place in society, and such feelings are particularly common among older adults.

The loneliness of the later years can be accentuated by the losses that come with age — loss of sight, hearing, memory, and strength. Older people may lose their jobs, hobbies, friends, and loved ones. A particularly difficult loss is the death of a spouse with whom they have been close for many years. In the face of such losses, a person may ultimately ask what reason remains for living. It may be no coincidence that many old people die soon after their spouses have died or shortly after their retirement.

A Husband's Grief over the Death of His Wife.   Charles, 65, lost his wife, Betsy, to cancer after a year's battle. During the last few months of Betsy's life, members of the local hospice organization helped Charles care for her at home. Here is an account of Charles's attempt to deal with her death.

Before Betsy's death she expressed a desire to talk to me about her impending death. I could not tolerate the reality of her illness and her dying. So, I never talked with her. Even though Betsy has been dead for some time, I still feel guilty for not listening to her and talking. When I look at her chair where

she sat, I feel an overwhelming sense of loneliness. At times I feel as though my heart is going to explode. I rarely sleep through the night, and I get up early in the morning and look for tasks to keep me busy. I feel lost and lonely, and it is difficult for me to be in the house where she and I lived together for more than 45 years. Her memories are everywhere. My friends continue to encourage me to talk about my feelings. Although my friends and neighbors are supportive, I'm worried that I'll be a burden for them. I wish that I had died instead of Betsy, for she would have been better able to deal with my being gone that I'm able to cope with her passing.

C. S. Lewis, in *A Grief Observed* (1961), poetically compares grief to a long and winding valley where any bend may reveal a totally new landscape. He writes about his own grief over observing the death of his wife from cancer:

And grief still feels like fear. Perhaps, more strictly, like suspense. Or like waiting; just hanging about waiting for something to happen. It gives life a permanently provisional feeling. It doesn't seem worth starting anything. I can't settle down.

I yawn, I fidget, I smoke too much. Up until this I always had too little time. Now there is nothing but time. Almost pure time, empty successiveness. (p. 29)

In his thought-provoking book *Learn to Grow Old,* Paul Tournier (1972) writes that the way we live earlier in life determines the quality of our years during old age and retirement. For him, growing old and retiring does not mean being condemned to loneliness. He believes that we need to prepare ourselves in the present for a meaningful life of work and leisure in our later years.

The pangs of aloneness or the feelings that life is futile reflect a drastic loss of meaning rather than an essential part of growing old. Viktor Frankl (1969) has written about the "will to meaning" as a key determinant of a person's desire to live. He notes that many of the inmates in the Nazi concentration camp where he was imprisoned kept themselves alive by looking forward to the prospect of being released and reunited with their families. Many of those who lost hope simply gave up and died, regardless of their age.

At least until recently our society has compounded the elderly person's loss of meaning by grossly neglecting the aged population. Although many elderly are well-taken care of in a convalescent home and are visited by their family members, many others are left alone in an institution with only minimal human contact.

Sometimes, however, older people choose a lonely existence, rather than participating in the activities and human relationships that could be open to them. Rudy is an example of an older man who feels basically lost and does not seem able to find a direction that brings him satisfaction. Rudy is 85 years old. His wife died 15 years ago, and he remained in his large house. He reports that he has real difficulty being at home for any length of time. He leaves the house early in the morning in his pickup truck and spends most of his day doing crossword puzzles, except for the time he spends walking a few miles. When he finally returns home late at night, he faces the loneliness he attempted to escape from early in the morning. He has few friends, dates women much younger than himself, and always worries that they are out to get his money. A solitary pleasure is going to the races. Although he has occasional contact with extended family at holiday gatherings, he rarely initiates contact with them during the rest of the year. He shies away from people out of his fear of burdening them. What he fails to realize is how much he still has to offer and how much others could benefit from their association with him. His inability to recognize and appreciate what he could offer to others keeps him a prisoner of his loneliness.

Those who specialize in the study of aging often make the point that if we have led a rich life in early adulthood, we have a good chance of finding richness in our later years. Certainly, if we have learned to find direction from within ourselves, we will be better equipped to deal with the changes that aging brings. A few years ago we had the good fortune to meet an exceptional man, Dr. Ewald Schnitzer, who retired from the University of California at Los Angeles in 1973 and moved to Idyllwild, California, a place that he considers his last and happiest home. He provides an outstanding model of how to productively face old age.

Dr. Schnitzer lives alone by preference and continues to find excitement and meaning in art, philosophy, music, history, hiking, writing, and traveling. He believes that his entire life has prepared him well for his later years. He has learned to be content when he is alone, he finds pleasure in the company of people, animals, and nature, and he enjoys many memories of his rich experiences. A few years ago he assumed a grandfatherlike role with two children of a neighboring couple. He takes great pleasure in being part of these children's lives. He can live fully now, without dreading the future. This spirit of being fully alive is well expressed in his book *Looking In* (1977): "It would be painful should frailty prevent me from climbing mountains. Yet, when that time comes, I hope I find serenity in wandering through valleys, looking at the realm of distant summits not with ambition but with loving memories" (p. 88). At age 85 he still takes short walks on the trails in the mountains.

We conclude this discussion of the later years — and, in a sense, this entire chapter on loneliness and solitude — by returning to the example of Anne Morrow Lindbergh. In her later years her lifelong courage in facing aloneness enabled her to find new and rich meaning in her life. We were extremely impressed with this woman when we first read her book *Gift from the Sea,* but our respect increased when we read the "Afterword" in the book's 20th anniversary edition (1975). There, she looks back at the time when she originally wrote the book and notes that she was then deeply involved in family life. Since that time her children have left and established their own lives. She describes how a most uncomfortable stage followed her middle years, one that she hadn't anticipated when she wrote the book. She writes that she went from the "oyster-bed" stage of taking care of a family to the "abandoned-shell" stage of later life. This is how she describes the essence of the "abandoned-shell" stage:

> Plenty of solitude, and a sudden panic at how to fill it, characterized this period. With me, it was not a question of simply filling up the space or the time. I had many activities and even a well-established vocation to pursue. But when a mother is left, the lone hub of a wheel, with no other lives revolving around her, she faces a total reorientation. It takes time to re-find the center of gravity. (p. 134)

In this stage she did make choices to come to terms with herself and create a new role for herself. She points out that all the exploration she did earlier in life paid off when she reached the "abandoned-shell" stage. Here again, earlier choices affect current ones.

Before her husband, Charles, died in 1974, Lindbergh had looked forward to retiring with him on the Hawaiian Island of Maui. His death changed her life abruptly but did not bring it to an end. Its continuity was preserved in part by the presence of her 5 children and 12 grandchildren; moreover, she continued to involve herself in her own writing and in the preparation of her husband's papers for publication. Here is a fine example of a woman who has encountered her share of loneliness and learned to renew herself by actively choosing a positive stance toward life.

Maya Angelou is another person who schedules time for herself so she can retain her center. She lives a very full life, and she finds ways to retain her vitality. She schedules one day a month for herself; nothing is scheduled and her friends know not to call her.

We hope you will welcome your time alone. Once you fully accept it, your aloneness can become the source of your strength and the foundation of your relatedness to others. Think about the examples of Maya Angelou and Anne Morrow

Lindbergh and consider how you can make time for yourself to take care of your soul. Taking time to *be* alone gives you the opportunity to think, plan, imagine, and dream. It allows you to listen to yourself and to become sensitive to what you are experiencing. In solitude you can come to appreciate anew both your separateness from and your relatedness to the important people and projects in your life. Sometimes you may get so busy attending to day-to-day routines that you forget to reflect and provide yourself with spiritual and emotional nourishment. Remember, if you are not a good friend to yourself, it will be difficult to find true friendship in the company of others.

➤ *Time Out for Personal Reflection*

Complete the following sentences by writing down the first response that comes to mind.

1. The loneliest time in my life was when _____

_____

2. I usually deal with my loneliness by _____

_____

3. I escape from loneliness by _____

_____

4. If I were abandoned by all those who love me, _____

_____

5. One value I see in experiencing loneliness is _____

_____

6. My greatest fear of loneliness is _____

_____

7. I have felt lonely in a crowd when _____

_____

8. When I'm with a person who is lonely, _____

_____

9. For me, being with others _____

_____

10. I feel loneliest when _____

_____

11. The thought of living alone the rest of my life _____

_____

Chapter Summary

We have a need to be with others that is best satisfied through many forms of intimate relationships. Yet another essential dimension of the human experience is to be able to creatively function alone. Unless we can enjoy our own company, we will have difficulty finding real joy in being with others. Being with others and being with ourselves are two sides of the same coin.

Some people fail to reach out to others and make significant contact because they are timid in social situations and are relatively unassertive. Many people report that they are troubled by shyness or have had problems with being shy in the past. Shyness can lead to feelings of loneliness, yet shy people can challenge the fears that keep them unassertive. Shyness is not a disorder that needs to be "cured," nor are all aspects of being shy negative. It is important to recognize that certain attitudes and behaviors can create much of the loneliness we sometimes experience.

Each period of life presents unique tasks to be mastered, and loneliness can be best understood from a developmental perspective. Particular circumstances often result in loneliness as we pass through childhood, adolescence, young adulthood, middle age, and the later years. Most of us have experienced loneliness during our childhood and adolescent years, and these experiences can have a significant influence on our present attitudes, behavior, and relationships. It helps to be able to recognize our feelings about events that are associated with each of these turning points.

Experiencing loneliness is part of being human, for ultimately we are alone. We can grow from such experiences if we understand them and use them to renew our sense of ourselves. Moreover, we don't have to remain victimized by early decisions that we made as a result of past loneliness. We do have choices. We can choose to face loneliness and deal with it creatively, or we can choose to try to escape from it. We have some choice concerning whether we will feel lonely or whether we will make connections with others. We can design our activities so that we reject others before they reject us, or we can risk making contact with them.

Activities and Exercises

1. Allocate some time each day to be alone and reflect on anything you wish. Note down in your journal the thoughts and feelings that occur to you during your time alone.

2. If you have feelings of loneliness when you think about a certain person who has been or is now significant to you, write a letter to that person expressing all the things you're feeling (you don't have to mail the letter). For instance, tell that person how you miss him or her or write about your sadness, your resentment, or your desire for more closeness.

3. Imagine that you are the person you've written your letter to, and write a reply to yourself. What do you imagine that person would say to you if he or she received your letter? What do you fear (and what do you wish) he or she would say?

4. If you sometimes feel lonely and left out, you might try some specific experiments for a week or so. For example, if you feel isolated in most of your classes, why not make it a point to get to class early and initiate contact with a fellow student? If you feel anxious about taking such a step, try doing it in fantasy. What are your fears? What is the worst thing you can imagine might happen? Record your impressions in your journal. If you decide to try reaching out to other people, record in your journal what the experience is like for you.

5. Recall some periods of loneliness in your life. Select important situations in which you experienced loneliness, and spend some time recalling the details of each situation and reflecting on the meaning each of these experiences has had for you. Now you might do two things:
   a. Write down your reflections in your journal. How do you think your past experiences of loneliness affect you now?
   b. Select a friend or a person you'd like to trust more, and share this experience of loneliness.

6. Many people rarely make time exclusively for themselves. If you'd like to have time to yourself but just haven't gotten around to arranging it, consider going to a place you haven't been to before or to the beach, desert, or mountains. Reserve a weekend just for yourself; if this seems too much, then spend a day completely alone. The important thing is to remove yourself from your everyday routine and just be with yourself without external distractions.

7. Try spending a day or part of a day in a place where you can observe and experience lonely people. You might spend time near a busy downtown intersection, in a park where old people congregate, or in a large shopping center. Try to pay attention to expressions of loneliness, alienation, and isolation. How do people seem to be dealing with their loneliness? Later, you might discuss your observations in class.

8. Imagine yourself living in a typical rest home—without any of your possessions, cut off from your family and friends, and unable to do the things you now do. Reflect on what this experience would be like for you; then write down some of your reactions in your journal.

9. Select one or more of the following books for further reading on the topics explored in this chapter: *Listening to Your Inner Voice: Discover the Truth Within You and Let It Guide Your Way* (Block, 1991); *Gift from the Sea* (Lindbergh, 1975); *Loneliness* (Moustakas, 1961).

12

Death and Loss

Contemplate death if you would learn how to live.

✔ *Prechapter Self-Inventory*

Use the following scale to respond: 4 = this statement is true of me *most* of the time; 3 = this statement is true of me *much* of the time; 2 = this statement is true of me *some* of the time; 1 = this statement is true of me *almost none* of the time.

_____ 1. The fact that I must die makes me take the present moment seriously.

_____ 2. I don't like funerals, because they make me dwell on a painful subject.

_____ 3. If I had a terminal illness, I'd want to know how much time I had left to live, so I could decide how to spend it.

_____ 4. Because of the possibility of losing those I love, I don't allow myself to get too close to others.

_____ 5. If I live with dignity, I'll be able to die with dignity.

_____ 6. One of my greatest fears of death is the fear of the unknown.

_____ 7. I've had losses in my life that in some ways were like the experience of dying.

_____ 8. There are some ways in which I'm not really alive emotionally.

_____ 9. I'm not especially afraid of dying.

_____ 10. I fear the deaths of those I love more than I do my own.

Introduction

Your awareness of death enables you to give meaning to your life. The reality of your finiteness can stimulate you to look at your priorities and to ask what you value most. In this way your willingness to come to terms with your death can teach you how to really live. To run from death is to run from life, for as Gibran (1923) writes, "Life and death are one, even as the river and the sea are one" (p. 71). Siegel (1993) believes that if we are living fully, then dying isn't a problem. His advice is, "If you want to live forever, love someone" (p. 219). He encourages us to "touch the edge of death" by accepting the fact that we are mortal. The key is living each day fully by focusing on what we can give. Siegel writes: "My definition of how you use your day isn't 'What can I get today?' but rather 'What can I give today?' When you become clear about how you want to love the world, then you will be living your life without being selfish" (p. 19).

Are you living *now* the way you want? Do you have goals you have yet to meet? What do you most want to be able to say that you have experienced or accomplished before you die? What are you doing today to have the kind of life you want?

In this chapter we invite you to look at your attitudes and beliefs about your own death, the deaths of those you love, and other forms of significant loss. Although the topic of this chapter might seem morbid or depressing, an honest understanding and acceptance of death and loss can lay the groundwork for a rich and meaningful life. If we fully accept that we have only a limited time in which to live, we can make choices that will make the most of the time we have.

We also ask you to consider the notion of death in a broader perspective and to raise such questions as "What parts of me aren't as alive as they might be?" "In what emotional ways am I dead or dying?" "What will I do with my awareness of the ways in which I'm not fully alive?" Finally, we discuss the importance of fully experiencing grief when you suffer serious losses.

This discussion of death and loss has an important connection with the themes of the previous chapter, loneliness and solitude. When we emotionally accept the reality of our eventual death, we experience our ultimate aloneness. This awareness of our mortality and aloneness helps us realize that our actions do count, that we do have choices concerning how we live our lives, and that we must accept the final responsibility for how well we are living.

This chapter is also a bridge to the next chapter, which deals with meaning and values. Awareness of death is a catalyst for the human search for meaning in life. Our knowledge that we will die can encourage us to ask ourselves whether we're living by values that create a meaningful existence; if not, we have the time and opportunity to change our way of living. As Siegel (1989) puts it: "Facing death is often the catalyst that enables people to reach out for what they want" (p. 241). You can see this emphasis on meaning in Norma's response to the question of how she would feel if she found that she had a short time to live.

> *I'm 53 years old, and I have accomplished more in my life than I ever thought possible. So far, my life has been rich and gratifying. I have a husband and four children with whom I generally have a good relationship. Although I know they have a need for me in their lives, they could function well without me. While I am not afraid of death, I would consider death at this time in my life as terribly unfair. There is so much more I want to do. Within me are many untapped talents that I haven't had time to express. Many of my present projects take an enormous amount of time, and while they are mostly satisfying, I've put on hold many other personal and professional aspirations. At times I feel an overwhelming sense of sadness and disappointment over the possibility of running out of time to do those things I was meant to do. Time seems to go by so fast, and I often wish I could stop the clock. It is my hope to live to an old age, yet I do confront myself with the reality that I may not be that fortunate, which provides me with the impetus to want to make changes in my life. The reality of mortality challenges me to reflect on what I would regret not having done if I were to die soon. This reality helps me not to postpone my plans to later, because there may not be a later. The greatest tragedy for me would be, if on my dying day, I would say that there is so much that I didn't take the time to do.*

Our Fears of Death

We may fear many aspects of death, including leaving behind those we love, losing ourselves, encountering the unknown, coping with the humiliation and indignity of a painful or long dying, and growing distant in the memories of others. For many people it's not so much death itself as the experience of dying that arouses fears. Here, too, it is well to ask what our fears are really about and to face them.

Siegel (1988) believes that the pain and fear of dying come primarily from unresolved conflict and unfinished business. One of Siegel's patients told him, "Death is not the worst thing. Life without love is far worse" (p. 207). Perhaps we fear dying because we might realize that we have never really lived.

At this point pause to reflect on your own fears of death and dying. What expectations seem to arouse the greatest fears in you? Do your religious beliefs assist you in dealing with your fear of dying? Do your fears involve death itself, or the experience of dying? How might your fears be affecting how you choose to live now? Have you had someone close to you die? If so, how did the experience of that person's death affect your feelings about death and dying?

If you consider yourself relatively young, you might ask: "Why should this topic interest me? I've got lots of time left, so why think about morbid subjects?" Even the very young can be at least temporarily shocked into the realization that they could die at any time. This happens when a classmate dies in an automobile accident, by drowning, by suicide, by cancer, by AIDS, or by some act of violence. Although it is not necessary to morbidly focus on your death, it is important for you to deal with your fears of it and to consider what death means to you in terms of *living fully* now.

Death and the Meaning of Life

The existentialists view the acceptance of death as vital to the discovery of meaning and purpose in life. One of our distinguishing characteristics as human beings is our ability to grasp the concept of the future and, thus, the inevitability of death. Our ability to do so gives meaning to our existence, for it makes our every act and moment count.

Rather than living in fear of our mortality, we can view death as a challenge and as an opportunity. Siegel (1989, 1993) maintains that death is not a failure, but failing to live fully is the worst outcome. His writings and lectures are permeated with the assumption that the knowledge of our eventual death is what gives meaning to life. For Siegel (1989), the realization that we will die is a wakeup call to appreciate the urgency and beauty of each day.

> The greatest gift of all is that we don't live forever. It makes us face up to the meaning of our existence. It also enables people who never took time for themselves in life to take that time, at last, before they die. (p. 234)

The Stoics of ancient Greece had a dictum: "Contemplate death if you would learn how to live." Seneca commented that "no man enjoys the true taste of life but he who is willing and ready to quit it." And Saint Augustine said, "It is only in the face of death that man's self is born." Thus, it is in facing the reality of our death that we find meaning in life.

A sharply defined example of facing the reality of death, and of giving meaning to what is left of life, is provided by those who are terminally ill. Their confrontation with death causes them to do much living in a relatively brief period of time. The pressure of time almost forces them to choose how they will spend their remaining days. Irvin Yalom (1980) found that cancer patients in group therapy had the capacity to view their crisis as an opportunity to instigate change in their lives. Once they discovered that they had cancer, their inner changes included:

- a rearrangement of life's priorities, paying little attention to trivial matters
- a sense of liberation; the ability to choose to do those things they really wanted to do
- an increased sense of living in the moment; no postponement of living until some future time
- a vivid appreciation of the basic facts of life; for example, noticing changes in the seasons and other aspects of nature
- a deeper communication with loved ones than before the crisis

■ fewer interpersonal fears, less concern over security, and more willingness to take risks (p. 35)

The irony of the situation is well summed up by one of the patients: "What a tragedy that we had to wait till now, till our bodies were riddled with cancer, to learn these truths" (p. 165). This example serves to make a central point: When we confront the reality that life does not go on forever, life becomes more precious. Siegel (1988) echoes this view that confronting death makes it possible to love life. He reminds us that we have a choice and encourages us to choose love and life.

> We have an infinite number of choices ahead, but a finite number of endings. They are destruction and death or love and healing. If we choose the path of love we save ourselves and our universe. (p. 225)

The meaning of our lives, then, depends on the fact that we are finite beings. What we do with our lives counts. We can choose to become all that we are capable of becoming and make a conscious decision to fully affirm life, or we can passively let life slip by us. We can settle for letting events happen to us, or we can actively choose and create the kind of life we want. If we had forever to actualize our potentials, there would be no urgency about doing so. Our time is invaluable precisely because it is limited.

Cultural and religious beliefs affect the way people view death. Some belief systems emphasize making the most of this life, for it is viewed as the *only* existence. Other belief systems focus on the natural continuity and progression of this temporal life into an afterlife. Just as our beliefs and values affect our fear of death, so do they affect the meaning we attribute to death. Regardless of your philosophical or spiritual views on the meaning of life and death, a wide range of choices is still open to you to maximize the quality of your present life.

➤ *Time Out for Personal Reflection*

1. What fears do you experience when you think about your own death? Check any of the following statements that apply to you:

_____ I worry about what will happen to me after death.
_____ I'm anxious about the way I will die.
_____ I wonder whether I'll die with dignity.
_____ I fear the physical pain of dying.
_____ I worry most about my loved ones who will be left behind.
_____ I'm afraid that I won't be able to accomplish all that I want to accomplish before I die.
_____ I worry about my lack of control over how and when I will die.
_____ I fear ceasing to exist.

_____   I worry about being forgotten.
_____   I worry about all the things I'll miss after I die.

List any other fears you have about death or dying.

_____

_____

_____

_____

2. How well do you think you're living your life? List some specific things you aren't doing now that you'd like to be doing. List some things you think you'd be likely to do if you knew that you had only a short time to live.

_____

_____

_____

_____

3. We've asked students to write a brief description of what they might do if they knew they had only six months left to live. If you're willing to, write down what occurs to you when you think about this possibility.

_____

_____

_____

_____

4. In what ways does the fact that you will die give meaning to your life now?

_____

_____

_____

_____

5. In what ways do you think your fears about death and dying might be affecting the choices you make now?

_____

_____

_____

_____

Suicide: Ultimate Choice or Ultimate Cop-Out?

Suicide is one of the leading causes of death in the United States, and it is on the increase. Suicide ranks among the top five causes of death for white males aged 10 to 55 and is the second-ranked cause of death for all males aged 15 to 24 (De-Spelder & Strickland, 1983).

People who attempt suicide simply do not want to go on in such deadening patterns, or they see life as unbearable. They may feel that the chances of change are slim. Although there are options for living differently, they are unable to see any. Is suicide an ultimate choice or an ultimate cop-out? This question is complex, with no easy answer. What seems essential is that we make conscious choices about how fully we are willing to live, realizing that we must pay a price for being alive. For some people ending their lives does seem like a cop-out, the result of not being willing to struggle or of being too quick to give up without exploring other possibilities. Shneidman (1984) indicates that a major shortcoming of suicide is that it answers a remediable challenge with a permanent negative solution. He adds that living involves a long-term set of resolutions that sometimes offers only fleeting results.

Consider these questions as a way of clarifying your views on suicide:

What does your personal experience reveal? At times you may have felt a deep sense of hopelessness, and you may have questioned whether it was worth it to continue living. Have you ever felt really suicidal? If so, what was going on in your life that contributed to your desire to end it? What factor or factors kept you from following through with taking your life? Would this act have been motivated by the feeling that you had no choices?

What hidden meanings does suicide have? Taking one's life is such a powerful act that we must look to some of its underlying messages and symbolic meanings:

- A cry for help: "I cried out, but nobody heard me!"
- A form of self-punishment: "I don't deserve to live."
- An act of hostility: "I'll get even with you; see what you made me do."
- An attempt to control and exert power over people: "I will make others suffer for the rest of their lives for having rejected me."
- An attempt to be noticed: "Maybe now people will talk about me and feel sorry for the way they treated me."
- A relief from a terrible state of mind: "Life is too stressful, and I'm fed up."
- An escape from a difficult or impossible situation: "I hate living in an alcoholic family, and death seems like one way to end this situation."
- A relief from hopelessness: "I see no way out of the despair I feel. Ending my life will be better than hating to wake up each morning."
- An end to pain. "I suffer extreme physical pain, which will not end. Suicide will put an end to this nightmare."

Can suicide be an act of mercy? Some victims of painful and terminal illnesses have decided *when* and *how* to end their lives. Rather than dying with cancer and enduring extreme pain, some people have actually called their families together and then taken some form of poison. For several years, Dr. Jack Kevorkian, the physician from Michigan known as the "suicide doctor," has been making the news with assisted suicide. Kevorkian is continually getting into trouble with the law because of his beliefs and practices regarding euthanasia. Although this doctor faced murder or manslaughter charges, he has continued to assert that he is providing people with a means for choosing to end their lives when there is no more hope.

One CBS program of "60 Minutes" featured a person who was devoting his life to assisting people with AIDS to die. He was about to be prosecuted, when he himself died of AIDS. These events that have become major news stories represent an outcry by people saying, "I don't want anybody to keep me alive when my quality of life has diminished." People fear being kept alive at all costs when they are ready to die, and hospital machines can obstruct this readiness. Lawyers report an increase in the number of people asking for living wills, in which they give directions about when to unplug life-support equipment. Do you think a person should have the choice to end his or her life when it is certain there is no chance of recovery? Do you have a living will? Do you think you should have one?

■ Reactions to Suicide

When a family member commits suicide, the immediate reaction is generally shock and distress. Soon afterwards those left behind experience a range of feelings such as denial, anger, shame, guilt, grief, depression, and fear. When family members are in denial, they may invent reasons that will contribute to their refusal to accept the death as a suicide. Anger is quite common, often directed toward the deceased: "Why did you shut me out and leave me?" It can also be aimed at medical agencies, friends, and other family members. There may be a sense of shame because of the stigma of suicide. Guilt is often experienced over what the survivors could and should have done to prevent the tragedy. "Maybe if I had been more sensitive and caring," they might feel, "this terrible thing wouldn't have happened." They also experience fear over the possibility that this act will be repeated by another family member or, perhaps, even by themselves.

In a discussion of how to help survivors deal with their reactions to youth suicide, Hawton (1986) emphasizes the significant role of counseling. The nature of the unfinished business, how it is handled, and how the survivor is affected by it all have an impact on the grief process. Typically, those who are left behind experience a deep sense of abandonment, loneliness, and isolation. If the family members are willing to seek counseling (either individually or as a family), they can be taught how to express feelings that they might otherwise have kept buried inside. Counseling encourages the survivors to talk about the things they may be rehearsing over and over in their heads, and it can help them to talk about their feelings with one another. Counseling can help correct distortions survivors may hold, prepare for their future, learn to let go of regrets and blame, and give expression to their anger. Because of their deep sadness, it may be difficult for family members to become aware of, much less express to one another, the anger that they may feel.

Freedom in Dying

The process of dying involves a gradual diminishing of the choices available to us. But even in dying, we can choose how we handle what is happening to us. The following account deals with the dying of Jim Morelock, a student and close friend of mine (Jerry's).*

Jim is 25 years old. He is full of life — witty, bright, honest, and actively questioning. He had just graduated from college as a human services major and seemed to have a bright future when his illness was discovered.

About a year and a half ago, Jim developed a growth on his forehead and underwent surgery to have it removed. At that time, his doctors believed the growth was a rare disorder that was not malignant. Later, more tumors erupted, and more surgery followed. Several months ago, Jim found out that the tumors had spread throughout his body and that, even with cobalt treatment, he would have a short life. Since that time he has steadily grown weaker and has been able to do less and less; yet he has shown remarkable courage in the way he has faced this loss and his dying.

Some time ago Jim came to Idyllwild, California, and took part in the weekend seminar that we had with the reviewers of this book. On this chapter, he commented that although we may not have a choice concerning the losses we suffer in dying, we do retain the ability to choose our attitude toward our death and the way we relate to it.

Jim has taught me a lot during these past few months about this enduring capacity for choice, even in extreme circumstances. Jim has made many critical choices since being told of his illness. He chose to continue taking a course at the university, because he liked the contact with the people there. He worked hard at a boat dock to support himself, until he could no longer manage the physical exertion. He decided to undergo cobalt treatment, even though he knew that it most likely would not result in his cure, because he hoped that it would reduce his pain. It did not, and Jim has suffered much agony during the past few months. He decided not to undergo chemotherapy, primarily because he didn't want to prolong his life if he couldn't really live fully. He made a choice to accept God in his life, which gave him a sense of peace and serenity. Before he became bedridden, he decided to go to Hawaii and enjoy his time in first-class style.

Jim has always had an aversion to hospitals — to most institutions, for that matter — so he chose to remain at home, in more personal surroundings. As long as he was able, he read widely and continued to write in his journal about his thoughts and feelings on living and dying. With his friends, he played his guitar and sang songs that he had written. He maintained an active interest in life and in the things around him, without denying the fact that he was dying.

More than anyone I have known or heard about, Jim has taken care of unfinished business. He made it a point to gather his family and tell them his wishes, he

*This account is being repeated as it appeared in this book's first edition. Many readers have commented to us about how touched they were as they read about Jim's life and his death, and in this way he seems to have lived on in one important respect.

made contact with all his friends and said everything he wanted to say to them, and he asked Marianne to deliver the eulogy at his funeral services. He clearly stated his desire for cremation; he wants to burn those tumors and then have his ashes scattered over the sea — a wish that reflects his love of freedom and movement.

Jim has very little freedom and movement now, for he can do little except lie in his bed and wait for his death to come. To this day he is choosing to die with dignity, and although his body is deteriorating, his spirit is still very much alive. He retains his mental sharpness, his ability to say a lot in a very few words, and his sense of humor. He has allowed himself to grieve over his losses. As he puts it, "I'd sure like to hang around to enjoy all those people that love me!" Realizing that this isn't possible, Jim is saying good-bye to all those who are close to him.

Throughout this ordeal, Jim's mother has been truly exceptional. When she told me how remarkable Jim has been in complaining so rarely despite his constant pain, I reminded her that I'd never heard her complain during her months on duty. I have been continually amazed by her strength and courage, and I have admired her willingness to honor Jim's wishes and accept his beliefs, even though at times they have differed from her own. She has demonstrated her care without smothering him or depriving him of his free spirit and independence. Her acceptance of Jim's dying and her willingness to be fully present to him have given him the opportunity to express openly whatever he feels. Jim has been able to grieve and mourn because she has not cut off this process.

This experience has taught me much about dying and about living. Through him, I have learned that I don't have to do that much for a person who is dying other than to be with him or her by being myself. So often I have felt a sense of helplessness, of not knowing what to say or how much to say, of not knowing what to ask or not to ask, of feeling stuck for words. Jim's imminent death seems such a loss, and it's very difficult for me to accept it. Gradually, however, I have learned not to be so concerned about what to say or to refrain from saying. In fact, in my last visit I said very little, but I feel that we made significant contact with each other. I've also learned to share with him the sadness I feel, but there is simply no easy way to say good-buy to a friend.

Jim is showing me that his style of dying will be no different from his style of living. By his example and by his words, Jim has been a catalyst for me to think about the things I say and do and to evaluate my own life.

► *Time Out for Personal Reflection*

1. If you were close to someone during his or her dying, how did the experience affect your feelings about your life and about your own dying?

_____

_____

_____

_____

2. How would you like to be able to respond if a person who is close to you were dying?

_____

_____

_____

_____

3. If you were dying, what would you most want from the people who are closest to you?

_____

_____

_____

_____

_____

The Stages of Death and Loss

Death and dying have become topics of widespread discussion among psychologists, psychiatrists, physicians, sociologists, ministers, and researchers. Whereas these topics were once taboo for many people, they are now the focus of seminars, courses, and workshops, and a number of books give evidence of this growing interest.

Dr. Elisabeth Kübler-Ross is a pioneer in the contemporary study of death and dying. In her widely read books *On Death and Dying* (1969) and *Death: The Final Stage of Growth* (1975), she discusses the psychological and sociological aspects of death and the experience of dying. In a more recent book, *AIDS: The Ultimate Challenge,* Kübler-Ross (1993) applies the stages of dying to people with AIDS. Thanks to her efforts, many people have become aware of the almost universal need the dying have to talk about their impending death and to complete their business with the important people in their lives. She has shown how ignorance of the dying process and of the needs of dying people — as well as the fears of those around them — can rob the dying of the opportunity to fully experience their feelings and arrive at a resolution of them.

A greater understanding of dying can help us come to an acceptance of death, as well as be more helpful and present to those who are dying. For this reason, we describe the five stages of dying that Kübler-Ross has delineated, based on her research with terminally ill cancer patients. She emphasizes that these are not neat and compartmentalized stages that every person passes through in an orderly fashion. At times a person may experience a combination of these stages, perhaps skip one or more stages, or go back to an earlier stage he or she has already experienced. In general, however, Kübler-Ross found this sequence: denial, anger, bargaining, depression, and acceptance.

To make this discussion of the stages of dying more concrete, we will examine these stages as they relate to Ann, a 30-year-old cancer patient. Ann was married and the mother of three children in elementary school. Before she discovered that she had terminal cancer, she felt she had much to live for, and she enjoyed life.

■ Denial

Ann's first reaction to being told she had only about a year to live was shock. She refused to believe that the diagnosis was correct. Even after obtaining several other medical opinions, she still refused to accept that she was dying. In other words, her initial reaction was one of *denial.*

Even though Ann was attempting to deny the full impact of the reality, it would have been a mistake to assume that she didn't want to talk about her feelings. Her husband also denied her illness and was unwilling to talk to her about it. He felt that talking bluntly might only make her more depressed and lead her to lose all hope. He failed to recognize how important it would have been to Ann to feel that she *could* bring up the subject if she wished. On some level she knew that she could not talk about her death with her husband.

During the stage of denial, the attitudes of a dying person's family and friends are critical. If these people cannot face the fact of their loved one's dying, they cannot help him or her move toward an acceptance of death. Their own fear will blind them to signs that the dying person wants to talk about his or her death and needs support. In the case of Ann it would not necessarily have been a wise idea to force her to talk, but she could have been greatly helped if those around her had been available and sensitive to her when she stopped denying her death and showed a need to be listened to.

■ Anger

As Ann began to accept that her time was limited by an incurable disease, her denial was replaced by anger. Over and over she wondered why *she*—who had so much to live for—had to be afflicted with this dreadful disease. Her anger mounted as she thought of her children and realized that she would not be able to see them grow and develop. During her frequent visits to the hospital for radiation treatments, she directed some of her anger toward doctors "who didn't seem to know what they were doing," and toward the "impersonal" nurses.

During the stage of anger it's important that others recognize the need of dying people to express their anger, whether they direct it toward their doctors, the hospital staff, their friends, their children, or God. If this displaced anger is taken personally, any meaningful dialogue with the dying will be cut off. Moreover, people like Ann have reason to be enraged over having to suffer in this way when they have so much to live for. Rather than withdrawing support or taking offense, the people who surround a dying person can help most by allowing the person to fully express the pent-up rage inside. In this way they help the person to ultimately come to terms with his or her death.

■ Bargaining

Kübler-Ross (1969) sums up the essence of the bargaining stage as follows: "If God has decided to take us from this earth and he did not respond to any angry pleas, he may be more favorable if I ask nicely" (p. 72). Basically, the stage of bargaining is an attempt to postpone the inevitable end.

Ann's ambitions at this stage were to finish her college studies and graduate with her bachelor's degree, which she was close to obtaining. She also hoped to see her oldest daughter begin junior high school in a little over a year. During this time she tried any type of treatment that offered some hope of extending her life.

■ Depression

Eventually Ann's bargaining time ran out. No possibility of remission of her cancer remained, and she could no longer deny the inevitability of her death. Having been subjected to radiation treatments, chemotherapy, and a series of operations, she was becoming weaker and thinner, and she was able to do less and less. Her primary feelings became a great sense of loss and a fear of the unknown. She wondered about who would take care of her children and about her husband's future. She felt guilty because she was demanding so much attention and time and because the treatment of her illness was depleting the family income. She felt depressed over losing her hair and her beauty.

It would not have been helpful at this stage to try to cheer Ann up or to deny her real situation. Just as it had been important to allow her to fully vent her anger, it was important now to let her talk about her feelings and to make her final plans. Dying people are about to lose everyone they love, and only the freedom to grieve over these losses will enable them to find some peace and serenity in a final acceptance of death.

■ Acceptance

Kübler-Ross found that if patients have had enough time and support to work through the previous stages, most of them reach a stage at which they are neither depressed nor angry. Because they have expressed their anger and mourning the impending loss of those they love, they are able to become more accepting of their death. Kübler-Ross (1969) comments: "Acceptance should not be mistaken for a happy stage. It is almost devoid of feelings. It is as if the pain has gone, the struggle is over, and there comes a time for 'the final rest before the long journey,' as one patient phrased it" (p. 100).

Of course, some people never achieve an acceptance of their death, and some have no desire to. Ann, for example, never truly reached a stage of acceptance. Her final attitude was more one of surrender, a realization that it was futile to fight any longer. Although she still felt unready to die, she did want an end to her suffering. It may be that if those close to her had been more open to her and accepting of her feelings, she would have been able to work through more of her anger and depression.

■ The Significance of Kübler-Ross's Stages

Kübler-Ross's description of the dying process is not meant to be rigid and should not be interpreted as a natural progression that is expected in most cases. Just as people are unique in the way they live, they are unique in the way they die. It is a mistake to use these stages as the standard by which to judge whether a dying person's behavior is normal or right. The value of the stages is that they describe and summarize in a general way what many patients experience and therefore add to our understanding of dying. Sometimes practitioners who work with the terminally ill forget that the stages of dying do not progress neatly, even though they cognitively know this reality. One practitioner told us: "Although I had read Kübler-Ross's book and knew the stages that a dying person was supposed to go through, many of my terminal patients had not read the same book!"

Patients who do not make it to the acceptance stage are sometimes viewed as failures. For example, some nurses get angry at patients who take "backward" steps by going from depression to anger, or they question patients about why they have "stayed so long in the anger stage." People die in a variety of ways and have a variety of feelings during this process: hope, anger, depression, fear, envy, relief, and anticipation. Those who are dying move back and forth from mood to mood. Therefore, these stages should not be used as a method of categorizing, and thus dehumanizing, the dying; they are best used as a frame of reference for helping them.

■ The Hospice Movement

There is a trend toward more direct involvement of family members in caring for a dying person. An example of this is the hospice program. The term *hospice* was originally used to describe a waiting place for travelers during the Middle Ages. Later, hospices were established for children without parents, the incurably ill, and the elderly. It was during the 19th century that a Catholic religious order began developing hospices for dying persons (Kalish, 1985). In recent years hospices have spread rapidly through Europe and North America.

The hospice movement came about in response to what many people perceived to be inadequate care for the dying in conventional hospitals. In recent years hospice programs have become a part of some of these hospitals. The hospice movement also gives permission to those who are losing a significant person to feel the full range of emotions during the bereavement process. Hospice centers typi-

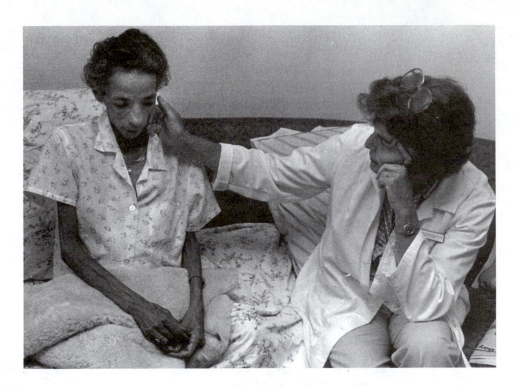

cally offer a variety of counseling services for those who survive the death of a loved one. Many of these survivors need the reassurance that they are not "going crazy," even though they may believe that they are.

According to Kalish (1985), the recent hospice movement has changed the attitude toward a dying person from "There is nothing more that we can do to help" to "We need to do what we can to provide the most humane care." This involves viewing patients and their family members as a unit. Caregivers do not separate the person who is dying from his or her family. Whenever possible, patients are kept at home as long as they wish. Both volunteers and a trained staff provide health-care aid, including helping the patient and the family members deal with psychological and social stresses. Hospices aim to provide services that help dying patients experience a sense of self-worth and dignity and to provide support for the family members so that they can prepare for the eventual separation. Although research on these programs is preliminary, hospice patients are more mobile and tend to report less general anxiety and fewer bodily symptoms than those being given traditional care. The spouse is able to spend more time in visiting and caring for the patient (Kalish, 1985).

Although a hospice is a humanitarian way of helping people die with dignity, hospice facilities are not always welcomed in the community. For example, in one neighborhood intense objections were raised to a hospice house for people dying of AIDS. Some of the residents had concerns about their property values falling, and others had reactions to bringing people who were afflicted with AIDS into their community.

Grieving over Death, Separation, and Other Losses

In a way that is similar to the stages of dying, people go through stages of grief in working through death and various other losses. *Grief work* refers to the exploration of feelings of sorrow, anger, and guilt over the experience of a significant loss. This process is often not an easy or simple one. Some people are never able to accept the death of a child or a spouse. They may get stuck by denying their feelings and by not facing and working through their pain over the loss. At some point in the grief process, people may feel numb or that they are functioning on automatic pilot. Once this numbness wears off, almost like novocaine, the pain seems to intensify. People who are going through this pain need to learn that they might well get worse before they feel better.

To put to rest unresolved issues and unexpressed feelings, we need to express our anger, regrets, guilts, and frustrations. When we attempt to deny pain, we inevitably wind up being stuck and are unable to express a range of feelings. This unexpressed pain tends to eat away at people both physically and psychologically and prevents them from accepting the reality of the death of a loved one. We are reminded of a woman who reported that she was overcome with emotions and could not stop crying at the funeral of an acquaintance. What surprised her was the way her reaction contrasted with her "strength and composure" over the death of her husband. What she didn't realize was that she had not allowed herself to grieve over the loss of her husband and that years later she was having a delayed grief reaction.

■ Allowing Yourself to Grieve

Grief is a necessary and natural process after a significant loss. However, there are forces in many cultures that make it very difficult for people to experience a complete grief process after they have suffered a loss. For example, in American society, there appears to be a cultural norm that fosters an expectation of a "quick cure," and oftentimes others cannot understand why it is taking "such a long time" for a grieving person to "get back to normal." As is the case with any emotion that does not get expressed, unresolved grief lingers in the background and prevents people from letting go of losses and from forming new relationships. Also, unresolved grief is considered a key factor in the onset of a variety of physical illnesses. Siegel (1988, 1989, 1993) cites numerous examples of people who developed cancer after a significant loss through death or divorce.

Most writers on the psychological aspects of death and loss agree that grieving is necessary. A common denominator of all these theories is that there is a general process of moving from a stage of depression to recovery. Although people may successfully work through their feelings pertaining to loss, it can be expected that the loss may always be with them. In successful grieving, however, people are not immobilized by the loss, nor do they close themselves off from other involvements. Another commonality in all these theories is that they recognize that not all people go through the grieving process at the same rate, nor do all people move neatly and predictably from one stage to another.

A chronic state of depression and a restricted range of feelings suffered by some people are often attributed to some unresolved reaction to a significant loss. Such individuals fear that the pain will consume them and that it is better to shut off their feelings. What they fail to realize is that they pay a price for this denial in the long run. This price involves excluding feelings of closeness and joy. At times these people can go on for years without ever expressing emotions over their loss, being convinced that they have adequately dealt with it. Yet they might find themselves being flooded with emotions for which they have no explanation. They may discover that another's loss opens up old wounds that they thought were successfully healed.

My [Marianne] father died six years ago. Although I grieved his death and found support from my friends and family, I find that even years later there are times when I am flooded with emotions of sadness over his loss. Sometimes these emotions take me by surprise, and I don't always know what triggered them. On several occasions when I felt the sadness I realized afterward that it was a particular anniversary date that had to do with his life and death. My unconscious was more in tune than was my conscious. Sometimes people who have lost a loved one expect to complete their grieving in a set time, such as one year. It is important to realize that there is no predictable schedule. Instead, people who are grieving need to experience their sadness and not tell themselves that they should be over this by now.

You might experience grief over many types of losses besides a death, such as the breakup of a relationship, the loss of a career, or the children leaving home. In learning to resolve grief, regardless of its source, people need to be able to talk about what they are telling themselves internally and what they are feeling. They typically need to express their feelings over the lack of fairness about their situation. They may eventually face up to the fact that there is no rational reason that will explain their loss.

If people who are experiencing a bereavement process are able to express the full range of their thoughts and feelings, they stand a better chance of adjusting to a new environment. Indeed, part of the grief process involves making basic life changes and experiencing new growth. If they have gone through the necessary cycle of bereavement, they are better equipped to become reinvested with a new purpose and a new reason for living.

What major losses have you had, and how have you coped with them? Have you lost a family member, a close friendship, a job that you valued, a spouse through divorce, a material object that had special meaning, a place where you once lived, a pet, or your faith in some person or group? Are there any similarities in how you responded to these different types of loss? Did you successfully work through your feelings about the losses? Or did you allow yourself to express your feelings to someone close to you? In recalling a particular loss, are the feelings still as intense as they were then?

A Young Woman's Denial of Grief.   Kelly is a 19-year-old community college student who recently enrolled in a course on death and dying. She let her instructor know privately that the course was touching her emotionally and confronting her with facing the death of her father five years before. She told him that when her father died in an airplane crash, she simply refused to believe that he was actually dead. Kelly convinced herself that he had gone away on a long vacation and would someday return to her. Very few tears were shared in the family, his name was rarely mentioned, no reminiscing was done by any of the family members, and none of them visited his grave. With her peers Kelly never acknowledged her father's death. Only a few close friends knew that she was without a father.

Kelly describes herself as never feeling extremely happy or very sad. She envies people whom she sees as spontaneous, joyous and, as she puts it, "really able to laugh." Since she began the class on death and dying, she has surprised herself with occasional crying spells, and she notices that she is often angry at the slightest provocation. She gave her instructor some poetry that she had recently written pertaining to how much she was missing her father. She has a desire to go and visit his grave but says that she is afraid of doing so. Kelly is just now, years after her father's death, beginning to allow herself to grieve over her loss. As she permits herself to feel pain, she will also be able to experience more joy in her life.

A Young Man's Acceptance of Grief.   Tony, who is 17 years old, told Marianne about the sudden death of his 57-year-old grandfather from a heart attack. He talked a lot about the kind of man his grandfather was and said he regretted not having had more contact. He is experiencing much sadness over his recent loss. It was interesting to hear his description of and reaction to his grandfather's funeral. Because his grandfather was well known, a surprisingly large crowd attended the funeral. Many people eulogized and spoke about the man. As Tony put it, there were many tears, and it was extremely difficult for him to witness all this emotionality. He asserts that when he dies, he does not want a funeral, because he wants to avoid putting people in such a painful position. What he does not realize is that although it is indeed difficult for him to feel his own pain and observe the pain of others, it is this very process that will enable him to deal more effectively with the loss of his grandfather. Even though Tony reacted negatively to the funeral, unlike Kelly he is not denying his feelings of grief over his loss.

Most cultures have rituals designed to help people with this grieving process. Examples are the funeral practices of the Irish, the Jewish, the Russians, and others, whereby painful feelings are actually triggered and released. Many cultures have a formal mourning period (usually a year). In these cultures an obvious pattern is the direct involvement of people in the funeral process.

In the American culture those who suffer from a loss are typically "protected" from any direct involvement in the burial. People are praised for not displaying overt signs of grief. Many of our rituals make it easy for us to deny our feelings of loss and therefore keep us from coming to terms with the reality of that loss. It has become clear that these practices are not genuinely helpful. Today, more emphasis is placed on providing ways for people to participate more directly in the dying process of their loved ones (such as the hospice movement) and the funeral process as well.

How My Family Dealt with a Death.   Earlier I (Jerry) wrote about Jim Morelock's dying. Let me share some of the stages our family went through in dealing with Jim's loss. When Jim first told me that his cancer was terminal, it was difficult for me to believe. I had thoughts that somehow he would win the battle. It was hard for me to understand why he would have to die, since he had so much to live for and to offer others. Although at times I was able to accept the reality of his impending death, at other times I would ask "Why him?" Together we talked about his dying, even though that was difficult. I took the opportunity to say good-bye to him.

At a memorial service many of Jim's friends recounted special times we had had with him. About a year later some close friends of his came to our home, and we planted an apple tree in his memory. We again reminisced and shared the ways we were missing him. As the years go by, the pain over his death becomes less intense. I find I bring him to my awareness in certain situations. He has now been dead for 19 years, yet his memory is still with me.

Our daughters developed a very special relationship with Jim over the years, seeing him as their big brother. During some visits he was very frank with them about his cancer, including telling them he might die. As he put it to them after one of his operations, "Well, I've won this battle, but that doesn't mean I've won the war yet." Cindy and Heidi were 9 and 10 at the time he was dying. They coped with his condition by talking to him, to us, to his mother, and to each other. Cindy wrote a detailed story with an unhappy ending. Heidi dreamed that she had "magic" ice cream that could cure anything. When she told us about her dream, she sadly added, "But there isn't any magic, is there?" Every doll that they had was operated on for cancer. These were the symbolic and direct ways in which our daughters dealt with the dying of a special friend. As parents we made ourselves available to them by listening to them and supporting them, yet we did not offer them false hope.

We still remember Jim and talk about him when we get together with people who knew him. We maintain contact with his mother and with some mutual friends. We share memories and recount some of the lessons each of us learned about living and dying through our contact with Jim. Marianne played an important role in being with Jim during the time he was dying. Jim taught her many lessons about how to relate to a dying person, which was of great value to her as she helped her father go through his dying. One key lesson was the importance of helping dying people retain a sense of dignity in the face of their losses. Another lesson pertained to listening to what the dying person is communicating, both verbally and nonverbally. Marianne also learned how essential it is to encourage the dying person to talk and to complete any unfinished business. Although dying is not easy, for the person dying or those who are assisting in this process, it is crucial that all concerned feel the freedom to talk about what they are experiencing.

■ Stages of Grief over a Divorce or a Significant Loss

The five stages of dying described by Kübler-Ross seem to have application to the severing of relationships and other significant losses, experiences that bear some similarity to dying. To illustrate, we describe a divorce in terms of the five stages. Of course, you can broaden this concept to see whether it applies to separation from your parents, the experience of breaking up with a girlfriend or boyfriend, or the process of seeing your children mature and leave home. The stages can also provide understanding of the process you go through after losing a job and facing the anxieties of unemployment. Although not all people who experience divorce, the breakup of a long-term relationship, or some other loss necessarily go through the stages in the same way, we've found that many people do experience a similar questioning and struggling.

Denial.   Many people who are divorcing go through a process of denial and self-deception. They may try to convince themselves that the state of their marriage isn't all that bad, that nobody is perfect, and that things would be worse if they did separate. Even after the decision is made to divorce, they may feel a sense of disbelief. If it was the other person who initiated the divorce, the remaining partner might ask: "Where did things go wrong? Why is she [he] doing this to me? How can this be happening to me?"

Anger.   Once people accept the reality that they are divorcing, they frequently experience anger and rage. They may say: "I gave a lot, and now I'm being deserted. I feel as if I've been used and then thrown away." Many people feel cheated and angry over the apparent injustice of what is happening to them. Just as it is very important for dying people to express any anger they feel, it's also important for people who are going through the grief associated with a divorce or other loss to express their anger. If they keep it bottled up inside, it is likely to be turned against them and may take the form of depression, a kind of self-punishment.

Bargaining.   Sometimes people hope that a separation will give them the distance they need to reevaluate things and that they will soon get back together again. Although separations sometimes work this way, it is often futile to wish that matters can be worked out. Nevertheless, during the bargaining stage one or both partners may try to make concessions and compromises that they hope will lead to a reconciliation.

Depression.   In the aftermath of a decision to divorce, a sense of hopelessness may set in. As the partners realize that a reconciliation isn't possible, they may begin to dwell on the emptiness and loss they feel. They may find it very difficult to let go of the future they had envisioned together. They may spend much time ruminating over what their lives might have been like if they had made their relationship work. It is not uncommon for people who divorce to turn their anger away from their spouse and toward themselves. Thus, they may experience much self-blame and self-doubt. They may say to themselves: "Maybe I didn't give our relationship a fair chance. What could I have done differently? I wonder where I went wrong? Why couldn't I do something different to make our relationship work?" Depression can also be the result of the recognition that a real loss has been sustained. It is vitally important that people fully experience and express the grief (and anger) they feel over their loss. Too often people deceive themselves into believing that they are finished with their sadness (or anger) long before they have given vent to their intense feelings. Unresolved grief (and anger) tends to be carried around with a person, blocking the expression of many other feelings. For instance, if grief isn't worked through, it may be extremely difficult for a person to form new relationships, because in some ways he or she is still holding on to the past relationship.

Acceptance.   If people allow themselves to mourn their losses, the process of grief work usually leads to a stage of acceptance. In the case of divorce, once the two persons have finished their grieving, new possibilities begin to open up. They can begin to accept that they must make a life for themselves without the other person and that they cannot cling to resentments that will keep them from beginning to establish that life. They can learn from their experience and apply that knowledge to future events.

In summary, these stages are experienced in different ways by each person who faces a significant loss. Some people, for example, express very little anger; others may not go through a bargaining stage. Nevertheless, the value of a model such as this one is that it provides some understanding of how we can learn to cope with the various losses in our lives. Whatever the loss may be and whatever stage of grieving we may be experiencing, it seems to be crucial that we freely express our feelings. Otherwise, we may not be able to achieve acceptance.

Being "Dead" Psychologically and Socially

We find it valuable to broaden the conception of death and dying to include being "dead" in a variety of psychological and social ways. What is dead or dying in us may be something we want to resurrect, or it may be something that *should* die to make way for new growth.

Brugh Joy (1979, 1990) believes that most of us live a highly restricted life, which means that many aspects of our being lie dormant. His workshops and books are designed to tilt people from their narrow vision of reality to a set of possibilities that is truly without limits. He writes about people who are ready to open themselves to an awakening process that allows them to be fully alive across the range of human experience. Such individuals "know at the deepest level of their awareness that they are ready for change from unfulfilling, culturally conditioned life patterns into states of consciousness that commit them to a path of self-realization . . . [and] are beginning to become aware that their intimate limitations are nothing but the restrictions set by their own minds" (1979, p. 9).

Sometimes growth requires that we be willing to let go of old and familiar ways of being, and we may need to mourn their loss before we can really move on. You may have experienced a letting go of the security of living with your parents, for example, in exchange for testing your independence by living alone and supporting yourself. In the process you may have lost something that was valuable to you, even if it was incompatible with your further development and growth. The following questions may help you to decide whether you're living as fully as you'd like to be.

■ Are You Caught Up in Deadening Roles?

Our roles and functions can eventually trap us. Instead of fulfilling certain roles while maintaining a separate sense of identity, we may get lost in our roles and in the patterns of thought, feeling, and behavior that go with them. As a result, we may neglect important parts of ourselves, limiting our options of feeling and experiencing. Moreover, we may feel lost when we're unable to play a certain role: a supervisor may not know how to behave when he or she isn't in a superior position to others, an instructor may be at loose ends when there are no students to teach, or a parent may find life empty when the children have grown.

Do you feel caught in certain roles? Do you depend on being able to identify with those roles to feel alive and valuable? Have you made the mistake of believing that who you are is expressed by a single role, no matter how much you value that role? Who and what would you be if your roles were stripped away one by one? Are you able to renew yourself by finding innovative ways of being and thinking? At this time in your life you might find that you're so caught up in the student role that you have little time or energy left for other parts of your life. When our roles begin to deaden us, we can ask whether we've taken on a function or identity that others have defined instead of listening to our own inner promptings.

■ Are You Alive to Your Senses and Your Body?

Your body expresses to a large degree how alive you are. It shows signs of your vitality or reveals your tiredness with life. Since your body doesn't lie, you can use it as an indication of the degree to which you're affirming life. As you look at your body, ask yourself: "Do I like what I see? Am I taking good care of myself physically, or am I indifferent to my own bodily well-being? What am I expressing by my posture? What does my facial expression communicate?"

You can also become deadened to the input from your senses. You may become oblivious to fragrances or eat foods without tasting or savoring them. Perhaps you rarely stop to notice the details of your surroundings. By contrast, taking time to be

alive to your senses can help you feel renewed and interested in life. You might ask yourself: "What sensations have particularly struck me today? What have I experienced and observed? What sensory surprises have enlivened me?"

■ Can You Be Spontaneous and Playful?

Can you be playful, fun, curious, explorative, spontaneous, silly? As an adult, it is likely that you take yourself too seriously at times and lose the ability to laugh at yourself. Siegel (1988) emphasizes the value of laughter, play, and humor in healing and staying healthy. Humor shakes us out of our patterned ways and promotes new perspectives. In his therapy groups for cancer patients, Siegel helps them release the child within, for those who cannot play and laugh are the ones who experience the most difficulty in healing. If you find that you're typically realistic and objective to the point that it's difficult for you to be playful or light, you might ask what inner messages are blocking your ability to let go. Are you inhibited by a fear of being wrong? Are you afraid of being called silly or of meeting with others' disapproval? If you want to, you can begin to challenge the messages that say: "Don't!" "You should!" "You shouldn't!" You can experiment with new behavior and run the risk of seeming silly or of "not acting your age."

■ Are You Alive to Your Feelings?

We can deaden ourselves to most of our feelings — the joyful ones as well as the painful ones. We can decide that feeling involves the risk of pain and that it's best to *think* our way through life. In choosing to cut off feelings of depression or sadness, we will most likely cut off feelings of joy. Closing ourselves to our lows usually means closing ourselves to our highs as well.

Because of the ways we sometimes insulate ourselves, we may find it difficult to recognize our flat emotional state. To begin assessing how alive you are emotionally, you might ask yourself:

- Do I let myself feel my sadness and grieve over a loss?
- Do I try hard to cheer people up when they're sad or depressed, instead of allowing them to experience their feelings?
- Do I let myself cry if I feel like crying?
- Do I ever feel ecstasy and true joy?
- Do I let myself feel close to another person?
- Do I suppress certain emotions? Do I hide my feelings of insecurity, fear, dependence, tenderness, anger, boredom?
- Do I keep myself from showing my feelings out of fear?

■ Are Your Relationships Alive?

Our relationships with the significant people in our lives have a way of becoming stale and deadening. It's easy to get stuck in habitual and routine ways of being with another person and to lose any sense of surprise and spontaneity. This kind of staleness is particularly common in long-term relationships. Of course, breaking out of predictable patterns in relationships can be fraught with anxiety. We have to decide whether we want security of vitality in our relationships. As you look at the significant relationships in your life, think about how alive both you and the other person in each relationship feel with each other. Do you give each other enough space to grow? Does the relationship energize you, or does it sap you of life? Are you settling into a comfortable, undemanding relationship? If you recognize that you aren't getting what you want in your friendships or intimate relationships, ask what *you* can do to revitalize them. Focus on how you can change yourself rather than getting others to change. You can also consider what specific things you'd like to ask from the other person. Simply talking about relationships can do a lot to bring new life into them.

■ Are You Alive Intellectually?

Children typically display much curiosity about life, yet somehow they lose this interest in figuring out problems as they grow older. By the time we reach adulthood, we can easily become caught up in our activities, devoting little time to considering *why* we're doing them and whether we even *want* to be doing them. It's also easy to allow our intellectual potential to shrivel up, either by limiting our exposure or by failing to follow our curiosity.

Take time to reassess the degree to which you keep yourself intellectually active in your classes. In the initial chapter we focused on ways to integrate mental and emotional dimensions of learning. One way of keeping mentally alert is by reflecting on how you can apply whatever you are learning in your classes to your personal development. How might you apply the notion of staying intellectually alive as a student? Have you given up on asking any real and substantive questions that you'd like to explore? Have you settled for merely going to classes and collecting the units you need to obtain a degree? Are you indifferent to learning? Are you open to learning new things? Are you changing as a learner?

■ Are You Alive Spiritually?

As a healer, Bernie Siegel (1988) views spirituality as encompassing the belief in some meaning or order in the universe. From his perspective, there is a loving and intelligent force behind creation. Regardless of what label is used for this force, contact with it allows us the possibility of finding peace and resolving seeming contradictions between the inner world and the outer. Siegel claims that spirituality means accepting what is.

> Spirituality means the ability to find peace and happiness in an imperfect world, and to feel that one's own personality is imperfect but acceptable. From the peaceful state of mind come both creativity and the ability to love unselfishly, which go hand in hand. Acceptance, faith, forgiveness, peace, and love are the traits that define spirituality for me. These characteristics always appear in those who achieve unexpected healing of serious illness. (p. 178)

How do you define spirituality for yourself? How do your spiritual beliefs give your life meaning and value? To what extent does spirituality play a role in your life now?

Siegel (1988) talks about "spiritual flat tires," referring to unexpected events that can have positive or negative outcomes, depending on how we respond to these situations. As a healer, Siegel has made it his mission to teach people about the inseparable link between mind and body. He finds that people who survive catastrophic illnesses use occasional spiritual flat tires to get refocused and to redirect their lives. Although they may have delays and redirections on the path of life, they don't experience such events as fatal mistakes. Siegel puts the matter of spiritual vitality poetically:

> My advice is to live your life. Allow that wonderful inner intelligence to speak through you. The blueprint for you to be your authentic self lies within. In some

mystical way the microscopic egg that grew to be you had the program for your physical, intellectual, emotional, and spiritual development. Allow the development to occur to its fullest; grow and bloom. Follow your bliss and be what you want to be. Don't climb the ladder of success only to find it's leaning against the wrong wall. Do not let your age limit your future growth as a human being. (p. xii)

► *Time Out for Personal Reflection*

1. How alive do you feel psychologically and socially? Check any of the following statements that apply to you.

_____ I feel alive and energetic most of the time.
_____ My body expresses aliveness and vitality.
_____ I feel intellectually curious and alive.
_____ I have significant friendships that are a source of nourishment for me.
_____ I can play and have fun.
_____ I allow myself to feel a wide range of emotions.
_____ I'm keenly aware of the things I see, smell, taste, and touch.
_____ I feel free to express who I am; I'm not trapped by my roles.

2. When do you feel most alive?

_____

_____

_____

_____

3. When do you feel least alive?

_____

_____

_____

_____

4. What specific things would you most like to change about your life so that you could feel more alive? What can you do to make these changes?

_____

_____

_____

_____

Taking Stock: How Well Are You Living Life?

It seems tragic that some people never really take the time to evaluate how well they are living life. Imagine for a moment that you're one of those people who get caught up in the routine of daily existence and never assess the quality of your living. Now assume that you are told that you have only a limited time to live. You begin to look at what you've missed and how you wish things had been different; you begin to experience regrets over the opportunities that you let slip by; you review the significant turning points in your life. You may wish now that you had paused to take stock at many points in your life, instead of waiting until it was too late.

One way to take stock of your life is to imagine your own death, including the details of the funeral and the things people might say about you. As an extension of this exercise, you might try actually writing down your own eulogy or obituary. This can be a powerful way of summing up how you see your life and how you'd like it to be different. In fact, we suggest that you try writing three eulogies for yourself. First, write your *actual* eulogy — the one you would give at your own funeral, if that were possible. Second, write the eulogy that you *fear* — one that expresses some of the negative things someone could say of you. Third, write the eulogy that you would *hope* for — one that expresses the most positive aspects of your life so far. After you've written your three eulogies, seal them in an envelope and put them away for a year or so. Then do the exercise again and compare the two sets of eulogies to see what changes have occurred in your view of your life.

Postscript: Taking Time

Before he died on August 10, 1977, Jim Morelock gave me (Jerry) a poster showing a man walking in the forest with two small girls. At the top of the poster were the words "Take Time." Jim knew me well enough to know how I tend to get caught up in so many activities that I sometimes forget to simply take time to really experience and enjoy the simple things in life. As I write this, I'm also remembering what one student wrote to me as we were writing what we hoped and wished for each person in the class. On one of my slips of paper was written, "I hope you will take the time to smell a rose." In another class one student gave each person an epitaph. Mine read: "Here lies Jerry Corey — a man who all his life tried to do too many things at once." I promised myself that I'd make a poster with those words on it and place it on my office wall as a reminder to slow down and enjoy life. I think many of us could use reminders like these frequently — especially since it took me almost a semester to get around to putting that poster up! In closing this chapter, the simple message is *take time.*

I wrote the preceding paragraph for the first edition of this book. Now, 19 years later, am I taking time to do fewer things at once and to enjoy life? Although I have been a slow learner in this respect, I am learning the value of taking time for what is important. I continue to reassess priorities and decide on what I want besides accomplishments. I am seeing that there is a whole other dimension besides the concrete, rational, and logical world I have been so comfortable in most of my life. Just now, at age 58, I am beginning to appreciate the ways life can continue to teach me important lessons if I pay attention. I have begun to look at the things I say and the things I do to determine if I am living in accordance with my nature. Still I do not find it easy to balance my work and leisure, nor have I discovered a way to do all the things that I say are important to me. To some extent, I am designing ways to keep my work projects in check. A part of me knows that there is more to life than I've allowed myself to sample, yet another part of me resists opening myself to untapped inner and outer resources.

Although Marianne and I work together in writing and doing workshops, I value spending personal time with her alone, as well as with our family and friends. Because I value my health and enjoy biking and hiking, I *make* time for these activities, even though it means working less. Although I still have some trouble taking as much time as I would like for fun, play, and relaxation, I have improved in this respect in the last five years. Yet I become anxious as I experience the weeks, months, and years passing too quickly. In the past few years I have been asking myself more often, "Is what I am doing now what I *really* want to be doing?" And before I accept a work project, I am lingering a bit longer and asking myself, "Do I want to accept this project, and what will I have to give up to make time for this new project?" It is getting easier to graciously turn down invitations that entail more work. I have begun to look at my behavior and evaluate the extent to which I am living in accordance with my priorities and by conscious choices. I am also learning how to appreciate the value of making time for quiet reflection, internal focusing, and getting centered, all of which are key in learning to listen to the wisdom within my inner being.

Chapter Summary

In this chapter we've encouraged you to devote some time to reflecting on your eventual death. Doing so can lead you to examine the quality and direction of your life and help you find your own meaning in living. The acceptance of death is closely related to the acceptance of life. Recognizing and accepting the fact of death gives us the impetus to search for our own answers to questions such as: "What is the meaning of my life?" "What do I most want from life?" "How can I create the life I want to live?" In addition, we've encouraged you to assess how fully alive you are right now.

Although terminally ill people show great variability in how they deal with their dying, a general pattern of stages has been identified: denial, anger, bargaining, depression, and acceptance. These same stages can apply to other types of loss, such as separation and divorce. People go through stages of grief in working through their losses. Grieving is necessary if we are to recover from any significant loss. Unless we express and explore feelings of sorrow, anger, and guilt over our losses, we are likely to remain stuck in depression and a feeling of numbness.

If we can honestly confront our fears of death, we have a chance to work on changing the quality of our lives and to make real changes in our relationships with others and with ourselves. We often live as though we had forever to accomplish what we want. Few of us ever contemplate that this may be the last day we have. The realization that there is an end to life can motivate us to get the most from the time we have. The fact of our finality can also be an impetus to take care of unfinished business. Thus, it is crucial that we live in a manner that will lead to few regrets. The more we fail to deal with immediate realities, the greater the likelihood that we will fear death.

Activities and Exercises

1. For at least a week take a few minutes each day to reflect on when you feel alive and when you feel "dead." Do you notice any trends in your observations? What can you do to feel more alive?
2. If you knew you were going to die within a short time, in what ways would you live your life differently? What might you give up? What might you be doing that you're not doing or experiencing now?
3. Imagine yourself on your deathbed. Write down whom you want to be there, what you want them to say to you, and what you want to say to them. Then write down your reactions to this experience.
4. For about a week write down specific things you see, read, or hear relating to the denial or avoidance of death in our culture.
5. Let yourself reflect on how the death of those you love might affect you. Consider each person separately, and try to imagine how your life today would be different if that person were not in it. In your journal you might respond to such questions as: Do I now have the relationships with my loved ones that I want to have? What's missing? What changes do I most want to make in my relationships?
6. Consider making some time alone in which to write three eulogies for yourself: one that you think *actually* sums up your life, one that you *fear* could be written about you, and one that you *hope* could be written about you. Write the eulogies as if you had died today; then seal them in an envelope, and do the exercise again in the future — say, in about a year. At that time you can compare your

eulogies to see in what respects your assessment of your life and your hopes and fears have changed.

7. After you've written your three eulogies, you might write down in your journal what the experience was like for you and what you learned from it. Are there any specific steps you'd like to take *now* to begin living more fully?

8. Investigate what type of hospice program, if any, your community has. Who is on the staff? What services does it offer? For a description of hospice programs in various communities, you can write to the National Hospice Organization, 765 Prospect Street, New Haven, CT 06511.

9. Select one or more of the following books for further reading on the topics explored in this chapter: *Death, Dying, and Bereavement* (Dickenson & Johnson, 1993); *On Death and Dying* (Kübler-Ross, 1969); *AIDS: The Ultimate Challenge* (Kübler-Ross, 1993); *Love, Medicine, and Miracles* (Siegel, 1988); *Peace, Love, and Healing* (Siegel, 1989).

13 Meaning and Values

*We need to develop the
ability to listen to our
inner selves and trust
what we hear.*

✔ *Prechapter Self-Inventory*

Use the following scale to respond: 4 = this statement is true of me *most* of the time; 3 = this statement is true of me *much* of the time; 2 = this statement is true of me *some* of the time; 1 = this statement is true of me *almost none* of the time.

_____ 1. At this time in my life I have a sense of meaning and purpose that gives me direction.

_____ 2. Most of my values are similar to those of my parents.

_____ 3. I have challenged and questioned most of the values I now hold.

_____ 4. Religion is an important source of meaning for me.

_____ 5. I generally live by the values I hold.

_____ 6. My values and my views about life's meaning have undergone much change over the years.

_____ 7. The meaning of my life is based in large part on my ability to have a significant impact on others.

_____ 8. I let others influence my values more than I'd like to admit.

_____ 9. I am willing to reflect on my own biases and prejudices, and to challenge them.

_____ 10. I welcome diversity more than being threatened by it.

Introduction

In this chapter we encourage you to look critically at the *why* of your existence, to clarify the sources of your values, and to reflect on questions such as these: "In what direction am I moving in my life? What have I accomplished in my life up to this point? Where have I been, where am I now, and where do I want to go? What steps can I take to make the changes I have decided on?"

Many who are fortunate enough to achieve power, fame, success, and material comfort nevertheless experience a sense of emptiness. Although they may not be able to articulate what is lacking in their lives, they know that something is amiss. The astronomical number of pills and drugs consumed to allay the symptoms of this "existential vacuum" — depression and anxiety — is evidence of our failure to find values that allow us to make sense of our place in the world. In *Habits of the Heart*, Bellah and his colleagues (1985) found among the people they interviewed a growing interest in finding purpose in their lives. Although our achievements as a society are enormous, we seem to be hovering on the very brink of disaster, not only from internal conflict but also from societal incoherence. Bellah and his associates assert that the core problem with our society is that we have put our own good, as individuals and as groups, ahead of the common good.

The need for a sense of meaning is manifested by an increased interest in religion, especially among young people in college. A student told us recently that in her English class of 20 students, 4 of them had selected religion as a topic for a composition dealing with a conflict in their lives. Other signs of the search for meaning include the widespread interest in Eastern and other philosophies, the use of meditation, the number of self-help and inspirational books published each year, the experimentation with different lifestyles, and even the college courses in personal growth!

Our Search for Identity

The discovery of meaning and values is essential to our achievement of identity as individuals. The quest for identity involves a commitment to give birth to ourselves by exploring the meaning of our uniqueness and our humanity. Many people have lost their sense of self, because they try to base their identity on acquiring material goods, producing, being approved of by everyone, and getting ahead at all costs. In their attempt to be liked and accepted by everyone, they have become finely tuned to what *others* expect of them but alienated from their *own* inner desires and feelings. As Rollo May (1973) observes, they are able to *respond* but not to *choose*. Indeed, May sees inner emptiness as the chief problem in contemporary society; too many of us, he says, have become "hollow people" who have very little understanding of who we are and what we feel. He cites one person's succinct description: "I'm just a collection of mirrors, reflecting what everyone expects of me" (p. 15).

To find out who we are, we may have to let parts of us die. We may need to shed old roles and identities that no longer give us vitality. Doing so may require a period of mourning for our old selves. Most people who have struggled with shedding immature and dependent roles and assuming a more active stance toward life know that such rebirth isn't easy and that it may entail pain as well as joy.

Jourard (1971) maintains that we begin to cease living when meaning vanishes from life. Yet too often we are encouraged to believe that we have only *one* identity, *one* role, *one* way to be, and *one* purpose to fulfill in a lifetime. This way of thinking can be figuratively deadly, for when our one ground for being alive is outgrown or lost, we may begin to die psychologically instead of accepting the challenge of reinventing ourselves anew. To keep ourselves from dying spiritually, we need to allow ourselves to imagine new ways of being, to invent new goals to live for, to search for new and more fulfilling meanings, to acquire new identities, and to reinvent our relationships with others. In essence, we need to allow parts of us to die so we can experience the rebirth necessary for growth.

Achieving identity doesn't necessarily mean stubbornly clinging to a certain way of thinking or behaving. Instead, it may involve trusting ourselves enough to become open to new possibilities. Nor is an identity something we achieve for all time; rather, we need to be continually willing to reexamine our patterns and our priorities, our habits and our relationships. Above all, we need to develop the ability to listen to our inner selves and trust what we hear.

Sometimes we may decide to go against our cultural upbringing to create an identity that is congruent with our own values. This was true for Jenny, a Vietnamese woman who developed a different set of values from her mother.

There were many instances when I wanted to be alone or to take time off from work to relax. There would be an attack of accusatory statements indicating that I was selfish, that I was wasting too much time on myself, and that I wasn't devoting enough time to my family obligations. Even the way I spent my money was met with criticism, because I did not save it for a better cause like my family. I spent many hours explaining to my mother about how much it meant to me to buy myself nice things and to spend some of my time enjoying life. In the eyes of my mother and her culture, I was the selfish one. I had to understand this perspective and edit it to my own values.

Our search for identity involves asking three key existential questions, none of which have easy or definite answers: "Who am I?" "Where am I going?" "Why?"

The question "Who am I?" is never settled once and for all; it will be answered differently at different times in our lives. When old identities no longer seem to supply a meaning or give us direction, we have to reinvent ourselves or risk a deadening existence. You must decide whether to let others tell you who you are or take a stand and define yourself anew.

"Where am I going?" This issue relates to our plans for a lifetime and the means we expect to use in attaining our goals. Like the previous question, this one demands periodic review. Life goals are not set once and for all. Will you show the courage it takes to decide for yourself where you are going, or will you look for a guru to show you a new path?

Asking the question "Why?" and searching for reasons is characteristic of being human. We face a rapidly changing world in which old values give way to new ones or to none at all. Part of shaping an identity requires an active search for meaning, trying to make sense of the world in which we find ourselves.

Pause now and assess how you experience your identity at this time in your life. The following "Time Out" may help you do so.

➤ *Time Out for Personal Reflection*

1. In the space below list the things you most like to do or the activities that have the most meaning for you.

   _____

   _____

   _____

   _____

2. How often do you do or experience each of the things you've just listed?

   _____

   _____

   _____

   _____

3. Does anything prevent you from doing the things you value as frequently as you'd like? If so, what?

   _____

   _____

   _____

   _____

4. What are some specific actions you can take to increase the amount of meaningful activity in your life?

   _____

   _____

_____

_____

5. Who are you? Try completing the sentence "I am . . ." ten different ways by quickly writing down the words or phrases that immediately occur to you. Use the spaces provided below.

I am:

_____

_____

_____

_____

_____

Our Quest for Meaning and Purpose

Humans are the only creatures we know of who can reflect on their existence and, based on this capacity for self-awareness, exercise individual choice in defining their lives. With this freedom, however, comes responsibility and a degree of anxiety. If we truly accept that the meaning of our lives is largely the product of our own choosing and the emptiness of our lives the result of our failure to choose, our anxiety is increased. To avoid this anxiety, we may refuse to examine the values that govern our daily behavior or to accept that we are, to a large degree, what we have chosen to become. Instead, we may make other people or outside institutions responsible for our direction. We pay a steep price for choosing a sense of security over our own freedom — the price of denying our basic humanness.

One obstacle in the way of finding meaning is that the world itself may appear meaningless. It's easy, when we look at the absurdity of the world in which we live, to give up the struggle or to seek some authoritative source of meaning. Yet creating our own meaning is precisely our challenge and task as human beings.

Yalom (1980) cites a number of psychotherapists who agree on one major point: Many clients who enter psychotherapy do so because they lack a clear sense of meaning and purpose in life. Yalom states the crisis of meaninglessness in its most basic form: "How does a being who needs meaning find meaning in a universe that has no meaning?" (p. 423). Along with Frankl, Yalom concludes that humans require meaning to survive. To live without meaning and values provokes considerable distress, and in its most severe form may lead to the decision for suicide. Humans appear to have a need for some absolutes in the form of clear ideals to which they can aspire and guidelines by which they can direct their actions.

Viktor Frankl is a European psychiatrist who has dedicated his professional life to the study of meaning in life. The approach to therapy that he developed is known as *logotherapy,* which means "therapy through meaning" or "healing through meaning." According to Frankl (1963, 1965, 1969, 1978), what distinguishes us as humans is our search for purpose. The striving to find meaning in our lives is a primary motivational force. Humans can choose to live and even die for the sake of their ideals and values. In *Man's Search for Meaning* (1963), Frankl shows how some element of choice is always possible. Frankl notes that "everything can be taken from a man but one thing: the last of the human freedoms — to choose one's attitude in any given set of circumstances, to choose one's own way" (p. 104). Frankl is fond of pointing out the wisdom of Nietzsche's words: "He who has a *why* to live for can bear with almost any *how*" (cited in Frankl, 1963, p. 164). Drawing on his experiences in the death camp at Auschwitz, Frankl asserts that inmates who had a vision of some goal, purpose, or task in life had a much greater chance of surviving than those who had no sense of mission. We are constantly confronted with choices, and the decisions we make or fail to make influence the meaning of our lives.

This relationship between choice and meaning is dramatically illustrated by Holocaust survivors who report that although they did not choose their circumstances, they could at least choose their attitude toward their plight. Consider the example of Dr. Edith Eva Eger, a 64-year-old clinical psychologist who practices in La Jolla, California, who was interviewed about her experiences as a survivor of a Nazi concentration camp (see Glionna, 1992). At one point, Eger weighed only 40 pounds, yet she refused to engage in the cannibalism that was taking place. She said, "I chose to eat grass. And I sat on the ground, selecting one blade over the other, telling myself that even under those conditions I still had a choice — which blade of grass I would eat." Although Eger lost her family to the camps and had her back broken by one of the guards, she eventually chose to let go of her hatred. She finally came to the realization that it was her captors who were the imprisoned ones. As she put it: "If I still hated today, I would still be in prison. I would be giving Hitler and Mengele their posthumous victories. If I hated, they would still be in charge, not me." Her example supports the notion that even in the most dire situations, it is possible to give a new meaning to such circumstances by our choice of attitudes.

■ Finding Meaning by Transcending Personal Interests

Many of us find meaning by striving to make a difference in the world. We want to know that we have touched the lives of others and that somehow we have contributed to helping others live more fully. Although self-acceptance is a prerequisite for meaningful interpersonal relationships, there is a quest to go beyond self-centered interests. Ultimately, we want to establish connections with others in society, and we want to make a contribution. Bellah and his colleagues (1985) conclude that meaning in life is found through intense relationships with others, not through an exclusive and narrow pursuit of self-realization. In their interviews with many people they found a desire to move beyond the isolated self. Our common life requires more than an exclusive concern with material accumulation. These authors maintain that reconstituting the social world is required; this involves a transformation of consciousness.

The Foundations of Meaning

■ Developing a Philosophy of Life

A philosophy of life is made up of the fundamental beliefs, attitudes, and values that govern a person's behavior. You may not have thought much about your philosophy of life, but the fact that you have never explicitly defined the components of your philosophy doesn't mean you are completely without one. All of us operate on the basis of general assumptions about ourselves, others, and the world. The first step in actively developing a philosophy of life is to formulate a clearer picture of your present attitudes and beliefs.

We have all been developing an implicit philosophy of life since we first began, as children, to wonder about life and death, love and hate, joy and fear, and the nature of the universe. We probably didn't need to be taught to be curious about such questions; raising them seems to be a natural part of human development. If we were fortunate, adults took time to engage in dialogue with us, instead of discouraging us from asking questions and deadening our innate curiosity.

During the adolescent years, the process of questioning usually assumes new dimensions. Adolescents who have been allowed to question and think for themselves as children begin to get involved in a more advanced set of issues. Many of the adolescents we've encountered in classes and workshops have at one time or another struggled with these questions:

- Are the values I've believed in all these years the values I want to continue to live by?
- Where did I get my values? Are they still valid for me? Are there additional sources from which I can derive new values?
- Is there a God? What is the nature of the hereafter? What is my conception of a God? What does religion mean in my life? What kind of religion do I choose for myself? Does religion have any value for me?
- What do I base my ethical and moral decisions on? Peer-group standards? parental standards? the normative values of my society?
- What explains the inhumanity I see in the world?
- What kind of future do I want? What can I do about actively creating this kind of future?

These are only a few of the many questions adolescents think about and try to answer for themselves.

A philosophy of life is not something we arrive at once and for all during our adolescent years. Developing our own philosophy of life continues as long as we live. As long as we remain curious and open to new learning, we can revise and rebuild our conceptions of the world. Life may have a particular meaning for us during adolescence, a new meaning during adulthood, and still another meaning as we reach old age. Indeed, if we don't remain open to basic changes in our views of life, we may find it difficult to adjust to changed circumstances. You may find the following suggestions helpful as you go about formulating and reforming your own philosophy:

- Frequently create time to be alone in reflective thought.
- Consider what meaning the fact of your eventual death has for the present moment.
- Make use of significant contacts with others who are willing to challenge your beliefs and the degree to which you live by them.
- Adopt an accepting attitude toward those whose belief systems differ from yours and develop a willingness to test your own beliefs.

We strongly recommend that you take time now to look at the outline in the "Activities and Exercises" section at the end of this chapter. This outline will help you clarify some key aspects of your philosophy of life, as will the following "Time Out."

➤ *Time Out for Personal Reflection*

Complete the following sentences by writing down the first responses that come to mind:

1. My parents have influenced my values by _____

   _____

2. Life would hardly be worth living if it weren't for _____

   _____

3. One thing that I most want to say about my life at this point is _____

   _____

4. If I could change one thing about my life at this point, it would be _____

   _____

5. If I had to answer the question "Who am I?" in a sentence, I'd say _____

   _____

6. What I like best about me is _____

   _____

7. I keep myself alive and vital by _____

   _____

8. I'm unique in that _____

   _____

9. When I think of my future, I _____

_____

10. I feel discouraged about life when _____

_____

11. My friends have influenced my values by _____

_____

12. My beliefs have been influenced by _____

_____

13. I feel most powerful when _____

_____

14. If I don't change, _____

_____

15. I feel good about myself when _____

_____

16. To me, the essence of a meaningful life is _____

_____

17. I suffer from a sense of meaninglessness when _____

_____

■ Religion and Meaning: A Personal View

Religious faith can be a powerful source of meaning and purpose. Religion helps many people make sense out of the universe and the mystery of our purpose in living. Like any other potential source of meaning, religious faith seems most authentic and valuable when it enables us to become as fully human as possible. Religion can help us get in touch with our own powers of thinking, feeling, deciding, willing, and acting. Reflect on the following questions about your religion to determine whether it is a constructive force in your life:

- Does my religion provide me with a set of values that is congruent with the way I live my life?
- Does my religion assist me in better understanding the meaning of life and death?
- Does my religion allow tolerance for others who see the world differently from me?
- Does my religion provide me with a sense of peace and serenity?
- Is my religious faith something I actively choose or passively accept?
- Do my religious beliefs help me live life fully and treat others with respect and concern?

- Does my religion help me integrate my experience and make sense of the world?
- Does my religion encourage me to exercise my freedom and to assume the responsibility for the direction of my own life?
- Are my religious beliefs helping me become more of the person I'd like to become?
- Does my religion encourage me to question life and keep myself open to new learning?

As you take time for self-examination, how able are you to answer these questions in a way that is meaningful and satisfying to you? If you are honest with yourself, perhaps you will find that you have not critically evaluated the sources of your spiritual and religious beliefs. Although you may hesitate to question your belief system out of a fear of weakening or undermining your faith, the opposite might well be true — demonstrating the courage to question your beliefs and values might strengthen them. As we have mentioned, increasing numbers of people seem to be deciding that a religious faith is necessary if they are to find order and purpose in life. At the same time, many others insist that religion only impedes the quest for meaning or that it is incompatible with contemporary beliefs in other areas of life. Acceptance or rejection of religious faith must come authentically from within ourselves, and we must remain open to new experience and learning.

Siegel (1993) makes a distinction between religion and spirituality. Although he acknowledges that religion can be a source of support and a vital part of the healing process, he says that religion can also be a destructive force. He refers to some of his patients whose religion taught them that they deserve to suffer and that disease is an appropriate punishment. Siegel believes that if we accept the messages of spirituality and love grace is available to all of us. He writes: "Spirituality is a healing force. With spirituality there are no rules related to God's love and God's ability to sustain us" (p. 172).

"Religion" may take the form of a system of beliefs and values concerning the ultimate questions in life rather than (or in addition to) membership in a church. People who belong to a church may not be "religious" in this sense, and others may consider themselves religious even though they are atheists or agnostics. True spirituality addresses the quest for order in the universe and meaning in life.

In my own experience, I (Jerry) have found religion most valuable as a challenge to broaden my choices and potential rather than a restrictive influence. Until I was about 30, I tended to think of my religion as a package of ready-made answers for all the crises of life, and I was willing to let my church make many key decisions for me. I now think that I was experiencing too much anxiety in many areas of life to take full responsibility for my choices. My religious training had taught me that I should look to the authority of the church for ultimate answers in the areas of morality, value, and purpose. Like many other people I was encouraged to learn the "correct" answers and conform my thinking to them. Now, when I think of religion as a positive force, I think of it as being *freeing* in the sense that it encourages me to trust myself, to discover the sources of strength and integrity within myself, and to assume responsibility for my own choices.

Although as an adult I've questioned and altered many of the religious teachings with which I was raised, I haven't discarded many of my past moral and religious values. Many of them served a purpose earlier in my life and, with modification, are still meaningful for me. However, whether or not I continue to hold the beliefs and values I've been taught, it seems crucial to me that I be willing to subject them to scrutiny. If they hold up under challenge, I can reincorporate them; by the same token, I can continue to examine the new beliefs and values I acquire.

My (Marianne's) religious faith has always been a positive force in my life. Sometimes people who are religious suffer from feelings of guilt and fears of damnation. When this is the case, religion ceases to be a positive and powerful force in one's life. Religion helps me with an inner strength on which I can rely and that helps me to overcome difficulties that life presents. Although religion was encouraged in my childhood, it was never forced on me. It was a practice that I wanted to emulate because I saw the positive effects it had on the people in my life. Religion was practiced more than it was preached. The questions we asked you to reflect on earlier are ones that I pose to myself as well. I want to be sure that I am aware of my beliefs and the necessity for making changes if I am not satisfied with my answers.

Our Values in Action

■ Values for Our Children

When our daughters Heidi and Cindy were growing up, we hoped they would come to share some important values with us. We hoped they would

- have a positive and significant impact on the people in their lives
- be willing to dare and not always choose caution over risk
- form their own values rather than unquestioningly adopting ours
- like and respect themselves and feel good about their abilities and talents
- be open and trusting rather than fearful or suspicious
- respect and care for others
- continue to have fun as they grew older
- be able to express their feelings and always feel free to come to us and share meaningful aspects of their lives
- remain in touch with their power and refuse to surrender it
- be independent and have the courage to be different from others if they want to be
- have an interest in a religion that they freely chose
- be proud of themselves, yet humble
- respect the differences in others
- not compromise their values and principles for material possessions
- develop a flexible view of the world and be willing to modify their perspective based on new experiences
- give back to the world by contributing to make it a better place to live
- make a difference in the lives of others

Our daughters graduated from college a number of years ago, and our hopes for them continue to be manifested. Indeed, Heidi, Cindy, and Jerry just completed a book entitled *Living and Learning* (Corey, Corey, & Corey, 1997). It deals with helping new college students define their values and explore the personal dimensions and meaning of their college experience. It is a personal book that we hope will help students actively shape the course of their educational journey.

We both enjoy sharing in our daughters' lives and being with them. They are now more independent from us, yet they continue to value time with us and invite us to be involved in their lives. Although their lives are not problem-free, they typically show a willingness to face and deal with their struggles and are succeeding in making significant choices for themselves. If you have children or expect to have children someday, you might pause to think about the values you would like them to develop, as well as the part you will need to play in offering them guidance.

■ Becoming Aware of How Your Values Operate

Your values influence what you do; your daily behavior is an expression of your basic values. We encourage you to take the time to continue examining the source of your values to determine if they are appropriate for you at this time in your life. Furthermore, it is essential that you be aware of the significant impact your value system has on your relationships with others. In our view, it is not appropriate for you to push your values on others, to assume a judgmental stance toward those who have a different view, or to strive to convert others to adopt your perspective on life. Indeed, if you are secure in your values and basic beliefs, you will not be threatened by those who have a different set of beliefs and values.

In *God's Love Song*, Maier (1991) wonders how anyone can claim to have found the only way, not only for himself or herself but also for everyone else. As a minister, Sam Maier teaches that diversity shared not only is beautiful but also fosters understanding, caring, and the creation of community. He puts this message in a powerful and poetic way:

> It is heartening to find communities where the emphasis is placed upon each person having the opportunity to:

- share what is vital and meaningful out of one's own experience;
- listen to what is vital and meaningful to others;
- not expect or demand that anyone else do it exactly the same way as oneself. (p. 3)

Reverend Maier's message is well worth contemplating. Although you might clarify a set of values that seem to work for you, we hope that you will respect the values of others that may be quite different from yours. One set of values is not right and the other wrong. The diversity of cultures, religions, and world views provides a tapestry of life that allows us the opportunity to embrace diverse paths toward meaning in life.

Whatever your own values are, they can be further clarified and strengthened if you entertain open discussion of various viewpoints and cultivate a nonjudgmental attitude toward diversity. You might raise questions such as:

- Where did I develop my values?
- Are my values open to modification?
- Have I challenged my values?

- Do I insist that the world remain the same now as it was earlier in my life?
- Do I feel so deeply committed to any of my values that I'm likely to push my friends and family members to accept them?
- How would I communicate my values to others without imposing those values?
- How do my own values and beliefs affect my behavior?
- Am I willing to accept people who hold different values?
- Do I avoid judging others even if they think, feel, or act in different ways from me?

Embracing Diversity

One barrier to forming meaningful connections with others is the existence of negative attitudes toward those who are different from us. We sometimes choose to live in an encapsulated world, seeking support from those who think and value as we do. This narrowness prevents us from learning from those who may have a different world view than our own, and it results in fewer options to participate fully in the human community.

Meaning in life can be found by paying attention to the common ground we all share and by becoming aware of universal themes that unite us in spite of our differences. In Chapter 1 we emphasized that a meaningful life is not lived alone but is the result of connectedness to others in love, work, and community. In our view, it is through acceptance and understanding of others that we are able to discover the deepest meaning in life. If we live in isolation, we are walling ourselves off from the possibilities of engaging in social interest.

In this section, we invite you to explore the costs to us all of prejudice and discrimination, which grow out of fear and ignorance, and encourage you to reflect on a philosophy of life that embraces understanding and acceptance of diverse world views. We ask you to think of behaviors you might be willing to change so you can demonstrate acceptance, respect, and tolerance for others, whether or not they are like or unlike you.

■ What Can You Do to Better the World?

Some claim that the world is getting worse and that humanity is doomed. Even if you do not accept this premise, you might find some evidence for the need for bettering humanity. But where can we start to make it better? Bettering humanity may seem like an overwhelming task, but it is less staggering if we start with ourselves. It is easier to blame others for the ills of the world than to accept that we might be contributing to this malady. It is well to ask ourselves, "What am I doing, even in the smallest way, that contributes to the problems in our society? And what can I do to become part of the solution to these problems?"

Prejudice, discrimination, hatred, and intolerance, especially toward those who are different from us, are all paths toward an empty existence. Prejudice, a preconceived notion or opinion about someone, can be overt or covert. People can

be obvious and blatant about their particular prejudices, or they can hide them. Prejudice is a very subtle thing, and it may occur outside of conscious awareness. Ridley (1995) reminds us that unintentional racism can be even more harmful than intentional racism. At least with blatant racists people know where they stand, whereas subtle forms of racism are often difficult to pinpoint.

Becoming aware of our own subtle prejudice and unintentional racism is the first step toward change. Laughing at or being impatient with someone who has an accent, telling or laughing at racial jokes, speaking in generalities about a whole group of people as though they are all the same, and assuming that our culture is superior to any other are all signs of prejudice founded on racist attitudes. If you want to become more tolerant, reflect on some of the ways you have acquired your beliefs about particular groups of people and begin to question the source of those beliefs.

Prejudice has negative consequences. For the victims, it results in acts of discrimination that keep them from participating fully in the mainstream of society. People often feel intimidated by differences, whether these are differences in skin color, lifestyle, or values embraced. At the root of prejudice is fear, low self-esteem, ignorance, and feelings of inferiority. If an outgroup is the target of hate and is treated in demeaning ways, the person with the prejudice can feel a sense of superiority. Prejudice can function as a defense mechanism. It protects individuals from facing undesirable aspects of themselves by projecting them onto others.

■ Building Connections by Reaching Out to Others

Living in a multicultural society, we are a people with many diverse backgrounds. It is a challenge to learn to embrace and appreciate diversity rather than be threatened by it. Unless we are able to accept this challenge, we remain isolated and separate from one another. Corey, Corey, and Corey (1997) list the following points to consider as ways of breaking down barriers that keep people separate:

- Acknowledge and understand your own biases and prejudices.
- Challenge your prejudices by looking for data that do not support your preconceived biases.
- Seek universal themes that unite you with others.
- Look for similarities that unite you with others who differ from you in certain ways.
- Avoid judging differences; view diversity as a strength.
- Be respectful of those who differ from you.
- Attempt to learn about cultures that differ from your own.
- Be open and flexible.
- Be willing to test, adapt, and change your perceptions.

The more you know about your own culture, the more you will be able to understand the cultures of others. And the more you know about diverse cultures, the better able you will be to connect with them in a positive way. If you recognize that you are somewhat culturally encapsulated, give yourself credit for acknowledging your limitations and then work to expand your viewpoint. You can't change all the ills in the world, but you can do something. You can certainly work toward becoming more tolerant of those who differ from you—and you might even be able to welcome diversity as a way of enriching your life.

One living example of welcoming diversity is found in Glide Memorial Church in San Francisco. The pastor of this church, the Reverend Cecil Williams, along with the executive director of the church, Janet Mirikitani, are committed to welcoming diverse people into their spiritual community, a community that truly embraces love and acceptance. Reverend Williams (1992) works to empower individuals who are recovering and provides assistance to troubled communities. The pastor does not see his congregation as a melting pot where all people are blended together. Instead, Glide Memorial Church is more akin to a salad bowl filled with different leaves. Reverend Williams does far more than preach about love to a packed congregation on Sunday; he is actively engaged in spreading the meaning of love. He demonstrates ways to find meaning and purpose in life through acts of love. Through the efforts of Glide, hundreds of homeless are fed each day, substance abusers are given hope of a new kind of life, and society's outcasts are welcomed into a loving community. By giving people unconditional love and acceptance, Reverend Williams and his people bring out the best in those they encounter.

Glide Memorial Church is an example of the value of reaching out to others and making a difference. We challenge you to reflect on ways you can augment the meaning of your life by making connections with others and striving to make a significant difference. Realize that you can change the world in small ways by touching the lives of others through your acts of kindness and generosity. The purpose of your life can take on expanded dimensions if you are interested in making the world a better place for all of us. This process of making a difference in the human community begins with seeing ways that diversity can enhance life.

The *Quick Discrimination Index* that follows can help you assess your attitudes toward cultural diversity. Even if you think you are free of prejudice toward others, you may discover some subtle biases. Once you are aware of them, you can begin working toward acceptance and tolerance.

The Quick Discrimination Index

We hope you'll take and score this social-attitude survey, which is designed to assess sensitivity, awareness, and receptivity to cultural diversity and gender equity. Since it is a self-assessment inventory, it is essential that you strive to respond to each item as honestly as possible. This inventory is not designed to assess how you should think about cultural diversity and gender equity issues; rather, its aim is to assess subtle racial and gender bias. You can use this inventory to become more aware of your attitudes and beliefs pertaining to these issues.

DIRECTIONS: Remember there are no right or wrong answers. Please circle the appropriate number to the right.

	Strongly disagree	Disagree	Not sure	Agree	Strongly agree
1. I do think it is more appropriate for the mother of a newborn baby, rather than the father, to stay home with the baby (not work) during the first year.	1	2	3	4	5
2. It is as easy for women to succeed in business as it is for men.	1	2	3	4	5
3. I really think affirmative-action programs on college campuses constitute reverse discrimination.	1	2	3	4	5
4. I feel I could develop an intimate relationship with someone from a different race.	1	2	3	4	5
5. All Americans should learn to speak two languages.	1	2	3	4	5
6. It upsets (or angers) me that a woman has never been president of the United States.	1	2	3	4	5
7. Generally speaking, men work harder than women.	1	2	3	4	5

(continued)

The Quick Discrimination Index (continued)

	Strongly disagree	Disagree	Not sure	Agree	Strongly agree
8. My friendship network is very racially mixed.	1	2	3	4	5
9. I am against affirmative-action programs in business.	1	2	3	4	5
10. Generally, men seem less concerned with building relationships than women.	1	2	3	4	5
11. I would feel OK about my son or daughter dating someone from a different race.	1	2	3	4	5
12. It upsets (or angers) me that a racial minority person has never been president of the United States.	1	2	3	4	5
13. In the past few years, too much attention has been directed toward multicultural or minority issues in education.	1	2	3	4	5
14. I think feminist perspectives should be an integral part of the higher education curriculum.	1	2	2	4	5
15. Most of my close friends are from my own racial group.	1	2	3	4	5
16. I feel somewhat more secure that a man rather than a woman is currently president of the United States.	1	2	3	4	5
17. I think that it is (or would be) important for my children to attend schools that are racially mixed.	1	2	3	4	5
18. In the past few years too much attention has been directed toward multicultural or minority issues in business.	1	2	3	4	5
19. Overall, I think racial minorities in America complain too much about racial discrimination.	1	2	3	4	5
20. I feel (or would feel) very comfortable having a woman as my primary physician.	1	2	3	4	5
21. I think the president of the United States should make a concerted effort to appoint more women and racial minorities to the country's Supreme Court.	1	2	3	4	5
22. I think white people's racism toward racial-minority groups still constitutes a major problem in America.	1	2	3	4	5
23. I think the school system, from elementary school through college, should encourage minority and immigrant children to learn and fully adopt traditional American values.	1	2	3	4	5
24. If I were to adopt a child, I would be happy to adopt a child of any race.	1	2	3	4	5
25. I think there is as much female physical violence toward men as there is male physical violence toward women.	1	2	3	4	5

The Quick Discrimination Index (continued)

	Strongly disagree	Disagree	Not sure	Agree	Strongly agree
26. I think the school system, from elementary school through college, should promote values representative of diverse cultures.	1	2	3	4	5
27. I believe that reading the autobiography of Malcolm X would be of value.	1	2	3	4	5
28. I would enjoy living in a neighborhood consisting of a racially diverse population (Asians, blacks, Latinos, whites).	1	2	3	4	5
29. I think it is better if people marry within their own race.	1	2	3	4	5
30. Women make too big a deal out of sexual-harassment issues in the workplace.	1	2	3	4	5

The total score measures overall sensitivity, awareness, and receptivity to cultural diversity and gender equality. Of the 30 items on the QDI, 15 are worded and scored in a positive direction (high scores indicate high sensitivity to multicultural/gender issues), and 15 are worded and scored in a negative direction (where low scores are indicative of high sensitivity). Naturally, when tallying the total score response, these latter 15 items need to be *reverse-scored*. Reverse scoring simply means that if a respondent circles a "1" they should get five points; a "2" four points, a "3" three points, a "4" two points, and a "5" one point.

The following QDI items need to be *reverse-scored*: 1, 2, 3, 7, 9, 10, 13, 15, 16, 18, 19, 23, 25, 29, 30.

Score range = 30 to 150, with high scores indicating more awareness, sensitivity, and receptivity to racial diversity and gender equality.

► *Time Out for Personal Reflection*

1. At this time, what are some of the principal sources of meaning and purpose in your life?

_____

_____

_____

_____

2. Have there been occasions in your life when you've allowed other people or institutions to make key choices for you? If so, give a couple of examples.

_____

_____

_____

_____

3. What role, if any, has religion played in your life?

_____

_____

_____

_____

4. If you were to create a new religion, what virtues and values would you include? What would be the vices and sins?

_____

_____

_____

_____

5. What are some of the values you'd most like to see your children adopt?

_____

_____

_____

_____

6. This is a list of some things different people value. Rate the importance of each one for you, using a five-point scale, with 1 meaning *extremely important* and 5 meaning *very unimportant.*

_____ companionship
_____ family life
_____ security
_____ being financially and materially successful
_____ enjoying leisure time
_____ work
_____ learning and getting an education
_____ appreciation of nature
_____ competing and winning
_____ loving others and being loved
_____ a relationship with God
_____ self-respect and pride
_____ being productive and achieving

_____	enjoying an intimate relationship
_____	having solitude and private time to reflect
_____	having a good time and being with others
_____	laughter and a sense of humor
_____	intelligence and a sense of curiosity
_____	opening up to new experiences
_____	risk taking and personal growth
_____	being approved of and liked by others
_____	being challenged and meeting challenges well
_____	courage
_____	compassion
_____	being of service to others

Now go back over your list and circle the things you'd like to have more of in your life. Think about what keeps you from having or doing the things that you value most.

7. To what extent are you threatened by people who think and believe differently from you? Do you tend to be drawn to human diversity, or do you tend to shy away from those with a different world view?

_____

_____

_____

8. What value do you place on diversity as part of your philosophy of life?

_____

_____

_____

9. What steps are you willing to take to move in the direction of challenging your prejudices or restricted ways of thinking?

_____

_____

_____

_____

10. What one action can you take to make a significant, even though small, difference in society? To what extent do you believe that you are able to influence others?

_____

_____

_____

_____

Chapter Summary

Seeking meaning and purpose in life is an important part of being human. Meaning is not automatically bestowed on you; it is the result of your active thinking and choosing. We've encouraged you to recognize your own values and to ask both how you acquired them and whether you can affirm them for yourself out of your own experience and reflection. This task of examining your values and purposes continues throughout your lifetime.

If you are secure about your value system, you will also be flexible and open to new life experiences. At various times in your life you may look at the world somewhat differently, which will indicate a need to modify some of your values. This is not to say that you will change your values without giving the matter considerable thought. Being secure about your values also implies that you do not need to impose them on other people. We hope you will be able to respect the values of others that may differ from your own. You can learn to accept other people who have a different world view from yours without necessarily approving of all of their behavior. If you are clear about the meaning in your own life, and if you have developed a philosophy of life that provides you with purpose and direction, you will be more able to interact with others who might embrace different value systems. Being able to talk openly with these people can be a useful avenue for your own personal growth.

In this chapter we have focused on the central role of values as a basis for meaning in life. In addition to finding meaning through projects that afford opportunities for personal growth, we have seen that meaning and purpose extend to the broader framework of forming linkages with others in the human community. Accepting others by respecting their right to hold values that may differ from your value system is a fundamental dimension of philosophy of life based on tolerance. Prejudice, based on fear and ignorance, is often a barrier that separates us from others instead of uniting us. The *Quick Discrimination Index* has given you some information about your attitudes toward human diversity. After you have assessed your attitudes, decide if you want to move more in the direction of welcoming diversity as a bridge to link yourself with others who differ from you. It may be overwhelming to think of solving the global problems of prejudice and discrimination, but you can begin in smaller but still significant ways by changing yourself. Once you recognize the barriers within yourself that prevent you from understanding and accepting others, you can take steps to challenge these barriers.

Activities and Exercises

1. Ask a few close friends what gives their lives meaning. How have they found their identities? What projects give them a sense of purpose? How do they think their lives would be different without this source of meaning?

2. Now that the course is coming to an end, discuss with other students what topics have meant the most to you. What did you learn about yourself from reading the book and taking the course? What do you think you will do with what you learned? Do you intend to make any specific behavioral changes? What questions were raised that are still open for you?

3. Writing a paper that describes your philosophy of life can help you integrate your thoughts and reflections on the topics raised in this chapter and throughout this book. Ideally, this paper will represent a critical analysis of who you are now and the factors that have been most influential in contributing to that person. If you attempted to write at least a part of your philosophy of life as you began this book, you have a basis for comparison if you now revise your philosophy of life. The following outline for your paper is very comprehensive, and writing such a paper can be a major project in a course. As you review the outline, you might select only one or two of the major topics and use them as a focus of your paper. Feel free to use or omit any part of the outline, and modify it in any way that will help you to write a paper that is personally significant. You might also consider adding poetry, excerpts from other writers, and pictures or works of art. If you take this project seriously, the assignment can help you clarify your goals for the future and the means to obtain them.

I. Who are you now? What influences have contributed to the person you are now?
   A. Influences during childhood:
      1. your relationship with your parents
      2. your relationship with your siblings
      3. important turning points
      4. successes and failures
      5. personal conflicts
      6. family expectations
      7. impact of school and early learning experiences
      8. your relationships with friends
      9. experiences of loneliness
      10. other
   B. Influences during adolescence:
      1. impact of your family and your relationship with your parents
      2. school experiences
      3. personal struggles
      4. critical turning points
      5. influence of your peer group
      6. experiences of loneliness
      7. successes and failures, and their impact on you
      8. influential adults other than parents
      9. your principal values
      10. other
   C. Love and sex:
      1. your need for love
      2. your fear of love

    3. the meaning of love for you
    4. dating experiences and their effect on you
    5. your view of gender roles
    6. expectations of others and their influence on your gender role
    7. attitudes toward the opposite sex
    8. meaning of sexuality in your life
    9. your values concerning love and sex
    10. other
  D. Intimate relationships and family life:
    1. the value you place on marriage
    2. how children fit in your life
    3. the meaning of intimacy for you
    4. the kind of intimate relationships you want
    5. areas of struggle for you in relating to others
    6. your views of marriage
    7. your values concerning family life
    8. how social expectations have influenced your views
    9. gender roles in intimate relationships
    10. other
  E. Death and meaning:
    1. your view of an afterlife
    2. religious views and your view of death
    3. the way death affects you
    4. sources of meaning in your life
    5. the things you most value in your life
    6. your struggles in finding meaning and purpose
    7. religion and the meaning of life
    8. critical turning points in finding meaning
    9. influential people in your life
    10. other
II. Whom do you want to become?
  A. Summary of your present position:
    1. how you see yourself now (strengths and weaknesses)
    2. how others perceive you now
    3. what makes you unique
    4. your relationships with others
    5. present struggles
  B. Your future plans for an occupation:
    1. nature of your work plans and their chances for success
    2. kind of work that is meaningful to you
    3. how you chose or will choose your work
    4. what work means to you
    5. what you expect from work
  C. Your future with others:
    1. the kind of relationships you want
    2. what you need to do to achieve the relationships you want

        3. plans for marriage or an alternative
        4. place for children in your future plans
    D. Future plans for yourself:
        1. how you would like to be ten years from now
           a. what you need to do to achieve your goals
           b. what you can do now
        2. your values for the future
        3. your view of the good life
           a. ways to achieve it
           b. how your view of the good life relates to all aspects of your life
        4. choices you see as being open to you now
           a. choices in work
           b. choices in school
           c. value choices
           d. other areas of choice in your life
4. Select one or more of the following books for further reading on the topics explored in this chapter: *Ethical and Spiritual Values in Counseling* (Burke & Miranti, 1992); *Man's Search for Meaning* (Frankl, 1963); *Joy's Way* (Joy, 1979); *Avalanche* (Joy, 1990).

Epilogue: Where to Go from Here — Pathways to Continued Growth

Avenues to personal growth are as varied as the people who choose them.

Before putting this book aside, we ask you to consider the personal meaning the book and this course have held for you. Throughout the book you've been invited to discover new choices you might like to make. One of the final challenges is to determine where you will go from here. Now that you've finished this book and are completing this course, will you stop here? Or will this be a commencement, a new beginning in the best sense? If you've invested yourself in the process of questioning your life, now is a good time to make a commitment to yourself (and maybe to someone else) to actively put to use what you've been learning about yourself.

As you consider what experiences for continued personal growth you are likely to choose at this time, be aware that your meaning in life is not cast in concrete. As you change, you can expect that what brings meaning to your life will also change. The projects you were deeply absorbed in at an earlier time in your life may hold little meaning for you today. And where and how you discover meaning today may not be the pattern for some future period.

You can deliberately choose experiences that will help you become the person you choose to be. Perhaps you remember reading a book or seeing a film that had a profound effect on you and really seemed to put things in perspective. Certainly, reading books that deal with significant issues in your life can be a growth experience in itself, as well as an encouragement to try new things.

Often, we make resolutions about what we'd like to be doing in our lives or about experiences we want to share with others, and then we fail to carry them out. Is this true of you? Are there activities you value yet rarely get around to doing?

Perhaps you tell yourself that you prize making new friendships, yet you find that you do very little to actually initiate any contacts. Or perhaps you derive satisfaction from growing vegetables or working in your garden, yet find many reasons to neglect this activity. You might tell yourself that you'd love to take a day or two just to be alone, yet never get around to arranging it. When you stop to think about it, aren't there choices you could be making right now that would make your life richer? How would you really like to be spending your time? What changes are you willing to make today, this week, this month, this year?

In addition to activities you enjoy but don't engage in as often as you'd like, there are undoubtedly many new things you might consider trying out as ways of adding meaning to your life and developing your potentials. You might consider making a contract with yourself to start now on a definite plan of action instead of putting it off until next week or next year. Here are some ways you might choose to challenge yourself to grow:

- find a hobby that develops a new side of yourself
- go to plays, concerts, and museums
- take a course in pottery making, wine tasting, guitar playing, or some other special interest
- get involved in exciting work projects or actively pursue forms of work that will lead to development of your hidden talents
- spend time alone to reflect on the quality of your life
- initiate contacts with others and perhaps develop an intimate relationship
- enroll in continuing education courses or earn a degree primarily for the satisfaction of learning
- do volunteer work and help make others' lives better
- experience the mountains, the desert, and the ocean — by hiking, sailing, and so on
- become involved in religious activities or pursue a spiritual path meaningful to you
- travel to new places, especially to experience different cultures
- keep a journal and record your feelings and dreams
- share some of your dreams with a person you trust

Any list of ways of growing is only a sample, of course; the avenues to personal growth are as various as the people who choose them. Growth can occur in small ways, and there are many things you can do on your own (or with friends or family) to continue your personal development. A few of the resources available to you for continued personal growth are outlined in the pages that follow. Different resources may fit your needs at different stages of your personal growth. We invite you to investigate any of these avenues that you feel are appropriate for you at this time.

■ Begin a Reading Program

One excellent way to motivate yourself to explore life is by reading good books, including selected self-help books. We caution you to beware of those self-help books that offer quick solutions, that promise a prescription for eternal happiness, or that give you steps to follow to find guaranteed success. We've provided a variety of self-help references in the "References and Suggested Readings" section at the end of this book that should give you a fine start on developing a personal reading program. Many students and clients tell us how meaningful selected books have been for them in putting into perspective some of the themes they have struggled with, and we encourage you to take advantage of this resource.

■ Establish a Writing Program

Along with setting up a reading and reflection program for yourself, another way to build on the gains you have made up to this point is to continue the practice of journal writing. If you have begun a process of personal writing in this book or in a separate notebook, keep up with this practice. Even devoting a short period a few times each week to reflecting on how your life is going and then recording some of your thoughts and feelings is useful in providing you with an awareness of patterns in your behavior. Without being self-critical you can learn to observe what you are feeling, thinking, and doing; then you have a basis for determining the degree to which you are successfully changing old patterns that were not working for you.

■ Contemplate Self-Directed Behavior Change

Now that you have finished this book, you have probably identified a few specific areas where you could do further work. If you recognize that you are not as assertive as you'd like to be in various social situations, for example, you can begin by doing some reading on the topic of assertiveness training. If you decide that you are frequently tense and that you do not generally react well to stress, you can construct a self-change program that will involve practicing relaxation methods and breathing exercises. The main point is that you identify some target areas for change, that you set realistic goals, that you develop some specific techniques for carrying out your goals, and that you practice selected behaviors that will help you make those changes.

■ Take Advantage of Support Groups

You can keep your programs of reading, writing, and self-directed change going by yourself. In addition to these avenues that you can pursue alone, consider how you can reach out to others as a source of continued challenge and support. Assume that you are having a difficult time in working through the loss of a loved one. Doing selected reading on death and loss as well as writing down your feelings in your journal can be of some help; if in addition you interact with a small group of others who have experienced loss, you can receive the empathy and support necessary to assist you in mourning and expressing your grief.

Most colleges and community mental health centers offer a variety of self-help groups that are facilitated by a person who has coped or is coping with a particular life issue. A good support group will help you see that you are not alone in your struggle. The experience can also provide you with alternatives that you may not be considering. Other examples of support groups include those that deal with rape or incest, consciousness-raising groups for women and for men, groups for reentry students, groups for people concerned about gay and lesbian issues, and medical self-help groups. As is the case with self-help books, you are advised to proceed with some caution in joining a support group. Take the time to ask questions about a group that you are considering joining and decide for yourself if this group is right for you at this time in your life.

■ Investigate Group or Individual Counseling

In Chapter 6 we discussed the value of counseling as a way to help you cope with your problems and as a pathway to self-understanding and wellness. We hope you'll remain open to the idea of seeking counseling for yourself at critical transition periods in your life or times when you feel particularly challenged with life events or choices to be made. Reading this book and participating in this kind of class may have raised personal issues that you were unaware of before. Taking this course has probably shown you that you are not alone with your struggles. To wrestle with choices about life is supremely human. While you are encouraged to trust yourself to make your own choices, even a few counseling sessions at the right time can assist you in clarifying your options and can provide you with the impetus to formulate action plans leading to change.

■ Practice Ongoing Self-Assessment

In Chapter 1 we indicated that this book is best considered an unfinished project. It is unfinished in that we hope you will reread at least portions of it and that you will continue to reflect on the topics we've covered. If you are keeping a journal, there is plenty of material for further reflection in the "Time Out" sections and the "Activities and Exercises" at the end of each chapter. Certain topics will have more appeal than others, so you can return to these chapters and see how any of your views and attitudes change over time.

Throughout this book you've been challenged to assess ways that you think, feel, and act on a variety of topics. Now would be a good time to review your responses to the prechapter self-inventories for each of the chapters and to look at your written responses to the "Time Out" exercises in the chapters. Taking time to consolidate your thoughts will do a great deal to enhance your learning—and will give you an indication of where you might want to go now that you are finishing this book and this course. Once you've done this review and made an assessment of where you see yourself now, you'll be in a much better position to determine future directions for yourself.

We strongly encourage you to consider implementing Bernie Siegel's five-part therapeutic program described in *Peace, Love, and Healing* (1989). Siegel started a form of individual and group therapy known as Exceptional Cancer Patients. As a result of his work with this population, Siegel believes he has learned a great deal about how to live to the fullest and how people can tap their own healing potential. Siegel recommends following this five-part program on a daily basis as a way to become what he calls an "exceptional human being":

- Keep a daily journal in which you write about your feelings and dreams.
- Join a therapy group that meets on a weekly basis where you can receive support, confrontation, and discipline.
- Make it a practice to meditate, do visualization (imagine yourself as being the way you would like to be), pray, reflect, or listen to quiet music as a way to break up the activities of your day four to six times. Make the time to refocus and get centered several times each day.
- Live one hour at a time. Paying attention to your feelings and reactions will eventually teach you that you are in charge of your feelings.
- Twice a day for fifteen minutes sit or stand naked in front of a mirror and work with the feelings that emerge for you.

Siegel believes that only truly exceptional human beings will commit themselves to the time and work involved in this therapeutic program aimed at change. He writes: "Once you do all of these things, however, you find that you begin to live more and more in the moment, and life becomes a series of moments that you are in charge of. Then joy will enter your life and you will be in heaven without dying" (1989, p. 226).

■ Dare to Dream

We encourage you to dream when you're awake as well as when you're asleep. Don Quixote dared "to dream the impossible dream." We encourage you to follow a similar path. The greatest hindrance to your growth may be a failure to allow yourself to imagine all the possibilities open to you. You may have restricted your vision of what you might become by not allowing yourself to formulate a vision or pursue your dreams. If you allow yourself to create dreams, a range of choices will unfold for you. We have met many people who continue to surprise themselves with what they have in their lives. At one time they would not have imagined such possibilities — even in their wildest dreams — but their dreams became reality for them. Having a vision of what you want is merely the beginning. Once you have a clearer picture of the person you want to become, of the relationships you want with others, and of the kind of world you would like to help create, it is essential to make choices and take action. But too many of us restrict our vision of the possible by not allowing ourselves the luxury of reflecting on an impossible dream. Dare to dream, and then have the courage to follow your passions.

■ Concluding Comments

As authors, we also consider our book an unfinished project in that our perspectives continue to evolve as we do. The spirit, general tone, and message of this sixth edition of *I Never Knew I Had a Choice* are basically the same as in the original version. However, with each of the prior editions, we have developed topics differently, in light of the changes in our times and our personal changes as well.

Now that you have finished reading and reflecting on *Choice* and now that your course is coming to an end, we hope you will not forget either the course or the book and that you won't see your work as finished. Rather, we hope that you are somewhat more aware of personal issues than you were when you began the course and that you are eager to continue on the path of self-examination and reflection.

We find that our students and people who attend our workshops sometimes expect dramatic transformations and feel disappointed if they do not make major changes in their lives. We often tell them that it is not the big changes that are necessarily significant; rather, it is the willingness to take small steps that lead to continued growth. Remember that it is essential to begin with yourself, as you can only change your own ways of thinking, feeling, and doing. Don't set yourself up to accomplish herculean feats; look instead at subtle ways of increasing your personal freedom.

Throughout this book we have encouraged you to open yourself to taking risks in thinking about yourself and others in new ways. Personal change is an ongoing process that really does not come to an end until you do. We sincerely wish you well in your commitment to take the steps necessary, no matter how small, in your journey to becoming the person you were meant to be. Remember that a journey of a thousand miles begins with the first step — so start walking!

References and Suggested Readings*

ADLER, A. (1958). *What life should mean to you.* New York: Capricorn.

ADLER, A. (1964). *Social interest: A challenge to mankind.* New York: Capricorn.

ADLER, A. (1969). *The practice and theory of individual psychology.* Paterson, NJ: Littlefield.

ALBERTI, A., & EMMONS, M. (1995). *Your perfect right: A guide to assertive living.* San Luis Obispo, CA: Impact Publishers.

AMADA, G. (1995). *A guide to psychotherapy.* New York: Ballantine.

AMERICAN ASSOCIATION FOR WORLD HEALTH. (1994). *AIDS and families* (resource booklet). Washington, DC: Author.

ANGELOU, M. (1968). *All God's children need traveling shoes.* New York: Random House.

BALCH, J. F., & BALCH, P. A. (1990). *Prescription for nutritional healing.* Garden City Park, NY: Avery.

*BASOW, S. A. (1992). *Gender: Stereotypes and roles* (3rd ed.). Pacific Grove, CA: Brooks/Cole.

BASS, E., & DAVIS, L. (1994). *The courage to heal: A guide for women survivors of child sexual abuse* (3rd ed.). New York: Harper Perennial.

BATESON, M. C. (1990). *Composing a life.* New York: Plume.

*BECKER, E. (1973). *The denial of death.* New York: Free Press.

*BELLAH, R. N., MADSEN, R., SULLIVAN, W. M., SWIDLER, A., & TIPTON, S. M. (1985). *Habits of the heart: Individualism and commitment in American life.* New York: Harper & Row (Perennial Library).

*BENSON, H. (1976). *The relaxation response.* New York: Avon Books.

BENSON, H. (1984). *Beyond the relaxation response.* New York: Berkeley Books.

*BERMAN, A. L., & JOBES, D. A. (1991). *Adolescent suicide: Assessment and intervention.* Washington, DC: American Psychological Association.

BERNE, E. (1975). *What do you say after you say hello?* New York: Bantam.

BETTELHEIM, B. (1967). *The empty fortress: Infantile autism and the birth of self.* New York: Free Press.

*BLACK, C. (1987). *It will never happen to me.* New York: Ballantine.

BLOCK, D. (1991). *Listening to your inner voice: Discover the truth within you and let it guide your way.* Center City, MN: Hazelden.

*An asterisk before an entry indicates a source that we highly recommend as supplementary reading.

*BLOOMFIELD, H. H., WITH FELDER, L. (1983). *Making peace with your parents.* New York: Ballantine.

*BLOOMFIELD, H. H., WITH FELDER, L. (1985). *Making peace with yourself: Transforming your weaknesses into strengths.* New York: Ballantine.

*BLY, R. (1990). *Iron John: A book about men.* New York: Random House (Vintage Books).

BLY, R. (1991a). Father hunger in men. In K. Thompson (Ed.), *To be a man: In search of the deep masculine* (pp. 189–192). Los Angeles, CA: Jeremy P. Tarcher.

BLY, R. (1991b). The need for male initiation. In K. Thompson (Ed.), *To be a man: In search of the deep masculine* (pp. 38–42). Los Angeles, CA: Jeremy P. Tarcher.

BLY, R. (1991c). What men really want. In K. Thompson (Ed.), *To be a man: In search of the deep masculine* (pp. 16–23). Los Angeles, CA: Jeremy P. Tarcher.

BOLLES, R. N. (1978). *The three boxes of life.* Berkeley, CA: Ten Speed Press.

*BOLLES, R. N. (1995). *What color is your parachute?* Berkeley, CA: Ten Speed Press.

BRAZIER, C. (1991). Men should embrace feminism. In K. Thompson (Ed.), *To be a man: In search of the deep masculine* (pp. 94–96). Los Angeles, CA: Jeremy P. Tarcher.

*BURKE, M. T., & MIRANTI, J. G. (1992). *Ethical and spiritual values in counseling.* Alexandria, VA: The American Counseling Association.

*BURNS, D. D. (1981). *Feeling good: The new mood therapy.* New York: New American Library (Signet).

*BURNS, D. D. (1985). *Intimate connections.* New York: New American Library (Signet).

*BUSCAGLIA, L. (1972). *Love.* Thorofare, NJ: Charles B. Slack.

BUSCAGLIA, L. (1982a). *Living, loving, and learning.* New York: Ballantine.

BUSCAGLIA, L. (1982b). *Personhood: The art of being fully human.* New York: Fawcett (Columbine).

BUSCAGLIA, L. (1992). *Born for love: Reflections on loving.* New York: Fawcett Columbine.

CAMERON, J. (1992). *The artist's way: A spiritual path to higher creativity.* New York: G. P. Putnam's Sons.

CANFIELD, J., & HANSEN, M. V. (1993). *Chicken soup for the soul.* Deerfield Beach, FL: Health Communications, Inc.

*CARNEY, C. G., & WELLS, C. F. (1995). *Discover the career within you* (4th ed.). Pacific Grove, CA: Brooks/Cole.

*CARR, J. B. (1988). *Crisis in intimacy: When expectations don't meet reality.* Pacific Grove, CA: Brooks/Cole.

CARTWRIGHT, R. D. (1991). Dreams that work: The relation of dream incorporation to adaptation to stressful events. *Dreaming, 1,* 3–9.

CARTWRIGHT, R. D., & LAMBERG, L. (1992). *Crisis dreaming.* New York: Harper Collins.

*CASEY, K., & VANCEBURG, M. (1985). *The promise of a new day: A book of daily meditations.* New York: Harper/Hazelden.

CENTERS FOR DISEASE CONTROL AND PREVENTION. (1993a). *Facts about condoms and their use in preventing HIV infection and other STD's.* Atlanta: Author.

CENTERS FOR DISEASE CONTROL AND PREVENTION. (1993b). *National AIDS Clearinghouse.* Atlanta: Author.

CENTERS FOR DISEASE CONTROL AND PREVENTION. (1994). *HIV/AIDS Surveillance Report, 6*(1), 1.

CHAPMAN, A. B. (1993). Black men do feel about love. In M. Golden (Ed.) *Wild women don't wear no blues: Black women writers on love, men and sex.* New York: Doubleday.

*CHARLESWORTH, E. A., & NATHAN, R. G. (1984). *Stress management: A comprehensive guide to wellness.* New York: Ballantine.

CHOPRA, D. (1992). *Creating health.* Boston: Houghton Mifflin.

CHOPRA, D. (1994). *Perfect health.* New York: Harmony Books.

CHOPRA, D. (1995). *Seven spiritual laws.* San Rafael, CA: New Work Library.

CLARK, D. (1987). *The new loving someone gay.* Berkeley, CA: Celestial Arts.

COREY, G. (1995). *Theory and practice of group counseling* (4th ed.). Pacific Grove, CA: Brooks/Cole.

COREY, G. (1996). *Theory and practice of counseling and psychotherapy* (5th ed.). Pacific Grove, CA: Brooks/Cole.

COREY, G., COREY, C., & COREY, H. (1997). *Living and learning.* Belmont, CA: Wadsworth.

COREY, M., & COREY, G. (1993). *Becoming a helper* (2nd ed.). Pacific Grove, CA: Brooks/Cole.

*COVEY, S. R. (1990). *The seven habits of highly effective people.* New York: Simon & Schuster (Fireside Books).

COWAN, C., & KINDER, M. (1985). *Smart women, foolish choices.* New York: New American Library.

DASS, R. (1978). *Journey of awakening: A meditator's guidebook.* New York: Bantam Books.

DAVIS, L. (1990). *The courage to heal workbook: For women and men survivors of child sexual abuse.* New York: Harper & Row.

DESPELDER, L., & STRICKLAND, A. (1983). *The last dance: Encountering death and dying.* Palo Alto, CA: Mayfield.

DICKENSON, D., & JOHNSON, M. (Eds.). (1993). *Death, dying, and bereavement.* Newbury Park, CA: Sage.

DONATELLE, R., SNOW-HARTER, C., & WILCOX, A. (1995). *Wellness: Choices for health and fitness.* Redwood City, CA: Benjamin/Cummings.

*DWORKIN, S. H., & GUTIERREZ, F. J. (Eds.). (1992). *Counseling gay men and lesbians: Journey to the end of the rainbow.* Alexandria, VA: American Counseling Association.

EDELMAN, M. W. (1992). *The measure of our success: A letter to my children and yours.* Boston: Beacon Press.

EDLESON, J. L., & TOLMAN, R. M. (1994). Group intervention strategies for men who batter. *Directions in Mental Health Counseling, 4*(7), 4–15.

*ELKIND, D. (1984). *All grown up and no place to go.* Reading, MA: Addison-Wesley.

*ELLIS, A. (1988). *How to stubbornly refuse to make yourself miserable about anything—Yes, anything!* Secaucus, NJ: Lyle Stuart.

ELLIS, A. (1994). *Reason and emotion in psychotherapy revised.* New York: Carol Publishing.

*ELLIS, A., & HARPER, R. A. (1975). *A new guide to rational living.* Englewood Cliffs, NJ: Prentice-Hall.

ERIKSON, E. (1963). *Childhood and society* (2nd ed.). New York: Norton.

ERIKSON, E. (1982). *The life cycle completed.* New York: Norton.

FALK, P. J. (1989). Lesbian mothers: Psychosocial assumptions in family law. *American Psychologist, 44*(6), 941–947.

FALUDI, S. (1991). *Backlash: The undeclared war against American women.* New York: Crown.

FASSINGER, R. E. (1991). The hidden minority: Issues and challenges in working with lesbian women and gay men. *The Counseling Psychologist, 19*(2), 157–176.

FINKLEHOR, D. (1984). *Child sexual abuse: New theory and research.* New York: Free Press.

*FORWARD, S., & BUCK, C. S. (1988). *Betrayal of innocence: Incest and its devastation.* New York: Penguin.

FORWARD, S., & TORRES, J. (1987). *Men who hate women and the women who love them.* New York: Bantam Books.

*FRANKL, V. (1963). *Man's search for meaning.* New York: Washington Square Press.

FRANKL, V. (1965). *The doctor and the soul.* New York: Bantam Books.

FRANKL, V. (1969). *The will to meaning: Foundation and applications of logotherapy.* New York: New American Library.

FRANKL, V. (1978). *The unheard cry for meaning.* New York: Bantam.

FREUD, S. (1949). *An outline of psychoanalysis.* New York: Norton.

FREUD, S. (1965). *The interpretation of dreams.* New York: Avon. (Original work published 1900)

FRIEDMAN, M., & ROSENMAN, R. H. (1974). *Type A behavior and your heart.* Greenwich, CT: Fawcett.

FRIEDMAN, M., & ULMER, D. (1985). *Treating Type A behavior and your heart.* New York: Ballantine (Fawcett Crest).

*FROMM, E. (1956). *The art of loving.* New York: Harper & Row (Colophon). (Paperback edition, 1974)

GARDNER, H. (1983). *Frames of mind: The theory of multiple intelligences.* New York: Basic Books.

GAYLIN, W. (1992). *The male ego.* New York: Viking.

GERSON, K. (1987). What do women want from men? Men's influence or women's work and family choices. In M. S. Kimmel (Ed.), *Changing men: New directions in research on men and masculinity.* Newbury Park, CA: Sage.

*GIBRAN, K. (1923). *The prophet.* New York: Knopf.

*GLASSER, W. (1985). *Control theory: A new explanation of how we control our lives.* New York: Harper & Row.

GLIONNA, J. M. (1992, January 12), Dance of life. *Los Angeles Times.*

GOLDBERG, H. (1976). *The hazards of being male.* New York: Nash.

GOLDBERG, H.(1979). *The new male.* New York: New American Library (Signet).

*GOLDBERG, H. (1987). *The inner male: Overcoming roadblocks to intimacy.* New York: New American Library (Signet).

GOLDEN, M. (Ed.). (1993). *Wild women don't wear no blues: Black women writers on love, men and sex.* New York: Doubleday.

GOOD, M., & GOOD, P. (1979). *20 most asked questions about the Amish and Mennonites.* Lancaster, PA: Good Books.

GORDON, S. (1991). *Prisoners of men's dreams.* Boston: Little, Brown.

GOULD, R. L. (1978). *Transformations: Growth and change in adult life.* New York: Simon & Schuster (Touchstone).

GOULDING, M., & GOULDING, R. (1979). *Changing lives through redecision therapy.* New York: Brunner/Mazel.

GOULDING, R., & GOULDING, M. (1978). *The power is in the patient.* San Francisco: TA Press.

GRAY, J. (1992). *Men are from Mars: Women are from Venus.* New York: Harper Collins.

GRIFFITH, H. W. (1990). *Complete guide to prescription and nonprescription drugs.* Los Angeles: The Body Press, A Division of Price Stern Sloan.

GRUSZNSKI, R., & BANKOVICS, G. (1990). Treating men who batter: A group approach. In D. Moore & F. Leafgren (Eds.). *Problem solving strategies and intervention for men in conflict* (pp. 201–211). Alexandria, VA: American Counseling Association.

HALES, D. (1987). *How to sleep like a baby.* New York: Ballantine.

HALES, D. (1997). *Invitation to health* (7th ed.). Pacific Grove, CA: Brooks/Cole.

HALL, C. S. (1984). Dreams. In R. J. Corsini (Ed.), *Encyclopedia of psychology: Vol. I* (pp. 388–390). New York: Wiley.

HAMACHEK, D. E. (1988). Evaluating self-concept and ego development within Erikson's psychosocial framework: A formulation. *Journal of Counseling and Development, 66,* 354–360.

HAMACHEK, D. (1990). Evaluating self-concept and ego status in Erikson's last three psychosocial stages. *Journal of Counseling and Development, 68*(6), 677–683.

HARLOW, H. F., & HARLOW, M. K. (1966). Learning to love. *American Scientist, 54,* 244–272.

HARR, G. L. (1995). *Career guide: Road maps to meaning in the world of work.* Pacific Grove, CA: Brooks/Cole.

HAVIGHURST, R. (1972). *Developmental tasks and education* (3rd ed.). New York: David McKay.

HAWTON, K. (1986). *Suicide and attempted suicide among children and adolescents.* Beverly Hills, CA: Sage.

HAY, L. L. (1987). *You can heal your life.* Carson, CA: Hay House.

HENDRICK, S. (1995). *Close relationships: What couple therapists can learn.* Pacific Grove, CA: Brooks/Cole.

*HENDRICK, S., & HENDRICK, C. (1992). *Liking, loving, and relating* (2nd ed.). Pacific Grove, CA: Brooks/Cole.

HERMAN, J. (1981). *Father-daughter incest.* Cambridge, MA: Harvard University Press.

HERR, E. L., & CRAMER, S. H. (1988). *Career guidance and counseling through the life span* (3rd ed.). Boston: Scott, Foresman.

HIRSHMANN, J. R., & HUNTER, C. H. (1995). *When women stop hating their bodies.* New York: Ballantine Books.

HODGE, M. (1967). *Your fear of love.* Garden City, NY: Doubleday.

HOLLAND, J. L. (1992). *Making vocational choices: A theory of vocational personalities and work environments.* Odessa, FL: Psychological Assessment Resources, Inc.

HOLLAND, J. L. (1994). *Self-directed search* (form R). Odessa, FL: Psychological Assessment Resources, Inc.

HOLMES, T. H., & RAHE, R. H. (1967). The social readjustment rating scale. *Journal of Psychosomatic Research, 11,* 213–218.

HOLMES, T. S., & HOLMES, T. H. (1970). Short-term intrusions into the life-style routine. *Journal of Psychosomatic Research, 14,* 121–132.

*HUGHES, L. (1996). *Beginnings and beyond: A guide for personal growth and adjustment.* Pacific Grove, CA: Brooks/Cole.

JAMES, M., & JONGEWARD, D. (1971). *Born to win: Transactional analysis with Gestalt experiments.* Reading, MA: Addison-Wesley.

JAMPOLSKY, G. G. (1981). *Love is letting go of fear.* New York: Bantam Books.

JOHNSON, E. M. (1992). *What you can do to avoid AIDS.* New York: Times Books.

JONES, L. (1996). *HIV/AIDS: What to do about it.* Pacific Grove, CA: Brooks/Cole.

JOURARD, S. (1971). *The transparent self: Self-disclosure and well-being* (rev. ed.). New York: Van Nostrand Reinhold.

JOURARD, S. (1975, July). Marriage is for life. *Journal of Marriage and Family Counseling,* 199–208.

*JOY, W. B. (1979). *Joy's way: A map for the transformational journey.* Los Angeles, CA: Jeremy P. Tarcher.

JOY, W. B. (1990). *Avalanche: Heretical reflections on the dark and the light.* New York: Ballantine.

JUNG, C. G. (1961). *Memories, dreams, reflections.* New York: Vintage Books.

JUSTICE, B., & JUSTICE, R. (1979). *The broken taboo: Sex in the family.* New York: Human Sciences Press.

KABAT-ZINN, J. (1990). *Full catastrophe living.* New York: Delacorte Press.

*KALISH, R. A. (1985). *Death, grief, and caring relationships* (2nd ed.). Pacific Grove, CA: Brooks/Cole.

*KEEN, S. (1991). *Fire in the belly: On being a man.* New York: Bantam.

KEILLOR, G. (1993). *The book of guys.* New York: Viking.

KIMMEL, M. S. (Ed.). (1987a). *Changing men: New directions in research on men and masculinity.* Newbury Park, CA: Sage.

KIMMEL, M. S. (1987b). Rethinking "masculinity": New directions in research. In M. S. Kimmel (Ed.), *Changing men: New directions in research on men and masculinity* (pp. 9–24). Newbury Park, CA: Sage.

KOBASA, S. C. (1979). Stressful life events, personality and health: An inquiry into hardiness. *Journal of Personality and Social Psychology, 37,* 1–11.

KOBASA, S. C., MADDI, S. R., & KAHN, S. (1982). Hardiness and health: A prospective study. *Journal of Personality and Social Psychology, 42*(1), 168–177.

*KÜBLER-ROSS, E. (1969). *On death and dying.* New York: Macmillan.

KÜBLER-ROSS, E. (1975). *Death: The final stage of growth.* Englewood Cliffs, NJ: Prentice-Hall (Spectrum).

KÜBLER-ROSS, E. (1981). *Living with death and dying.* New York: Macmillan.

KÜBLER-ROSS, E. (1993). *AIDS: The ultimate challenge.* New York: Collier Books (Macmillan.)

LAIDLAW, T. A., MALMO, C., & ASSOCIATES. (1990). *Healing voices: Feminist approaches to therapy with women.* San Francisco, CA: Jossey-Bass.

*LERNER, H. G. (1985). *The dance of anger: A woman's guide to changing the patterns of intimate relationships.* New York: Harper & Row (Perennial).

LERNER, H. G. (1989). *The dance of intimacy: A woman's guide to courageous acts of change in key relationships.* New York: Harper & Row (Perennial).

LEVANT, R. L., & POLLACK, W. S. (Eds.). (1995). *Foundations for a new psychology of men.* New York: Basic Books.

LEVINSON, D. J. (1978). *The seasons of man's life.* New York: Knopf.

LEWIS, C. S. (1961). *A grief observed.* New York: Seabury Press.

LEWIS, V. G., & BORDERS, L. D. (1995). Life satisfaction of single middle-aged professional women. *Journal of Counseling and Development, 74*(1), 94–100.

*LINDBERGH, A. (1975). *Gift from the sea.* New York: Pantheon. (Original work published in 1955)

LOCK, R. D. (1996a). *Taking charge of your career direction: Career planning guide, Book I* (3rd ed.). Pacific Grove, CA: Brooks/Cole.

LOCK, R. D. (1996b). *Job search: Career planning guide, Book 2* (3rd ed.). Pacific Grove, CA: Brooks/Cole.

LOCK, R. D. (1996c). *Student activities for taking charge of your career direction and job search: Career planning guide, Book 3* (3rd ed.). Pacific Grove, CA: Brooks/Cole.

LONG, V. O. (1996). *Facilitating personal growth in self and others.* Pacific Grove, CA: Brooks/Cole.

LOTT, B. (1994). *Women's lives: Themes and variations in gender learning* (2nd ed.). Pacific Grove, CA: Brooks/Cole.

LUNDEN, J. (1995, September). The courage to change. *Good Housekeeping,* pp. 73–75.

MADDI, S. R., & KOBASA, C. S. (1984). *The hardy executive: Health under stress.* Homewood, IL: Dow Jones-Irwin.

*MAIER, S. (1991). *God's love song.* Corvallis, OR: Postal Instant Press.

MALTZ, W. (1991). *The sexual healing journey: A guide for women and men survivors of sexual abuse.* New York: Harper Collins.

MALTZ, W., & HOLMAN, B. (1987). *Incest and sexuality: A guide to understanding and healing.* Lexington, MA: D. C. Heath (Lexington Books).

MASLACH, C. (1982). *Burnout: The cost of caring.* Englewood Cliffs, NJ: Prentice-Hall (Spectrum).

MASLOW, A. (1968). *Toward a psychology of being.* New York: Van Nostrand Reinhold.

MASLOW, A. (1970). *Motivation and personality* (2nd ed.). New York: Harper & Row.

MASLOW, A. (1971). *The farther reaches of human nature.* New York: Viking.

MAY, R. (1973). *Man's search for himself.* New York: Dell (Delta).

MCKAY, G. D., & DINKMEYER, D. (1994). *How you feel is up to you.* San Luis Obispo, CA: Impact Publishers.

MEISELMAN, K. C. (1978). *Incest: A psychological study of causes and effects with treatment recommendations.* San Francisco, CA: Jossey-Bass.

MEISELMAN, K. C. (1990). *Resolving the trauma of incest: Reintegration therapy with survivors.* San Francisco, CA: Jossey-Bass.

MILLMAN, D. (1984). *Way of the peaceful warrior: A book that changes lives.* Tiburon, CA: H. J. Kramer, Inc.

*MOORE, T. (1994). *Care of the soul: A guide for cultivating depth and sacredness in everyday life.* New York: Harper Perennial.

MORNELL, P. (1979). *Passive men, wild women.* New York: Ballantine.

MORRIS, M. (1984). *If I should die before I wake.* New York: Dell.

MORRISSEY, M. (Ed.) (1995, June). ACA's 44th annual convention coverage. *Counseling Today, 37*(12), 22, 46.

MOSAK, H. H. (1989). Adlerian psychotherapy. In R. J. Corsini & D. Wedding (Eds.) *Current psychotherapies* (4th ed.) (pp. 64–116). Itasca, IL: F. E. Peacock.

*MOUSTAKAS, C. (1961). *Loneliness.* Englewood Cliffs, NJ: Prentice-Hall (Spectrum).

MOUSTAKAS, C. (1972). *Loneliness and love.* Englewood Cliffs, NJ: Prentice-Hall (Spectrum).

MOUSTAKAS, C. (1977). *Turning points.* Englewood Cliffs, NJ: Prentice-Hall (Spectrum).

NAISBITT, J. (1984). *Megatrends.* New York: Warner Books.

NAISBITT, J., & ABURDENE, P. (1991). *Megatrends 2000.* New York: Avon.

*NAPIER, A. Y. (1990). *The fragile bond: In search of an equal, intimate and enduring marriage.* New York: Harper & Row (Perennial Library).

ORSBORN, C. (1986). *Enough is enough: Exploring the myth of having it all.* New York: Putnam.

PARHAM, T. A. (1993). *Psychological storms: The African American struggle for identity.* Chicago, IL: African American Images.

*PECK, M. S. (1978). *The road less traveled: A new psychology of love, traditional values and spiritual growth.* New York: Simon & Schuster (Touchstone).

*PECK, M. S. (1987). *The different drum: Community making and peace.* New York: Simon & Schuster (Touchstone).

PERLS, F. S. (1969). *Gestalt therapy verbatim.* New York: Bantam Books.

PERLS, F. S. (1970). Four lectures. In J. Fagan & I. L. Shepherd (Eds.), *Gestalt therapy now* (pp. 14–38). New York: Harper & Row (Colophon).

PHYSICIANS' DESK REFERENCE. (1994). *The PDR family guide to women's health and prescription drugs.* Montvale, NJ: Medical Economics.

*RABINOWITZ, F. E., & COCHRAN, S. V. (1994). *Man alive: A primer of men's issues.* Pacific Grove, CA: Brooks/Cole.

*RAINWATER, J. (1979). *You're in charge! A guide to becoming your own therapist.* Los Angeles: Guild of Tutors Press.

RANDAHL, G. J. (1991). A typological analysis of the relations between measured vocational interests and abilities. *Journal of Vocational Behavior, 38,* 333–350.

*RICE, P. L. (1992). *Stress and health* (2nd ed.). Pacific Grove, CA: Brooks/Cole.

RIDLEY, C. R. (1995). *Overcoming unintentional racism in counseling and psychotherapy.* Thousand Oaks, CA: Sage.

RIGER, S. (1991). Gender dilemmas in sexual harassment policies and procedures. *American Psychologist, 46*(5), 497–505.

RINPOCHE, S. (1994). *Meditation.* San Francisco: Harper.

ROBINSON, E. A. (1943). *The children of the night.* New York: Scribner's.

ROBINSON, F. P. (1970). *Effective study* (4th ed.). New York: Harper & Row.

ROGERS, C. R. (1961). *On becoming a person: A therapist's view of psychotherapy.* Boston: Houghton Mifflin.

ROGERS, C. R. (1980). *A way of being.* Boston: Houghton Mifflin.

ROGERS, C. R. (1983). *Freedom to learn for the 80's.* Columbus, OH: Charles E. Merrill.

ROSENMAN, R. H. (1991). Type A behavior pattern and coronary heart disease: The hostility factor? *Stress Medicine, 7*(4), 245–253.

RUBIN, T. I. (1969). *The angry book.* New York: Macmillan.

RUSH, F. (1980). *The best kept secret: Sexual abuse of children.* Englewood Cliffs, NJ: Prentice-Hall.

RUSK, T., WITH MILLER, D. P. (1991). *Instead of therapy.* Carson, CA: Hay House, Inc.

SAN FRANCISCO AIDS FOUNDATION (1990). *AIDS in the workplace* (pamphlet). San Francisco, CA: Impact AIDS.

SCHAFER, W. (1992). *Stress management for wellness* (2nd ed.) Orlando, FL: Harcourt Brace Jovanovich.

SCHNITZER, E. (1977). *Looking in.* Idyllwild, CA: Strawberry Valley Press.

SCHULTZ, D., & SCHULTZ, S. E. (1994). *Theories of personality* (5th ed.). Pacific Grove, CA: Brooks/Cole.

SHARF, R. S. (1993). *Occupational information overview.* Pacific Grove, CA: Brooks/Cole.

SHEEHY, G. (1976). *Passages: Predictable crises of adult life.* New York: Dutton.

SHEEHY, G. (1981). *Pathfinders.* New York: Morrow.

SHEEHY, G. (1992). *The silent passage.* New York: Random House.

*SHEEHY, G. (1995). *New passages: Mapping your life across time.* New York: Random House.

SHNEIDMAN, E. S. (Ed.). (1984). *Death: Current perspectives.* Palo Alto, CA: Mayfield.

*SIEGEL, B. (1988). *Love, medicine, and miracles.* New York: Harper & Row (Perennial Library).

*SIEGEL, B. (1989). *Peace, love, and healing. Bodymind communication and the path to self-healing: An exploration.* New York: Harper & Row.

SIEGEL, B. (1993). *How to live between office visits: A guide to life, love and health.* New York: Harper Collins.

SIKULA, L. (1994). *Changing careers: Steps to success.* Pacific Grove, CA: Brooks/Cole.

SINGER HARRIS, A. (1996). *Living with paradox: An introduction to Jungian psychology.* Pacific Grove, CA: Brooks/Cole.

SLEEK, S. (1994). Psychology looks at a new masculinity. *The APA Monitor, 25*(11), 6–7.

STEINER, C. (1975). *Scripts people live: Transactional analysis of life scripts.* New York: Bantam Books.

*TANNEN, D. (1987). *That's not what I meant: How conversational style makes or breaks relationships.* New York: Ballantine.

*TANNEN, D. (1991). *You just don't understand: Women and men in conversation.* New York: Ballantine.

TAURIS, C. (1992). *The mismeasure of women.* New York: Simon & Schuster (Touchstone).

TERKEL, S. (1975). *Working.* New York: Avon.

THOMPSON, K. (Ed.). (1991). *To be a man: In search of the deep masculine.* Los Angeles, CA: Jeremy P. Tarcher.

TOURNIER, P. (1972). *Learn to grow old.* New York: Harper & Row.

TRACY, V. M. (1993). *The impact of childhood sexual abuse on women's sexuality.* Unpublished doctoral dissertation. La Jolla University: San Diego, CA.

TRAVIS, J. W., & RYAN, R. S. (1994). *Wellness workbook* (3rd ed.). Berkeley, CA: Ten Speed Press.

U.S. DEPARTMENT OF HEALTH AND HUMAN SERVICES (1987, Spring). *Facts about AIDS* (pamphlet). Washington, DC: U.S. Government Printing Office.

U.S. DEPARTMENT OF HEALTH AND HUMAN SERVICES (1988a). *Understanding AIDS* (pamphlet). Washington, DC: U.S. Government Printing Office.

U.S. DEPARTMENT OF HEALTH AND HUMAN SERVICES (1988b). *Women, sex, and AIDS* (pamphlet). Washington, DC: U.S. Government Printing Office.

U.S. DEPARTMENT OF HEALTH AND HUMAN SERVICES (1989). *Many teens are saying no* (pamphlet). Washington, DC: U.S. Government Printing Office.

U.S. DEPARTMENT OF HEALTH AND HUMAN SERVICES (1991a). *AIDS and you* (pamphlet). Washington, DC: U.S. Government Printing Office.

U.S. DEPARTMENT OF HEALTH AND HUMAN SERVICES (1991b). *Caring for someone with AIDS* (pamphlet). Washington, DC: U.S. Government Printing Office.

U.S. DEPARTMENT OF HEALTH AND HUMAN SERVICES (1991c). *HIV infection and AIDS: Are you at risk?* (pamphlet). Washington, DC: U.S. Government Printing Office.

U.S. DEPARTMENT OF HEALTH AND HUMAN SERVICES (1991d). *How you won't get AIDS* (pamphlet). Washington, DC: U.S. Government Printing Office.

U.S. DEPARTMENT OF HEALTH AND HUMAN SERVICES (1991e). *Voluntary HIV counseling and testing: Facts, issues, and answers* (pamphlet). Washington, DC: U.S. Government Printing Office.

U.S. DEPARTMENT OF LABOR. (1979). *Guide for occupational exploration.* Washington, DC: U.S. Government Printing Office.

U.S. DEPARTMENT OF LABOR. (1991). *Dictionary of occupational titles* (4th ed., revised). Washington, DC: U.S. Government Printing Office.

U.S. DEPARTMENT OF LABOR. (1994). *Occupational outlook handbook, 1994–1995*. Washington, DC: U.S. Government Printing Office.

VANDERBILT, H. (1992, February). Incest: A four-part chilling report. *Lear's, 4*(12), 49–77.

VANZETTI, N., & DUCK, S. (1996). *A lifetime of relationships*. Pacific Grove, CA: Brooks/Cole.

VERGEER, G. E. (1995). Therapeutic applications of humor. *Directions in Mental Health Counseling, 5*(3), 4–11.

WATSON, D. L., & THARP, R. G. (1993). *Self-directed behavior: Self-modification for personal adjustment* (6th ed.). Pacific Grove, CA: Brooks/Cole.

WEHRLY, B. (1995). *Pathways to multicultural counseling competence: A developmental journey*. Pacific Grove, CA: Brooks/Cole.

WEITEN, W. (1995). *Psychology: Themes and variations* (3rd ed.). Pacific Grove, CA: Brooks/Cole.

WEITEN, W., & LLOYD, M. A. (1994). *Psychology applied to modern life: Adjustment in the 90s* (4th ed.). Pacific Grove, CA: Brooks/Cole.

WESTRA, M. (1996). *Active communication*. Pacific Grove, CA: Brooks/Cole.

WHITE, J. L., & PARHAM, T. A. (1990). *The psychology of blacks: An African-American perspective*. Englewood Cliffs, NJ: Prentice-Hall.

WILLIAMS, B., & KNIGHT, S. M. (1994). *Healthy for life: Wellness and the art of living*. Pacific Grove, CA: Brooks/Cole.

WILLIAMS, C. (1992). *No hiding place: Empowerment and recovery for our troubled communities*. San Francisco: Harper.

WITKIN, G. (1994). *The male stress syndrome: How to survive stress in the '90s* (2nd ed.). New York: Newmarket Press.

WOLFE, S. M., FUGATE, L., HULSTRAND, E. P., & KAMIMOTO, L. E. (1988). *Worst pills, best pills*. Washington, DC: Public Citizen Health Research Group.

WRIGHT, L. (1988). The Type A behavior pattern and coronary artery disease. *American Psychologist, 43*(1), 2–14.

*YALOM, I. D. (1980). *Existential psychotherapy*. New York: Basic Books.

*ZIMBARDO, P. G. (1987). *Shyness*. New York: Jove.

Index

Photo Credits

TO THE OWNER OF THIS BOOK:

We hope that you have enjoyed *I Never Knew I Had a Choice* (Sixth Edition) and found it meaningful. We'd like to know as much about your experiences with the book as you care to offer. Your comments can help us make it better for future readers. Thank you.

School:_____

Your instructor's name: _____

 1. What did you like *most* about this book? _____

_____

 2. What did you like *least* about this book? _____

_____

 3. How much personal value did you find in the "Time Out for Personal Reflection" sections?

_____

_____

 4. Of how much interest and value were the end-of-chapter "Activities and Exercises"?

_____

 5. Specific topics in the book you thought were most relevant and important:

_____

 6. Specific suggestions for improving the book: _____

_____

 7. Some ways you used this book in class: _____

_____

 8. Some ways you used this book out of class: _____

_____

 9. The name of the course in which you used this book: _____

_____

10. In a separate letter, if you care to write one, please let us know what other comments about the book you'd like to make. We welcome your suggestions!

Optional:

Your name: _____ Date: _____

May Brooks/Cole quote you, either in promotion for *I Never Knew I Had a Choice* (Sixth Edition) or in future publishing ventures?

Yes: _____ No: _____

Sincerely,

Gerald Corey
Marianne Schneider Corey

FOLD HERE

BUSINESS REPLY MAIL

FIRST CLASS   PERMIT NO. 358   PACIFIC GROVE, CA

POSTAGE WILL BE PAID BY ADDRESSEE

ATT: *Gerald Corey and Marianne Schneider Corey*

Brooks/Cole Publishing Company
511 Forest Lodge Road
Pacific Grove, California 93950-9968

FOLD HERE

Brooks/Cole is dedicated to publishing quality publications for education in the human services fields. If you are interested in learning more about our publications, please fill in your name and address and request our latest catalogue.

Name: _____

Street Address: _____

City, State, and Zip: _____

FOLD HERE

FOLD HERE